Race, Gender, and
the Labor Market

Race, Gender, and the Labor Market

Inequalities at Work

Robert L. Kaufman

LYNNE
RIENNER
PUBLISHERS

BOULDER
LONDON

Published in the United States of America in 2010 by
Lynne Rienner Publishers, Inc.
1800 30th Street, Boulder, Colorado 80301
www.rienner.com

and in the United Kingdom by
Lynne Rienner Publishers, Inc.
3 Henrietta Street, Covent Garden, London WC2E 8LU

Library of Congress Cataloging-in-Publication Data
Kaufman, Robert L.
Race, gender, and the labor market : inequalities at work / Robert L. Kaufman.
    p.   cm.
  Includes bibliographical references and index.
  ISBN 978-1-58826-710-8 (hardcover : alk. paper)
  1. Labor market. 2. Discrimination in employment. 3. Sex discrimination
against men. 4. Sex discrimination against women. I. Title.
  HD5706.K318   2010
  331.4—dc22

                        2009053719

British Cataloguing in Publication Data
A Cataloguing in Publication record for this book
is available from the British Library.

Printed and bound in the United States of America

The paper used in this publication meets the requirements
of the American National Standard for Permanence of
Paper for Printed Library Materials Z39.48-1992.

5 4 3 2 1

To Laurie,
without whose love, support, advice,
encouragement, and gentle nudges
this book would likely have never been published

Contents

List of Tables and Figures   ix
Acknowledgments   xiii

1 Why Study Race and Gender Labor Market Inequality?   1

2 Perspectives on Segregation and Earnings Gaps   17

3 Analyzing Labor Market Disparities   57

4 The Segregation of Groups Across Labor Market Positions   77

5 Stereotypical Work Conditions and Race-Sex Earnings Gaps   111

6 Regional Variation in Labor Market Inequality   137

7 Conclusion   163

Appendix A: Supplementary Details on Data and Methods   181
Appendix B: Numeric Results Tables   217
References   247
Index   263
About the Book   277

Tables and Figures

Tables

2.1	Hypothesized Effects on Employment Segregation of General Skill and Training, Growth and Employment, Race-Gender Typing, Product Market Structure, and Linkages to Other Actors	44
2.2	Hypothesized Effects on Earnings Gaps (Ratios) Between Race-Sex Groups of Net Employment Segregation, General Skill and Training, Growth and Employment, Race-Gender Typing, Product Market Structure, and Linkages to Other Actors	45
3.1	Occupational Segments Classification Scheme	60
3.2	Industrial Sectors Classification Scheme	61
3.3	Weighted Sample Sizes of Race-Sex Groups from PUMS, 1990	63
3.4	Measurement of Position-Level Variables	70
4.1	Predictions and Summary of Results for the Analyses of Employment Segregation	81
4.2	How Growth, Profitability, and Market Power Moderate the Effects of Race-Gender–Typing Indicators	98
4.3	How Race-Gender–Typing Indicators Moderate the Effects of Growth, Market Power, and Profitability	100
5.1	Predictions and Summary of Results for Analyses of Earnings Levels with Order of Effects by Race-Sex Group	115
5.2	Predictions and Summary of Results for the Analyses of Earnings Ratios	122
5.3	How Growth, Market Power, and Profitability Moderate the Effects of Race-Gender–Typing Indicators on Earnings Ratios	129
5.4	How Race-Gender–Typing Indicators Moderate the Effects of Growth, Market Power, and Profitability on Earnings Ratios	130
6.1	Summary of Results for the Analyses of Employment Segregation by Region	143

6.2   Summary of Results for the Analyses of Earnings Ratios
        by Region   155
A.1   Measurement of Worker-Level Variables   184
A.2   Estimates of Between-Equation Error Correlations
        for Base Models of Employment Segregation and
        Earnings Gaps   199
A.3   1990 Census Occupations and Segment Codes   200
A.4   1990 Census Industry Codes and Segment Classification   210
B4.1   SUR-EGLS Regressions of Employment Segregation
        on Skills, Growth and Employment Rates, Race and
        Gender Typing, Product Market Structure, and Linkages
        to Other Actors   218
B4.2   SUR-EGLS Regressions of Employment Segregation on
        Skills, Growth and Employment Rates, Race and Gender
        Typing, Product Market Structure, and Linkages to Other
        Actors with Significant Interactions   221
B5.1   Two-Stage EGLS Regressions of Earnings Levels on
        Skills and Growth, Race and Gender Typing, Desirable
        Employment, Product Market Structure, and Linkages
        to Other Actors   225
B5.2   SUR-EGLS Regressions of Earnings Gaps on Skills,
        Growth and Employment Rates, Race and Gender Typing,
        Product Market Structure, and Linkages to Other Actors   228
B5.3   SUR-EGLS Regressions of Earnings Gaps on Skills and
        Growth, Desirable Employment Rates, Race and
        Gender Typing, Product Market Structure, Linkages to
        Other Actors, and Significant Interactions   231
B6.1   SUR-EGLS Regressions of Employment Segregation on
        Skills and Growth, Race and Gender Typing, Desirable
        Employment, Product Market Structure, and Linkages
        to Other Actors—Northern States   235
B6.2   SUR-EGLS Regressions of Employment Segregation on
        Skills and Growth, Race and Gender Typing, Desirable
        Employment, Product Market Structure, and Linkages to
        Other Actors—Southern States   238
B6.3   SUR-EGLS Regressions of Earnings Gaps on Skills,
        Growth and Employment Rates, Race and Gender Typing,
        Product Market Structure, and Linkages to Other Actors—
        Northern States   241
B6.4   SUR-EGLS Regressions of Earnings Gaps on Skills,
        Growth and Employment Rates, Race and Gender Typing,
        Product Market Structure, and Linkages to Other Actors—
        Southern States   244

Figures

1.1	Employment Segregation for Occupations, 1980–2000	5
1.2	Employment Segregation for Occupation by Industry, 1980–2000	6
1.3	Observed and Net Aggregated Employment Segregation, 1990	7
1.4	Decomposition of Earnings Gaps Among Race-Sex Groups, 1980 and 1990	9
2.1	The Relative Importance of Qualifications and Race-Sex Status	39
2.2	Hypothetical Example of Earnings Devaluation for Black Men and White Men	40
2.3	Two-Level Model of Segregation and Earnings Gaps	42
2.4	Hypothetical Example of Different Earnings Returns for Black Women and White Men	47
3.1	Process Used to Define Labor Market Positions	59
3.2	Observed and Adjusted Earnings Ratios Among Race-Sex Groups, Garbage Collectors in Sanitary Services	68
4.1	Explained Variance in Employment Segregation, SUR-EGLS Base Model	79
4.2	Skill Effect on Employment Segregation by Growth Rate	85
4.3	Growth Rate Effect on Employment Segregation by Skill	86
4.4	Status in Interaction and Employment Segregation	89
5.1	Explained Variance in Earnings Level, Two-Stage EGLS Regression	114
5.2	Explained Variance in Earnings Ratios, SUR-EGLS Base Model	121
6.1	Explained Variance in Employment Segregation by Region, SUR-EGLS Base Model	139
6.2	Effect of Growth Rate on Employment Segregation of Black Men to White Men and of White Women to White Men, Moderated by Skill in the South	147
6.3	Explained Variance in Earnings Gaps by Region, SUR-EGLS Base Model	151

Acknowledgments

Support for this research was provided by grants to the author from the W. E. Upjohn Institute for Employment Research (Grant no. 2000-68) and the National Science Foundation (Grant no. SBR-9422800). Large parts of a first draft were completed during a sabbatical while I was at Ohio State University, with the encouragement of my colleagues there, Lauren Krivo and Ruth Peterson. I am grateful for the able research assistance provided over the years by Andrew Cognard-Black, Beckett Broh, Lori Campbell, Martha Crowley, Tamara Heald-Moore, Casey Paragin, and Jeffrey J. Sallaz, and for the extensive programming work performed by Barbara House. Portions of this manuscript were previously published, in a different form, in the journal *American Sociological Review* and as a chapter in the book *Sourcebook on Labor Markets: Evolving Structures and Processes,* edited by Ivar Berg and Arne L. Kalleberg. I would also like to thank the editorial staff at Lynne Rienner Publishers (Lesli Brooks Athanasoulis, Karen H. Brown, and Andrew Berzanskis) for their careful, cheerful, and thoughtful assistance in taking this manuscript through the publication process. It is difficult to express how much of a debt I owe to the reviewers for Lynne Rienner Publishers, not only for their careful reading of an earlier version, but for the incredibly constructive and detailed suggestions and advice that they offered. I believe that the end result does justice to their hard work, but any remaining errors or lack of clarity are my responsibility.

Race, Gender, and
the Labor Market

1

Why Study Race and Gender Labor Market Inequality?

A beginning is the time for taking the most delicate care
that the balances are correct.
—Frank Herbert (1965: 3)

Perhaps the most straightforward answer to the question posed by the chapter title is simply that such inequalities persist despite considerable social changes. This is true whether one considers ethnographies of the everyday experience of minorities and women in the workplace, studies of the success or failure of job seekers in local labor markets, or large-scale statistical analyses of employment representation and earnings using nationally representative data such as the focus of the research reported in this book.

To my mind, the most convincing evidence for continuing status-based discrimination comes from audit studies. Bendick (2007: 4) succinctly describes the logic and method of audit studies as "a systematic research procedure for creating controlled experiments analyzing employers' candid responses to employees' personal characteristics." Although popular opinion may discount the existence of preferential evaluations and treatment, Bendick's survey of thirty recent audit analyses demonstrates how these careful studies have verified the continued operation of preferential evaluations, both in employment and other settings (see also Bertrand and Mullainathan 2004; Fix and Struyk 1993; Pager 2003; Pager 2007; Pager and Quillian 2005; Pager, Western, and Bonikowski 2009; Turner, Fix, and Struyk 1991; Braddock and McPartland 1987; Yinger 1995). For example, in the Turner, Fix, and Struyk study, sets of black and white job candidates were paired, given equivalent credentials, and sent to apply for the same entry-level jobs. The study's results were as systematic as they are startling to popular opinion:

> It found that black applicants were less likely to receive an interview than their white counterparts. If they got an interview, they were likely to have a shorter one and to encounter more negative remarks. They were more likely to be denied

a job and more likely to be steered to less desirable jobs. (http://www.urban
.org/pubs/catalog/discrim.htm)

A recent variation on this methodology (Pager 2003; Pager, Western, and
Bonikowski 2009) focused on the role an applicant's criminal record plays in
the hiring process. Having a criminal record substantially reduces call-backs
after the initial application, and this is significantly more pronounced for black
than for white applicants among certain types of employers (e.g., suburban employers or when applicants had personal contact with the employer). Overall,
this work documents the persisting and substantial preference of employers for
white applicants, *even if they have criminal records* (Pager 2003: 960): "Blacks
are less than half as likely to receive consideration by employers, relative to
their white counterparts, *and black nonoffenders fall behind even whites with
prior felony convictions*" (emphasis added).

This last finding is a powerful reminder of just how pervasive and how
strong the social forces are that maintain and create privileged treatment in the
labor market based on observable status characteristics.

In this book, I thus begin by focusing on the mechanisms by which race-sex
groups are allocated and segregated into labor market positions. I then explore
how such employment segregation affects earnings determination, how this differs across race-sex groups, and how these processes are contingent on economic
and social contexts. My use of the term *race-sex groups* is purposeful in order to
recognize the necessity of considering the intersection between race and sex rather
than treating race and sex as separable phenomena. Thus I develop my ideas and
design my analyses around comparisons among black women, black men, white
women, and white men.[1] In the next section, I describe four different jobs that illustrate the kinds of inequalities and issues that I explore in this research.

Food for Thought:
Profiles of Some Race-Gender–Typed Jobs

Consider two pairs of jobs. Each pair requires similar levels of general skill and
training but differs in terms of some of the specific skills required, the nature
of the work performed, and the context within which work occurs.[2] The first pair
includes pressing machine operatives in laundries and garbage collectors for
sanitary services. Both are routine, relatively low-skilled jobs, with poor physical working environments, a history of moderate declines in the number of jobs
available, above-average levels of unemployment, and a high level of unionization. They differ in that garbage collecting offers more opportunity to work full
time, requires more physical exertion but less physical dexterity, and takes place
in a somewhat noncompetitive market compared to the very competitive market
for laundries. The second pair comprises registered nurses in hospitals and pilots

and navigators in air transport. Both are relatively autonomous and high-skilled jobs, with stable employment opportunities and below-average unemployment, and require about average physical exertion but above-average levels of clerical perception. The jobs in this pair differ in that work as a pilot involves worse physical environmental conditions and has a much higher union presence, requires even higher physical dexterity and math skills but lacks the requirement for nurturing skills that nurses must have, and takes place in a somewhat noncompetitive market compared to the oligopolistic market for hospitals, with a correspondingly lower level of profitability.

Why are these varying profiles of interest? Because the pairs of jobs also differ in their employment opportunities and their consequences for workers by race and by sex. Even taking into account human capital, family/marital structure, and geographic residence, there are marked differences in which race–sex group members are employed in each of these jobs.[3] Black women disproportionately work as pressing machine operatives in laundries in many parts of the country, as do black men as garbage collectors for sanitary services, white women as registered nurses in hospitals, and white men as pilots and navigators in air transport. These jobs differ not only in who is more likely to find employment in them, but they vary as well in the outcomes for workers employed in them. Despite considerable similarities in their profiles within pairs, there are substantial earnings disparities between the jobs in each pair. Garbage collectors earn more than twice as much as pressers, just as pilots do compared to registered nurses. Moreover, earnings gaps among race-sex groups vary systematically across these four positions, taking into account individual and group differences in human capital, family structure, geographic residence, and labor supply.[4] The race and gender disparities are greatest among pilots and least among nurses (with one minor exception), with only somewhat larger gaps among pressers and garbage collectors than among nurses.

How can we explain such differences? Some scholars focus on workers' characteristics and argue that such employment segregation and earnings gaps result from skill deficits among race-sex groups or from workers' choices and preferences for kinds of work. Others emphasize the nature and context of work and workplaces and argue that disparities result from market structures and forces, from race-sex stereotyping of work and queuing mechanisms, and from devaluation processes. My approach, laid out in Chapter 2, integrates ideas from each perspective, but emphasizes constraints *on* workers more so than it does choices *by* workers. The empirical analyses in Chapters 4 and 5 suggest that the operation of race-sex stereotyping and devaluation processes, as moderated by external pressures and internal resources, are of central importance.

A skeptical reader might well question (with good reason) whether such "cherry-picked" evidence really indicates the existence of widespread labor market disparities among race-sex groups. In the next section, I overview trends in employment segregation and earnings gaps among race-sex groups and present some summary evidence in an effort to reassure such a reader.

Evidence of the Persistence of Labor Market Differences

Employment Segregation

The classic and simple way of documenting differences in the sorting of groups into labor market positions is to use the index of dissimilarity (Reskin 1993).[5] This measures the proportion of a group who would have to trade labor market positions with members of the other group so that both groups had identical distributions across positions. Studies most commonly use occupations to define labor market positions. A good summary of trends in occupational segregation through the 1990s is provided by King (1992), whose findings I have updated to include 2000 (see Figure 1.1). These results indicate that

- From 1940 through 1960, differences between the occupational distributions of African Americans and whites were fairly substantial and roughly stable at around 40–45% for black men versus white men and 60–65% for black women versus white women.
- From 1960 to 1980, the differences declined substantially to about 30–34% for both African American men and women.
- From 1980 to 1990, and again from 1990 to 2000, there have been small declines of about another 2–3% each decade.
- Sex segregation within racial groups is consistently much higher than racial segregation within sex groups and has generally shown a lower rate of decline. In fact the decline from 1990 to 2000 was less than 1% among whites and about 1.5% among blacks.

Such findings actually underestimate the extent of labor market segregation because they mask segregation that occurs within occupations by *both* sex (Bielby and Baron 1986; Jacobs 2001; Peterson and Morgan 1995; Tomaskovic-Devey 1993) and race (King 1992; Tomaskovic-Devey 1993). One way of showing this is to calculate segregation using more detailed definitions of labor market positions. Figure 1.1 presents indices of dissimilarity among race-sex groups for 1980, 1990, and 2000 using three-digit census occupations (nearly 400 in number), while Figure 1.2 presents indices of dissimilarity using six-digit census industry-occupation combinations (about 40,000 in number).[6]

The indices calculated for more detailed labor market positions in Figure 1.2 show notably higher levels of segregation, especially by race, than do those in Figure 1.1 for occupations alone. On average, the extent of racial segregation is 20–30% higher and the degree of sex segregation is 10–15% higher for the more finely grained positions. Overall, these results suggest that about 33% of blacks (or whites) would have to change their labor market placement in order to achieve an even distribution of racial groups across detailed labor market positions and that, within racial groups, nearly 60% of women (or men) would

Figure 1.1 Employment Segregation for Occupations, 1980–2000

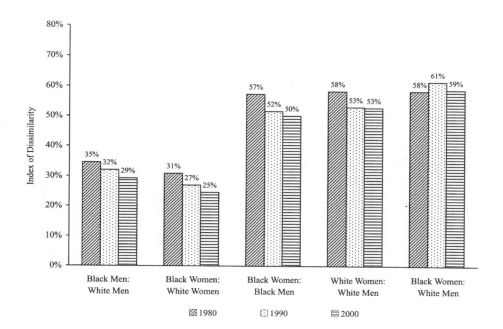

have to change their labor market placement in order to achieve an even distribution of sex groups across positions. Note also that there were much smaller changes in sex segregation between 1990 and 2000 in contrast to the rate of decline across the prior thirty years.

Some might argue, however, that such measures *overstate* the extent of racial inequality because they fail to take into account racial differences in labor market inputs (such as education, experience, and family status) or geographic location (region and metropolitan residence) that influence placement into labor market positions. In reality, although such factors are consequential for individual success in the labor market, they explain only part of the racial or gender differences in occupational distributions. To illustrate, Figure 1.3 presents results from the 1990 Census using 107 industry-occupation groups.[7] It shows the index of dissimilarity for both the *observed* industry-occupation distributions for race-sex groups and the *net* industry-occupation distributions for race-sex groups. (Note that the absolute levels of observed segregation are smaller than those in the prior figures due to the higher degree of aggregation.) Observed segregation is measured by the index of dissimilarity for the *actual* distribution of pairs of race-sex groups across the 107 industry-occupation cells. I calculated net segregation as the index of dissimilarity for the *predicted* distribution of pairs of

Figure 1.2 Employment Segregation for Occupation by Industry, 1980–2000

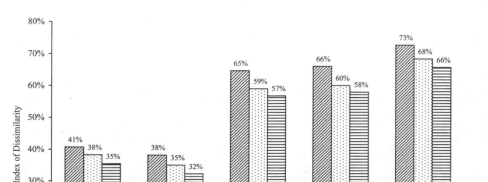

groups across the 107 cells, where the prediction takes into account how groups differ in human capital, family structure, and geographic residence.[8] What is most important in this figure is the difference between observed and net segregation. Adjusting the labor market placement of race-sex groups to reflect group differences in the control variables reduces segregation by at most three percentage points (a 12% reduction). Indeed, for sex segregation among whites, the net segregation is actually higher than the observed. Thus, moderate to high levels of racial and gender employment segregation still exist, and relatively little of this segregation is due to differences in human capital, family status, or geographic residence.

One factor that these analyses do not fully address is the role of individual preferences and the self-selection of women and minorities into certain types of jobs (e.g., a preference for public-service employment among minorities). Family status is often assumed to constrain women's preferences, and thus the variables for family status partially control for the influence of women's preferences. As I discuss in more detail later, self-selection is of secondary importance because, while it does narrow choices by job seekers, they are equally if not more constrained by the limited set of jobs actually offered. In fact, there is little

Figure 1.3 Observed and Net Aggregated Employment Segregation, 1990

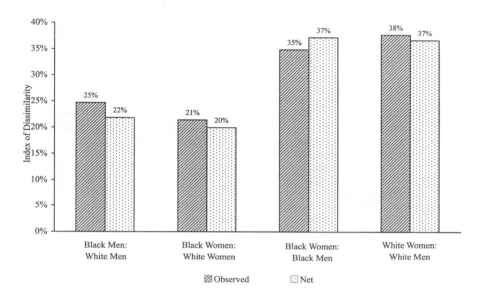

evidence that such value differences influence sex differences in the jobs selected (Barry 1987; Bielby and Bielby 1988; Glass 1990; Glass and Camarigg 1992; Padavic 1991).[9]

There is little reason to consider a comparable argument concerning race differences in job selection. To the best of my knowledge, a differential values or rational-choice argument about job selection by race has not been made in the literature. Indeed Tomaskovic-Devey (1993: 40) noted that it "would be a potentially racist assumption." Furthermore, research finds at most minimal differences between blacks and whites in job or work values (Day and Rounds 1998; Gupta, Tracey, and Gore 2008; Johnson 2002).

Earnings

What implications does such segregation have for labor market rewards? It is commonly argued that a share of the differences in earnings among race-sex groups can be attributed to differences in the earnings of the labor market positions into which they have been sorted (Beck, Horan, and Tolbert 1980; Council of Economic Advisers 1998; Darity and Myers 1998; England 1992; Glass, Tienda, and Smith 1988; Kaufman 1983; Marini 1989; Parcel and Mueller 1989; Taylor, Gwartney-Gibbs, and Farley 1986; Tomaskovic-Devey 1993). The basic premise is that minorities and women occupy jobs that typically have lower levels of earnings than those jobs occupied by white men and that this fact can explain some part of the earnings differences among groups.

How large are the earnings gaps among race-sex groups, how have these changed over time, and how much of the gaps can be attributed to segregation as opposed to other causes? The Council of Economic Advisers reported that (for full-time workers):

> Wages of white men continue to exceed those of all other groups of workers (Labor Markets [Tables] 4, 5, and 6). Studies indicate that black men's wages rose relative to white men's between the early 1960s and the mid-1970s, especially in the South. But this trend reversed sometime in the mid- to late 1970s, and black men's relative pay declined for at least 10 years. The evidence of the last 10 years is mixed. . . .
>
> After reaching near parity in the mid-1970s, black women's wages have fallen relative to those of white women. . . . Young, college-educated black women reached pay parity with their white counterparts in the early 1970s but have seen their relative wages fall about 10 percentage points since then (Labor Markets [Tables] 5 and 7). (1998: 23)

According to the data in this report, among full-time workers in 1997 black men earned 74% of what white men earned, while black women earned 83% of what white women earned. Thus racial earnings gaps have persisted and even increased to some degree. Although gender-wage gaps have decreased, women still earned only 75% of what men earned among whites, but 84% of what men earned among blacks.

While the Council of Economic Advisers (COEA) acknowledges the importance of the link between labor market segregation and earnings (1998: 24), they did not directly assess its impact or whether declines in segregation have led to a lessened contribution of segregation as a source of disparity. Figure 1.4 presents data on earnings by race-sex group for 1980 and 1990 that make clear the interplay between employment segregation and earnings gaps. Although some of the magnitudes differ from the COEA report (because the sample includes all workers, not just full-time workers), it shows similar patterns and trends overall. The size of the total gap among groups (the height of each bar) was relatively stable between 1980 and 1990, but showed opposite trends for race gaps than for sex gaps. Within sexes, the race gap in earnings increased, but much more so for men than for women. Within racial groups, the sex gap in earnings decreased, but much more so for blacks than for whites.

These gaps in annual earnings remained fairly substantial in 1990, aside from the very small gap between white women and black women.[10] On average, white men earned much more than the other three race-sex groups. Black men earned $11,000 less, or 62% of white men's earnings, a sharp contrast from the small race gap in earnings among women. Both white women and black women earned about $16,000 less than white men, or about half of what they

Figure 1.4 Decomposition of Earnings Gaps
Among Race-Sex Groups, 1980 and 1990

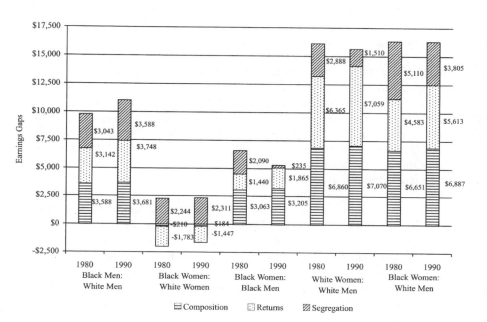

earned. There was also a notable sex gap among blacks. Black women earned about $5,300 less than black men, or about 25% less.

What are the sources of these gaps? The typical way to think about these discrepancies attributes between-group earnings gaps to only two sources: one due to differences among groups in their average levels of, say, human capital; and one due to differences among groups in the return to human capital which they receive (see, for example, Althauser and Wigler 1972; England et al. 1994; Featherman and Hauser 1976; Kaufman 1983). However, I have refined this approach (Kaufman 1983) to distinguish a third source, that amount due to segregation of groups into jobs that pay better or worse. More formally, then, the three sources of earnings gaps are defined as follows:

1. *Composition* is the share of the gap attributable to between-group mean differences in factors that affect earnings (e.g., differences in average education between groups). This component captures "compensable" differences between groups, including those due to pre–labor market discrimination (e.g., in educational attainment).

2. *Returns* is the share of the gap attributable to between-group differences in the payoff to factors that affect earnings (e.g., different returns to education for groups). This component captures discrimination in the form of unequal payoffs for labor inputs to some extent, although it is recognized that this is not "smoking gun" evidence of discrimination.

3. *Segregation* is the share of the gap attributable to "the impact of the differential distribution of the groups across labor divisions coupled with the differential earnings of employment in the various labor market divisions" (p. 589)—for example, differences in mean earnings between skilled craft positions (disproportionately employing white men) and low-skilled household service positions (disproportionately employing black women). This component thus captures the extent to which an unequal distribution of groups across positions creates inequality in earnings, *even if there were no earnings discrimination against groups within positions.*

Figure 1.4 reports the results of applying this three-component decomposition to data from the 1980 and 1990 Censuses. In this analysis, the predictors of earnings included measures of human capital, family structure, geographic residence, and labor supply. Including labor supply is a somewhat conservative strategy (i.e., maximizing the composition component and minimizing the return component) because labor-supply indicators mix together involuntary with voluntary reduction of supply by some workers (e.g., some women).

Although the total gaps in earnings were very stable (the total height of the bars for each pair), the same is not true of the sources of the gap. The *returns* and *segregation* components were more volatile than the total gaps. But the *composition* component was nearly constant. Aside from the very small reversal of the gap between white women and black women,[11] the *composition* bars in Figure 1.4 show that group differences in the mean of the earnings-generating characteristics contributed to the gap in both 1980 and 1990 by about $3,600 for black men compared to white men; $7,000 for white women compared to white men; $3,100 for black women compared to black men; and $6,700 for black women compared to white men.

In proportionate terms, the share of the gap due to group differences in *composition* was also fairly stable, aside from a large increase in the share of the gap between black men and black women. In 1990, group differences in *composition* ranged from 33% of the earnings gap between black men and white men to 60% of the earnings gap between black women and black men. Clearly pre–labor market differences were an important source of earnings gaps between groups, especially of the sex gaps within race groups.

In contrast to this stability, the size of the *returns* component increased between 1980 and 1990 for all group comparisons, although the component is still negative for black women compared to white women.[12] All else constant, there was a larger earnings gap between groups in 1990 than in 1980 because of changes in the returns paid to group members. For black men compared to white men, the gap increased by $700 to over $3,700; for white women compared to white men, the gap rose by $700 to nearly $7,100; for black women compared to black men, the gap increased by $400 to nearly $1,900; and for black women compared to white men, the gap jumped by over $1,000 to $5,600.

In 1980, the *returns* component ranged from 22% of the earnings gap between black women and black men to 40% of the earnings gap between white women and white men. By 1990, this proportionate share had also increased, now ranging from 34% to 45%. Although the larger group differences in returns cannot be unambiguously attributed solely to increasing discrimination, it is important to note that this formulation of the decomposition model measures group differences in returns *within* sets of similar labor market positions. Thus, within-position differences in payoffs produced a sizable and growing component (both absolute and relative) of the earnings gap among groups. Moreover, it equaled or exceeded the proportionate share of the gap due to pre–labor market *composition* for black men compared to white men and for white women compared to white men.

The *segregation* component showed opposite trends for race gaps than for sex gaps (the top black bars in Figure 1.4). Within sex groups, the *segregation* component increased the black-white gap in earnings from 1980 to 1990, especially for men. For black men compared to white men, the gap rose by $500 to nearly $3,600; for black women compared to white women, the gap increased by under $100 to $2,300. However, the *segregation* component decreased the sex gap in earnings from 1980 to 1990, especially between black men and women. For black women compared to black men, the gap dropped by $1,900 to $200; for white women compared to white men, the gap fell by $1,400 to $1,500; and for black women compared to white men, the gap decreased by $1,300 to $3,800. By 1990, the *segregation* component was only a minor part of the earnings gap between sex groups. Thus, some part of the increases in the proportionate share of the *returns* component (especially for black women compared to black men) were due to the reduction in the contribution of the *segregation* component. But the *segregation* component remained a substantial component of the race gaps, $2,300 for women and nearly $3,600 for men. Indeed, for black men compared to white men, each of the three components accounted for about a one-third share of the total gap.

The value of these decomposition results is that they clearly indicate the role that labor markets play in reproducing prior inequality as well as producing inequality among race-sex groups through their participation in the labor market. Except for black women compared to white women, a substantial share of the earnings gaps among groups can be explained by pre–labor differences (from 33% to 60%). Thus pre–labor market group differences and inequalities are strongly reproduced within the labor market as earnings inequalities among groups. But the labor market is not just a passive generator of inequality. Fully

40–67% of the earnings gaps are not simply reproduced from preexisting differences. This remainder can be attributed to more active labor market processes creating race and sex inequality, including those of discrimination and segregation.

Contributions to Gaps in What We Know

Given the evidence presented in this chapter, how can we make sense of such patterns of inequality? I suggest that the starting point is to examine the mechanisms that sort race-sex groups into labor market positions, to analyze how employment segregation and other labor market processes affect earnings determination and the production of earnings gaps among race-sex groups, and how the latter may differ across race-sex groups. Over the past twenty-five years, sociologists and economists alike have explored a wide variety of explanations for the persistent employment and compensation differentials between men and women and between blacks and whites. However, despite considerable speculation and empirical study, generalizable knowledge about the processes generating such labor market inequalities remains limited for several reasons.

Perhaps the most critical shortcoming has been the lack of theoretical and empirical attention to the intersection of race and gender (for an exception see the work by McCall (2000a,b, 2001a,b): "The extant scholarship focuses either on gender composition or on race composition; we found almost no research that simultaneously takes gender and race into account to examine, for example, what establishment characteristics are associated with the employment of women of color" (Reskin, McBrier, and Kmec 1999: 356–357). This is surprising given the marked differences in race employment-segregation levels within sexes but comparable sex-segregation levels within races noted above. This constrains researchers' ability both to test theory and to formulate policy recommendations if, as many scholars argue should be the case, the effects of race and sex are not additive but interactive. Consequently, I give due consideration to the intersection of race and gender in developing theoretical expectations, designing the analyses, and interpreting results.

Second, despite the large volume of research in this area, studies have tended to be piecemeal, testing a few factors, rather than providing comprehensive empirical evaluations. And there are still unanswered questions and some critical shortcomings of the commonly used research designs. For example, an unresolved issue of long debate in the earnings-gap literature is why the "femaleness" of a job decreases wages (Groshen 1991). Past research has documented wage disparities among female-dominated, sex-integrated, and male-dominated jobs and speculated about the reasons for disparities, but such speculations are rarely tested explicitly. Human capital deficiencies are insufficient to explain these differences (England 1992; Groshen 1991; Kilbourne et al. 1994a) and a compensating differentials explanation is inconsistent with the empirical findings (Groshen 1991; Jacobs and Steinberg 1990). The literature suggests that workplace discrimination is key, but direct and comprehensive tests of the processes argued to create and underlie workplace discrimination are few.

Similarly, trends in and levels of workplace segregation by race or by sex (but rarely both) have been studied extensively but systematic research is lacking on how the conditions of work and workplace characteristics affect workplace segregation. Even for such a central criterion as general skill, Reskin, McBrier, and Kmec review (1999: 339) found that "little research exists on how the skills establishments require affect its [race and sex] composition." To move beyond the plethora of narrow or mono-causal models, I draw on an eclectic literature in sociology and economics to develop theoretical expectations: dual economy and segmented markets, race segregation, sex segregation, statistical discrimination, queuing approaches, human capital, Becker's theory of discrimination, comparable worth, cultural feminism, and gendered evaluation of work. I use segmented market theory and race-sex queuing theory as complementary perspectives to integrate ideas from these varied approaches as detailed in Chapter 2.

A third shortcoming, especially in the employment-segregation literature, has been the use of overly broad or circularly defined labor market segments to define the positions across which workers are segregated and within which earnings gaps are measured. For example, virtually all studies of employment segregation define labor market positions using occupations, rather than using more finely grained labor market positions that also take into account the economic sector within which workers are employed.[13] Unlike past categorizations of labor market segments, I use a combination of detailed occupation and detailed industry of employment to define labor market positions that embody the race-and sex-segregated contours of the labor market without resorting to a circular definition using the observed race or sex composition of positions (see Chapter 3). Disaggregating occupations by economic sector is only a partial step toward the ideal of analyzing jobs (i.e., specific job titles in particular firms) and it provides a varying degree of within-occupation detail and variation. For example, registered nurses work overwhelmingly in a limited set of health-care industries (hospitals, doctor's offices, etc.) whereas janitors and cleaners work in virtually every industry. I have chosen to use this definition of positions and data because of the advantages they provide in terms of generalizability across geographic locales and the full range of positions as well as providing data at both the worker and position level (see the next point).[14]

A related concern is that for a long time virtually all studies of employment segregation analyzed aggregate units (occupations or industries) but failed to control appropriately for worker-level determinants (e.g., human capital or family status) that affect the matching of workers to positions.[15] Only a few such studies controlled for these at all, introducing substantial specification error. If

such factors were controlled, they were typically included as worker characteristics aggregated to the position level (e.g., England, Allison, and Wu 2006),
a strategy that suffers from a type of ecological fallacy (Krivo and Kaufman 1990).
More recently, a body of work on segregation has developed using job- and/or
establishment-level data that avoids this problem (e.g., Fernandez and Mors
2008; Fernandez and Sosa 2005; Holzer, Raphael, and Stoll 2004; Kmec
2005; Petersen and Saporta 2004; Stainback 2008). As I describe in Chapter
3, I employ a two-step procedure to control properly for worker-level factors,
resulting in an appropriate measurement of position-level differentials among
race-sex groups.

A Brief Guide to the Rest of the Book

In the next chapter, I lay out the details of my integrated perspective and apply
it to develop the series of hypotheses empirically assessed in subsequent chapters. In Chapter 3, I discuss the census and other data sources that I used to develop the measures for these analyses and the statistical techniques I employ.
The following three chapters present and describe the results of analyses that
seek to answer two initial questions posed in Chapter 2:

   1. How do the working conditions and task requirements of labor market
positions, the nature of industrial product and labor markets in which they are
embedded, and their linkages to other actors (e.g., the government and unions)
affect the degree and type of employment segregation in 1990 among race-sex
groups, taking into account worker differences in human capital, family structure, and geographic residence? In particular, do race- and gender-typing of task
requirements create corresponding employment segregation by race and sex
(assessed using the base model in Chapter 4)?
   2. Similarly, how do these factors affect the earnings gaps among race-sex
groups? Can (stereotypic) working conditions and skills/task requirements
explain the effects of race-sex composition on earnings gaps, again giving due
consideration to the effects of differential human capital, family structure, and
geographic residence (explored using the base model in Chapter 5)?

I elaborate these initial questions and analyses by arguing that there are economic and social contexts across which such processes may vary systematically.
Thus I assess two further issues:

   3. How are the determinants of employment segregation and earnings gaps
moderated by (interact with) economic contexts such as market power and observed changes in demand for labor? Specifically, do market power and other
forms of economic buffering from market pressures intensify the effects of

normative factors (e.g., race- and gender-typed tasks and working conditions) and does employment growth diminish such effects (elaborated in the extended models in Chapters 4 and 5)?

4. How are the determinants of employment segregation and earnings gaps moderated by (interact with) larger societal contexts, specifically regional differences between the North and South? Given the documented regional differences in levels of racial prejudice, are segregation and earnings gaps higher in the South and are the effects of race-typed tasks and working conditions larger in the South (assessed in Chapter 6)?

The concluding chapter reexamines the contributions of this research, highlights major findings and their implications for the multiple theoretical perspectives that I summarize in Chapter 2, provides some suggestions for future research, and identifies some policy implications of the results.

Notes

1. As I discuss in Chapter 3, I exclude other race-ethnic groups (e.g., Hispanic and Asian subgroups) from my analyses because their inclusion would have required using an overly aggregated definition of labor market positions. In Chapter 7, I speculate about how the processes and results I find might apply to other groups.

2. The following characterizations use the measures of general skills and training, race- and gender-typed tasks, and other characteristics of labor market positions discussed in Chapter 3. For a quick overview of how these are defined, see Table 3.4.

3. For details of how such employment representation measures are constructed, see the discussion in Chapter 3.

4. For details of how the earnings gaps, net of the controls for individual factors, are constructed, see the discussion in Chapter 3.

5. The index of dissimilarity is calculated as (Duncan and Duncan 1955):

$$\frac{1}{2} \sum_{Occ=1}^{0} \left| \frac{n_{Occ,\,Group\,1}}{N_{Group\,1}} - \frac{n_{Occ,\,Group\,2}}{N_{Group\,2}} \right|$$

6. These data use occupation and industry comparably coded to the 1990 Census standard codes for all three censuses by the Integrated Public Use Microdata Series (IPUMS) project. The number of actual occupation-industry combinations in the data varied by census: 43,276 in 1980; 46,473 in 1990; 39,293 in 2000.

7. These groupings are aggregations of the six-digit industry occupations. The industry groups are defined by product type (using Browning and Singlemann's 1978 classification) and by the extent of industrial market power (concentration of sales). The occupation groups are defined by skill type (combinations of working with people, data, or things) and by skill level. See Chapter 3 for more detail on these indicators.

8. The net distributions were derived from the effects of race-sex group membership on labor market position from a log-linear analysis controlling for the effects of human capital, family structure, and geographic residence on labor market position.

These race-sex effects were used to adjust the observed distributions to remove the effects of differences among race-sex groups in the control variables (for details of this procedure see Kaufman and Schervish 1986).

9. Even preferences for typical work are only weakly associated with job choices (Jacobs 1989; Rosenfeld 1983; Rosenfeld and Spenner 1992), and many scholars argue that these preferences often reflect the influence of past labor market discrimination (Reskin 1993; Marini 1989).

10. This is much smaller than the gap among full-time workers because black women are much more likely to work full time than are white women.

11. The negative component for black women compared to white women indicates that, rather than decreasing, the gap increases by about $200 after adjusting for differences in composition.

12. For black women compared to white women, the gap *decreased* by $400 *less,* to over $1,400.

13. A related concern in the employment-segregation literature is that the few existing analytic studies that do use a more detailed definition of employment positions are difficult to generalize because they rely on restricted samples (or case studies). For example, Bielby and Baron's (1986) classic analysis of job segregation by sex is limited to job titles in mixed-sex occupations for a sample of California establishments overrepresenting manufacturing industries and excluding some major industries. Similarly, Tomaskovic-Devey (1993) analyzes job-level sex segregation and racial segregation for a North Carolina sample.

14. Although scholars have long recognized that for studying labor market mechanisms the ideal definition of positions would be jobs (e.g., Baron and Bielby 1986; Tomaskovic-Devey 1993; Petersen and Morgan 1995), there are trade-offs in balancing this against other concerns. For example, job-level studies are harder to generalize as they are typically limited by geographic locale (Baron and Bielby 1986; Tomaskovic-Devey 1993; analyses of the Multi-City Study of Urban Inequality [MCSUI] data [Bobo et al. 2000]) or to a subset of industries or occupations (Baron and Bielby 1986; MCSUI analyses; Petersen and Morgan 1995). And many, but not all, of the job-level studies lack data on worker characteristics, which are a key factor in understanding labor market processes and outcomes.

15. Tomaskovic-Devey (1993) has both worker-level and organization-level data, but he analyzes them separately. His job-level segregation analyses do not control for the effects of worker characteristics, nor do the worker-level analyses control for job/firm characteristics.

2

Perspectives on Segregation and Earnings Gaps

We became especially conscious, in our joint labors,
of the urges we both have felt to understand the tensions
we experienced from our earliest years between the
individualistic search for opportunities, so often and so
widely celebrated in America, and the roles of structural and
institutional arrangements that block (or mock) some persons'
progress even as those arrangements help to reward others'
individual aspirations and the tactics chosen to fulfill them.
—Kalleberg and Berg (1987: xi)

Over the past thirty years, sociologists and economists alike have explored explanations for the persistent employment and compensation differentials between men and women and between blacks and whites. This set of perspectives exhibit the same tension between individual and structural factors so aptly described by Kalleberg and Berg, often portrayed as a contrast between supply-side approaches and demand-side approaches. Put most simply, supply-side explanations focus on the nature of the individuals supplying labor: the traits that workers bring to the labor market, such as skills, credentials, preferences, and orientations. In contrast, demand-side explanations emphasize the nature of the workplace demanding labor: the characteristics of the setting in which work occurs, such as job requirements and content, market and organizational structure, queuing and personnel practices, and the wider social and economic contexts in which they are embedded. In this chapter I will first overview the major supply-side and demand-side perspectives and the evidence supporting them and then propose an integrated approach drawing on ideas from a variety of perspectives that partially bridges this distinction using queuing processes as a linchpin. As this discussion will make clear, the tension between individual and structural factors also arises within some of these perspectives.

17

Supply-Side Perspectives

Supply-side explanations for racial differences in employment and compensation have long emphasized differences in qualifications, training, and credentials between blacks and whites from a human-capital perspective in economics and a status-attainment one in sociology. More recently, spatial mismatch (which bridges the individual-structural divide) has proposed that differences in the residential location of blacks and whites can also be consequential. In contrast, explanations for sex segregation and sex-wage gaps have focused predominantly on varying choices, preferences, and family roles between women and men (Padavic and Reskin 2002).

Human Capital/Status Attainment

These approaches try to explain segregation and earnings gaps as a function of group differences in education, experience, and skills (Marini and Fan 1997; Moss and Tilly 2001; Padavic and Reskin 2002; Turner, Fix, and Struyk 1991). The human-capital approach in economics argues that workers forgo present earnings to invest in themselves through training and skill development. Sociologists using a status-attainment or life-course perspective (Blau and Duncan 1967; Buchmann 2006; Featherman and Hauser 1976; Ganzeboom, Treiman, and Ultee 1991; Sewell, Haller, and Portes 1969) similarly propose that achievements at earlier stages of the life course are the central determinants of later attainments. Both approaches thus argue that education, experience, and skills are crucial predictors of the matching of workers to jobs. To the extent that race-sex groups differ in their average human capital, this could explain group differences in the type of jobs and rewards attained.

Research has consistently documented continuing but at best slowly converging racial differences in general human capital such as education and work experience as well as in occupationally specific human capital such as on-the-job training or reading, math, and science achievement tests (Council of Economic Advisers 1998; Haveman, Bershadker, and Schwabish 2003; Jaynes and Williams 1989; Hedges and Nowell 1998; and other studies in Jencks and Phillips 1998). Among employers there is also a distinct perception that blacks and whites differ in "soft" skills such as interpersonal interaction and motivation/effort (Moss and Tilly 2001; Neckerman and Kirschenman 1991). However, Moss and Tilly (2001: 247) caution that it is not clear whether this perception reflects employers' stereotyping or real racial differences in skills.

In contrast, sex differences in human capital are much more limited (Haveman, Bershadker, and Schwabish 2003; Padavic and Reskin 2002; Tomaskovic-Devey 1993). Currently men and women in the United States have about the same average number of years of schooling, with slightly fewer men than women having completed high school and obtained associate degrees, but somewhat more men than women having completed baccalaureate and graduate/professional degrees (US Bureau of the Census 2009). However, such static statistics conceal the fact that the long-standing advantage of men with respect to baccalaureate degrees reversed in the 1980s, with a growing advantage at the baccalaureate level accruing to women (DiPrete and Buchmann 2006). More substantial, but continuing to decline, are sex differences in work experience and on-the-job training (Padavic and Reskin 2002) and mathematical achievement test scores (Muller 1998).

Clearly human capital and skills are important predictors of the jobs people get and the earnings they receive, but the group differences noted above are not sufficient to explain employment disparities. Studies have consistently shown that, even accounting for such differences (which do explain large portions of initial race but not sex disparities; see, for example, Farkas et al. 1997), sizable race and sex gaps remain in the kinds of jobs and earnings that workers attain.[1] For example, Raudenbush and Kasim (1998) find that, even taking into account family social origins, human capital, and cognitive skills, African American men's earnings are only 85% of white men's earnings; for women the race gap is not significant. The net sex gap in earnings is much larger among whites (65%) than among blacks (85%). Moreover, the source of two-thirds of these gaps are *within occupations,* which neither cognitive skills nor preferences for types of work can explain.

Some of the most compelling evidence on racial discrimination in hiring comes from audit studies (see the extensive review of studies in Bendick 2007 or Pager 2007). For example, in the studies by Turner, Fix, and Struyk (1991), carefully matched pairs of black and white job seekers applied for the same entry-level jobs in three large cities. Each pair presented equivalent credentials and skills to employers, and they underwent extensive training to behave similarly during job interviews. A summary of their progress through the application and hiring process paints a stark picture of the reality of discriminatory processes in the labor market:

> The hiring audit demonstrates that unequal treatment of black job seekers is entrenched and widespread, contradicting claims that hiring practices today either favor blacks or are effectively color blind. Specifically, in one out of five audits, the white applicant was able to advance farther through the hiring process than his equally qualified black counterpart. In other words, the white was able to submit an application, receive a formal interview, or be offered a job when the black was not. Overall, in one out of eight—or 15 percent—of the audits, the white was offered a job although his equally qualified black partner was not. (p. 2)

More recent studies using variations of this audit methodology (Bertrand and Mullainathan 2004; Pager 2003; Pager and Quillian 2005) have confirmed the persistence of such processes. Thus past research shows that group differences in human capital and skills, while important, are far from the whole story for the existence and persistence of gaps in employment and earnings.

Spatial Mismatch

According to this perspective, racial differences in the labor market stem in part from a discontinuity between the residential location of blacks and the geographic location of jobs (Ihlanfeldt and Sjoquist 1998; Kain 1968, 1992; Raphael and Stoll 2006; Wilson 1996). The continuing concentration of blacks in the central cities of large metropolitan areas coupled with the growing density of employment outside the central city create a mismatch that restricts the kinds of jobs to which many black job seekers have ready access. And high (albeit declining) residential segregation constrains blacks' ability to be geographically mobile to follow jobs. Several other factors also contribute to the mismatch process: (1) the difficulty if not impossibility of commuting via public transportation; (2) a lack of information on suburban job opportunities; and (3) greater employment discrimination by suburban employers (Ihlanfeldt and Sjoquist 1998). Mismatch can create segregation in the kinds of jobs workers obtain as well as "crowding" in the jobs remaining in the central cities, which should lower wages and exacerbate racial wage gaps. This approach is neither purely supply side nor demand side. It combines characteristics of workers (residential location) and employers (business location) as well as non–labor market factors (residential segregation and transportation infrastructure).

Research has shown moderate support for the spatial mismatch thesis. Ihlanfeldt and Sjoquist's (1998) review found that twenty-one of twenty-eight studies report results in support of the spatial mismatch hypothesis, echoing similar, earlier reviews. Recent evidence indicates that blacks have longer commutes (Gabriel and Rosenthal 1996); that job decentralization increases the length of time spent unemployed for urban blacks (Holzer, Ihlanfeldt, and Sjoquist 1994); that areas with higher residential segregation have greater spatial mismatch (Raphael and Stoll 2006); that job access explains a notable share of the employment differential between young white and black males (Raphael 1998); and that spatial mismatch declined by only a modest amount (13%) during the 1990s (Raphael and Stoll 2006).

McCall (2001a) proposes a different way of thinking about spatial processes and labor market inequality. She suggests that there are four ideal-typic configurations of inequality in local labor markets, which have resulted from the economic restructuring of local economies. She finds that specific forms of inequality (by race, sex, or class) spatially cluster with distinct levels across locales, which suggests that it is more fruitful to explore class differences within sex than race differences within sex. For example, in the industrial configuration (e.g., the traditional Rust Belt), sex inequality is low among those lacking college credentials but high among those with college degrees, and racial inequality is uniformly high. But the opposite pattern of high and low inequality characterizes post-industrial local economies (e.g., the large polarized service sector). Moreover, the effects of industrial restructuring indicators on the forms of inequality vary both across configurations and across the forms (McCall 2000a, 2001a,b).

Worker Preferences

These approaches concentrate on social and cultural differences among workers from different race-sex groups that create preferences for different types of labor market positions and thus lead to segregation and earnings gaps among groups by choice (England 1992; Marini and Fan 1997). Although such a "choice" explanation is often proposed for sex differences in labor market outcomes, it has not been accepted or used in the literature on race inequality (Padavic and Reskin 2002; Tomaskovic-Devey 1993). Two distinct types of preferences have been suggested as a source of sex differences in job selection: preferences for work that can accommodate family responsibilities; and preferences for work with certain types of skills and working conditions.

Family responsibilities. The empirical reality is that women still bear the primary burden for family labor although this has diminished somewhat over the last thirty years (Bianchi et al. 2000). Research consistently shows that sex is the most influential factor in understanding the household division of labor (Shelton and John 1996; Bianchi et al. 2000). Even among dual-earner households, employed wives still spend significantly more time on housework than employed husbands (Ferree 1991; Goldscheider and Waite 1991; Shelton 1992; Sayer 2005). Moreover, husbands and wives undertake gender-specific tasks, with men much less likely to do the everyday, "must do" work. For example, men do, at best, between 25% to 33% of the cooking and meal cleanup, laundry, and housecleaning in married-couple households (Goldscheider and Waite 1991; Shelton 1992). Bianchi et al. (2000) find that, since 1965, the amount of time women devote to housework has declined substantially (from thirty hours to less than twenty hours per week in 1995), while men's time on housework has increased somewhat (from about five hours to ten hours per week). Shelton and John's (1996) review finds contradictory evidence about a more egalitarian division of labor among blacks than whites. But the growing prevalence of single-mother households as a family type puts more of an onus for family responsibilities on women, especially among blacks.

Economists and sociologists offer very different explanations for these disparities. Neoclassical economists typically argue that men and women specialize in the division of family labor because it is a rational way to maximize family utility (e.g., Becker 1991; O'Neill 2003). Specifically, women undertake primary responsibility for child-rearing and other family labor, while men take primary responsibility for wage earning. Such a division of labor is more efficient for families because men and women specialize in either home or work, and each invests in different but complementary human capital. Women specialize in nonmarket work because they have a "comparative advantage" over men stemming from their biological role as mothers. It is also rational because, on average, a woman can expect lower labor market rewards. Further, she is argued to have less time and energy for paid employment, to be less likely to invest in on-the-job training, and either to be more likely to acquire less valuable general skills or to experience skill depreciation of specific skills due to labor force interruptions for child-rearing (O'Neill 2003). According to this perspective, mothers choose work that accommodates their family responsibilities, are less productive workers, and accordingly are paid less.

Sociologists have argued instead that the sex-based division of labor in the home results from time demands and constraints, from power dynamics, and/or from the operation of a broader system of gender relations (Berk 1985; Bianchi et al. 2000; Shelton and John 1996). Demands for household labor (presence and age of children) and constraints on providing such labor (hours of paid work) are perhaps the strongest predictors of the amount of household labor done by individuals. But this does not explain why such predictors are much more consequential for women than men or why women but not men would engage in less paid work (Bianchi et al. 2000; Shelton and John 1996). Neither can it explain why there have long been smaller differences in labor force participation among black women and men than among white women and men.

The household power dynamics approach, on the other hand, suggests that partners' relative resources explains the gendered allocation of household labor (Brines 1993; Shelton and John 1996). Greater resources (e.g., income) confer greater power in bargaining over the division of labor, such that the partner with fewer resources performs more of the household labor, especially "core," everyday tasks. While this holds true for women who are more economically dependent in marriages, the reverse holds for economically dependent men, suggesting that men react to dependency by reinforcing gender-typicality in other realms (Brines 1994). And the smaller sex gap in earnings among blacks than whites (Padavic and Reskin 2002) would imply a more egalitarian division of household labor in black families, but the evidence for this is mixed (Shelton and John 1996).

A gender relations perspective focuses on the explicitly gendered nature of the processes creating and maintaining the division of household work (Berk 1985; Bianchi et al. 2000; Brines 1994; Greenstein 1996; West and Zimmerman 1987). This complements the other approaches by emphasizing the importance of patriarchy, of childhood gender-role socialization, adult gender ideologies, and of the household as an arena in which both men and women "do gender" by creating and re-creating gender relations.

Thus, economists and sociologists have both proposed, albeit for vastly different reasons, that women self-select into positions that offer flexibility in scheduling tasks or hours. One consequence could be wage gaps between women and men. The human capital thesis of compensating differentials proposes that workers make a trade-off between wages and the amenities or disamenities of a job (Brown 1980). Workers accept lower wages for jobs with desired amenities but require a wage premium for jobs with disamenities. This would suggest that women may exchange wages for the amenity of job conditions accommodating family responsibility. If so, this could explain some part of the aggregate wage differences between women and men and would predict larger *within*-position wage gaps for some jobs. If these job conditions are not amenities for men, then they would not accept a wage discount, as women would do, leading to greater sex wage gaps within such positions.

However, aside from the availability of part-time work, there is no evidence of compatibility between women's actual employment conditions and the accommodation of family responsibility (Padavic and Reskin 2002). Female-typed jobs offer less flexibility in scheduling tasks, provide less free time during work, and require more effort (Glass 1990). Further, women working thirty hours or more per week are *not* more likely than men to be in jobs offering such ease and flexibility (Glass and Camarigg 1992). Similarly, research has not supported the compensating differentials thesis, either in general (Brown 1980; Kilbourne et al. 1994a) or as applied to sex wage gaps (Jacobs and Steinberg 1990; Kilbourne et al. 1994a).[2] Alternatively, some economists have suggested that women anticipate having a discontinuous labor force participation in order to raise families and that they will choose jobs accordingly (O'Neill 2003; Mincer and Polachek 1974). If so, they should self-select into jobs that do not experience depreciation of human capital over time or that have higher entry wages but flat experience-earnings profiles. However, past research has provided little support for either skill depreciation or for a scenario of high starting wages but flat experience-earnings profiles (England 1992).

Preferences for certain skills and working conditions. As far as I can determine, a preference or values argument about job selection by race has not been made in the literature (Reskin 1993; Tomaskovic-Devey 1993). But there is a lively debate about whether women choose jobs with "female-typed" skills and working conditions (as discussed here) or whether they are restricted to such jobs (as discussed later). Gender-role socialization approaches argue that men and women develop preferences for work with varying skills and conditions during childhood and adult gender socialization (England 1992; Jacobs 1989; Marini and Fan 1997; Padavic and Reskin 2002; Tomaskovic-Devey 1993). As early as ages two to three, children begin to differentiate their choices of activities, toys, and playmates in a gendered fashion and develop a sense of their own gender identity by age six (Stockard 1999). It is generally accepted that such differences have a limited biological basis: "As ethnomethodologists have demonstrated, this process is almost entirely socially constructed despite its apparent 'naturalness'" (Ridgeway 1997: 219).

Recent work suggests that one result of socialization is that children (and adults) learn and develop sets of cognitive schemas to "provide an efficient way to organize new knowledge and information and help individuals maintain consistency and predictability in new situations" (Stockard 1999: 219). *Gender* schemas categorize and organize information by gender categories and are one of a few "superschemas" that are first invoked in perceptual processes. Although a gender schema may be tangential to the focus of perception or interaction, it can be activated in response to the sex of the others in an interaction or in response to gender cues embedded in the objects or activities of the interaction (Ridgeway 1997).[3]

Women and men may make employment choices based upon such a gender schema, categorizing certain types of skills and conditions as female or male "appropriate." If so, there would be greater segregation between men and women in positions that require either "female" skills and conditions (such as physical dexterity, clerical perception, the performance of nurturant or subservient tasks, and pleasant working conditions) or "male" skills and working conditions (such as mathematical skills, heavy physical labor, status-superior interactions with men, and extreme environmental conditions). Bielby and Baron's (1986) analysis of job segregation in mixed-sex occupations in a restricted sample of California firms found such segregation, but there is not comparable research across the full range of occupations and industries.[4]

Two different mechanisms could turn sex-segregated choices of jobs into sex-linked wage differences. Despite the lack of empirical support noted above, a compensating differentials approach theoretically could explain lower wages for female-dominated jobs if working in a job with female-typed skills and conditions provides amenities to women. Note that the same logic (which to my knowledge has not been applied this way) would suggest that wages should also be lower for male-dominated jobs, a result at odds with the consistent finding of a negative linear effect of percent female on male earnings (Budig 2002; Catanzarite 2003; Cohen and Huffman 2003b). Crowding is another process by which segregated work (by sex or by race) could result in lower wages for jobs (Bergmann 1974, 1986; Sorenson 1990; Taeuber, Taeuber, and Cain 1966), although it does not rely on choice as the mechanism producing segregation. If the set of segregated positions is sufficiently restricted such that the supply of workers outstrips the demand for workers, such crowding should reduce wages if the oversupply is not transient.

However, the plausibility of preferences as an explanation for segregation and wage gaps relies on a rather weak empirical underpinning in terms of actual sex differences in work values and preferences and how these affect job choice. As Rowe and Snizek (1995) argued, there is a myth about the magnitude of sex differences in work values: Sex differences in occupational and work values are in fact small and typically explain little of the variation in occupational values (see also Tolbert and Moen 1998). Similarly, there are at most small black-white differences in work values (Day and Rounds 1998; Gupta, Tracey, and Gore 2008; Johnson 2002), the direction of which would not suggest that blacks select less desirable jobs. Johnson (2002), for example, finds that African Americans (especially women) value nearly all forms of job rewards more highly than whites. Moreover, the rank order of what is most highly valued is very similar for men and women, correlating between .85 to .99 (Bridges 1989; Herzog 1982; Lueptow 1980; Rowe and Snizek 1995), with some studies finding no such differences (Cassirer and Reskin 2000; Jencks, Perman, and Rainwater 1988; Loscoco 1990).

Turning to preferences for specific types of jobs or skills, there are similarly limited sex differences in vocational interests. Many studies (e.g., Betz, Harmon, and Borgen 1996; Day and Rounds 1998; Gupta, Tracey, and Gore 2008; Johnson 2002; Lippa 1998; Mullis, Mullis, and Gerwels 1998; Tracey 1997; Wagner 1982) have examined race-sex group differences in vocational interests using Holland's six-component RIASEC typology (the acronym standing for realistic, investigative, artistic, social, enterprising, and conventional components) as well as its two underlying dimensions of people-things and data-ideas.[5] They consistently find no sex or race-ethnic group differences in the overall structure of preferences; neither does the structure vary within race-ethnicity by sex or vice versa. But the magnitude of group differences in scale scores on the components are variable across studies, ranging from none to sometimes more substantial. Although Lippa's (1998) analyses of three small samples finds that men express a stronger vocational interest in things and women express more interest in people, they do not differ along the data-ideas dimension and there is considerable overlap in the score distributions of men and women. In contrast, Day and Rounds (1998) find no appreciable differences along these dimensions for ten race-sex groups in their analysis of a very large national sample. Research using other ways of measuring specific interests also find minimal or no sex differences (Browne 1997; Filer 1986; Gati, Osipow, and Givon 1995; Judd and Oswald 1997). Although both sexes continue to stereotype the gender appropriateness of jobs (see the review by Phillips and Imhoff 1997), they still rate the same jobs as desirable (see, for example, Judd and Oswald 1997).

Finally, there is limited evidence that such personality and value differences actually affect sex differences in the jobs selected (Barry 1987; Fernandez and Mors 2008; Fernandez and Sosa 2005; Filer 1986; Glass and Camarigg 1992; Padavic 1991). On the one hand, some studies find evidence for both applicant self-segregation and employer steering into sex-segregated jobs (Fernandez and Mors 2008; Fernandez and Sosa 2005). In contrast, Filer (1986: 423), for example, concludes that "in general, the small magnitude of the changes in the estimated co-efficients [*for race and sex*] when personalities and tastes are incorporated into the analysis suggests that their importance lies primarily in providing additional information rather than in correcting the possible biases discussed above." Even preferences for gender-typical work are only weakly related to job choice (Rosenfeld and Spenner 1992; Jacobs 1989), and many argue that such preferences reflect the effect of past market discrimination (Marini 1989; Reskin 1993).

Demand-Side Perspectives

The demand-side perspectives typically acknowledge the importance of some supply-side factors (in particular qualifications, training, and other sources of human capital) but argue that other processes also must be operative because supply-side traits are insufficient to explain race and sex differences in employment outcomes. Among these perspectives, neoclassical economic explanations of race and sex differences highlight the role of "tastes for discrimination" as constrained by rational decisionmaking in the hiring process. The segmented market approach used by both sociologists and economists focuses on the operation of product-market and organizational factors as they affect labor market processes and also assume that tastes for discrimination play a role. A recent outgrowth from the segmented markets approach has been an emphasis on the role of staffing and recruitment practices to inhibit or facilitate sex-segregated hiring and staffing. Race-sex queuing and devaluation theories in sociology emphasize how workers in the labor queue for jobs are evaluated according to their race and sex as "master" statuses rather than solely by their credentials and qualifications and how job rewards partly depend on the race-sex composition of jobs' incumbents.

Discrimination and Rational Decisionmakers

Preeminent here is Becker's (1971) competitive theory of discrimination (see also Arrow 1972, 1973; Cain 1975) developed to explain racial labor market differentials. A second well-known approach is the theory of statistical discrimination, which has been widely applied to both race and sex differences by economists and sociologists alike (Arrow 1972, 1973; Baron and Bielby 1986; Bielby and Baron 1986; Doeringer and Piore 1971; Marini 1989; Reskin 1993; Thurow 1975; Tomaskovic-Devey and Skaggs 1999).

Competitive theory of discrimination. Becker (1971) argues that "tastes for discrimination" can be exercised by employers, workers, or customers. Assuming widespread tastes for discrimination against blacks and competitive product markets leads to different results depending on the source of discrimination. When the source is employers' tastes for discrimination, this results in discriminating firms paying white workers a wage premium, which is offset by blacks being paid a discounted wage in the short run. But competition in the product and labor markets should, in the long run, give nondiscriminating firms a competitive advantage and force discriminating firms to either change their wage offers (i.e., stop discriminating) or be driven out of business. When there are workers' tastes for discrimination, this could also create transient wage discrimination if there were a shortage of workers. In the long run, however, such workers' tastes for discrimination should not lead to discrimination in wages but rather to segregation of blacks and whites into different firms, all paid the same wage. In contrast, only customers' tastes for discrimination can result in long-run wage discrimination that is resistant to competitive market pressures.

In light of this argument and the widespread persistence of discrimination, Becker contends that discrimination must be due to various product market imperfections (lack of competition). Becker also argues that labor unionization, due to white workers' tastes for discrimination, should lead to greater discrimination among unionized than among nonunionized (competitive) sectors. In particular, Becker argues that monopolistic discriminating employers do not face competitive pricing pressures that could drive competitive discriminating employers out of business. Monopolists could, in fact, use some of their excess (monopoly) profits to indulge their taste for discrimination without affecting the price at which goods are offered (Becker 1971; Cain 1975).

Even within the neoclassical framework, the competitive theory of discrimination is problematic as a general explanation for wage gaps. Absent market imperfections, only consumer preferences can lead to enduring discrimination. And consumer preferences cannot generally explain discrimination because consumers do not usually know who (which race) produced the good being purchased. And if there are sufficient market imperfections to create the observed degree of discrimination, then the amount of market imperfection is large enough that it can no longer be assumed that the US economy basically operates in competitive markets. Research on the effect of market power on segregation and wage inequality has been contradictory; some studies find greater inequality in monopolistic than in competitive sectors while others find the opposite.[6] Moreover, all the studies still show substantial discrimination in competitive sectors, suggesting that competition does *not* eliminate discrimination.

More fundamentally, a question can be raised about the logic of the "taste" for discrimination thesis invoked by this approach (and by the segmented markets perspective discussed later). These tastes are presumed to be expressed through the creation of physical segregation of groups: the total exclusion of particular race-sex groups from a workplace. A much more plausible expression would be the creation of social distance among groups in a workplace rather than physical distance between workplaces (Reskin 1988, 1993; England 1992; Kaufman 1986; Marshall 1974): in other words, the assignment of white men to the more desirable jobs in a workplace and the assignment of members of other race-sex groups to the less desirable jobs.

Statistical discrimination. The supply-side approach to human capital suggests that disparities in employment and earnings outcomes are due in part to *individual* differences in human capital among race-sex groups. Statistical discrimination is often proposed by economists and sociologists alike as a mechanism that links rational employment decisions to groups' *aggregate* levels of human capital (Arrow 1972, 1973; Baron and Bielby 1986; Bielby and Baron 1986; Doeringer and Piore 1971; Marini 1989; Reskin 1993; Thurow 1975; Tomaskovic-Devey and Skaggs 1999). According to this thesis, there is a "statistical" reason for employers to discriminate. For example, employers may believe (correctly or not) that race-sex groups have different distributions of (unmeasured) productivity. Employers then use a worker's race and/or sex as an inexpensive screening device in hiring for jobs, particularly skilled jobs, in the belief that race and sex status are related to productivity. That is, individual workers are stereotyped as qualified or not based on their identification with a race and sex group rather than on their own qualifications. Profiling workers according to their race and sex group membership is assumed to reduce firms' information costs.

Employers might rationally conclude that individual blacks and whites differ in their average (unmeasured) productivity because, as groups, blacks and whites do differ in their average levels of various "objective" indicators of productivity (e.g., education and work experience). Employers then use race as a low-cost "screen" either to filter out less productive workers or as a rationalization for paying black workers less. A more sophisticated variant argues that employers might believe that blacks have greater variability in their potential productivity than whites because blacks exhibit greater variability in their distribution on the "objective" indicators of productivity. If so, there is less chance of making an error (greater reliability) in judging the productivity of whites to be greater than that of blacks. Thus, employers either will give preferential treatment to whites in hiring or will discount blacks' wage offers to guard against paying them more than their productivity.

Statistical discrimination is also used to explain sex differences in employment and earnings, but with a twist. It is often argued that employers' beliefs about sex differences may not be factually correct but may form the basis for their behavior nonetheless (Bielby and Baron 1986; England 1992; Tomaskovic-Devey and Skaggs 1999). That is, employers believe that the potential productivity of women is less than that of men and will act on that belief. Consequently employers either hire men preferentially or pay women a discounted wage. It is plausible that the dual statuses of black women would intensify employers' use of statistical discrimination by providing reinforcing reasons to question their productivity.

Unlike the competitive theory of discrimination, it is not clear that competitive market pressures are an effective counteractive force to statistical discrimination. Statistical discrimination entails some costs to employers, primarily the losses associated with hiring some workers who are less productive than those not offered a job. But it also may provide some savings by lowering the costs of screening job applicants. If the costs of more accurately determining the productivity of individual workers and paying workers strictly according to productivity are less than the costs of statistical discrimination, then competition theoretically could be effective in eliminating discrimination. But if such information costs are greater, then competition cannot eliminate statistical discrimination.

There is fairly consistent support in the literature for statistical discrimination as one source of employment and earnings differences among groups. It is often cited as a principal cause of occupational segregation and wage gaps (Arrow 1972; Baron and Bielby 1986; Bielby and Baron 1986; Marini 1989; Neumark 1999; Reskin 1993; Thurow 1975; Tomaskovic-Devey and Skaggs 1999). However, statistical discrimination has proven more useful as a tool applied by other perspectives (which specify the conditions under which it is likely to occur) than as a general explanation for employment and earnings inequalities.

Segmented Market Perspectives

Labor market segmentation is the idea that there are sets of positions in the labor market whose characteristics systematically differ in ways that affect their recruitment, hiring, promotion, and reward processes (Hodson and Kaufman 1982; Kalleberg and Berg 1994; Lang and Dickens 1994; Sakamoto and Chen 1991). It recognizes that matching people to jobs has implications for understanding how and why inequality in labor market rewards is distributed across groups. One of the original, motivating questions was to understand and explain racial differences in labor market outcomes (Bluestone 1970; Gordon 1972; Hodson and Kaufman 1982; Kaufman 1983), but this approach has frequently been applied to analyses of sex differences as well (Baron and Newman 1990; Bielby and Baron 1986; Bridges 1982; England 1992; Huffman and Velasco 1997; McBrier 2003; Wallace and Chang 1990; Wharton 1986).

Segmented market theory proposes that labor market outcomes for individuals (especially their earnings) depends on the structural context of their jobs (Baron and Bielby 1980; Domanski 1990; Hachen 1992; Hodson and Kaufman 1982; Sakamoto and Chen 1991; Tigges 1987; Tolbert, Horan, and Beck 1980). Its guiding principle is that product and labor markets are not open, homogeneous, and competitive but rather form distinct segments, which vary in their exposure to or insulation from market and nonmarket pressures. Both the average level of earnings in positions and the returns paid to workers' traits (particularly human capital) are determined by the nature of the factors that segment product and labor markets.

It is well established that employment in larger firms or in industries with larger establishment size raises workers' earnings (Brown, Hamilton, and Medoff 1990; Hodson 1983; Kalleberg, Wallace, and Althauser 1981; Villemez and Bridges 1988). Similarly, firms in oligopolistic product markets can set product prices and wages, whereas firms in competitive markets must accept market-driven prices and wages. Such markets give rise to different resources and vulnerabilities for firms and workers (Hodson and Kaufman 1982), which creates the potential for very different labor market structures and remuneration practices. Workers' wages thus reflect not only the investments they make in themselves (human capital) but also the premiums and discounts paid according to the "location" of their job in particular markets. One implication is that the linking of wages to market segments can explain wage gaps among race-sex groups if women and minorities are segregated into lower-paid labor market segments.

Segmented market theories often conceptualize the matching process using a queuing model, either explicitly (Doeringer and Piore 1971; Kaufman 1986; Sakamoto and Chen 1991; Sorensen and Kalleberg 1981; Thurow 1975) or implicitly (Beck, Horan, and Tolbert 1978; Bibb and Form 1977; Hodson and Kaufman 1982; Tolbert, Horan, and Beck 1980). Unlike the race-sex queuing model discussed next, queuing is argued to characterize only jobs in protected labor markets while jobs in unstructured labor markets are open to competition (Lang and Dickens 1994). Initial entry into such protected markets is beneficial to workers in terms of both immediate rewards and job security and promotion prospects. As Braddock and McPartland (1987) point out, discrimination against African Americans is greatest at this entry stage and can have long-term consequences in creating and maintaining racial inequality. Similarly, Marini and Fan (1997: 592) argue that "women and men with the same formal employment credentials may be triaged by personnel officers into different jobs, and these different job placements may have important implications for earnings and future career mobility." Indeed they find that sex differences in initial placement explain substantially more of the sex gap in initial earnings (42%) than do sex differences in human capital, family structure, and occupational aspirations combined (30%).

Like Becker's competitive theory of discrimination, segmented market approaches argue that employers' preference for white men is one source of segregation by race and/or sex. But they also fruitfully use statistical discrimination to explain how queuing can give rise to segregation and wage disparities. The future costs and consequences of hiring less productive workers are argued to be higher for jobs and sectors of the economy in protected market segments. Typically, work in a protected segment requires longer training time (often through on-the-job training by other workers) and work is often interdependent, making it impossible to measure individual productivity. To encourage workers to train their own replacements and to discourage slacking and turnover, employers offer incentives such as job rights for workers, promotion opportunities, and higher earnings. If employers mistakenly hire less productive workers, they face one of two costly choices. Either they keep them and forgo the profit that a more productive worker would create, or they fire them and pay high replacement costs. Thus statistical discrimination should be more likely in these segments because of the higher cost consequences of selecting less productive or higher-turnover workers. The result should be either greater segregation in these segments, discounted wages for women and minorities in these segments, or both. As I noted above, such results should be disproportionately more pronounced for black women.

But this exclusionary process has been disputed empirically and conceptually. Studies of the effects of economic buffering (market power) and slack resources (profitability) on black employment representation have found inconsistent effects (compare Becker 1971; Comanor 1973; Coleman 2004; Galle, Wiswell, and Burr 1985; Kaufman 1986; Kaufman and Daymont 1981; Shepherd 1970). Reskin (1993) notes that there has been very mixed evidence for the influence of economic buffering and economic structure on sex segregation. As I argued in discussing Becker's approach, employers' expression of a "taste" for discrimination is much more likely to result in segregation within a workplace than to create segregation between workplaces. Moreover, it is important to consider countervailing pressures. Antidiscrimination pressure by the government and citizens' groups has generally targeted larger, more visible economic arenas (Hirsh and Kornrich 2008; Holzer 1998; Kaufman 1986; Marshall 1974; Szafran 1982). Even absent such targeting, changes in employment regulations and in public opinion promoting nondiscrimination can offset economic buffering by changing employers' preferences and reducing the salience of discriminatory preferences (Reskin 1993; Szafran 1982). Speculatively, firms attempting to change in response to pressure might be especially proactive in hiring black women, as they "double-count." Although firms with market power or slack resources can most easily afford to change their labor practices (Kaufman 1986; Szafran 1982), these factors also provide resources to resist market and external pressures.

Staffing and Recruitment Practices

There is a bourgeoning literature exploring the mechanisms by which employment segregation occurs at the establishment level and its consequences for earnings, much of it focused on the role of staffing and recruitment practices (e.g., Holzer, Raphael, and Stoll 2004; Fernandez and Sosa 2005; Fernandez and Fernandez-Mateo 2006; Fernandez and Mors 2008; Kmec 2005; Kmec and Trimble 2009; Petersen and Sapporta 2004; Petersen, Sapporta, and Seidel 2000; Stainback 2008). As Kmec (2005: 324) so aptly argues and summarizes, there are a variety of ways in which organizational practices can facilitate or inhibit employment segregation. These include whether or not they limit hiring agents' (1) knowledge of an applicant's race and sex; (2) discretionary decisionmaking and favoritism; and (3) use of stereotypes or personal beliefs to evaluate an applicant's performance or behavior. A recurrent theme in this literature is that informal recruitment practices, in particular the use of employee referrals, should reproduce the existing race-sex composition of the workplace because it provides the employer knowledge of the applicant's race and sex, thus permitting discretion and exposing applicants to stereotyping in hiring decisions. In addition, the high degree of race-sex homophily of networks means that an applicant's contacts are more likely to provide information about similarly segregated jobs. In contrast, formal advertising methods could diversify the applicant pool by providing information about openings to members of groups not traditionally employed in the establishment, especially if they rely on referrals from outside agencies. A related argument is that applicants' use of social network contacts to find jobs provides access to good jobs differentially by race and sex; however the evidence for this point is mixed (see the studies reviewed by Kmec and Trimble 2009). What has been more consistently established is that an initial screening of candidates into queues for different positions by race and sex can be consequential for pay differentials in the aggregate but not within positions (Fernandez and Mors 2008; Petersen and Sapporta 2004; Petersen, Saporta, and Seidel 2000).

Race-Sex Queuing Theory

Reskin and Roos (1990) extended traditional queuing theory by proposing *gender queues* to explain sex-linked labor market processes, in particular job segregation and integration. The basic premise of queuing theory is that the matching of workers to jobs results from the intersection of two queues: a *job queue,* in which individuals rank jobs according to their desirability; and a *labor queue,* in which employers rank potential employees according to their desirability. Thus, an employer (or his/her agent) offers employment to the most highly ranked candidate in the labor queue of potential workers, and individuals choose their most highly ranked job in the job queue of offered jobs. Economic and sociological approaches have emphasized employers' judgment of the "trainability" and productivity of an individual as a key determinant of how they rank candidates (Lang and Dickens 1994; Sakamoto and Chen 1991; Reskin and Roos 1990; Sorensen and Kalleberg 1981; Thurow 1975). Such judgments are presumed to rely heavily on a candidate's human capital and employment history. Individuals' ranking of jobs typically reflects an attempt "to maximize income, social standing, autonomy, job security, congenial working conditions, and the chance for advancement" (Reskin and Roos 1990: 38). As noted above for labor market segmentation, a queuing process is assumed to apply only to some jobs.

In contrast, Reskin and Roos (1990) argue that queuing processes also incorporate evaluations of employer preferences for sex (race) groups and that such evaluations are applied to work in *all* labor market positions, not just positions in sheltered or structured labor markets. They assert that labor queues have three structural properties: (1) the ordering principle for the elements of the queue; (2) the intensity of preferences; and (3) the shape of the queue.

Research on queuing and race-sex inequality has focused primarily on the first structural property. The *ordering principle* for the labor queue refers to the criteria employers use to order workers in the labor queue. Beyond using a candidate's credentials, trainability, or productivity, employers may also order candidates according to their race and sex for varied reasons. Some jobs may be stereotyped as "appropriate" for some groups and as "inappropriate" for others; for example, labeled as male or female jobs. Statistical discrimination may prompt employers' use of a race-sex ordering principle for some jobs, especially if productivity is hard to measure or if uncertainty about a candidate's productivity has costly consequences. Or employers may apply a race-sex ordering principle in response to worker or customer discrimination (in Becker's terms). Reskin and Roos (1990) describe the expected consequence of ordering labor queues by race and sex: "If employers tend to favor group X, then the Xs will be concentrated in the best jobs and the non Xs largely relegated to the least desirable ones" (p. 31).

While the race-sex ordering of the labor queue is the most central structural property, the other structural properties are also important to understand how queues and market segmentation produce racial and sex inequality. The *intensity of preferences* refers to the strength of rankers' preferences for the different criteria used to rank the elements in the queue. For some jobs, credentials and trainability may be given the most weight, with little or no use made of race-sex status, while for other jobs race-sex status is of paramount importance. The *shape* of a queue refers to the size of the queue itself (the number of elements) and the relative sizes of the elements in the queue. Changes in the shape of the job queue can influence the distribution of race-sex groups across jobs. For example, a job experiencing growth can open opportunities for less-favored groups if there is a scarcity of qualified members of a more preferred group. Indeed, as I argue later, employment growth should moderate the influence of other processes, enhancing some but diminishing others.

There has been surprisingly little research directly testing race-sex queuing theory. Aside from a consistent finding that employment growth (the shape of the job queue) diminishes segregation (e.g., Fields and Wolff 1991 and the studies reviewed by Reskin 1993: 251), the results have been mixed. In part, this may stem from the fact that the research has been case-study driven. For example, Wright and Jacobs's (1994) study of computer workers did not find support for a queuing explanation of feminization, while Roos and Manley's (1996) study of human-resource management did. A limitation of this approach is the implicit assumption that (white) men are preferred for all jobs, whereas the reality is that for certain kinds of jobs they are the least preferred. What images are invoked in most people's minds when they think about nurses, laundry pressers, or garbage collectors? Moreover, there has been no method proposed to determine for which jobs race-sex ordering principles are salient or more intense. As I argue more fully below, the race-sex ordering of the queue for jobs varies systematically with the nature and work tasks of jobs, as does the intensity and salience of the ordering principle.

Devaluation Perspective

With respect to earnings gaps, scholars agree that many gender- or race-typed work tasks and conditions are important determinants of the earnings given to positions and their incumbents but disagree over their implications for sex differences. The debate has centered on whether they represent "compensable differences" or a "gendered devaluation of work." As I discussed earlier, the compensating-differentials perspective holds that such tasks are either skills or amenities/disamenities differentially valued and chosen by women and men

and thus that corresponding sex-wage gaps are compensable (socially and economically legitimate).

In contrast, the devaluation perspective argues that the evidence for the compensating-differentials approach is weak (aside from risks of death and injury),
that there is little evidence of sex differences in the valuation of amenities/
disamenities, and that skill and the skill-earnings relationship are socially constructed (e.g., Baron and Newman 1990; England et al. 1994; England 1992;
Glass 1990; Jacobs and Steinberg 1990; Parcel 1989; Parcel and Mueller 1989;
Reskin 1988; Steinberg 1990). Rather, many of the skills that women use at
work (e.g., nurturing skills) are not rewarded as skills or are evaluated less
highly, even negatively, while many of the skills that men use at work (e.g., authority) are positively valued and hence rewarded. Unlike the compensating-
differentials approach, which applies only to women in gender-typed jobs, this
devaluation mechanism applies to *all* workers in race- or gender-typed jobs.
That is, the extent to which the work tasks in a job are female-typed and black-
typed should be associated with lower earnings for members of *all* race-sex
groups in that job.

Developing an Integrated Perspective

Reskin and Roos's elaboration of the structural properties of queues provides the
linchpin that I use to integrate it with the human-capital perspective's emphasis
on credentials, productivity, and family status, with segmented market theory's
emphasis on job and firm characteristics, and with the devaluation perspective's
emphasis on race- and gender-typing of work tasks and conditions. However, I
add a fourth structural property of queues. Closely related to the intensity of
preferences is the *salience of preferences,* which refers to the power or incentives of rankers to achieve their preferences. The importance of considering
both factors was highlighted sixty years ago by Merton (1949) in his seminal
work on prejudice and discrimination: Unprejudiced individuals may choose
to engage in discriminatory behavior just as prejudiced individuals may opt to
practice nondiscriminatory behavior, if there are sufficient forces working to
make their preferences less salient. Similarly Reskin (2003: 12) argues that organizational practices "can check or permit the effects of intrapsychic and interpersonal mechanisms." In the case of the labor queue, the intensity and
salience of preferences manifest themselves in the extent to which the ordering
of potential employees reflects the race-sex group preferences of rankers (or of
others with power) relative to the qualifications of individuals. Thus some factors (like regional location) should affect the intensity of preferences, whereas
others (like market concentration) should affect the salience of preferences.

This integrated explanation of race and sex inequality is applicable to all
labor market positions. I argue that race-sex queues can explain how members

of race-sex groups are segregated and how this sorting into jobs with different locations in product and labor markets in turn can explain differential earnings among race-sex groups beyond individual differences in credentials, productivity, and trainability. My approach is founded on six fundamental principles:

1. The matching of workers to jobs is governed by a queuing process for *all* jobs, not just those in protected market segments.
2. Labor queues have "structural" properties (order, shape, intensity and salience of preferences), some of which vary according to the characteristics of the corresponding product and labor markets in which a position is located.
3. Job queues also have these structural properties, some of which vary across potential workers, but I assume that they are invariant between blacks and whites in the aggregate and are "relatively" invariant between men and women in the aggregate.
4. Queuing processes specify that human capital is a central ordering principle for labor queues and that queues reproduce premarket differences among race-sex groups as inequality in employment and earnings.
5. By including a race-sex ordering principle for labor queues, this approach recognizes and models the role played both by various forms of discrimination (e.g., societal, employer, or statistical) and by human capital in determining how race-sex groups are differentially evaluated and offered jobs.
6. Because the operation of race-sex queues results in the segregation of race-sex groups into positions that systematically differ in the characteristics of their product and labor markets, these queuing processes can also explain earnings gaps among race-sex groups.

In the next section I briefly elaborate these six principles, and in the following section I apply them more systematically to develop the general expectations that guide the empirical evaluation of this integrated perspective in later chapters.

The Six Principles Explained

1. Queuing applies to all jobs. The ranking of workers in labor queues always embodies a race-sex ordering principle, even where employers are relatively indifferent to candidates' credentials, training, and productivity. Jobs carry race- and gender-typed labels that normatively identify them as "appropriate" or "inappropriate" for blacks and women. For example, a job requiring a high level of general skills as well as nurturant skills would be white female–typed, whereas if it required mathematical instead of nurturant skills, it would be white male–typed. Analogously, a job requiring menial work as well as manual dexterity would be black female–typed, whereas if it required physical strength instead of manual dexterity it would be black male–typed. Because the evaluation of workers for all jobs is subject to race-sex ordering, a queuing process is relevant to understanding the matching of workers to jobs for all jobs.

2. *The structural properties of labor queues vary across product and labor markets.* The ordering principle, shape, and the intensity and salience of preferences for a labor queue vary according to the characteristics of the corresponding product and labor markets in which a position is located. In particular, the ordering principle for a job's labor queue varies according to the required work tasks. In the labor queue, workers will be ranked not only according to the fit between their credentials and the required work tasks but also according to their race and/or sex status because the labeling of jobs as race- or gender-appropriate is affected by the specific content of the required work tasks. In some cases, the race-sex ordering is the result of statistical discrimination by employers in response to real or stereotypical group differences in credentials. Beyond this, jobs carry race- and/or gender-typed labels that identify them as "appropriate" or "inappropriate" for blacks and women. Because such labels are socially constructed, they are influenced by the nature of the work tasks required by the job. And these characteristics of the job affect the race-sex ordering of the labor queue aside from any real or stereotypical differences among groups in productivity or trainability. Thus, employers' preferences for race-sex groups are not uniform across jobs but vary systematically according to the characteristics of the job.

Similarly, the salience of employers' preferences is affected by different aspects of product and labor markets. Product market structures that give employers slack resources (such as the possession of market power or higher levels of profitability) should increase the salience of their preferences because these resources can be used to indulge their preferences. In contrast, employment growth should decrease the salience of preferences to the degree that growth restricts the available supply of preferred workers with the necessary skills. The actions of other labor market actors, such as union contracts and government regulation, may also affect the salience of employers' preferences.

3. *The structural properties of job queues vary across potential workers.* Although the ordering principle applied in the job queue and the intensity of preferences vary across potential workers, I assume that they are invariant between blacks and whites in the aggregate and are "relatively" invariant between men and women in the aggregate. Given that neither theory nor empirical findings suggest that there are racial differences in how individuals evaluate the desirability of jobs, the assumption of racial invariance is not controversial.

The assumption of relative invariance between women and men is more subject to debate. By relative invariance, I mean that there are slight differences between men and women in terms of how they rank jobs, largely restricted to a preference for part-time employment among some women with family responsibilities. Although several of the perspectives discussed above theoretically emphasize the importance of sex differences in preferences, the empirical support for this is limited. There are only small sex differences in general occupational values and work values, and gender explains very little of the individual variation in these values. Moreover, aside from part-time employment, there is no evidence to suggest that women self-select into work that accommodates family responsibilities. And while there is some evidence to indicate that, in the aggregate, men have more of a vocational preference for working with things and that women have more of a vocational preference for working with people, there is little evidence that such sex differences in preferences play much of a role (if any) in how workers choose jobs.

Theoretically, sex differences in preferences for types of work tasks and working conditions (e.g., women prefer female-typed tasks and conditions) should be reproduced as differences in how women and men rank jobs in their job queue and, thus, which jobs they choose. As such, this offers a competing explanation for sex segregation (but not for race segregation) to the proposed operation of a sex-based ordering principle in the labor queue. However, I just noted that the sex differences in preferences are small and that prior research has provided at most qualified support for a weak link between gender-typed preferences and job selection. I would further argue that the importance of workers' preferences is secondary because they mainly influence choices among the jobs offered. The constraints employers impose on the types of jobs offered are causally prior to workers' choices, severely limit the types of jobs that can be chosen, and even can be a primary cause of expressed preferences (Padavic and Reskin 2002). Thus, in the empirical applications in later chapters, I emphasize the race-sex ordering principle of the labor queue in interpreting results. But given that applicant preferences do affect to which openings they will apply, I will also consider how the empirical findings could be explained by sex differences in the ordering principle of the job queue.

4. Queuing and the role of human capital. Credentials, experience, and skills are crucial predictors of how workers are matched to jobs because they are a primary ordering principle used by employers to rank workers in the labor queue and thus determine how likely a candidate is to receive a job offer. In turn, how likely applicants are to accept an offer depends on where they rank the job in their job queue, which depends primarily on job rewards. The end result is that candidates with better qualifications will be matched to jobs with higher earnings and other job rewards. As reviewed in the earlier discussion of human capital, there are some differences between race-sex groups in their average human capital, especially between blacks and whites. These individual differences (many of which reflect processes of pre–labor market discrimination) should be reproduced by queuing processes as race-sex group differences in the types of jobs offered and correspondingly in the job rewards received. Thus, some share of the observed levels of segregation and earnings gaps are due to group differences in human capital.

5. *The race-sex ordering of labor queues, human capital, and segregation.* First, the race-sex ordering property of the labor queue reflects employers' use of socially normative labeling of jobs as appropriate or inappropriate for members of particular race-sex groups. Second, it may result from statistical discrimination based on employers' presumptions (whether correct or not) of lower average productivity and higher variability (uncertainty) in productivity for minorities and women. As described above, statistical discrimination is most likely for jobs in protected market segments, jobs requiring high levels of skill and long training times, or interdependent jobs for which individual contributions to productivity cannot be measured. Finally, the race-sex ordering property may incorporate more context-specific discrimination including that due to customer aversion, resistance or hostility from current workers, or even custom.

All of these suggest ways that candidates' race-sex status affects how employers rank them in the labor queue. I am not arguing that job applicants' human capital is not relevant. However, the precise role human capital and race-sex status play in determining job matching and earnings depends on the content of the race-sex ordering principle in the labor queue, the intensity and salience of employers' preferences for a race-sex ordering principle in the labor queue, and on the shape (size) of the *job* queue.

Consider the ranking of workers in two hypothetical labor queues shown in Figure 2.1 (modeled after a similar display in Reskin and Roos [1990: 33]). In both labor queues, workers are ranked by their qualifications, but employers also order workers according to a preference for whites over blacks and, within race, for men over women. In the first labor queue, employers' preferences for whites and men is so intense and salient that they would hire white men with low qualifications over candidates from any other race-sex group, then white women, then black men, and lastly black women. In the second labor queue, employers' preferences are much less intense or salient and they use race-sex status only to break ties among job applicants with approximately equal qualifications.

But the shape of the job queue ultimately determines how far down the labor queue an employer goes in making job offers. Theoretically, the first labor queue could be nearly cleared if the demand for workers were high enough, resulting in little apparent role of race-sex status or of human capital, whereas job offers in the second labor queue might never go beyond white men if the demand for workers were low enough, resulting in a larger apparent role of race-sex status and of human capital. This suggests that employment growth should be of crucial importance in understanding the role of human capital and of race-sex status in matching workers to jobs.

6. *The operation of race-sex queues and earnings gaps.* A central implication of the existence of the race-sex ordering of labor queues is that this should concentrate members of the most preferred groups (whites and men) in the best and most desirable jobs and largely limit the members of other groups into worse and less desirable jobs (Reskin and Roos 1990). Thus the employment

Figure 2.1 The Relative Importance of Qualifications and Race-Sex Status

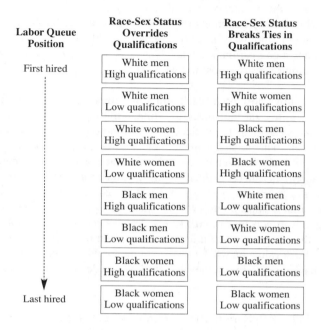

Labor Queue Position	Race-Sex Status Overrides Qualifications	Race-Sex Status Breaks Ties in Qualifications
First hired	White men High qualifications	White men High qualifications
	White men Low qualifications	White women High qualifications
	White women High qualifications	Black men High qualifications
	White women Low qualifications	Black women High qualifications
	Black men High qualifications	White men Low qualifications
	Black men Low qualifications	White women Low qualifications
	Black women High qualifications	Black men Low qualifications
Last hired	Black women Low qualifications	Black women Low qualifications

segregation of whites (men) into better-paying jobs and of blacks (women) into lower-paying jobs should explain some share of the earnings gaps among race-sex groups at the aggregate level.

But this is quite different from understanding how the size of the earnings gap varies across labor market positions. At the labor market position level, I would first argue that differential treatment breeds differential treatment. Predispositions (whether individual or structural) to create social distance among race-sex groups should manifest themselves both in the ordering of race-sex groups in the labor queues for positions and in the differential treatment (reward) of race-sex groups within positions. This is one reason why positions with an overrepresentation of men (whites) should also exhibit larger earnings gaps among race-sex groups. Secondly, a greater concentration of blacks and women should globally "devalue" the level of earnings of a position for all race-sex groups. Moreover, in accord with past research, I expect that such devaluation should occur at a higher rate for men and whites, in part because their base earnings are higher.[7] Logically, then, depressing the earnings level of all groups in a position should also decrease the extent of differentials among race-sex groups within that position. Consider the following data-based but hypothetical example:

1. Black men's base earnings are discounted by 12.8% compared to white men with equivalent characteristics (human capital, family structure, geographic residence, and labor supply).
2. White men's earnings are devalued at a rate of $459 per percentage point of employees in a position who are black.
3. Black men's earnings are devalued at a rate of $294 per percentage point of employees in a position who are black.[8]

Figure 2.2 shows how both black and white men's earnings would decrease while the earnings ratio of black-to-white earnings would increase (denoting less inequality) as the percent black of a position rises.

However, such global devaluation of earnings levels and its effects on earnings inequality may be overshadowed by how race- and gender-typed skills and work requirements are (de)valued and by how the returns to such characteristics vary across race-sex groups. I expect that skills and tasks that are stereotyped as black or female "appropriate" will be specifically devalued; that is, they will have negative effects on earnings levels. As has been found for global devaluation (i.e., the effects of percent female and percent black), I also anticipate that such specific devaluation will be more extreme for whites and men. White (male) workers have more to lose if they are employed in devalued positions compared

Figure 2.2 Hypothetical Example of Earnings Devaluation for Black Men and White Men

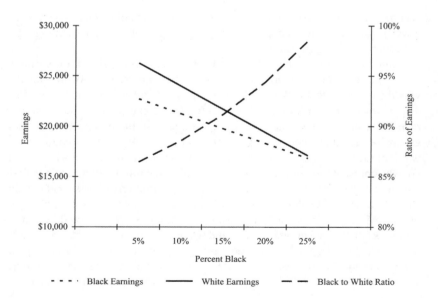

to whites (men) not working in such jobs. Thus, similar to the devaluing effects of employment segregation shown in Figure 2.2, black- and female-typed skills and conditions should decrease earnings gaps (increase earnings ratios).

In contrast, I expect that skills and tasks typed as white- or male-appropriate will have positive effects on earnings levels and that the within-group payoff to these earnings-enhancing characteristics should be more beneficial for whites (men). In many ways this is just the flip side of the specific devaluation argument, making explicit that men's skills are positively valued in the labor market. But it is also consistent with a statistical discrimination argument that employers discount earnings for women and blacks who are employed in more skilled positions. As a result, earnings inequality should be higher (lower earnings ratios) at higher levels of white- or male-typed skills and conditions.

The Six Principles Applied: A Two-Level Model

The integrated model specifies that employment segregation and earnings gaps are determined by factors at two different levels of analysis: workers and positions. As shown in Figure 2.3, this can be conceived as a two-level model. Hypothetically, employment segregation and earnings gaps each can be analyzed separately with a single statistical model of the two levels (workers nested within labor market positions) using multilevel analysis modeling techniques (Raudenbush and Bryk 2002; Goldstein 1995). But these techniques are not feasible to implement, in part due to the very large sample size for level one (5,979,937 workers) and the large number of level-two units (1,917 labor market positions).[9] Moreover, multilevel techniques for the analysis of a structural equation model such as that portrayed at the position level are still in the developmental stages. Instead, as detailed in Chapter 3 and Appendix A, I utilize a statistical approach that allows me to handle appropriately the key dilemmas of a multilevel data structure: "aggregation bias, mis-estimated precision, and the 'unit of analysis' problem" (Raudenbush and Bryk 2002: 5). My method also permits the estimation of a structural equation model for the relationship between employment segregation and earnings gaps at the position level while properly taking into account how race-sex group differences in worker characteristics contribute to segregation and earnings disparities. In brief, I separately analyze each level of the two-level model portrayed in Figure 2.3. The dashed arrows between the two levels indicate that the position-level outcomes are constructed from prior analyses of the corresponding worker-level outcomes. That is, the employment segregation of race-sex groups and the earnings gaps among race-sex groups in each position are statistically adjusted to remove the effects of differences between groups in the worker-level factors. These adjusted measures then become the endogenous variables in a structural equation model at the position level.

The Level 1 model in the top panel of Figure 2.3 identifies the five sets of worker characteristics that affect the labor market position in which workers

Figure 2.3 Two-Level Model of Segregation and Earnings Gaps

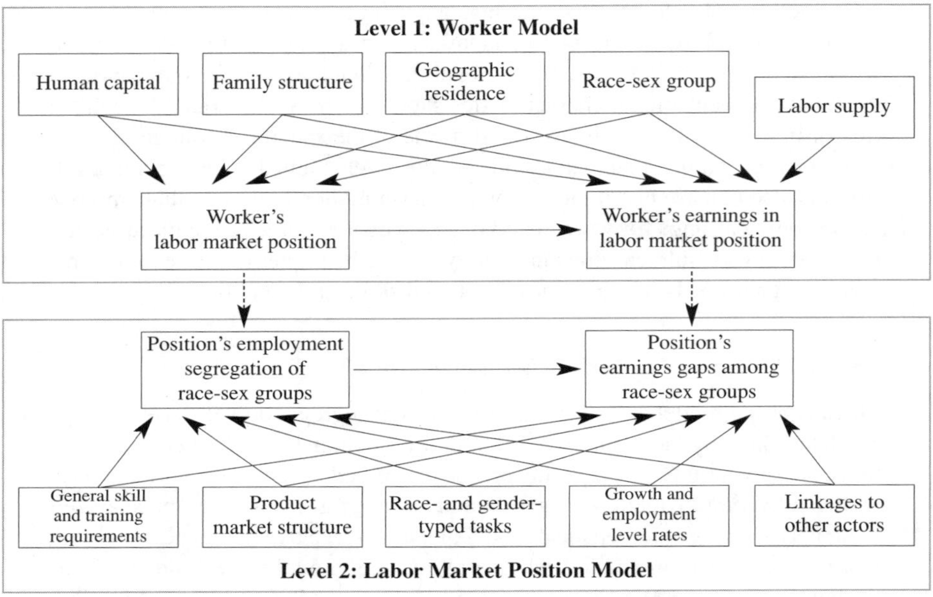

Level 1: Worker Model

| Human capital | Family structure | Geographic residence | Race-sex group | Labor supply |

Worker's labor market position → Worker's earnings in labor market position

Position's employment segregation of race-sex groups → Position's earnings gaps among race-sex groups

| General skill and training requirements | Product market structure | Race- and gender-typed tasks | Growth and employment level rates | Linkages to other actors |

Level 2: Labor Market Position Model

are employed and the earnings that they receive from their position. *Human capital* is obviously a central predictor as it is one of the primary principles used to match workers to job requirements and to determine their earnings. The effects of *family structure* on labor market position outcomes are theoretically ambiguous because they combine both choice by workers (e.g., some women choose only jobs that accommodate family responsibilities) and constraints imposed by employers (e.g., some employers rank women with family responsibilities low in the labor queue for the most valued jobs). By specifying that family structure affects outcomes at the worker level, I indirectly control for a major source of potential sex differences in job preferences. I include *geographic residence* in the model to acknowledge the possible role of spatial mismatch in producing race-sex differences. This serves to adjust for differences across locales in the availability of kinds of work, the supply (size) of race-sex groups, and the levels of remuneration. Because the empirical analysis at the worker level uses workers' annual earnings rather than wage rates (as discussed in the next chapter), I specify that *labor supply* (hours and weeks worked) also affects earnings. *Race-sex group* status effects in this worker-level model are in essence indicators of employer discrimination. These effects capture only those differences among race-sex groups in employment and earnings that are not due to differences among groups in human capital, family structure, geographic residence, and labor supply (this last factor is used only for earnings).

The Level 2 model in the bottom panel of Figure 2.3 uses labor market positions as the unit of analysis. As described in Chapter 3, positions are defined as industry-occupation combinations that are fairly homogeneous in the key characteristics of labor and product markets that "segment" work (Kalleberg and Berg 1994; Tomaskovic-Devey 1993; Hachen 1992; Kaufman 1986; Hodson and Kaufman 1982; Baron and Bielby 1980; Tolbert, Horan, and Beck 1980). The bottom panel identifies the five sets of labor market position characteristics that affect the extent of employment segregation and earnings gaps among race-sex groups in a position. According to my integrated perspective, these factors affect the structural properties of labor queues (and job queues) and thus affect how members of race-sex groups are matched to positions, independent of their individual qualifications. They also indirectly affect earnings gaps among groups because they concentrate whites (men) into better-paid work and blacks (women) into lower-paid work. In addition, they have a direct link to earnings gaps because they index either situations in which statistical discrimination is more (or less) likely to occur, contexts where work and hence earnings are devalued, or jobs for which the intensity and salience of preferences for race-sex groups will vary. In the following sections, I discuss each set of factors and how they should influence segregation and earnings gaps. Tables 2.1 and 2.2 provide convenient summaries of these expectations for segregation and earnings gaps (ratios) respectively. As discussed in Chapter 3, the earnings gap measures are the ratios of earnings for a subordinate group to a superordinate group; for example, black women to white men. Consequently, a positive effect of, say, employment growth increases the ratio and thus decreases the disparity between groups.

General skill and training requirements. The level of skills required and the time needed for training are among the most important determinants of job wage levels (England et al. 1994; Tomaskovic-Devey 1993; Jacobs and Steinberg 1990; Parcel and Mueller 1989). Thus, if these factors affect how groups are differentially segregated across positions, then clearly they will also affect the aggregate earnings gaps among groups. In fact, general skills and training requirements should affect the ordering of race-sex groups in the labor queue by employers as well as the intensity of their preferences, irrespective of applicants' qualifications. The literature on racial occupational segregation argues that skilled work is stereotyped as inappropriate for blacks and other minorities and that unskilled work is stereotyped as appropriate (Kaufman 1986; Lyson 1985; Reskin 1988). This implies that the ranking of blacks (both men and women) in the labor queue for jobs with high skill would be low and that their ranking in the labor queue for jobs with low skill would be high.[10] In contrast, no such stereotyping by skill level is expected to operate for white women as past research has found no *general* skill-level differences between men's and women's positions. Skill differences by sex inhere instead in the *types* of skills male and female workers exercise (England et al. 1994; Reskin 1993, 1988; England 1992; Steinberg 1990).

Table 2.1 Hypothesized Effects on Employment Segregation of General Skill and Training, Growth and Employment, Race-Gender Typing, Product Market Structure, and Linkages to Other Actors

Predictors	Black Women: White Men	Black Men: White Men	White Women: White Men	Black Women: Black Men	Black Women: White Women
General skill and training					
Skill and training scale	−	−	−	−	−
Skill and training × growth	+	+	+	+	+
Growth and employment					
Employment growth rate	+/0	+/0	+/0	+/0	+/0
Sufficient work hours	−	−	−	−	−
Unemployment rate	+	+	+	+	+
Self-employment rate	−	−	−	−	−
Race-gender typing					
Environmental conditions	+/−	+	−	−	+
Physical exertion	+/−	+	−	−	+
Routinization	+	+			+
Status in interaction	−	−	−	−	−
Authority	−	−	−	−	−
Gender typing only					
Physical dexterity	+		+	+	
Nurturant skill	+		+	+	
Clerical perception	+		+	+	
Math skill	−		−	−	
Product market structure					
Market power	+	+	+	+	+
Profitability	+	+	+	+	+
Economic scale					
Capital intensity					
Foreign involvement					
Productivity					
Linkages to other actors					
Industry unionization	+/0	+/0	+/0	+/0	+/0
Occupation unionization	+/0	+/0	+/0	+/0	+/0
Percent public sector	+	+	+	+	+
Federal purchases	+/0	+/0	+/0	+/0	+/0

Note: + Positive effect − Negative effect 0 No effect +/− Opposing predictions Blank No prediction

Beyond the influence of such stereotyping, statistical discrimination should also be relevant to both sex and race segregation in jobs requiring greater skill levels, especially those requiring longer periods of specific vocational training. As discussed above, there are likely to be greater costs associated with hiring less productive workers for such jobs and, hence, greater motivation for employers to reduce costs by profiling workers by race and sex, especially to profile black women. In addition, blocking access to valuable training has long been argued to be one of the primary routes through which an advantaged group maintains and legitimizes its favored position (Bonacich 1976; Hartmann 1976; Reskin 1993, 1988; Schutt 1987; Taeuber, Taeuber, and Cain 1966). As job skill levels rise and training times increase, then, the rank order placement of blacks

Table 2.2 Hypothesized Effects on Earnings Gaps (Ratios) Between Race-Sex Groups of Net Employment Segregation, General Skill and Training, Growth and Employment, Race-Gender Typing, Product Market Structure, and Linkages to Other Actors

Predictors	Black Women: White Men	Black Men: White Men	White Women: White Men	Black Women: Black Men	Black Women: White Women
Net employment segregation	+	+	+	+	+
General skill and training	+/–	+ /–	+ /–	+/–	+/–
Growth and employment					
Employment growth rate	+	+	+	+	+
Sufficient work hours	+	+	+	+	+
Unemployment rate	+	+	+	+	+
Self-employment rate	–	–	–	–	–
Race-gender typing					
Environmental conditions	+/–	+ /–	+/–	+ /–	+/–
Physical exertion	+	+	+	+	+
Routinization	+	+	+/0	+/0	+
Status in interaction	–	–	–	–	–
Authority	–	–	–	–	–
Gender typing only					
Physical dexterity	+	+	+	+	+
Nurturant skill	+	+	+	+	+
Clerical perception	+	+	+	+	+
Math skill	–	–	–	–	–
Product market structure					
Market power	+	+	+	+	+
Profitability	+	+	+	+	+
Economic scale					
Capital intensity					
Foreign involvement					
Productivity					
Linkages to other actors					
Industry unionization	+	+	+/0	+/0	+
Occupation unionization	+	+	+/0	+/0	+
Percent public sector	+	+	+	+	+
Federal purchases	+/0	+/0	+/0	+/0	+/0

Note: + Positive effect – Negative effect 0 No effect +/– Opposing predictions Blank No prediction

and women in the labor queue should decrease *and* this preference should become more intense.

Given the large effects of skills and training on earnings, the segregation of blacks into jobs with lower levels of skill and training will contribute to the total earnings gaps between blacks and whites. Without taking such segregation into account, measuring total earnings gaps net of job skill (not individual skills) would overestimate the extent to which group differences are equitable or compensable because it assumes that the sorting of race-sex groups into jobs by skill is equitable. Moreover, this pattern of concentration of race-sex groups should devalue earnings in positions into which women and minorities are crowded (like ones with low skill and training) and "over"-value earnings in positions into which men and whites are funneled (like those with higher skill and training). One consequence could be that employment in more highly skilled positions has a higher payoff for women (blacks) than for men (whites) relative to their employment in low-skilled positions. Kilbourne, England, and Beron (1994b) did in fact find that general skill has a greater positive effect on earnings for blacks and women than for white men. On the other hand, if employers are practicing statistical discrimination in their hiring for highly skilled positions, then they may pay wage discounts to blacks and women at high levels of skill and training rather than segregating workers.

What does this imply about how the degree of earnings gaps among race-sex groups varies with the skill level of labor market positions? In the first scenario, earnings gaps would be smaller (higher earnings ratios) for highly skilled positions than for less-skilled positions, while the opposite effect would characterize the operation of statistical discrimination in the form of wage discounts. The empirical analysis of earnings gaps will help adjudicate between these competing explanations. Keep in mind that statistical discrimination in wage setting is an alternative to statistical discrimination in hiring and promotion. Thus, evidence against statistical discrimination in wages does not imply the absence of statistical discrimination in employment.

Growth and employment levels. A central argument of queuing theory is that changes in the shape of the job queue (the number of positions available at any point in time) should be directly related to the access of the less preferred race-sex groups (those ranked lower in the labor queue). Employment growth in a position by definition means that employers must now take more workers from lower-ranked positions within the labor queue. Employment growth thus signals a change in the shape of the queue that should increase access for blacks. There is consistent evidence for a positive impact of occupational growth, but the evidence for industrial growth is mixed (Baron, Mittman, and Newman 1991; Glass, Tienda, and Smith 1988; Kaufman 1986; Reskin 1993; Reskin and Roos 1990).

But growth should have more than just direct effects. The shape of the labor queue also has implications for the race-sex ordering principle of the queue because it may change the intensity and salience of employers' preferences for race-sex groups (Reskin and Roos 1993). When the demand for workers increases, employers either must wait until additional members of their preferred race-sex group obtain the necessary training or employ workers from race-sex groups further down the labor queue. This logic suggests that the effects of growth on segregation are not necessarily the same for all jobs but may be moderated by other factors. The higher the skill level and the longer the training time, the less salient and intense will be employers' preferences and the greater the incentive will be to hire from less preferred race-sex groups. But among low-skill positions requiring little training, employers can meet employment demand by hiring from their preferred group, white men. Indeed, Turner, Fix, and Struyk (1991) audit studies of hiring show the existence of employers' preference for white men for low-skill jobs, as does Moss and Tilly's (2001) study of employers' description of their hiring process. Thus, I would expect that growth should reduce segregation among positions with higher skills and longer training times, but increase segregation among low-skilled positions. Correspondingly, the effects of skill and training time to diminish access should be smaller when employment growth is high. Moreover, the positive effect of growth for a particular race-sex group should also be larger for positions that are race- and gender-typed as "appropriate" for that group. The race- and gender-typed nature of work should increase the intensity and salience of employers' preferences in times of employment growth because it provides an additional incentive to hire preferred workers. As the later analyses demonstrate, the direct and moderating effects of growth are a key contribution to understanding queuing processes.

With respect to earnings gaps among race-sex groups in a position, growth should decrease the earnings gaps (especially among recent hires) because it favors the bargaining position of workers vis-à-vis employers at the same time as it decreases the saliency of employer preferences. In addition, growth should most increase access by less-favored groups to more desirable (better rewarded) positions and thus have a higher payoff for them than for white men. As Figure 2.4 illustrates, this should result in smaller gaps (higher earnings ratios).[11]

Figure 2.4 Hypothetical Example of Different Earnings Returns for Black Women and White Men

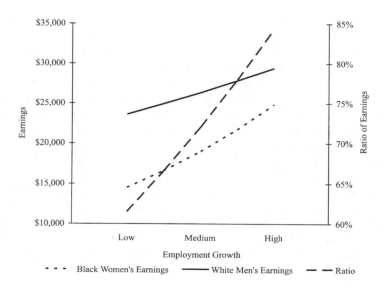

Besides growth, there are other characteristics of a position's employment level that should affect segregation and earnings gaps. I argued above that a job's "desirability" should increase employment segregation among groups because the matching of the job and labor queues will generally favor the group ranked highest in the labor queues for the most desired jobs. Individuals rank highly not only jobs with higher earnings and skills, but also jobs providing sufficient work hours, job security, autonomy in setting hours and working free from supervision, and benefits (Jencks, Perman, and Rainwater 1988). Thus, the matching process should increase race and sex segregation in jobs with corresponding desirable employment levels: a greater availability of sufficient work hours; a lower unemployment rate; or a higher self-employment rate.

Turning to earnings gaps, the unemployment rate indicates undesirable work conditions, and its effects on earnings gaps should follow a process of specific devaluation. That is, it should devalue (depress) earnings for all groups, with the effects being larger for white men, leading to the prediction that the unemployment rate should reduce earnings gaps among groups (increase earnings ratios). In contrast, the availability of sufficient work hours should increase earnings, especially for blacks and women, with the result being a reduction in earnings gaps (higher earnings ratios). Finally, self-employment opportunities should similarly increase earnings levels. As others have found (Hundley 2000; McCrary 1998; Sullivan and McCracken 1988), I expect whites and men to have greater payoffs to self-employment due partly to customer discrimination (Becker 1971) and partly to access to less segregated and more lucrative networks. Self-employment opportunities thus should heighten earnings gaps (depress earnings ratios).

Race- and gender-typed work tasks. A fundamental premise of my approach is that there exist socially normative definitions (stereotypes) of certain kinds of work tasks and kinds of skills as being "appropriate" or "inappropriate" for blacks and women. When applied to race (but not sex) segregation, this explanation is well accepted as representing constraints imposed on black job seekers by employers, due to employers' preferences and in reaction to other actors in the labor market. These constraints arise from employers' and societal beliefs about the roles black and whites should fill, employers' desire to minimize conflict if integration is opposed by white workers or customers, employer efforts to disrupt worker solidarity, and efforts by advantaged workers to protect their privileges. Specifically, employers order race-sex groups in the labor queue according to their appropriateness given the race-typed character of the job.

Past research suggests that the following characteristics capture the normatively based constraints imposed on black workers. Stereotypically "appropriate" work would be jobs requiring heavy physical labor, poor working conditions, and the performance of menial tasks or subservient tasks. "Inappropriate" work would be jobs requiring status-discrepant interactions in which a worker is in a superior status over (nonminority) workers or clientele; that is, work involving formal authority, informal authority based on technical expertise or specialization (high skill), or other status-superior interactions with coworkers or clientele. Thus the "appropriateness" of a job for blacks should affect the ordering of blacks and whites in the labor queue; it should increase black representation in stereotypically "appropriate" labor market positions and decrease their representation in stereotypically "inappropriate" positions. As discussed below, it is also important to consider how gender-typing intersects with race-typing.

Tomaskovic-Devey (1993) notes the curious fact that, even though the constraint explanation is well accepted for understanding the stereotypic nature of race segregation, it is often contested by a choice (preference) explanation when applied to sex segregation (see also Padavic and Reskin 2002). For the reasons elaborated earlier, I argue that the constraints imposed by employers (and others) take precedence over workers' preferences. Because individuals' job choices are restricted by their rank in the labor queue for different jobs, gender-typed work tasks and conditions affect segregation primarily by determining how women and men are ranked by employers in the labor queue, with a limited role played by workers' preferences. There is some overlap between the characteristics that define work as gender-typed and those identified above that define it as race-typed. Stereotypically "appropriate" work for women are jobs requiring physical dexterity, clerical perception, nurturant skills, or the performance of subservient (subordinate) tasks. "Inappropriate" work would be jobs requiring status-superior interactions with men, heavy physical labor, extreme environmental conditions, or mathematical skills. The "gender appropriateness" of a job for women should affect the degree to which women or men are more highly ranked in the labor queue for a job. This should increase women's representation in stereotypically "appropriate" labor market positions and decrease their representation in stereotypically "inappropriate" positions.

The employment representation of black women compared to black men embodies the results of both race stereotyping and gender stereotyping of appropriate and inappropriate work. For most of the stereotyping indicators, the predictions from race and gender stereotyping are either additive and consistent with each other or only one applies. But contradictory predictions arise for poor working conditions and greater physical exertion. Race stereotyping would suggest that these should increase the representation of blacks, whereas gender stereotyping would suggest that they should decrease the representation of women.

As discussed earlier, there are several mechanisms linking the race and gender stereotyping of work to variation across positions in race-sex wage gaps. The very process of segregation should reproduce itself in terms of earnings gaps within positions by devaluing the work performed in race- and gender-typed work contexts. Devaluation can occur through several distinct processes that may operate simultaneously. First, the rewards for a job should be "globally" devalued when the race-sex composition of its workforce labels it as a "female" or a "black" job. Similarly, the rewards may be "specifically" devalued to the degree that specific task requirements create such labeling. Moreover, rewards could also be devalued if female-typed skills are not considered as skills or are valued less highly (even negatively) than comparable male-typed skills and conditions. For example, if the societal belief is that nurturing is an innate trait of all women, then employers may not define it as a skill and may undervalue earnings in jobs requiring nurturant skills.

Thus, both the kind of segregation of other race-sex groups from white men and the extent to which the work tasks in a position are race and gender typed should affect a position's level of earnings. Because the negative effects of devaluation on earnings levels should be larger for whites (men) than for blacks (women), race and sex earnings gaps should be smallest in both globally and specifically devalued positions. Consequently, earnings gaps should be smaller (higher earnings ratios) in positions with an overrepresentation of blacks and women and in positions characterized by black- and female-typed skills and requirements (see Figure 2.2 above). In contrast, the positive effects on earnings levels of white male–typed skills and requirements should be smaller for blacks and women. Concomitantly, earnings gaps should be greater in positions characterized by white male–typed skills and requirements.

Note that there are competing predictions for environmental conditions. On the one hand, work in poor environmental conditions is stereotyped as black appropriate, and such typing should give rise to specific devaluation and thus to smaller wage gaps. On the other hand, such work is also typed as male appropriate, and the disamenity of hazardous work should be positively compensated.[12] Both of these should give rise to specific valuation of such work and thus larger wage gaps.

Product market structure. Although there is a larger set of factors that have been identified as key characteristics of product market structure, I focus particular attention on market power and profitability. Conceptually, these aspects of product markets are the most closely linked to employer motivations, resources, and decisionmaking. Empirically, they also have been the most frequently studied.

Market power (economic buffering) and profitability (slack resources). There has been much argument but little agreement over the role of these central features of product market structure. Early market segmentation approaches and the neoclassical theory of discrimination assumed societal-wide "tastes for discrimination" that would create a preference for white men in the labor queue for all jobs. But these "tastes" can be exercised (become more intense and salient, in my terms) only where market power provides economic buffering from competition or where profitability supplies slack resources. This "preferencing" should result in greater exclusion of other race-sex groups from employment in such firms and product markets or, alternatively, their inclusion and the payment of a premium to white men (or a discount to other race-sex groups). But empirical studies of the exclusionary process have found contradictory effects that raise doubts about this prediction.

I also have more fundamental questions about the underlying logic of how tastes for discrimination will manifest themselves as employer actions. First, these tastes are presumed to be a desire for the *physical* segregation of groups: the total exclusion of particular race-sex groups from a workplace. A much more plausible expression of such "tastes" would be the creation of social distance among groups in the workplace rather than physical distance between workplaces (Reskin 1993, 1988; England 1992; Reskin and Roos 1987; Kaufman 1986; Marshall 1974). There are two obvious ways employers can create social distance among race-sex groups in the workplace: (1) pay premiums to whites (men) or discounts to blacks (women) who are employed in the *same* position, or (2) order whites (men) higher in the labor queue for the superior-status, better-paid jobs and order blacks (women) higher in the labor queue for subordinate-status, lower-paid jobs.

Following this social-distance logic, I might be tempted to argue that buffering and slack resources should create greater wage gaps among race-sex groups and should make employers' preferences for imposing a race-sex ordering on labor queues more intense and salient. Before doing so, it is important to consider countervailing pressures or changes that could affect employers' preferences or make them less intense or salient. In particular, antidiscrimination pressure by the government and citizens' groups has generally targeted larger, more visible economic arenas as the place to contest past discrimination (Kaufman 1986; Leonard 1994; Marshall 1974; Reskin 1993; Szafran 1982), and certainly a high degree of market power and high rates of profit create visibility. Even absent such targeting, changes in employment regulations and in public opinion promoting nondiscrimination can offset economic buffering by changing employers' preferences or by reducing the salience of discriminatory preferences (Reskin 1993; Szafran 1982). Similarly, exogenous societal forces may limit the intensity and salience of employers' preferences, as occurred during World War II, resulting in expanded employment opportunities for women and minorities. Although firms that are economically buffered or have slack resources are the most able to use these reserves to change their employment practices (Kaufman 1986; Szafran 1982), these same factors provide resources to resist market and external pressures.

In sum, greater economic buffering and slack resources should increase the salience of employers' preferences for race-sex groups in the labor queue, whether that preference is to impose a race-sex ordering or not, but their influence can be counterbalanced by other forces. Clearly, then, the relationship of economic buffering and slack resources to segregation and earnings gaps should change over time in response to changes in political pressures by the government and citizens' groups, changes in public opinion on racial and sexual egalitarianism, and exogenous forces such as war. Prior to the mid-1960s, there was a preponderance of inegalitarian beliefs and little if any government and other public pressure against discrimination. From the mid-1960s through the late 1970s, antidiscrimination pressures consistently grew as did more egalitarian public opinion, but since the late 1970s political pressures have slackened (Reskin 1993; England 1992; DiPrete and Grusky 1990; Bound and Freeman 1989; Jaynes and Williams 1989). Some of the empirical inconsistency of past research may well reflect such changing market environments. This suggests that market power and profitability should have increased employment segregation and earnings gaps before 1970 but that these effects might reverse thereafter as these resources provide employers greater latitude to accommodate to external pressures and societal changes. Additionally, I would expect the earnings payoff of employment in positions with high market power and profitability to be greater for women and blacks, further suggesting that these should decrease earnings gaps (increase earnings ratios).

Other aspects of product market structure. Economic scale, capital intensity, foreign involvement, and productivity are also key aspects of product market structure commonly used in the economic segmentation literature (Wallace and Chang 1990; Kalleberg and Berg 1987; Hodson and Kaufman 1982; Tolbert, Horan, and Beck 1980) but there is little clear theoretical or empirical justification for how they should affect segregation and earnings gaps, although they should all have positive effects on the level of earnings. For example, economic scale has been claimed as a proxy for a variety of other processes, with contradictory predictions. These include: (1) formalization that restricts discretionary decisionmaking and curtails subjectivity in evaluating workers and job candidates; (2) departmentalization and differentiation, which facilitate tastes for discrimination by creating more opportunities to segregate; (3) structural inertia that inhibits change; (4) visibility to public pressure and applicability of federal employment regulations that should inhibit tastes for discrimination; and (5) power to resist external pressures. There are similar contradictions about its empirical effects, with some studies finding that it increases segregation (Bielby and Baron 1986; Kaufman 1986; Leonard 1984), others that it decreases or has a U-shaped effect on segregation (Lyson 1985; Tomaskovic-Devey 1993; Wallace and Chang 1990), and one that it has no effect (Wharton 1986). Thus, I include indicators of these aspects of product market structure in the analyses reported in later chapters because of their centrality in this literature and to allow for change or unanticipated effects, but I have no clear expectations that they are empirically important.

Linkages to other actors. This final set draws attention to the two major actors (other than employers and workers) who can influence queuing and wage-determination processes, namely labor unions and the public (government) sector.

Unions. A few scholars (from widely divergent approaches) have argued that, in the context of pervasive racism and sexism, most unions act as instruments to create market barriers protecting the privileged interests of white male workers (e.g., Beck 1980; Hartmann 1976; Becker 1971). But these approaches fail to consider the importance of distinguishing between craft-type and industrial-type unions. Craft-type unions typically exercise substantial control over the size and composition of the labor pool for select positions, which in turn permits them to keep wages high. Historically, craft-type unions usually were able to maintain such power without including women and minorities (Bonacich 1976, 1975; Kessler-Harris 1985; Libeau 1977; May 1985; Schutt 1987); indeed limiting supply by excluding such groups was often in the unions' short-term self-interest.

In contrast, industrial-type unions have much weaker and limited control over access to jobs, limited to negotiating over hiring and promotion rules. The power of industrial-type unions derives from their role as agents for collective bargaining, relying on the threat of strikes and other collective actions (such as "banking" individual grievances to use in contract negotiations). Since the resurgence of industrial unionism in the 1930s, most industrial-type unions have recognized that the success of collective action has been contingent upon the inclusion of blacks, women, and other minorities who were employed in the workplace, and they began to act in this self-interest (Gabin 1990, 1985; Milkman 1987, 1985; Bonacich 1976; Marshall 1965). Thus industrial-type unions began to encourage minority and female membership and to support racial- and sex-neutral employment and wage practices. Given that industrial-type unions typically have less influence over worker selection (and thus the ordering of race-sex groups in the labor queue) than over wages and work rules, the impact of unions should be more relevant to understanding earnings gaps than employment segregation.

The evidence for the effects of unionization is mixed. A few studies have found evidence of a negative impact of unions on race-sex inequality (Beck 1980; Hartmann 1976; Becker 1971). But the vast majority of studies have found that the extent of industrial-type (but *not* craft-type) unionization has either a beneficial or a neutral impact on the level of racial and sexual inequality (Kaufman 1993; Baron and Newman 1990; Gabin 1990; Bridges and Nelson 1989; Milkman 1987; Kaufman 1986; Strom 1985; Leonard 1985; Bridges 1982; US Commission on Civil Rights 1982; Kaufman and Daymont 1981; Libeau 1977; Bonacich 1976; Marshall 1974, 1965; Hill 1974; Ashenfelter 1972).

The public sector. The government is an actor with a role both as an employer and as an agent of the social "will" as expressed in employment legislation. Scholars agree that, since the mid-1960s, the public sector has been more favorably disposed to the employment of blacks and women than the private sector (DiPrete 1989; Kaufman 1986; King 1992; Leonard 1984; Hodson and Kaufman 1982; Reskin and Roos 1993; Shepherd 1970; Smith and Welch 1977;

Wharton 1989), in part as a result of actions by the executive branch, such as the institution of preferential hiring of veterans, the job-training provisions of President Johnson's War on Poverty (Jacobs and Skocpol 2005), or Executive Order 11246 authorizing affirmative action as part of federal-contract compliance. A more egalitarian ranking of race-sex groups in the labor queue should thus characterize positions located in the public sector. In terms of lower wage gaps, public sector employment should follow a specific devaluation process in which the negative effect of public relative to private employment on earnings levels should be more detrimental for whites (men). Thus earnings gaps should be smaller in the public than in the private sector.

But the public sector can also influence the race-sex ordering of the labor queue by private employers through efforts to make employers' preferences less salient by enforcing antidiscrimination legislation and executive orders and the monitoring of large establishments' annual Equal Employment Opportunity (EEO-1) reports on the race-sex makeup of their employees. Through the efforts of the Equal Employment Opportunity Commission (EEOC) and the Office of Federal Contract Compliance (OFCC), the government has the capability both to affect the ranking of race-sex groups in the labor queue and to influence wage inequality. The OFCC has been responsible for enforcing nondiscriminatory employment and wage treatment among federal contractors since the 1960s. The earliest studies of the impact of the OFCC revealed little effect (Burman 1973; Kaufman and Daymont 1981; Smith and Welch 1977). Studies of somewhat later time periods indicated that it did make a difference, even though enforcement was haphazard (Gunderson 1989; Kaufman 1986; Leonard 1984; Reskin 1993). Research for the most recent times, however, has suggested that it has been largely ineffectual (Hirsh 2008, 2009; Hirsh and Kornrich 2008; Padavic and Reskin 2002; Leonard 1994). For example, Hirsh and Kornrich (2008) found that regulatory agents are more forgiving of federal contractors than nonfederal contractors in determining the legitimacy of discrimination claims, especially by race but also by sex. In sum, as Hirsh (2009: 245) concluded, "To the extent that EEO enforcement encourages organizational change, it does so indirectly, operating through establishments' industrial and legal environments."

What's Next?

The remainder of the book is devoted to using data to evaluate the ideas developed in this chapter. In line with the model shown earlier in Figure 2.4, I first assess how my approach aids in understanding employment segregation among race-sex groups. I then examine how well it applies in predicting wage gaps among groups. In each of the chapters reporting and discussing the results of this evaluation, I begin with a base model, which I then complicate by studying how employment growth, market power, and profitability affect the intensity and salience of employers' preferences for a race-sex ordering principle. That is, I consider how these three factors moderate the effects of the race- and gender-stereotyping indicators. In later chapters I evaluate how variations in social context and cultural beliefs, broadly defined, influence the determinants of segregation and wages gaps. A comparison of the models predicting segregation and earnings gaps in the southern region of the United States to the rest of the country should reveal indirectly the influence of regional variation in beliefs about race relations and gender roles.

If you are interested in all the details behind the data and methods that I use for these evaluations, you should read the next chapter and Appendix A carefully. If not, you should still read some sections of the next chapter and skim the remainder so that you have an appreciation of what is behind the later charts and tables that present the results of the evaluations. What I think you must read seriously are the introductory section, the section on defining labor market positions, the subsection on data sources and sample selection for the worker-level analyses (and the synopsis of indicators in Table A.3 of the appendix), and the subsection on data sources, sample selection, and the summary on measurement in Table 3.4 for the position-level analyses.

Notes

1. A few studies of narrowly defined samples (e.g., a single cohort or only recent college graduates) find relatively small sex gaps in wages. For example, O'Neill (2003) analyzes workers aged thirty-five to forty-three from the National Longitudinal Survey of Youth (NLSY) and finds that the female-male wage ratio is reduced to 91% (from 78%) after taking into account education, cognitive skills, experience, and family structure.

2. There is support for a compensating differential for extremely hazardous work (i.e., life threatening) but not for any other type of amenity or disamenity (Brown 1980).

3. For an online demonstration of the power of such cognitive schema, try doing one of the implicit association tests at http://implicit.harvard.edu/implicit/demo/.

4. Their sample of firms overrepresents manufacturing and excludes major industries such as construction, banking, and department stores.

5. The RIASEC components are scored using responses from the Strong Interest Inventory.

6. There is a great deal of inconsistency among studies in the effect of market power on black representation (compare Becker 1971 and Shepherd 1970 to Kaufman 1986, Kaufman and Daymont 1981, and Comanor 1973). There is a similar inconsistency in the effect of "marginal industry" characteristics (competitive markets, low profits, labor-intensive, small size) on the representation of women (compare Bridges 1982 to Wharton 1986 to Wallace and Chang 1990). Nor have differences in the racial and sex composition of the core and periphery been consistently found (compare Beck, Horan, and Tolbert 1980, Bibb and Form 1977, and Lyson 1985 to Hodson 1983 and Zucker and Rosenstein 1981).

7. A larger devaluing effect of percent female has often but not always been found for men than for women, while a similar effect of percent black has been even less consistently found for whites compared to blacks (Cotter et al. 1997; England et al. 1994;

England, Reid, and Kilbourne 1996; Johnson and Solon 1986; Kilbourne et al. 1994a; McCall 2001b; Macpherson and Hirsch 1995; Parcel 1989; Reid 1998; Tomaskovic-Devey 1993).

8. The discount rate was calculated from comparing the average (across labor market positions) of the "adjusted" earnings of black men and white men, where the effects of differences between black and white men in levels of human capital, family structure, geographic residence, and labor supply were statistically removed. The devaluation rates were calculated by regressing the adjusted earnings for each group on the percent black males in the position. The definition of labor market positions and the measurement of these sets of factors are described in Chapter 3.

9. The MLwiN program for fitting multilevel models, for example, requires that the full data set fits within an internal worksheet, and the size of my data set would exceed program limits. Even aside from such issues, the iterative analytic techniques used by any of the multilevel programs and the model size (number of parameters to estimate) would take a prohibitive amount of time, especially to predict the allocation of workers into the 1,917 categories of labor market positions. There is an additional difficulty in trying to estimate a two-level model of employment segregation. The Level 1 outcome (worker's position) is identical to the Level 2 unit (labor market position), so there is no variation in the outcome (or its error) within the Level 2 units. This is a "degenerate" and "unestimable" multilevel logistic model given how the estimation procedure "linearizes" the Level 1 outcome (Raudenbush et al. 2001: Eq. 5.33). The linearization requires dividing by the error variance within Level 2 units, which would mean dividing by zero, yielding an undefined calculation.

10. Such restriction of opportunities could depress educational aspirations among minority youth (an "education can't help me" attitude). But African American youth in fact express higher levels of educational and occupational aspirations than do comparable white youth (Ainsworth-Darnell and Downey 1998).

11. It could be argued that growth will move less favored groups into positions in which there has been a legacy of discrimination (including wage discrimination) against them. This might suggest that growth would increase within-position earnings gaps. Indeed, several studies suggest that greater equity in employment access initially increases the extent to which wage discrimination within positions accounts for race-sex group inequality (Glass, Tienda, and Smith 1988; Tienda, Smith, and Ortiz 1987; Kaufman 1983; Beck, Horan, and Tolbert 1980; Grodsky and Pager 2001). However, the empirical analyses of wage gaps control for the legacy of employment discrimination, which makes this line of argument implausible.

12. As I argue elsewhere, the only consistent empirical support for the compensating-differential approach is that there is higher compensation for hazardous working conditions.

3

Analyzing Labor Market Disparities

"My mind," he said, "rebels at stagnation. Give me problems,
give me work, give me the most abstruse cryptogram, or the most
intricate analysis and I am in my proper atmosphere."
—Sir Arthur Conan Doyle (1960: 91–92)

A quick look back at Figure 2.3 in Chapter 2 makes it clear that two different kinds of data are needed to evaluate this model of segregation and earnings gaps. For the worker-level model shown in the upper panel, data about workers' individual characteristics and the positions in which they are employed were used, taken from the 1990 Census of Population Public Use Microdata Samples (PUMS) (US Bureau of the Census 1994a, 1994b). The 1990 Census sample includes nearly six million workers (5,979,937 to be exact). For the position-level model shown in the lower panel, data about the features of their labor market positions were taken from a variety of sources. For 1990, over nineteen hundred positions were analyzed (1,917 to be precise). As this chapter's title suggests, data are available on a huge number of workers employed in many different positions.

You may be wondering at this point what exactly is meant by a labor market position? How is a worker's human capital or a position's employment growth measured? What statistical methods are applied in these analyses? (You might also be wondering how crazy I am to work with so many cases.[1]) The short answer to the first question is that I define labor market positions as a combination of the occupation and the industry in which people work. The census data describe workers' jobs by classifying them into one of 503 occupations and into one of 228 industries. I use these detailed three-digit codes to define labor market positions (for example, pressing machine operatives (occupation code 747) who are employed in the laundry, cleaning, and garment-services industry (industry code 771) define one of my labor market positions). How and why these occupations came to be defined as positions is described in the next section. Following this description of labor market positions, I discuss what you need to know about the worker-level analyses: the sample of workers from the 1990 Census; the measurement of worker characteristics; the statistical techniques used to predict how workers are matched to positions and how their earnings are determined; and finally how I used these results to measure segregation and earnings gaps among race-sex groups at the position level. In the final section, I describe the basics about the position-level analyses: the variety of data sources on occupational and industrial characteristics that I used; how I measure the characteristics of positions used as predictors; how I define the sample of positions; and the statistical techniques I apply to evaluate the position-level models of segregation and earnings gaps among race-sex groups. In Appendix A, I provide more details (especially technical ones) on all of these issues.

Defining Labor Market Positions

Figure 3.1 provides a visual summary of the process I used to define labor market positions. In brief, I define a labor market position as either a single six-digit occupation-industry combination or as a set of occupation-industry combinations that have fairly homogeneous occupational and industrial characteristics. Specifically, I used occupational and industrial characteristics to define labor market positions from the 54,279 occupation-industry pairs that were reported by workers in the 1990 Census sample described in the next section. These combinations were initially classified into 840 cells defined by the cross-classification of 42 occupational groupings (segments) and 20 industrial groupings (sectors). The occupational segments are relatively homogeneous in their skills and work tasks, and the industrial sectors are relatively homogeneous in their product market structure. As detailed below, positions are defined by occupation-industry pairs in the same cell or, in some cases, combined with pairs in cells with similar industrial or occupational characteristics.

Occupational Segments

I defined the forty-two occupational segments using three key aspects of the skills and work tasks performed by occupational incumbents: the types of skills needed, the level of skills and training required, and the "potential" stereotyping of task requirements and working conditions.[2] As Table 3.1 portrays, I applied these criteria in a hierarchical fashion, classifying first by types of skill, then by level of skill, and then by potential stereotyping. The first distinction uses four categories of the general types of skill required: (1) working with only things, (2) working with both people and things, (3) working with both people and data, or (4) working with both data and things. Within skill types, I classify

Figure 3.1 Process Used to Define Labor Market Positions

54,279 Occupation-industry pairs

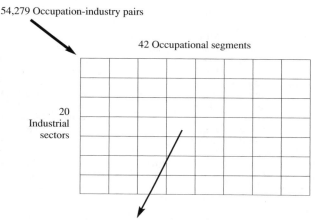

42 Occupational segments

20
Industrial
sectors

Cell of occupations that are low-skilled, black-typed, mixed-gender-typed, and work with things in industries that are small size and provide personal services in competitive domestic markets:

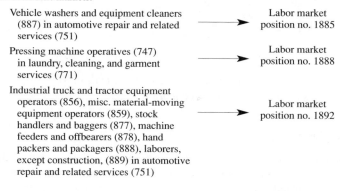

Vehicle washers and equipment cleaners (887) in automotive repair and related services (751) → Labor market position no. 1885

Pressing machine operatives (747) in laundry, cleaning, and garment services (771) → Labor market position no. 1888

Industrial truck and tractor equipment operators (856), misc. material-moving equipment operators (859), stock handlers and baggers (877), machine feeders and offbearers (878), hand packers and packagers (888), laborers, except construction, (889) in automotive repair and related services (751) → Labor market position no. 1892

occupations as requiring low, medium, or high levels of general skills and training. Within skill types and skill levels, I distinguish occupations by whether or not the work task requirements or working conditions create the potential for race typing and/or the potential for gender typing of the position to ensure that I map the critical boundaries for possible race and sex segregation. I define three categories of the potential for gender typing: female typed, male typed, and mixed typing. Analogously, I delineate three categories of the potential for race typing: black typed, white typed, and mixed typed. In principle, this classification system could define up to ninety-eight occupational segments, but not all combinations of race typing and skill level are logically possible. Appendix A details how each of these criteria are operationalized and applied to define the segments, and Appendix

Table 3.1 Occupational Segments Classification Scheme

Skill Type	Skill Level	Gender Typing	Race Typing	Skill Type	Skill Level	Gender Typing	Race Typing
Things	Low	Mixed	Mixed	Data and people	Low	Female	Mixed
	Low	Male	Black		Low	Mixed	Black
	Low	Mixed	Black		Low	Mixed	Mixed
	Medium	Male	Black		Medium	Female	Mixed
	Medium	Male	Mixed		Medium	Male	White
	Medium	Mixed	Black		Medium	Mixed	Black
	Medium	Mixed	Mixed		Medium	Mixed	White
Data and things	Low	Male	Black		Medium	Mixed	Mixed
	Low	Mixed	Black		High	Female	White
	Low	Mixed	Mixed		High	Mixed	White
	Medium	Female	Black		High	Mixed	Mixed
	Medium	Female	Mixed	People and things	Low	Female	Black
	Medium	Male	Black		Low	Female	Mixed
	Medium	Male	White		Low	Mixed	Black
	Medium	Male	Mixed		Low	Mixed	Mixed
	Medium	Mixed	Black		Medium	Female	Mixed
	Medium	Mixed	White		Medium	Male	White
	Medium	Mixed	Mixed		Medium	Male	Mixed
	High	Female	White		Medium	Mixed	Mixed
	High	Female	Mixed				
	High	Mixed	White				
	High	Mixed	Mixed				

Table A.1 presents the occupational segment classification for all 503 occupations as well as their 1990 Census occupation codes.

Industrial Sectors

To define the twenty industrial sectors, I grouped together industries that are relatively homogeneous in terms of four central indicators of the type, power, and resources of industries in the economic segmentation literature (Hodson and Kaufman 1982; Kalleberg and Berg 1987; Kaufman, Hodson, and Fligstein 1981; Tolbert, Horan and Beck 1980). As Table 3.2 shows, I applied these four criteria hierarchically, categorizing first by product type, followed by market scope, market power, and economic scale. I initially grouped industries using Browning and Singelmann's (1978) definition of broad product types: extractive, transformative, distributive services, producer services, social services, and personal services. Within product type, I classified industries into three categories according to the scope of the markets in which they operate: international, domestic, and domestic with a significant presence of foreign competitors. Within product type and scope, I grouped industries by the extent of their power and presence in markets. Market power consisted of two categories: oligopolistic versus competitive. Economic scale had two categories: large versus small to

Table 3.2 Industrial Sectors Classification Scheme

Product Type	Market Scope	Concentration	Economic Scale
Extractive	International	Oligopolistic	Small-medium
	Domestic	Oligopolistic	Small-medium
	Domestic	Competitive	Small-medium
Transformative	International	Oligopolistic	Large
	International	Oligopolistic	Small-medium
	Domestic	Oligopolistic	Mixed
	Domestic	Competitive	Small-medium
	Domestic, foreign penetration	Oligopolistic	Large
	Domestic, foreign penetration	Competitive	Small-medium
Distributive service	International	Oligopolistic	Small-medium
	Domestic	Oligopolistic	Large
	Domestic	Oligopolistic	Small-medium
	Domestic	Competitive	Small-medium
Producer service	Domestic	Oligopolistic	Small-medium
	Domestic	Competitive	Small-medium
Social service	Domestic	Oligopolistic	Small-medium
	Domestic	Competitive	Small-medium
	Public	Public	Public
Personal service	Domestic	Oligopolistic	Small-medium
	Domestic	Competitive	Small-medium

medium size. I also include a public sector by theoretical fiat, given both the hypothesized differences in outcomes for the private and public sectors and the divergence in their use of profitability as a motivating goal. Thus, this approach could define up to seventy-three sectors, but only twenty combinations empirically exist in my data. Appendix A provides more detail on the definition of the industrial segments, and Appendix Table A.2 presents the industrial sector classification for all 228 industries as well as their 1990 Census industry codes.

Defining Positions from the Cells of the Segment by Sector Cross-Classification

My ideal goal was to define a labor market position with a minimum of fifty workers from each of the four race-sex groups. Each occupation-industry combination in the same cell of the segment by sector cross-classification was examined to determine if it had sufficient numbers of each race-sex group to define that combination as a position. For example, pressing machine operatives (occupation code 747) in laundry, cleaning, and garment services (industry code 771) defines a labor market position, as do garbage collectors (875) for sanitary services (471), registered nurses (95) in hospitals (831), and airplane pilots and navigators (226) in air transport (421). More than one labor market position could be defined from within the same cell because each cell contained multiple occupation-industry pairs, as Figure 3.1 illustrates. For example, three other occupation-industry pairs in the same cell as pressing machine operatives in laundries had sufficient cases to treat each as a separate position.

If there were insufficient cases for some groups, then an occupation-industry pair was combined with other occupation-industry pairs in the same cell or, if there were still insufficient cases, with those in "similar" cells to achieve sufficient cases. Consider two examples of positions defined by combinations within the same cell. In the oil and gas extraction industry (42), mining machine operators (616) were combined with mining occupations not elsewhere classified (617). A more complex combination of six occupations in the automotive repair and related services industry (751) was created as well.

I used the following rules to determine which six-digit combinations could be aggregated to define positions:

1. Combinations had to be in cells with the same broad industrial product type.
2. Combinations had to be in cells with the same occupational skill type.
3. Within the above restrictions, I combined across cells according to their similarity on the other industrial and occupational factors used to define the cells.

If the goal of fifty workers had been strictly applied for black women, it would have created a very high level of aggregation, as this group is the most segregated (Carlson 1992; King 1992; Reskin and Padavic 1999). I relaxed this restriction for black women if there were sufficient numbers for the other groups, but made efforts to maintain a variety of positions with sufficient black women for stable estimation of the dependent measures. Using these rules, I initially defined 1,967 labor market positions. Thirty-six percent of these are single detailed occupation-industry pairs, while the median number of combinations to form a position is fifteen pairs. I eventually excluded fifty of these positions from the analysis because they had too few black women.[3]

Data and Methods for the Worker-Level Analyses

Data Source and Sample Selection

I use the 1990 Census Public Use Microdata Samples (PUMS) to measure the worker-level dependent variables (labor market position in which the worker is employed and annual earnings from the position) and the worker-level predictors (human capital, family status, geographic residence, and labor supply) of these outcomes. For 1990, I combine the 5% PUMS with the 1% PUMS.[4] I limited the PUMS samples to blacks and whites, aged twenty-five and older, and in the labor force. Other race-ethnic groups (e.g., Hispanic and Asian subgroups) were excluded due to sample sizes in many positions that were too small for reliable estimation of group differentials within labor market positions.[5] The age restriction excludes both those people in the earliest years of labor force participation, during which employment and job attachment tend to be highly volatile (Rindfuss, Swicegood, and Rosenfeld 1987), and those who are still completing their formal education. Table 3.3 shows the sample size for each of the four race-sex groups in 1990.

Why use 1990 Census data rather than 2000 Census data? Beyond the fact that the 1990 Census was the only data available when I began this project, there are other substantive reasons not to use the more recent census data. There was a major revision of the coding of occupation in the 2000 Census such that it is not possible to define labor market positions comparably across censuses. This precludes constructing good measures of employment growth and decline between 1990 and 2000. Furthermore, many of the other occupational characteristics described later in this chapter, particularly those used as indicators of race and gender typing, are not available for the 2000 Census coding of occupations. Thus, the absence of these measures would seriously limit my research given the crucial theoretical role of growth in queuing theory, the centrality of race and gender typing to my approach, and because a key expectation from my integrated perspective is that growth moderates the effects of race and gender typing. Moreover, I would expect the theoretical processes to be relatively invariant over time, as I found to be the case from supplementary analyses (not reported) of 1980 labor market positions.

Measurement

For reasons I detail below, I use log-linear analysis to predict the matching of workers to labor market positions and a type of regression analysis to predict workers' earnings from their positions. Keep in mind that the main purpose of these worker-level analyses is to construct two outcome measures at the labor market position level—employment segregation and earning gaps among race-sex groups—net of the effects of workers' human capital, family status, geographic residence, and, for predicting earnings, labor supply.

Table 3.3 Weighted Sample Sizes of Race-Sex Groups from PUMS, 1990

	Number	Percentage
Black women	338,064	5.7
Black men	298,920	5.0
White women	2,431,168	40.7
White men	2,911,784	48.7

Note: PUMS stands for the Public Use Microdata Samples of the 1990 Census.

For the employment analysis, the outcome measure is a categorical variable whose 1,917 categories indicate the labor market position in which a worker is employed. The labor market outcome measure for the earnings analysis is the worker's annual earnings in the preceding calendar year measured in dollars (i.e., for the 1990 PUMS this is annual earnings for 1989). The predictors are measures of four core concepts:

1. *Human capital* indicators are education and potential work experience.
2. *Family structure* measures include marital status, the number of young children, and the number of older children.
3. *Geographic residence* indicators are metropolitan residence and state of residence.
4. *Labor supply* (used only in the earnings analyses) measures include weeks worked and employment level (hours).

See Appendix A for a detailed discussion of the operationalization of these variables.

Predicting Employment in Labor Market Positions

The purpose of predicting workers' employment in labor market positions is to use the results to measure employment segregation, taking into account race-sex groups' differences in the worker-level predictors. To do this, I use procedures developed in my past research on the employment representation of black and white men (Kaufman 1986; Kaufman and Daymont 1981; Daymont and Kaufman 1979). I first predict a worker's labor market position based on his or her human capital, family structure, geographic residence, and race-sex group membership. The "net" effects of race-sex group membership from this multivariate analysis are thus adjusted for (purged of) group differences in the other predictors. I then use these net effects to construct measures of employment segregation among race-sex groups.

Specifically, I applied log-linear analysis to the eight-dimensional cross-tabulation of labor market position, race-sex group membership, education, potential experience, marital status, number of children, metropolitan residence, and southern residence. I performed a separate log-linear analysis for each labor market position; the dependent variable was a dichotomy (D_j) indicating if workers were employed in the jth labor market position or elsewhere.[6] This set of nearly two thousand analyses was repeated for the regional model used to estimate segregation in the South and the non-South.

Measuring employment segregation from the worker-level results. Although the index of dissimilarity is the most commonly used measure of employment segregation (Reskin 1993), it is ill suited for the hypotheses I outlined in Chapter 2 for several reasons. What I need are measures of the over- or under-representation of race-sex groups in each labor market position that are adjusted for the differences between groups in human capital, family structure, and geographic residence. The index of dissimilarity is typically calculated from the *observed* distribution of two groups, say black women and white men, across a set of positions and does not allow for controls for differences in education, experience, and so on between black females and white males.[7] A second, more consequential problem is that the index of dissimilarity is a nondirectional measure indicating only, for example, whether there is an unevenness in the representation of black women and white men but not whether black women are overrepresented or underrepresented. Moreover, it is an aggregate measure of unevenness *across* a set of positions rather than a measure of unevenness *within* a position.

In place of the index of dissimilarity, I use the results of the log-linear analyses to construct the kind of measures I need: indicators of the relative employment representation in a labor market position for pairs of race-sex groups adjusted for group differences in human capital, family structure, and geographic residence. The basis for my measure is an odds ratio comparing, say, the odds of a black woman being employed as a presser in a laundry to the odds of a white man being employed in that position. Using the observed distribution of these groups yields an odds ratio of 24.99.[8] That is, black women are almost twenty-five times more likely to be employed in this position than are white men. Similar calculations would show that black women are 4.61 times as likely as white women, and 4.59 times as likely as black men, to work in this position.

These examples are all *observed* odds ratios. I use instead *net* odds ratios calculated from the parameters for the race-sex group by position association from the log-linear analyses for each position (Kaufman and Schervish 1987) for five paired comparisons among race-sex groups: black women to white men, black men to white men, white women to white men, black women to black men, and black women to white women. For each comparison, I calculated the odds ratio contrasting: (1) the odds of a member of group 1 being employed in a position versus employment in any other position to (2) the odds of a member of group 2 being employed in the position versus employment elsewhere, net of the effects of the other predictors. For example, the net odds ratio comparing black women's (BW) and white men's (WM) net chances of being employed as a presser in a laundry (position 1888) would be:

Eq. 3.1 $$\textit{Net Odds Ratio}_{BW:WM} \textit{ for position 1888} =$$

$$\frac{\textit{Predicted Odds}_{BW} \textit{ for position 1888}}{\textit{Predicted Odds}_{WM} \textit{ for position 1888}}$$

If you are interested in learning exactly how these net odds ratios are calculated, you should consult Appendix A. In the analyses in later chapters, I use the log of the odds ratio. Logging the odds ratio changes it to an additive metric and further ensures that the order of comparison (black women to white men versus white men to black women) does not affect the magnitude of the indicator. Thus, a positive value of the logged measure would indicate, for example, a greater representation of black women than white men employed in a position, while a negative value would indicate a greater representation of white men.

The net odds ratios for black women for this particular position are slightly different from the observed ones given above: 26.84 compared to white men, 4.18 compared to white women, and 5.26 compared to black men. So you might wonder if the controls for worker characteristics lead to any substantial differences in practical terms. I conducted parallel analyses using logged odds ratios calculated from the observed distribution of groups. In each analysis, discussed later, there was at least one predictor that was significant using the *net* odds ratio that was not significant for the *observed* odds ratio and vice versa. And even though the net and observed measures are highly correlated, there were a number of positions for which the magnitude of the difference between the observed and net measures was notable, especially for black-white comparisons. For either black men compared to white men or black women compared to white women, the net and observed measures differed by more than one-third of a standard deviation for 35% of the positions. The number of positions that showed such difference in magnitudes was much smaller for the other comparisons (3–9%).

I used an analogous procedure to construct the region-specific employment segregation measures using the results from the regional log-linear model. In this situation, I calculated two odds ratios for each pair of race-sex groups in each position, one measuring employment segregation in the South and the second employment segregation in the non-South.

Predicting Earnings from Labor Market Positions

The purpose of predicting the earnings workers receive from their labor market position is to use the results to measure earnings gaps among race-sex groups, taking into account group differences in the worker-level predictors of earnings. For each race-sex group, I first predict a worker's earnings using indicators of his or her human capital, family structure, geographic residence, labor supply, and the labor market position in which he or she is employed. I then use regression standardization (Althauser and Wigler 1972) to predict the average adjusted earnings for each race-sex group in a labor market position under the hypothetical condition that all groups have the same average values for the predictors.

Specifically, I ran a separate regression for each race-sex group of workers' earnings on the worker-level predictors (X), state of residence (*State*), and labor market position (*LMP*). This permits the returns to these characteristics to vary across race-sex groups. I further specified that the returns to these predictors vary across occupational segments (*Occ*) and industrial sectors (*Ind*) within each group.[9] Thus, the regression for each group takes the form:

Eq. 3.2 $\quad Earn = \alpha + \beta_1 X + \beta_2 X * Occ + \beta_3 X * Ind + \beta_4 State + \beta_5 LMP + \varepsilon$

Given the numerous labor market positions, I estimated these regressions using an "unbalanced" fixed-effects model for the effects of labor market position (Greene 1997; Judge et al. 1985) as detailed in Appendix A. This provides a more convenient alternative to estimating a regression with 1,916 dummy variables for labor market position.

In addition to this model, I also used a regional model to specify that the earnings determination process could be different in the South than in the non-South. For each race-sex group, I ran separate regressions for those residing in the South and in the non-South. The regression model is identical to that in Eq. 3.2, except that the South regressions include only dummy variables for the southern states and the non-South regressions include only dummy variables for the nonsouthern states.

Measuring adjusted earnings gaps. I construct adjusted earning gaps (*EG*) for five paired comparisons among race-sex groups in a labor market position: black women to white men, black men to white men, white women to white men, black women to black men, and black women to white women. My measure is the ratio of the regression-standardized earnings in a labor market position for the pair of groups. The regression-standardized earnings is the predicted value of earnings from the worker-level earnings model in Eq. 3.2, using each group's own coefficients but the same set of values for the predictors (the total sample means) for each group. For example, I used the coefficients from the fixed-effect regression (Eq. 3.2) for black men (BM), for white men (WM), and the total sample mean of the predictors to calculate the adjusted earnings gap for black men compared to white men in position 318 (garbage collectors in sanitary services) as:

Eq. 3.3 $\qquad Earnings\ Gap_{BM:WM}\ for\ position\ 318 =$

$$\frac{Predicted\ Earnings_{BM}\ for\ position\ 318}{Predicted\ Earnings_{WM}\ for\ position\ 318}$$

Consult Appendix A for details on the calculation of the predicted earnings for each race-sex group in each position. In the analyses in later chapters, I use the log of the earnings gap in Eq. 3.3 as the outcome variable. Logging the earnings gap changes it to an additive metric and also ensures that the order of comparison (BM to WM versus WM to BM) does not affect the magnitude of the indicator. Thus, a positive value of the logged earnings gap would indicate, for example, higher earnings for black men than white men in a position, while a negative value would indicate higher earnings for white men. Supplementary analyses also use the levels of predicted race-sex group specific earnings (such as those used in Eq. 3.3 to calculate the earnings gap) as the outcome.

Continuing the example, the *adjusted* earnings ratio for black men to white men in position 318 is 0.837. That is, after adjusting for differences in education, experience, and so on, black men earn 83.7 cents for each dollar earned by white men working as garbage collectors in sanitary services. As Figure 3.2 shows, the adjustment results in a leveling of the earnings gap in comparison to the *observed* earnings ratio of 0.788, suggesting that almost one-quarter of the earnings gap can be attributed to differences in human capital, family structure, geographic residence, and labor supply. However, the same is not equally true for all the race-sex group comparisons in this position, as shown in Figure 3.2. For black women in comparison to any other group, the earnings ratios are all smaller (the gaps are larger) and a larger share of the gap is due to differences between black women and the other groups in their average characteristics. However, a large earnings gap remains as shown by the distance of the white bars for adjusted earnings from a level of equality (a ratio of 1.0). For white

**Figure 3.2 Observed and Adjusted Earnings Ratios
Among Race-Sex Groups, Garbage Collectors in Sanitary Services**

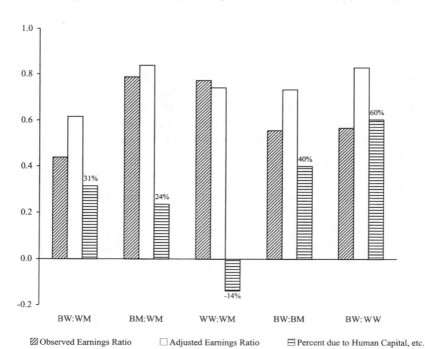

women, there is little difference between the observed and the adjusted earnings ratios, and the adjusted ratio is actually smaller than the observed, indicating that the earnings gap in this position is not at all due to differences between white men and women in human capital and the other predictors.

I followed a parallel set of steps to construct the region-specific adjusted earning gaps for the five paired comparisons among race-sex groups in a labor market position. For each race-sex group, I calculated the regression-standardized earnings for a position in the South as the predicted earnings using the race-sex group's coefficients from the South version of the earnings model in Eq. 3.2, again using the total sample means as the "standard" values for the predictors. The analogous calculation for a position in the non-South used each race-sex group's coefficients from the non-South version of the earnings model in Eq. 3.2 and the total sample means. I also experimented with the specification of the "standard" values for the predictors by using region-specific means rather than total sample means, but the resulting adjusted earnings ratios were virtually indistinguishable with correlations above 0.99.

Data and Methods for the Position-Level Analyses

Data Sources and Sample Selection

Beyond the census PUMS data, I used a variety of sources for the industrial- and occupational-level variables as detailed in Appendix A (see the note at the bottom of Table 3.4 for a list). The industry-level data that I compiled and use for this analysis are publically available on the Web through the Inter-University Consortium for Political and Social Research (ICPSR).[10] The sample size of labor market positions is 1,917, which excludes forty-nine positions for which there were too few workers from any of the race-sex groups to obtain stable estimates of the labor market positions outcome measures of employment segregation and earnings gaps. Specifically, I excluded positions if there were fewer than five workers from any of the race-sex groups.

Measurement

Table 3.4 presents summary information on the measurement of the position-level variables, including the data source(s) used for each. Given the large number of indicators, I highlight key points about measurement for each cluster of variables below and provide full information on operationalizing them in Appendix A. Note that some of these variables are characteristics of the industry in which a worker is employed and some are characteristics of their occupation. For multi-item scales, I constructed each scale by first creating a standardized indicator for each component and then calculating the mean of the standardized indicators for each industry (occupation).[11]

Table 3.4 Measurement of Position-Level Variables

Variable	Measurement	Data Sources
General skills and training		
General skills	Complexity of working with people, Complexity of working with data, Complexity of working with things, General educational development	DOT
Training	Specific vocational preparation time in months	DOT
Growth and employment rates		
Employment growth	Log of the ratio of employment in labor market position in 1990 to employment in labor market position in 1980	PUMS
Sufficient work hours	Percent of labor force working more than 30 hours per week	PUMS
Unemployment rate	Percent of labor force unemployed	PUMS
Self-employment rate	Percent of labor force self-employed	PUMS
Race- and gender-typed tasks		
Physical exertion	Physical demands and strength items	DOT
Environmental conditions	Presence of six environmental conditions (cold, heat, wetness, noise, hazardous work, and fumes/odors)	DOT
Routinization	Repetitive or short-cycle job, Job has a variety of duties (reverse coded), Routine task preference	DOT
Status in interaction	Complexity in dealing with people (reverse coded)	DOT
Authority	Dummy indicator coded 1 if occupation is supervisory and 0 if not, from England et al. (1994) for 1980 Occupations, revised for 1990	EKHRM
Physical dexterity	Manual dexterity, Finger dexterity, Motor coordination (all reverse coded)	DOT
Nurturant work	Dummy indicator coded 1 if nurturant work is a major task and 0 if not, from England et al. (1994) for 1980 Occupations, revised for 1990	EKHRM
Clerical aptitude	Clerical perception (reverse coded)	DOT
Math skills	Numerical aptitude (reverse coded)	DOT

continues

Table 3.4 continued

Variable	Measurement	Data Sources
Product market structure		
Market power	Eight-firm employment concentration ratio, Eight-firm sales concentration ratio	ES
Physical size	Workers/firm, Percent of firms with >5,000 workers, Percent of firms with >10,000 workers, Percent of workers in firms with >5,000 workers, Percent of workers in firms with >10,000 workers	ES
Financial size	Sales/firm, Assets/firm, Net income/firm, Value added/firm	ES, IO, SOI
Profitability	Three-year averages of net income/assets and of net income/receipts	SOI
Capital intensity	Total assets/employee and depreciable assets/employee	ES, SOI
Foreign involvement	Foreign dividends/firm, Foreign tax credits/firm, Exports/firm	ES
Foreign penetration	Imports/firm, Imports as a percent of industry's total commodity output, Imports as a percent of total imports across all industries, Content coded indicator of extent of foreign competition in domestic market	ES, IO, IOL
Productivity	Value added/employee and value added as a percent of total output	ES, IO
Linkages to other actors		
Industry unionization	Proportion of industry labor force who were union members	CPS
Occupation unionization	Proportion of occupational labor force who were union members	CPS
Public sector	Percent of labor force in public sector	PUMS
Federal purchases	Federal purchases as a percent of total output, Federal purchases/firm	ES, IO

Sources: The data source codes are: *CPS, Current Population Surveys, May file, 1985–1989; March DOT, Dictionary of Occupational Titles* (4th ed.); *EKHRM,* England, Kilbourne, Herbert, Reid, and Megdal (1994); *ES, 1987 Enterprise Statistics; IO,* the *Input-Output Structure of the United States, 1987; IOL, U.S. Industrial Outlook: 1990; PUMS, 1980 and 1990 Public Use Micro Samples;* and *SOI, Statistics of Income: Corporation Income Tax Returns for 1989–1991.*

As I described earlier, many of the labor market positions are aggregates of detailed occupation-industry codes, so the scales were aggregated in a corresponding fashion. For these positions I calculated the industrial indicators for each position as a weighted sum of the indicator values for the component industries, with weights proportional to the total number of workers in the component industries. I used an analogous procedure for the occupational measures, weighting proportional to the number of workers in the component occupations. There were some missing data, primarily due to coverage limitations for service industries in the industrial data sources. The measurement of the industrial measures was further complicated by the fact that each archival source used its own unique set of industry codes. Luckily, each source also reported the equivalency between its coding and Standard Industrial Classification (SIC) codes. I used these equivalencies to translate each coding scheme into census industry codes (which also have SIC code equivalents) as a common scheme because the census codes provide the link to the worker-level data.[12]

General skills and training. I initially constructed separate measures of the general skills required and of the training time required to obtain skills. I combined these into a single measure of *General Skills and Training* because their separate use created severe collinearity problems; supplementary analyses (not reported) using either skill complexity alone or training time alone indicated that each affects the outcomes similarly.

Growth and employment type rates. Employment growth (or decline) over the last decade is a central indicator from a queuing perspective, denoting changes in the size of the job queue. I use the log of the ratio of 1990 employment over 1980 employment to specify that growth and decline represent equivalent metric changes and to reduce skewness. The other three indicators in this set measure three different aspects of the availability of desirable jobs: those offering sufficient levels of employment (more than thirty hours per week); those providing small likelihood of job insecurity (low unemployment); and those offering the opportunity to be your own boss (self-employment).

Race- and gender-typed work tasks. As proposed in Chapter 2, race-typed tasks and conditions are those jobs requiring heavy physical labor, poor working conditions, menial (routine/repetitive) or subservient tasks, status-superior interactions, authority, and skill. Except for skill, these also define gender-typed tasks and conditions, which additionally include physical dexterity, nurturant skills, clerical perception, and mathematical skills.

Product market structure. The core of this cluster provides indicators of the power, resources, and nature of the production process of industries: market power (concentration), physical size, financial size, profitability, capital intensity, and productivity. I combined the physical and financial dimensions of size into a single measure of economic scale because their separate use created collinearity problems and because preliminary analyses suggested that each affects the outcomes similarly. I also constructed measures of economic globalization: the degree to which domestic industries operate in non-US markets and the degree to which non-US industries operate in domestic markets. Note that the foreign penetration scale was used in the definition of industrial sectors but not as a predictor.

Linkages to other actors. This final cluster of measures taps into two different sets of external actors who can influence labor market processes: unions and government. I use separate indicators for the presence of unions in industries and in occupations because no data exist to measure unionization reliably at the level of industry-occupation combinations. I measure government linkages in terms of a labor market position's degree of exposure to two different roles of the government: as an employer (percent employed in the public sector) and as a potential regulator of federal contract nondiscrimination provisions (percent of federal purchases).

Estimation Issues

In this section I address five statistical problems that are present in the regression models for predicting employment segregation and earnings gaps. I first discuss the two simpler issues, missing data for some of the predictors and collinearity among the predictors. I then discuss the use of estimated generalized least squares (EGLS) regression to correct for heteroskedasticity of the errors across positions and correlated errors between pairs of positions. Finally, I consider the issue of between-equation correlated errors; that is, correlation of the errors in predicting employment segregation with the errors in predicting earnings gaps. Readers who are not statistically inclined might want to skim or skip these last two subsections, depending on your tolerance for more technical material.

In the discussion below, I use as a concrete example the following typical model of the two outcomes that compare white women (WW) to white men (WM) in terms of employment segregation (*ES*) and earnings gaps (*EG*) in Eq. 3.4a and 3.4b as well as the group-specific predicted earnings for white women and white men (Eârn) in Eq. 3.4c and 3.4d:

Eq. 3.4a
$$ES_i{}^{WW:WM} = \underline{\beta}_1{}' \underline{X}_{1,i} + \varepsilon_{1,i}$$

Eq. 3.4b
$$EG_i{}^{WW:WM} = \gamma_2 ES_i{}^{WW:WM} + \underline{\beta}_2{}' \underline{X}_{2,i} + \varepsilon_{2,i}$$

Eq. 3.4c
$$E\hat{a}rn_i{}^{WW} = \gamma_3 ES_i{}^{WW:WM} + \delta_3 ES_i{}^{BM:WM} + \underline{\beta}_3{}' \underline{X}_{3,i} + \varepsilon_{3,i}$$

Eq. 3.4d
$$E\hat{a}rn_i{}^{WM} = \gamma_4 ES_i{}^{WW:WM} + \delta_4 ES_i{}^{BM:WM} + \underline{\beta}_4{}' \underline{X}_{4,i} + \varepsilon_{4,i}$$

Missing data. Data are missing for some of the position-level predictors (X_1, X_2, X_3, or X_4), primarily due to coverage limitations for service sector industries in the industrial data sources. Listwise exclusion of positions with missing data would have reduced the sample size considerably as well as disproportionately excluding positions in the service sectors.[13] In Appendix A, I describe Cohen and Cohen's (1983: 284–289) procedure to include all cases.

Collinearity. Collinearity is a situation in which two or more of the predictors are so highly correlated that it is impossible to get good estimates of their separate effects (Greene 1997: 420). I assessed the presence and impact of collinearity using Belsley, Kuh, and Welsch's (1980) diagnostic procedures. As I noted above, preliminary analyses using these diagnostics indicated collinearity problems that I resolved by combining general skills and training time into a single scale and by combining physical size and financial size into a single scale. No other collinearity issues were consequential.

Heteroskedasticity, correlated errors within an equation, and EGLS estimation. To apply ordinary least squares (OLS) regression to any of the models in Eq. 3.4a–d, I would have to assume that the error variances for, say, $\varepsilon_{1,i}$ in Eq. 3.4a, are homoskedastic (have equal variance across positions) and have zero autocorrelation (are not correlated between pairs of positions). In Appendix A, I discuss both the reasons to suspect that these two problems are likely to occur in my analyses and how I tested for their presence. In all of the analyses reported later, the diagnostic tests indicate that there is in fact both heteroskedasticity and autocorrelation. The consequence of this violation of the assumptions is that the OLS estimator remains unbiased but is inefficient for correctly calculated standard errors (Greene 1997: 498). However, the coefficient standard errors and significance tests that are *actually* reported by any statistical software using OLS in this situation are biased (Greene 1997: 498–499). Consequently, I use estimated generalized least squares (EGLS), which provides unbiased and efficient estimates. Appendix A details the exact specification of the EGLS models that I estimated.

Correlated errors between equations. Because the models for the earnings gap in Eq. 3.4b and for the group-specific earnings levels in Eq. 3.4c and 3.4d include other endogenous variables as predictors (employment segregation between the groups), an additional statistical problem is possible when estimating these models. If the errors for two equations (say, $\varepsilon_{1,i}$ and $\varepsilon_{2,i}$ in Eq. 3.4a and 3.4b) are correlated, then equation-by-equation OLS (or EGLS) estimates of the employment segregation and earnings gap models are biased and inconsistent (Greene 1997: 710). For some of the analyses, this issue is inconsequential because the magnitude of the correlations between $\varepsilon_{1,i}$ and $\varepsilon_{2,i}$ is small enough to ignore, but in others the correlation differs significantly from zero. Appendix

A describes how I determined which was the case for each analysis. When the correlated errors are significant for the earnings gap analyses, I use a seemingly unrelated regressions (SUR) model (Greene 1997: 737). For estimating the models for group-specific earnings levels (Eq. 3.4c and 3.4d) I instead use a two-stage least squares (2SLS) approach (Greene 1997: 710–711). In Appendix A, I discuss the rationale for choosing the SUR versus the 2SLS models for these analyses.

Notes

1. If you really want an answer to this question, you will have to chat with me in person and make up your own mind about it.

2. You might wonder if using these indicators of the potential for stereotyping means that I must find that such occupations in fact have high levels of race or sex segregation. The answer is no. I do *not* use the actual race or sex composition of occupations to define occupations as similar, which obviously would be circular. Instead, I group together occupations that are similar in terms of a particular set of task requirements and working conditions, those specific ones that my theory suggests should create race or gender typing.

3. All but one of these positions had fewer than five black women. The other position had more than five black women but fewer than five black men and few cases overall.

4. For measuring employment growth for the position-level analyses, I also use the 1980 5% PUMS data with the same sample selection criteria. A 1% PUMS with geographic coding parallel to the 5% PUMS is not available for 1980.

5. The exclusion of Asians and Hispanics is unfortunate as the inequality literature continues to pay relatively little attention to their place in the US stratification system. And when they are included in analyses, it is often as pan-ethnic groups, which ignores the fact that the history and treatment in the United States of Mexican Americans differs from that of Cuban Americans, of Puerto Ricans, and so on. Their inclusion would have added richness to this study by providing an opportunity to validate (or falsify) the theoretical expectations hypotheses developed in Chapter 2 against a wider variety of situations. While I would expect the same processes to be operable, some differential expectations would also be necessary. For example, the details of how jobs are "race typed" would vary for these groups in line with differences in how these groups are stereotyped in the United States.

6. Ideally, I would have run a single analysis simultaneously predicting in which of the 1,917 positions a worker is employed. But this would require analyzing a crosstabulation with 3,680,640 cells, which is beyond the program capabilities of current statistical software and would have taken an extreme amount of time even if it were not.

7. This shortcoming could be overcome by using the net effects of race-sex group membership from the log-linear analyses to construct the adjusted (rather than observed) distribution of each group across positions (Kaufman and Schervish 1986), but would not solve the other problems.

8. The observed proportion of black women employed as pressers in laundries is 0.00299, while the proportion of white men employed as pressers in laundries is 0.00012. Thus the odds ratio is calculated as $\dfrac{\dfrac{0.00299}{(1-0.00299)}}{\dfrac{0.00012}{(1-0.00012)}}$, which equals 24.99.

9. As described in Appendix A, I used an aggregated version of the industrial sectors and occupational segments in these regressions.

10. The ICPSR Web address is http://www.icpsr.umich.edu/. The data are archived as Study Number 1225, *1980 and 1990 Industrial Structure Measures*. Users of these data should acknowledge my research support from the National Science Foundation (Grant no. SBR-9422800) and the role of ICPSR as distributor of the data.

11. A standardized indicator is a *z*-score calculated as $z = \dfrac{x - Mean\ of\ x}{Standard\ deviation\ of\ x}$. This converts each component to an equivalent metric of measurement. The standardized indicators each have a mean of zero and a standard deviation of one.

12. This translation required different manipulations of the data from each source when multiple industries were combined into a single census industry, depending on whether the reported variables were raw counts and amounts or aggregate statistics. Raw counts and amounts were simply summed across the component industries. For aggregate statistics, I calculated the weighted mean of the aggregate statistic across the component industries, with weights defined by the number of reporting units (typically firms or establishments) in each component industry.

13. The sample size would be reduced from 1,917 to 1,425.

4

The Segregation of Groups Across Labor Market Positions

Self-evident data are patient, they let theories chatter about them,
but remain what they are. It is the business of theories to conform to data.
—Edmund Husserl (1931: 89)

In this chapter, I begin the process of evaluating how well my approach can answer the questions with which I introduced this book. Or, in Husserl's terms, it is time to see how well my approach conforms to the data that I described in the last chapter. Specifically, I discuss results from models predicting the degree and kind of employment segregation among race-sex groups that characterized labor market positions in 1990. I analyze five dependent variables, each measuring the differential employment representation for a paired comparison of the race-sex groups: black women to white men, black men to white men, white women to white men, black women to black men, and black women to white women. The first three outcomes contrast the employment representation of white males to each of the other three groups. The other two outcomes are technically redundant (i.e., these outcomes are linear functions of the first three outcome measures),[1] but their results are useful to present separately in order to compare race segregation between men and women and to compare sex segregation between blacks and whites.

I start with a base model, corresponding to Figure 2.4 in Chapter 2.[2] This base model specifies that the effect of each predictor on employment segregation is constant; that is, it does not depend on (vary with) the value of the other predictors. The sole exception is for the combined effects of employment growth and general skill and training requirements, which are integrally linked in affecting the clearing of labor queues. As discussed earlier, the effect of growth on segregation should be different for high versus low skill/training requirements and the effect of skills/training on segregation should be different in growing versus declining positions. Thus, these factors are specified as an "interaction effect" in which each moderates the influence of the other. Given how many expectations I test in these base analyses, I divide the discussion of the base model results into two sections. In the first section (Core Findings), I direct the reader's attention to the two sets of results most central to my integrated perspective—the interactive relationship between employment growth and general skills/training and the effects of the race- and gender-typing indicators. These results uniformly demonstrate a high degree of support for my race-sex queuing approach and highlight the importance of stereotyping processes and countervailing forces. In the second section (Supplementary Findings), I discuss the findings for the remaining sets of factors—desirable employment, product market structure, and linkages to other actors—which show fewer effects of interest and relevance. I end this section by reflecting on the implications of the findings for the various perspectives I reviewed in Chapter 2 and for what they reveal about the intersection of race and sex.

I then complicate this base model by considering the somewhat more speculative implication of my approach, which is that employment growth, profitability, and market power more broadly moderate the effects of race- and gender-typed work tasks on employment segregation. Although the common practice is to interpret only one side of an interaction (e.g., how growth moderates the effect of skill), I discuss both sides. Statistically, the interaction model actually specifies each variable as moderating the effect of the other on the outcome. And conceptually, I am also interested in how race-gender typicality may condition the effects of growth and economic resources on segregation. As you will see, these extended analyses reinforce the conclusion from the initial analyses that offsetting pressures can either diminish or enhance race-gender stereotyping effects but that the direct effects of these forces themselves consistently increase the representation of "less preferred" groups across a variety of race- and gender-typed work settings.

Base Model Results

A first, natural question is to ask how well the base model explains the five types of employment segregation. The charts in Figure 4.1 provide a summary for each outcome of the extent to which the base model as a whole explains the variation in segregation (the pie charts) and the relative importance of the five sets of predictors (the associated bar charts).[3] Generally, the base model explains somewhat less than half of the variation across positions for race segregation within sex (black men to white men and black women to white women) but more than half of the variation for sex segregation within race (white women to white men and black women to black men) and for the combined race and sex segregation contrast (black women to white men). This finding foreshadows what we will see in detail later; the process segregating black women from white men appears to correspond more to processes of sex segregation than to processes of race segregation.

Figure 4.1 Explained Variance in Employment Segregation, SUR-EGLS Base Model

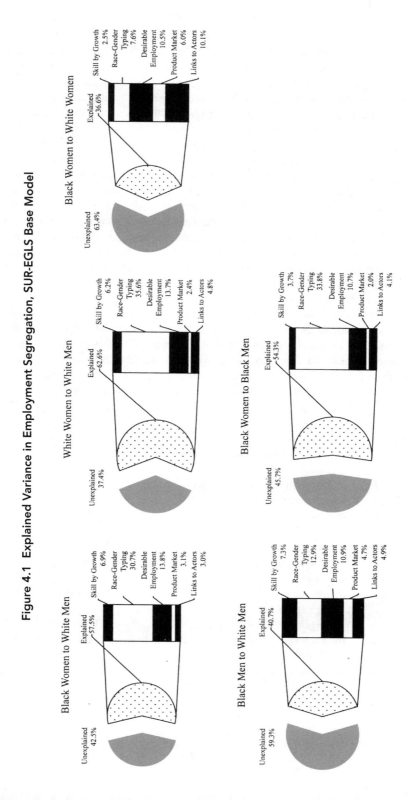

Black Women to White Men

Unexplained
42.5%

Explained
57.5%

Skill by Growth
6.9%

Race-Gender
Typing
30.7%

Desirable
Employment
13.8%

Product Market
3.1%

Links to Actors
3.0%

White Women to White Men

Unexplained
37.4%

Explained
62.6%

Skill by Growth
6.2%

Race-Gender
Typing
35.6%

Desirable
Employment
13.7%

Product Market
2.4%

Links to Actors
4.8%

Black Women to White Women

Unexplained
63.4%

Explained
36.6%

Skill by Growth
2.5%

Race-Gender
Typing
7.6%

Desirable
Employment
10.5%

Product Market
6.0%

Links to Actors
10.1%

Black Men to White Men

Unexplained
59.3%

Explained
40.7%

Skill by Growth
7.3%

Race-Gender
Typing
12.9%

Desirable
Employment
10.9%

Product Market
4.7%

Links to Actors
4.9%

Black Women to Black Men

Unexplained
45.7%

Explained
54.3%

Skill by Growth
3.7%

Race-Gender
Typing
33.8%

Desirable
Employment
10.7%

Product Market
2.0%

Links to Actors
4.1%

Indeed, the pattern of relative contributions of each set of predictors is very similar for the three sex-segregation outcomes and somewhat distinct from that for race segregation within sex. For sex segregation, the race-gender–typing set clearly dominates, with the desirable employment set explaining only about one-third to one-half as much and the remaining three sets together explaining about as much as the desirable employment rate set. In contrast, the sets of factors have more similar contributions in explaining race segregation within sex. For men, race-gender typing and desirable employment are the largest contributors, followed fairly closely (about two-thirds the size) by the skill-growth set, with the product market and links to other actors sets similarly contributing about two-thirds what skill-growth does. For women, desirable employment and links to other actors are the most important predictors of race segregation, with race-gender typing and product markets somewhat less predictive (60–75%) and skill-growth a distant last place. Despite these differences across outcome measures, note that the race-gender–typing set and the desirable employment set are always the two most influential sets, except that race-gender typing falls to third place for race segregation among women.

For those readers who want to see the detailed numeric results, Appendix Table B4.1 contains the EGLS-SUR results for the base model.[4] In contrast, discussion of the results is oriented here around visual summaries of these findings presented in Table 4.1. For each segregation outcome, this table presents a pair of columns: (1) the "predict" column lists the predicted effect of the explanatory variables, and (2) the "result" column indicates whether the results support or contradict the hypotheses. I use the following symbols to report predictions and results.

In the "predict" columns:
+	means a positive effect is predicted
–	means a negative effect is predicted
+/–	means there are opposing predictions
0	means a zero effect is predicted
Blank	means there is no prediction

In the "results" columns:
✔	means that the predicted effect is significant in the predicted direction
✗	means the effect is significant but the direction is the opposite of the prediction
∪	means the effect is nonlinear, specifically it is U shaped
✚	means a significant positive effect is found when there was no prediction
–	means a significant negative effect is found when there was no prediction
Blank	means no significant effect found

Table 4.1 Predictions and Summary of Results for the Analyses of Employment Segregation

Predictors	Black Women: White Men		Black Men: White Men		White Women: White Men		Black Women: Black Men		Black Women: White Women	
	Predict	Result	Predict	Result	Predict	Result	Predict	Result	Predict	Result
Panel A: General skill and growth										
Skill and training scale	–	✓	–	✓	–	✓	–	✓	–	✓
Skill and training × growth	+	✓	+	✓	+	✓	+		+	
Employment growth rate	+/0		+/0		+/0		+/0		+/0	
Panel B: Race-gender typing										
Environmental Conditions	+/–	▌	+	✗	–	✓	–		+	
Physical exertion	+/–	▌	+	✓	–	✓	–	✓	+	
Routinization	+	✗	+	✓		▌		▌	+	
Status in interaction	–	⊃	–	⊃	–	⊃	–	⊃	–	⊃
Authority	–		–		–	✗	–	✗	–	
Panel C: Gender typing only										
Physical dexterity	+	✓			+	✓	+	✓		
Nurturant skill	+	✓		▌	+	✓	+	✓		
Clerical perception	+	✓			+	✓	+	✓		
Math skill	–	✓		▌	–	✓	–	✓		▌

continues

Table 4.1 continued

Predictors	Black Women: White Men		Black Men: White Men		White Women: White Men		Black Women: Black Men		Black Women: White Women	
	Predict	Result	Predict	Result	Predict	Result	Predict	Result	Predict	Result
Panel D: Desirable employment										
Sufficient work hours	−	✓	−	✓	−	✓	−	✓	−	✗
Unemployment rate	+	✓	+	✓	+	✓	+	✓	+	✓
Self-employment rate	−	✓	−	✓	−	✓	−	✓	−	✓
Panel E: Product market structure										
Market power	+	✓	+	✓	+	✓	+	✓	+	✓
Profitability	+	✓	+		+	✓	+	✓	+	
Economic scale										
Capital intensity										
Foreign involvement		−				−		−		
Productivity										**+**
Panel F: Linkages to other actors										
Industry unionization	+/0	✗	+/0		+/0	✗	+/0	✗	+/0	✓
Occupation unionization	+/0		+/0		+/0	✗	+/0		+/0	✓
Percent public sector	+	✓	+	✓	+		+	✗	+	✓
Federal purchases	+/0	✗	+/0	✗	+/0	✗	+/0	✗	+/0	

Notes:

Predicted effects
+ Positive − Negative +/− Opposing predictions 0 No effect Blank No prediction

Findings
✓ Predicted effect significant ✗ Opposite of prediction significant ∪ U-shaped effect
+ Positive significant effect **−** Negative significant effect Blank No significant effect

To illustrate how to read Table 4.1, consider the predictions and results for the effects of physical exertion (in the race-gender–typing set). Keep in mind that the outcomes are coded such that a positive effect increases the relative representation of blacks compared to whites or of women compared to men, while a negative effect decreases their relative representation. For race segregation within sex, the predicted effect is positive; greater exertion requirements should increase the representation of blacks. For sex segregation within race, the predicted effect is negative; greater exertion requirements should decrease the representation of women. The results indicate that for three of these four predictions, the effect is significant in the expected direction (exertion does not affect the representation of black to white women). For black women to white men (which involves both a race and a sex comparison) there are opposing predictions, and the finding is a significant negative effect. In sum, exertion increases the employment representation of blacks relative to whites only for men but decreases the representation of women to men in all three contrasts of women to men.

Core Findings

General skills and training by growth. I argued earlier that neither general skill and training nor employment growth should have a constant effect on race-sex employment segregation. Higher skill requirements should decrease the employment representation of blacks relative to whites and of women relative to men. In part it is stereotyping by employers of highly skilled work as "inappropriate" for women and blacks that places them lower in the labor queue for such jobs, and in part it represents statistical discrimination based on the stereotyping of blacks and women as less qualified. However, if the demand for workers from a preferred race-sex group is greater than the supply, employers either must wait for members from their preferred group to acquire the needed skills and training or must hire from race-sex groups further down the labor queue. The skill effect thus should be smaller when demand for workers in a position is growing because growth increases the incentive for employers to hire from less-preferred groups. The flip side of this argument is that employment growth marks a change in the shape of the labor queue, which should decrease the salience and intensity of employers' preferences for race-sex groups in a position. Growth should open employment to those ranked lower in the queue, even more so if they have the necessary skills but are ranked low solely due to statistical discrimination by race or sex. Among high-skill positions, then, growth should *increase* the representation of blacks relative to whites and of women relative to men because growth diminishes employers' preference for white men. But among low-skill positions (stereotyped as appropriate for blacks and women), growth should *decrease* the representation of blacks relative to whites and of women relative to men because growth diminishes employers' preference for these groups.

For all five forms of employment segregation, there is a strong, negative main effect of a position's general skill demands as predicted (Panel A of Table 4.1). I found the expected moderating effect of employment growth only for the segregation of the other race-sex groups from white men and not for the other two outcomes. As Figure 4.2 illustrates, the negative effects of skill are muted by employment growth. The overall skill effects indicate that black women, black men, and white women are overrepresented compared to white men in positions with lower levels of general skill and training requirements but are underrepresented in higher skill positions. Keep in mind that these effects control for the influence of differences among race-sex groups in workers' human capital, family structure, and geographic residence. But the skill effect in high-growth positions (the solid thin line) is less than it is in positions experiencing large employment declines (the solid thick line).[5] Comparing the high-skill endpoints of the lines, it is clear that white men are overrepresented (a negative relative representation) in high-skill positions but much less so if there is high employment growth than if there is no growth or a decline. Similarly, the low-skill endpoints of the lines indicate that black women, black men, and white women are overrepresented (positive predicted representation) in low-skill positions but much less so for high employment-growth positions than for others. The muting of the effects of general skill and training requirements by employment growth suggests the influence of race-sex queuing processes. Employment growth diminishes but does not eliminate the salience and intensity of a widespread preference for white men in higher skilled positions.[6] But the negative skill effects are not muted for sex segregation among blacks, or for race segregation among women.

Turning to the results for employment growth, the main effect of growth is not significant for any of the five outcomes. This is not totally unanticipated because I expected the growth effect to be conditioned by skill level such that the growth effect is positive for high-skill positions but negative for low-skill ones. In this model, the main effect of growth is the effect of growth for positions with average skill and training requirements.[7] And it is not surprising that this effect is zero given the significant interaction of growth and skill for the segregation of the other race-sex groups from white men. Indeed, as Figure 4.3 shows for these three comparisons, the moderating effects of skill on employment growth are much more dramatic than vice versa. The top dashed line in each diagram represents the effect of employment growth on segregation in low-skill positions, while the bottom solid line is the effect of growth among high-skill positions.[8] As expected, the dashed lines show that, as growth increases, the representation of black women, black men, and white women relative to white men decreases in low-skill positions. In contrast, for high-skill positions the solid lines demonstrate an opposite effect of growth: As growth increases, the representation of black women, black men, and white women relative to white men *increases*. For each of these groups, the growth effect changes from negative to positive not far from the average level of skill and training requirements.[9]

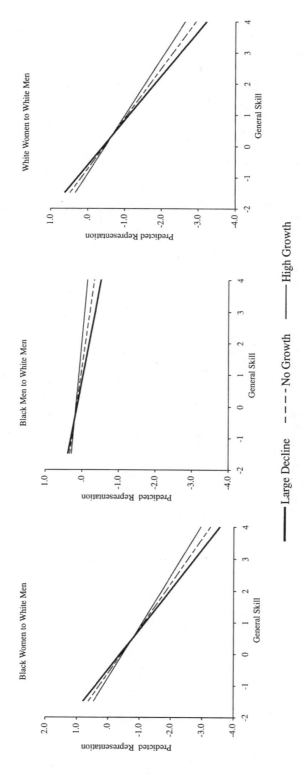

Figure 4.2 Skill Effect on Employment Segregation by Growth Rate

Black Women to White Men

Black Men to White Men

White Women to White Men

—— Large Decline — — – No Growth —— High Growth

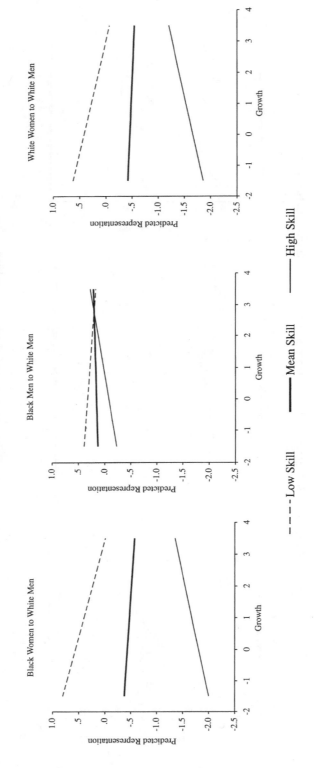

Figure 4.3 Growth Rate Effect on Employment Segregation by Skill

Such a pattern indicates that growth has little effect on their segregation from white men among the many positions with near-average skill requirements. The change in sign of the growth effects provides strong support for the argument that employment growth reduces the salience and intensity of employers for a particular race-sex group in a position. Among high-skill positions this means that growth weakens employers' preference for white men, but among low-skill positions growth diminishes the preference for the other race-sex groups. However, employment growth is important only for the segregation of the other race-sex groups from white men. It affects neither sex segregation among blacks nor race segregation among women.

Race-gender typing. A prime tenet of my approach is that the race-sex ordering principle is not constant across labor queues but rather varies according to how a position's task and working conditions are stereotypically labeled as race-gender "appropriate" or "inappropriate." This implies that the representation of a race-sex group in a position should depend on the whether the position's tasks and work conditions are group appropriate or inappropriate. The effects of the nine race- and gender-typed skill and working conditions indicators are nearly all consistent with this principle, shown as thirty-three predicted effects in Panels B and C of Table 4.1. For these predictions, the results indicate that twenty-two match the hypotheses in whole or part, seven have no significant effects, and only four are significant in a contrary direction. There were also twelve effects for which no prediction was made, in two cases because of opposing race versus sex expectations for black women relative to white men, and the remainder because the predictor indicated gender (race) stereotyping but the outcome embodied only a race (sex) comparison. Among these, there are seven significant effects.

The "male-typed" indicators (extreme environmental conditions, physical exertion, and math skills) decrease the representation of women, except that environmental conditions do not affect sex segregation among blacks (see the result columns for black women: white men; white women: white men; and black women: black men). Analogously, the "female-typed" indicators (dexterity, nurturant skills, and clerical perception) all increase the relative representation of black women or white women. It is noteworthy that several of these indicators also affect the representation of black men in accord with a "menial work/brute force" stereotypic image of black men.[10] Thus, the representation of black men in a position is higher when it requires heavy physical exertion and lower when dexterity or math skills are required.[11] These last results are particularly important because, unlike the effects of these gender-typing indicators on sex segregation, these latter cannot be attributed to worker preferences.

The results for the remaining race- and gender-typing indicators provide somewhat mixed support for stereotyping processes. The effects of relative status in interaction are largely but not wholly consistent with the stereotyping of more subservient work as "appropriate" for women and blacks and more superordinate work as "appropriate" for white men, given that the effect is U-shaped. The bubble plots in Figure 4.4 demonstrate that the effect is predominantly negative, except for black to white women. The size of the bubbles is proportionate to the number of positions at each level of relative status in interaction. Note that the low-relative-status end of the plots have the largest bubbles and a negative slope to the trend line. The overwhelming majority of positions lie below the point at which the effect turns positive, especially for sex segregation.[12] The negative effect is less pronounced for race segregation among men. And, contrary to expectations, the effect of relative status on race segregation among women is positive.

The positive routinization effect on the representation of black men to white men corresponds to a race-typing explanation, but the negative effects of routinization on the representation of both black and white women do not. Similar to the upper tail of the status-in-interaction effects, the authority effect on sex segregation among both whites and blacks surprisingly contradicts what would be expected, with women having a higher representation relative to men in positions of authority. It is worth noting that the bivariate effect of authority is in fact negative and significant, but changes once the extent of self-employment and sufficient hours are introduced into the analysis.[13] A partial explanation for this might lie in the continuing growth of employment in female-dominated clerical and service jobs coupled with a process of resegregation among positions with supervisory or managerial status. Women who do achieve authority positions supervise predominantly female workers (Reskin and Padavic 1999; Reskin and Ross 1992) or are nominal supervisors who exercise no real power (Tomaskovic-Devey 1993).

Overall, the results for the race-gender–typing indicators provide strong support for the operation of stereotyping processes, despite a few contrary results. In particular, the gender-typing indicators have significant effects on nearly every male-female comparison in the predicted direction. Although this pattern of findings provides substantial credibility for my argument that this demonstrates employers' use of a race-sex ordering principle to rank workers in the labor queue, I discuss later the extent to which a worker preference approach is a plausible alternative explanation.

Supplementary Findings

Desirable employment. Early versions of queuing approaches used the implicit assumption that white men were the preferred group for all positions. This implies that white men would be concentrated in the most desirable employment situations and that others would be relegated to less advantageous ones. My argument is more nuanced. Some characteristics of positions stereotype them as appropriate for blacks or women, but these are not characteristics that necessarily define employment as desirable. Beyond such stereotyping, I also assume

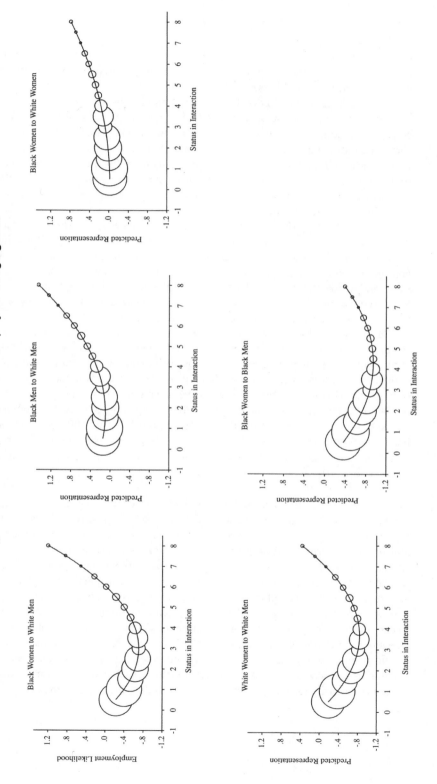

Figure 4.4 Status in Interaction and Employment Segregation

a general employer preference for whites and men. And thus I similarly expect that, controlling for the effects of stereotyping, whites and men are more likely to be in the more desirable positions.

The findings in Panel D of Table 4.1 accord closely with this expectation. Higher levels of sufficient work hours and self-employment and lower rates of unemployment define better work situations in which I expect that whites and men should be more highly represented. Of the fifteen effects, twelve are significant in the predicted direction, two are not significant, and only one (sufficient hours for black women to white women) is significant in a contrary direction. Given the generally uniform preferences among race-sex groups for such desirable employment situations, these results suggest that employers have a preference for whites and men and that they funnel them into the more desired work situations. Fernandez and Mors's (2008) analyses suggest that one mechanism through which this can occur is human resource managers' use of their own stereotypic notions of job appropriateness to steer applicants into labor queues differentially by race-sex status and job desirability. Similarly, when employers recruit using employee referrals, gender-homophilous social networks will tend to reproduce themselves as referrals to sex-segregated jobs (Fernandez and Sosa 2005).

However, preferences for part-time work are not uniform among race-sex groups. More women than men express a desire for part-time work (Bridges 1989; Padavic and Reskin 2002), which offers a competing or complementary explanation for the effects of sufficient hours on sex segregation but not on race segregation. Historically, black women have had higher rates of labor force participation and commitment than white women, suggesting a greater preference or need for more work hours (Council of Economic Advisers 1998; Reskin and Padavic 1999). Such a preference could explain the unexpected finding that sufficient hours has a negative rather than positive effect on the representation of black to white women.

Product market structure. As the "predict" columns in Panel E of Table 4.1 show, I expected market power and profitability to have positive effects on the representation of women and minorities. Large market shares and high profitability provide firms buffering from economic forces and slack resources to respond to external pressures. But the issue is how employers use such power to respond to antidiscrimination pressure from the government and the public: resistance or compliance. Market power has a significant positive effect on all five outcomes, as does profitability for the three outcomes involving a sex comparison. These positive effects are consistent with the argument that antidiscrimination pressure since the 1970s targeted firms in such visible arenas, which used their slack resources to respond by increasing access to employment for women and blacks. Contrary to the neoclassical theory of discrimination, such barriers to competition are not necessarily also employment barriers. Rather, they can facilitate access if there are incentives to do so. These results suggest that in the decades preceding 1990, public pressure provided such an incentive.

I had no firm predictions for the remaining aspects of product market structure, and only capital intensity affected multiple outcomes. For each of the measures of sex segregation, higher capital intensity decreases the representation of women relative to men. This could correspond to a stereotyping of manufacturing and factory work as a male domain as well as inertia in employment practices given the decline in manufacturing employment.

Linkages to other actors. This final set of results provides limited support for my hypotheses. Concerning unions as labor market actors, I argued that unions have long recognized that their collective self-interest lies in representing *all* workers and thus should increase (or at least not affect) the representation of minorities and women. Because unions have little if any direct control over access to employment (aside from the numerically few craft-style unions), I suggested that unionization effects would be more likely for earnings gaps than for employment segregation. Six of ten unionization effects are significant, but only two are in the predicted direction (see Panel F of Table 4.1). Industry unionization has a negative effect on the three sex contrasts, as does occupation unionization for sex segregation among whites. Higher unionization is thus associated with a lower representation of women relative to men. It is impossible to know from this study whether this reflects active measures by unions to exclude women from unionized markets or a passive failure to press for more egalitarian treatment in those markets where, historically, unions have had a strong presence but women have not. In contrast, both unionization measures do have positive effects on race segregation among women, increasing the representation of black women to white women. Overall, these effects suggest that unionization has been detrimental to the representation of women relative to men but, among women, beneficial to the employment representation of blacks relative to whites.

The government is the other important labor market actor. Since the 1960s, it has generally represented the broader social will to foster more egalitarian employment practices, both as an employer of its own labor force and as an enforcer of antidiscrimination legislation. Thus I expected positive effects for both public sector employment and for federal purchases. But the two indicators of government linkages have opposite effects. Public sector employment has a positive effect on the three racial contrasts, with blacks showing a higher relative representation in public sector than in private sector positions. But it has a negative effect on the representation of women to men among blacks. As others have found (e.g., Asher and Popkin 1984; Blank 1985; DiPrete 1989), the public sector operates with a much more egalitarian ordering of the labor queues by race but not always by sex.

In contrast, federal purchases as a predictor has a significant negative effect on four of the comparisons and no effect on that of black women to white women. This indicates that a greater degree of federal contracting corresponds to a lower representation of women to men and of black men to white men, contrary to findings from earlier studies. One possibility is that enforcement of non-discrimination clauses in federal contracts has been anything but successful in recent times. Reskin and Padavic (1999) argue that such enforcement was not a priority of the Reagan and Bush administrations during the 1980s and noted that segregation increased among federal contractors in those years, "suggesting that federal contractors had reverted to the discriminatory practices that had prompted President Nixon to issue the executive order in the first place" (p. 355; see also Leonard 1994). Other scholars have suggested instead that over time the existence of federal contract regulations has in fact provided legal cover to contractors (Edelman 2004; Hirsh 2008; Hirsh and Kornrich 2008). That is, the existence of long-time affirmative action plans can serve to legitimize contractors' current practices because they have a formal antidiscrimination mechanism in place.

Implications for Other Explanations of Employment Segregation

Could the findings just described be explained by the other perspectives on employment segregation that I reviewed in Chapter 2? The answer is that they can, but in a piecemeal fashion and to a limited degree at best. The *product market structure* demand-side approaches are pertinent to only a few predictors, and about the same number of effects supports them as contradicts them. The "competition reduces discrimination" arguments used by both Becker's neoclassical theory of discrimination and the dual/segmented markets approaches receive little support. The positive effects of market power and profitability indicate that the relative representation of blacks compared to whites and of women relative to men is higher in more protected product markets and lower in more competitive markets. This flatly disputes the contention that discrimination occurs in economic arenas buffered from market forces while economic competition reduces discrimination. However, the moderating effect of employment growth on skills (discussed in more detail below) suggests that competition for workers (not for profits) can reduce discrimination but only in highly skilled positions. The negative unionization effects on the representation of women to men are consistent with Becker's argument that unions create market imperfections in which discrimination can occur, but the positive effect of unionization on the representation of black women to white women contradicts this. Economic scale (as a proxy for formalization and bureaucratization) has no effect.

From the supply side, human capital and status attainment approaches would suggest focusing on skill disparities among race-sex groups. Such a *skill deficits approach* is applicable to a somewhat broader array of predictors and does receive somewhat greater support, albeit some of this relies on speculative and unproven skill differentials among race-sex groups. The clearest support for a skill deficits approach comes from the negative effect of math skills on both sex and race segregation, given the documented differences in tested math skills among groups (Jaynes and Williams 1989; Jencks and Phillips 1998; Muller 1998), although more recent studies suggest that sex differences among youth and young adults are becoming negligible (see the studies reviewed by Barres 2006). The negative general-skill effects on racial representation are also consistent with this explanation but only to the degree that there are general (not specific) skill differences that were not captured by the control for differences in worker human capital. But the negative effects on gender representation cannot be attributed to general-skill deficits as research has repeatedly found no sex differences in levels of general skills (England et al. 1994; Reskin 1993; Steinberg 1990). Further, the interaction between general skill and employment growth partly contradicts a skill deficits approach, which would predict that employment growth among low-skill positions should increase the representation of black men and black women because these groups on average have lower general skills. Figure 4.3 showed that at below-average skill levels there is in fact a significant negative effect of growth that decreases rather than increases the representation of black men and black women relative to white men.

The positive effects of several "female" skill indicators (dexterity, nurturant skill, and clerical perception) on sex segregation could also be due to a skill deficit, but only if one assumes that men in fact have lower levels of such skills than women. But for black men neither the negative effect of dexterity nor the positive effect of clerical perception can be plausibly explained by skill deficits. Similarly, a skill deficit could explain the negative effect of physical exertion on sex segregation but is not plausible for its positive effect on the representation of black men.

A supply-side *worker preference interpretation* is a competing explanation for many of the gender-typing effects on the sex segregation outcomes. This approach argues that women prefer jobs with "female-typed" skills and conditions. In my terms, this implies that the effects of gender typing on sex segregation results from how women rank such jobs more highly in the job queue rather than how employers rank workers in the labor queue. It is certainly true that the results for these factors are predominantly consistent with this approach. As would be expected, female-typed skills and working conditions (dexterity, nurturant skills, and clerical perception) have a positive effect on the representation of women relative to men in labor market positions, while male-typed skills and working conditions (math skills, physical exertion, extreme environmental conditions, and sufficient [longer] work hours) all have a negative effect. Capital intensity also has a negative effect, which could be attributed to a female preference against factory work settings.

Yet almost all of these also affect race segregation, which cannot plausibly be attributed to preferences.[14] Furthermore, some have an opposite effect on the representation of black men (physical exertion and dexterity) to that on the representation of women. Moreover, several effects contradict what a preference approach would predict. Self-employment provides a high degree of flexibility in scheduling work, yet it has a negative effect on the representation of black and white women as well as black men. There are fairly similar preferences among race-sex groups for steady work and job security.[15] And yet the unemployment rate has a negative effect on the representation of both black women and black men.

As I argued in more detail in Chapter 2, I discount this competing explanation for several reasons, even though the selection of openings to which people apply will reflect their preferences. Theoretically, the importance of workers' preferences should be diminished because workers are limited in the end to choices among the jobs offered. The constraints employers impose on the types of jobs offered are causally prior to workers' choices among jobs, severely limit the types of jobs that can be chosen, and even can be a primary cause of expressed preferences (Reskin and Padavic 1999). Second, several gender-typing indicators (dexterity, exertion, and math skills) also affect race segregation among men, and these effects cannot plausibly be imputed to worker preferences. Finally, the plausibility of preferences as an explanation relies on a somewhat mixed empirical underpinning in terms of actual sex differences in work values and preferences and how these affect job choice. Although the research I reviewed in Chapter 2 suggested that there are at most small sex differences in work-related preferences, a few case studies of firms have found that both applicant preferences for sex-segregated jobs and employer steering contribute to sex-segregated hiring (Fernandez and Mors 2008; Fernandez and Sosa 2005). However, many argue that such worker preferences reflect the effect of past market discrimination (e.g., Marini 1989; Reskin 1993). And others, like Padavic (1991), have found that women are quite willing to transfer from "clean" women's work to men's "dirty" jobs if they can increase their pay.

In summary, my race-sex queuing perspective is more widely applicable than the other explanations to the full set of predictors of employment segregation, and, aside from a few anomalies, the base model results are consistent with nearly all of its expectations. In particular, the interactive effects of general skill and employment growth can be fully explained only by this approach. While a preference interpretation is also consistent with many of the empirical findings, it has a somewhat narrower applicability to the range of factors. A skill deficits approach has even more limited relevance to the full range of predictors, but the results are largely consistent with it for those few predictors to which it applies. The product market structure approaches are similarly limited but receive even less support from the analysis. Becker's theory and the segmented markets perspective are consistent only with the negative effects of unionization for the representation of black and white women relative to white men. They are contradicted by the positive unionization effects on the representation of black women to white women and by the finding of egalitarian rather than discriminatory effects of market power and profitability.

The Intersection of Race and Sex

In the discussion above, I focused on how well the results support my predictions about employment segregation, but these results also have implications for the interplay between race and sex in the creation of employment segregation. The analyses indicate that the predictors' effects on sex segregation among both whites and blacks are relatively similar to each but somewhat different from their effects on race segregation among either men or women. Of the twenty-two predictors that have a significant effect, only seven affect both race and sex segregation in the same direction, eight affect both race and sex representation but with opposite effects, five affect only sex contrasts, and two affect only race comparisons. In addition, the analysis of the relative representation of black women to white men (embodying both a race and sex contrast) has a pattern of effects much more similar to that for sex segregation among whites than for race segregation among women.

Even though there is considerable similarity between the analyses of the employment segregation of black women and of white women, each contrasted to white men, the analysis of the representation of black women to white women highlights a number of differences in these processes. Skill, self-employment, and math skills all decrease the representation of black women to white women, just as they decrease the representation of each group relative to white men. But the negative effect of skill is not moderated and muted by employment growth, nor does employment growth have a significant effect. The representation of black to white women is increased by higher levels of sufficient hours, unemployment, status in interaction, market power, foreign involvement, industry unionization, occupation unionization, and public sector employment. Of particular note here is that several predictors have opposite signed effects on the representation of black women to white women than on the representation of either to white men: the availability of sufficient hours, status in interaction, industry unionization, and occupation unionization.[16]

These differences do not simply reflect a uniform process of racial segregation among men and women, as can be seen from a comparison of the results for the segregation of black women from white women to those for the segregation of black men to white men. Considerably fewer predictors have effects on the representation of black to white women than of black to white men, and their explanatory power is much less. Only skill, unemployment, self-employment, math skills, market power, and public sector employment similarly affect both forms of race segregation, while two others have opposite effects. Both the availability of sufficient hours and higher status in interaction increase the relative representation of black women to white women but decrease the representation of black men to white men. The two unionization indicators each increase the representation of black women but have no significant effect on black men. It is also noteworthy that while higher general-skill requirements decrease the relative representation of both black women and black men, this effect is muted by employment growth only for black men. From a queuing perspective, this implies that when employment demand lessens the salience of employers' preferences for a race-sex ordering of workers in the labor queue, it may do so more for black men and white women than it does for black women.

Extending the Base Model: Moderating Factors

The results from the base model suggest that the race-sex queuing perspective is widely applicable for understanding employment segregation among race-sex groups, despite a few anomalies. In particular, the set of race-gender–typing indicators has the strongest predictive power in four of the five base model analyses, all but the relative representation of black to white women. The extended model more widely explores how external pressures and resources mute or enhance the influence of such race-gender stereotyping. There are both empirical and substantive reasons for this extension. Empirically, the interaction between employment growth and general skill is one of the more interesting substantive findings from the base model and illustrates how other factors can moderate the influence of race-gender stereotyping. As shown earlier in Figures 4.2 and 4.3, employment growth mutes the negative effects of general skill on the representation of women and blacks relative to white men, and employment growth has opposite effects among high-skill than low-skill positions. Specifically, employment pressures appear to diminish employers' use of a race-sex ordering principle, whether it is to favor white men or other race-sex groups. Recall how the effect of growth is quite different for high-skill than for low-skill positions. Although high-skill positions have a greater relative representation of white men than other race-sex groups, the degree of overrepresentation decreases in high-skill positions with higher employment growth. Analogously, low-skill positions have a higher relative representation of other race-sex groups, but their overrepresentation is smaller in low-skill positions with high employment growth.

   Theoretically, a parallel rationale could be applied to each of the race-gender–typing indicators to develop an expectation that growth should diminish the salience of the race-sex ordering principle. That is, growth should moderate the effects of the race-gender–typing indicators on employment segregation and the race-gender–typing indicators should condition the effects of growth. For example, among positions stereotyped as female-appropriate, growth should decrease the relative representation of women, but among positions stereotyped as male-appropriate, growth should increase the relative representation of women. Further, I argued in Chapter 2 that economic buffering and slack resources should heighten the salience of employers' preferences for race-sex groups for a position, whatever those preferences might be. This similarly implies that market power and profitability should moderate the effects of the race-gender–typing indicators and vice versa.

I evaluate these speculations by testing for interaction effects between the set of race-gender–typing indicators and growth, profitability, and market power. The extended models reported below retain only those interactions that were significant. To preview the findings, growth and profitability interact with the race-gender–typing measures only in the analyses of sex segregation, while market power has significant interactions for both race and sex segregation. Although the magnitude of the effects of growth, profitability, and market power on employment segregation vary somewhat across the race-gender–typed work situations, the fairly consistent effect of each is to increase the representation of the stereotypically less-preferred groups. On the flip side of the interactions, growth, profitability, and market power do not systematically mute the effects of the race-gender–typing indicators on employment segregation. In some cases, they increase the stereotyping effect and in others they reduce it.

For interested readers, Appendix Table B4.2 lists the detailed numeric EGLS-SUR results for the extended model.[17] I discuss instead Tables 4.2 and 4.3, which present visual/verbal summaries of the significant interactions from the extended models. Table 4.2 describes how the effects of the race-gender–typing indicators on employment segregation change according to the levels of growth, market power, and profitability that characterize a position's context. Table 4.3 complements this by depicting how the effects of growth, market power, and profitability vary across race-gender–typed settings. For each of the five segregation contrasts, a table entry indicates a significant interaction and describes the effect of a predictor on the relative representation of the two groups and how it differs between two opposing levels of the moderating variable. A plus sign (+) indicates that a predictor increases the representation of the specified race-sex group (relative to the other group in the contrast), whereas a minus sign (–) means that the predictor reduces the representation of that group. A zero (0) denotes that the effect becomes zero in a moderating condition, and a U-shaped relationship is shown by (∪). When the size of a plus or minus symbol varies across the levels of the moderating variable, this means that the magnitude of a predictor's effect varies correspondingly. For example, the results in Panel B of Table 4.2 for physical exertion indicate that market power reduces gender typing according to physical exertion. For each of the three sex-segregation outcomes, physical exertion decreases the representation of women relative to men but this effect is larger for positions in competitive industries and smaller for positions in oligopolistic industries.

Table 4.2 How Growth, Profitability, and Market Power Moderate the Effects of Race-Gender-Typing Indicators

		Black Women: White Men	Black Men: White Men	White Women: White Men	Black Women: Black Men	Black Women: White Women
	Growth level[a]	R-G-T effect	R-G-T effect	R-G-T effect	R-G-T effect	R-G-T effect
Panel A: Growth moderation of						
Environmental conditions	Decline	▬ BW		▬ WW	▬ BW	
	Growth	+ BW		+ WW	+ BW	
Routinization	Decline	0 BW		0 WW	0 BW	
	Growth	▬ BW		▬ WW	▬ BW	
Nurturant skill	Decline			0 WW		
	Growth			+ WW		
Math skill	Decline			– WW		
	Growth			▬ WW		
	Profit level[a]	R-G-T effect	R-G-T effect	R-G-T effect	R-G-T effect	R-G-T effect
Panel B: Profitability moderation of						
Clerical perception	Loss	+ BW		+ WW	+ BW	
	Gain	+ BW		+ WW	+ BW	
Nurturant skill	Loss	0 BW			▬ BW	
	Gain	+ BW			+ BW	
Routinization	Loss	▬ BW				
	Gain	▬ BW				
Status in interaction with others	Loss				▬ BW	
	Gain				∪ BW	

continues

Table 4.2 continued

	MP level[a]	Black Women: White Men — R-G-T effect	Black Men: White Men — R-G-T effect	White Women: White Men — R-G-T effect	Black Women: Black Men — R-G-T effect	Black Women: White Women — R-G-T effect
Panel C: Market Power (MP) moderation of						
Physical exertion	Low	**–** BW		**–** WW	**–** BW	
	High	– BW		– WW	– BW	
Authority	Low	0 BW		– WW	0 BW	
	High	**–** BW		**–** WW	**–** BW	
Nurturant skill	Low			0 WW		
	High			**+** WW		
Status in interaction with others	Low		∪ BW			**+** BW
	High		+ BW			0 BW
Environmental conditions	Low		**–** BM			
	High		0 BM			

Note: a. The levels of the moderating variables are defined as the mean of the moderating variable plus or minus twice its standard deviation. If the "low" value was less than the variable's minimum then the minimum was used. Similarly, if the "high" value was greater than the variable's maximum, then the maximum was used.

Table 4.3 How Race-Gender-Typing Indicators Moderate the Effects of Growth, Market Power, and Profitability

	R-G-T level[a]	Black Women: White Men — Growth effect	Black Men: White Men — Growth effect	White Women: White Men — Growth effect	Black Women: Black Men — Growth effect	Black Women: White Women — Growth effect
Panel A: Growth moderated by						
Environmental conditions	Poor	**+** BW		**+** WW	**+** BW	
	Good	**–** BW		+ WW	**–** BW	
Routinization	Low	**+** BW		**+** WW	**+** BW	
	High	**–** BW		**–** WW	**–** BW	
Nurturant skill	No			+ WW		
	Yes			**+** WW		
Math skill	Low			**+** WW		
	High			**–** WW		

	R-G-T level[a]	Black Women: White Men — Profit effect	Black Men: White Men — Profit effect	White Women: White Men — Profit effect	Black Women: Black Men — Profit effect	Black Women: White Women — Profit effect
Panel B: Profitability moderated by						
Clerical perception	Low	**+** BW		**+** WW	**+** BW	
	High	0 BW		0 WM	**+** BW	
Nurturant skill	No	+ BW			**+** BW	
	Yes	**+** BW			**+** BW	
Routinization	Low	**+** BW				
	High	+ BW				
Status in interaction with others	Low				**+** BW	
	High				**+** BW	

continues

Table 4.3 continued

R-G-T level[a]		Black Women: White Men MP effect	Black Men: White Men MP effect	White Women: White Men MP effect	Black Women: Black Men MP effect	Black Women: White Women MP effect
Panel C: Market power (MP) moderated by						
Physical exertion	Low	+ BW		0 WW	0 BW	
	High	+ BW		+ WW	+ BW	
Authority	No	+ BW		+ WW	+ BW	
	Yes	0 BW		0 WW	− BW	
Nurturant skill	No			+ WW		
	Yes			+ WW		
Status in interaction with others	Low		0 BM			+ BW
	High		+ BM			0 BW
Environmental conditions	Poor		0 BM			
	Good		+ BM			

Note: a. For nurturant skill and authority, the levels of the moderating variables are defined as the absence (0) or presence (1) of the attribute. Otherwise, the levels of the moderating variables are defined as the mean of the moderating variable plus or minus twice its standard deviation. If the "low" value was less than the variable's minimum then the minimum was used. Similarly, if the "high" value was greater than the variable's maximum then the maximum was used.

Moderated Effects of Growth
and Race-Gender–Typing Indicators

How growth conditions the effect of race-gender typing. The first panel of Table 4.2 presents the results for the moderating effect of employment growth. Notice that growth only moderates effects on sex segregation, not on race segregation. Growth conditions the effects of environmental conditions and routinization on all three sex contrasts but, for sex segregation among whites, growth also conditions the effects of nurturant skills and math skills. Specifically, employment pressure seems to reduce the salience of gender typing according to a position's environmental conditions but it appears to intensify the gender-typing effects of the other variables. Under conditions of low growth or decline, poorer environmental conditions reduce the relative representation of women to men. As the level of employment growth increases, this effect becomes smaller. When there is very high growth, the opposite effect occurs: Poorer working conditions slightly *increase* the relative representation of women. In contrast, growth strengthens the effects of the other race-gender–typing indicators. The negative effect of routinization on sex segregation is small or zero for positions with declining employment but routine work reduces the representation of women to men as employment pressure rises.

Among whites, math skill requirements decrease the representation of women to men but do so even more in high-growth positions; and nurturant skill requirements increase white women's representation, except in positions with employment decline. Unlike the interaction of general skill and growth, where growth mutes gender typing by general skill, growth intensifies the gender-typing effects of these specific skills. Although this is unexpected, a partial explanation for these effects may lie in the relative abundance of workers with the needed skills. As measured using the *Dictionary of Occupational Titles,* even the highest level of math skills is not especially scarce, with 10% of workers having the requisite aptitude and one-third having the aptitude needed for the top two math skill levels. It is speculated that nurturant skill is similarly widely present among workers. If the specific skill needed for a growing position is widely enough present in the labor pool, employers can add workers from their preferred race-sex group without changing the race-sex ordering principle used to rank workers in the labor queue. In such a case, the representation of the preferred group would rise.

How race-gender typing conditions the effect of growth. The results in Panel A of Table 4.3 reveal a simple and largely consistent picture of how the effect of growth is moderated by the race-gender–typing indicators. Greater employment pressure generally increases the representation of the "less preferred" race-sex group in a contrast. For positions with poor environmental conditions (stereotyped as male appropriate), growth increases women's relative representation. But the effects of growth change dramatically for positions with good working conditions (typed as female appropriate): It has a much smaller positive effect on white women's representation and changes sign to decrease the representation of black women relative to either white or black men. Among whites, growth mainly increases the representation of women relative to men. This positive effect is somewhat smaller for positions with good working conditions than for those with poor working conditions and for positions not requiring nurturant skills than for those needing such skills.

Despite a few exceptions, the effect of growth on sex segregation largely corresponds to the expectation that employment pressure should open access to race-sex groups ranked lower in the labor queue.[18] If the demand for workers increases sufficiently, employers must either refrain from hiring or must hire from race-sex groups less preferred for certain types of positions. However, the way in which nurturant skills and math skills condition the effect of growth on sex segregation among whites hints that employment growth in a position can deepen employment disparities between women and men if the specific skills needed are both widely available and gender typed. In the same vein, while growth mutes the stereotyping effects of physical exertion requirements on sex segregation, it enhances the stereotyping effects of routinization and, for whites, of nurturant skills and math skills.

Moderated Effects of Profitability and Race-Gender–Typing Indicators

How profitability conditions the effect of race-gender typing. Like employment growth, profitability and some of the race-gender–typing indicators only condition each other's effect on the three sex-segregation measures, not the two measures of race segregation within sex. For all three comparisons, greater profitability suppresses the gender-typing effect of clerical perception (see Panel B of Table 4.2). Although clerical requirements increase the representation of women relative to men, this effect is smaller in more profitable industries. Similarly, among blacks, the negative effect of status in interaction on women's representation is muted by profitability, changing from a totally negative effect in industries with a loss to a U-shaped effect in profitable industries. In other cases, profitability strengthens gender-typing effects. For black women compared to either white or black men, nurturant skills increase black women's representation but only when profitability is higher, and the negative effect of routinization on black women's representation relative to white men is larger when profitability is higher.

How race-gender typing conditions the effect of profitability. Profitability's effects on sex segregation vary somewhat across race-gender–typed contexts, but greater profitability almost always increases the representation of women to men. Of the fourteen effects shown in Panel B of Table 4.3, twelve are positive and only two are zero. For all three sex comparisons, profitability increases women's representation more when the requirements for clerical work are low, and the effect is zero or smaller when there are more clerical requirements. For black women relative to white men, profitability also has a positive effect, which is larger when nurturant skills are required or when the work is *not* routine than otherwise. For black women contrasted to black men, profitability's positive effect is larger when nurturant skills are required or when the worker has subordinate status in interaction than when not.

Overall, profitability consistently increases the relative employment of women, even more uniformly than do growth or market power (discussed next). And this positive effect changes only slightly across race-gender–typed work contexts. These results correspond to the argument that profitability provides resources that employers can use to respond to public pressure for more egalitarian employment processes, at least with respect to gender. Recall that profitability does not affect race segregation. But profitability is not necessarily a panacea for reducing gender typing in employment. As a moderating factor, profitability has more mixed effects in that it mutes the gender-typing effects of clerical perception and status in interactions, but it intensifies the gender-typing effects of nurturant skills and routinization.

Moderated Effects of Market Power and Race-Gender–Typing Indicators

How market power conditions the effect of race-gender typing. Panel C of Table 4.2 reveals that market power moderates the effects of some race-gender–typing indicators on all five employment-segregation outcomes. For the three measures contrasting women to men, market power similarly moderates the effects of physical exertion and authority, and also conditions the effect of nurturant skill for white women. Market power attenuates the degree of gender typing created by physical exertion demands but heightens the gender-typing effects of authority and nurturant skills. Greater physical exertion requirements reduce women's representation, but this effect is muted among positions in industries with a high degree of market power. While authority also decreases women's representation, its effect is larger in high market-power settings and is either negligible or small in more competitive industries. For white women, nurturant skill increases their representation but only in high market-power contexts.

For the two measures of race segregation within sexes, market power reduces the effects of status in interaction and, for black men, of environmental conditions. For black men, status in interaction has a pronounced U-shaped effect on their representation relative to white men in competitive contexts that flattens to a smaller but consistently positive effect in high market-power settings. The effect of environmental conditions on black men's representation is similarly muted, changing from a negative effect in competitive industries to no effect in ones that are more oligopolistic. For black women, status in interaction has a positive effect on their representation relative to white women in competitive market settings, which diminishes to no effect as market power rises.

How race-gender typing conditions the effect of market power. Although the magnitude of market power's effect does vary across race-gender–typed settings, market power consistently increases the representation of women relative to men or of blacks relative to whites. Panel C of Table 4.3 contains nine pairs of market power effects on employment segregation, each pair contrasting the market power effect on the outcome for low versus high levels of a race-gender–typing indicator. Note that of the eighteen market power effects on race and sex segregation, eleven are positive, indicating that market power increases the representation of women relative to men or of blacks relative to whites in those contexts. Only once is market power's effect negative, decreasing black women's representation relative to black men among positions with authority, and in the remaining five settings the market power effect is negligible.

The size of the effect of market power on sex segregation varies by a position's requirements for physical exertion or possession of authority and, for white women, by nurturant-skill needs. For positions without authority, market power increases the representation of women to men for all three outcomes involving a sex contrast. But for positions with authority, market power *decreases* women's representation among blacks and has no effect on the representation of either black or white women relative to white men. Market power's effect on sex segregation also varies with a position's requirements for physical exertion. For positions with greater demands for exertion, market power increases the representation of women to men and has either a much smaller or a negligible effect on women's representation if there is little need for physical exertion. For white women, the market power effect is also smaller if nurturant skills are not required than if they are. Thus, although market power generally diminishes sex segregation, this is limited to positions without authority or those requiring greater physical exertion.

Similarly, market power broadly increases blacks' representation relative to whites, but the magnitude of these effects does vary by the status in interaction of a position and, for black men, by environmental conditions. Comparing black men to white men, market power increases black men's representation but only for positions with superior status vis-à-vis others or for positions with good environmental conditions. Among positions with low status or poor working conditions, market power has no effect. For black women, the opposite pattern occurs. Market power increases their representation relative to white women for subordinate positions and has no effect among superordinate positions.

In sum, market power broadly reduces segregation by both sex and by race, although in some race- or gender-typed settings it has little or no effect. Perhaps the most interesting of these variations is that market power increases women's relative representation only among positions lacking authority and, among women, only increases the representation of blacks to whites in positions subordinate to others in interaction. These both lend credence to the idea that employers with market power open access to employment in such firms but at the same time create social distance among workers within them. However, the finding that among men, market power increases the representation of blacks to whites in positions superordinate to others in interaction runs counter to this explanation. Moreover, market power as a conditioning context does not consistently increase or decrease the effects of the race-gender–typing indicators. In a few cases (like the effects of authority and nurturant skills), market power intensifies the gender-typing effect of the indicators. But more commonly, market power reduces the race-gender–typing effects of other predictors.

Implications of the Extended Model Results

These findings highlight the importance of external pressures and internal resources as determinants of race and sex segregation in employment. Employment pressures usually increase the representation of women relative to men, although there are a few gender-typed settings in which the reverse occurs. Remember also from the base model results that in high general-skill positions, growth decreases the representation of white men relative to the other race-sex groups, but, in low-skill positions, growth increases the relative representation of white men. That is, growth typically results in a greater representation of the race-sex group that is "less preferred" for the race-gender type of the position. This set of findings provide a clear, and I hope convincing, illustration of the fundamental way in which the race-sex ordering principle of a labor queue for a position can be partially overridden by external pressure.

Profitability and market power provide slack resources, which can be used to respond more readily to external pressures, either by resisting them or accommodating them. As I argued earlier, whether this creates more or less adherence to a race-sex ordering principle depends in part on the existence of other incentives. Market power in particular creates visibility to both the general public and the government, which in turn makes such work settings more likely targets of public or governmental demands and actions. Such visibility and pressure provide an incentive to use slack resources to accommodate rather than resist external pressures. The results from the extended model provide a great deal of support for the view that, in recent times, slack resources have been used to increase access to employment by blacks and women. Market power consistently increases the representation of women to men or of blacks to whites, aside from a few race- or gender-typed settings in which it has little or no effect. Profitability even more uniformly raises women's representation relative to men, whereas it has no effect on race segregation. Herring (2009) argues that workforce diversity can increase a business's profitability by increasing the variety of perspectives brought to bear on its operations and practice, which can result in higher creativity, better problem-solving, and an ability to reach more diverse markets. This provides an incentive other than public pressure to use slack resources to lessen adherence to a race-sex ordering principle. The fact that profitability affects sex but not race segregation might imply a lesser profit motive to diversify by race given the smaller size of the black workforce than the female workforce.

But, as I noted above, neither condition should be seen as a panacea for segregation. While market power and profitability diminish the effects of some forms of race or gender typing in the operation of labor queues, they intensify the effects of others. Higher profitability mutes the gender-typing effects of clerical perception and status in interaction. And greater market power suppresses the gender-typing effect of physical exertion and the race-typing effects of environmental conditions and status in interaction. On the other hand, the gender-typing effect of nurturant skills is heightened in either high profit or high market-power contexts. A similar intensification occurs for the effect of routinization in high-profit industries and for the effect of authority in high market-power settings.

What's Next?

In this chapter, I evaluated how well my race-sex queuing perspective works for understanding employment segregation among race-sex groups. Except for a few anomalies (most notably the effect of government enforcement), findings from the base model corroborate nearly all of the hypothesized effects. In addition, the extended model illustrates the complex ways in which growth, market power, and profitability moderate the effects of race-gender typing and how their effects on segregation, in turn, depend on the race-gender–typed context of work. In the next chapter, I evaluate how well my perspective applies to the subsequent outcome in my model, earnings gaps among race-sex groups.

Notes

1. For example, the logged outcome measuring the relative representation of black women to black men is equal to the logged relative representation of black women to white men minus the logged relative representation of black men to white men.

2. The analyses presented in this chapter are similar but not identical to those on employment segregation that I have previously published (Kaufman 2002). The base model results differ in that they are estimated as part of a system of interrelated outcomes—employment segregation and earnings gaps—using an SUR (seemingly unrelated regression)

technique (see Chapter 3), whereas in Kaufman (2002) the corresponding results were estimated from a single-equation EGLS technique. More importantly, I extend the prior analyses in several significant ways: (1) in this chapter, I explore how growth, profitability, and market power moderate the effects of the race-gender–typing indicators on employment segregation; (2) in Chapter 5, I analyze earnings disparities; and (3) in Chapter 6, I examine the moderating effects of region in analyses of both employment segregation and earnings gaps.

3. There is no unique way to divide up the contributions to explained variance (R^2) among the sets of predictors because some portion of it is shared among the predictors; in these analyses about half of the total explanatory power is shared. One common way to define the contribution of a set is to calculate the change in R^2 when the set is removed from the final model. This attributes any shared explanatory power to the other predictors. A second way to define the contribution of a set is to calculate the change in R^2 when the set is added first to the analysis, which attributes any shared explanatory power to this set. The results I present are the average of these alternative ways of attributing shared explanatory power, but rescaled so that they sum to the actual R^2.

4. These appendix tables also provide results for the diagnostic tests I used to assess the problems of heteroskedasticity and correlated errors for each outcome. The significant Lagrange multiplier (LM) statistics indicate that both error components (correlated errors within industry sectors and correlated errors within occupation segments) are different from zero and should be specified as part of the error structure. The significant Breusch-Pagan (BP) statistics for the initial error variance indicate heteroskedasticity by group size and by sector location. The nonsignificant BP statistics for the error variance adjusted for group size and segment location suggest that heteroskedasticity is properly modeled in these analyses.

5. High employment growth is defined as two standard deviations above the point of neither growth nor decline. A large decline in employment growth is defined as two standard deviations below the no growth point.

6. For the representation of black women or white women relative to white men, the skill effect stays negative even at the maximum growth rate observed in the data. For black men compared to white men, the skill effect turns positive at a point near the maximum growth rate. Only three of the 1,916 positions in 1990 had a growth rate at or above this point.

7. Technically this is the effect of growth when skill equals zero, but skill is scaled such that the mean skill is approximately zero (0.008) with a standard deviation of about one (0.968).

8. High skill is defined as two standard deviations above the mean skill level. Low skill is defined as the minimum skill level observed in the data, about one-and-a-half standard deviations below the mean skill level.

9. This occurs at one-third of a standard deviation below the mean for black men, one-third of a standard deviation above the mean for black women, and almost one-half of a standard deviation above the mean for white women.

10. Negative attributions about black men stereotypically identify them as "lazy," "irresponsible," and "violent," while positive traits, which they stereotypically lack, include "intelligent," "hard working," "dependable," and "determined to succeed" (Levine, Carmines, and Sniderman 1999).

11. For some entry-level jobs, an alternative explanation for this pattern could be the use of criminal records checks by employers. Holzer, Raphael, and Stoll's (2004) study suggests that employers' use of a criminal records screen actually increases the hiring of blacks into such jobs (especially ones requiring personal contact). Because the overwhelming majority of blacks do not have a criminal record, the check will counter employers' stereotypes and increase black employment opportunities.

12. For black women to white men, 86% of the positions lie below the turnover point, for white women to white men the value is 94%, for black men to white men the figure is 61%, and for black women to black men it is 96%.

13. These changes in effect are not due to collinearity. The bivariate correlations among these variables are at most .25, the standard error for authority does not change appreciably when the other two predictors are removed from the model, and the Belsley, Kuh, and Welsch collinearity diagnostics give no indication of problems with these variables.

14. The math-skills effect on race segregation, for example, could be in part due to documented skill deficits among African Americans resulting from parental or neighborhood disadvantages or school-related factors such as tracking, differences in school quality, the racial mix of teachers and students, and so on (see the studies in Jencks and Phillips 1998).

15. Both men and women value job security relative to other job rewards similarly, although men have a slightly higher absolute valuation (Tolbert and Moen 1998). Blacks value job security more highly than do whites, as has been generally found for extrinsic types of job rewards (Martin and Tuch 1993).

16. Unlike its effect on the other four outcomes, relative status in interactions has a predominantly positive effect on the representation of black women to white women. Although it is technically U-shaped, the effect is positive for 93.4% of the labor market positions.

17. These appendix tables also provide results for the diagnostic tests I used to assess the problems of heteroskedasticity and correlated errors for each outcome. The significant LM statistics indicate that both error components (correlated errors within industry sectors and correlated errors within occupation segments) are different from zero. The significant BP statistics for the initial error variance indicate heteroskedasticity by group size and by sector location. The nonsignificant BP statistics for the error variance adjusted for group size and segment location suggest that heteroskedasticity is properly modeled in these analyses.

18. The pattern of growth fostering a greater representation of the underrepresented group does not hold for all settings. Earlier results from the base model indicated that highly routinized work corresponded to a male domain while work with low levels of routine are female typed. In low-routine (female) settings, growth increases women's representation whereas growth decreases women's representation in high-routine (male) settings. Moreover, among whites, although growth increases women's representation in low math-skill positions, growth decreases women's representation in male-typed positions requiring greater math skills.

5

Stereotypical Work Conditions and Race-Sex Earnings Gaps

Some circumstantial evidence is very strong,
as when you find a trout in the milk.
—Thoreau (1927: 246)[1]

It is a truism that the conditions and task requirements of jobs affect the level of compensation that workers receive. But there is much less agreement about *how* they affect earnings differences among race and sex groups. "Comparable worth" and "cultural feminist" perspectives (e.g., Reid 1998; England et al. 1994; Kilbourne et al. 1994a; England 1992; Jacobs and Steinberg 1990; Steinberg 1990; Baron and Newman 1990; Glass 1990; Parcel 1989; Parcel and Mueller 1989; Reskin 1988) assert that the effects of many conditions and task requirements reflect a "gendered devaluation of work." They argue that skill and the skill-earnings relationship are socially constructed and that many of women's skills (e.g., nurturance, dexterity, clerical perception) are not accepted as skills and hence are unrewarded or are evaluated less highly, even negatively.

However, this research has focused on devaluation processes as an explanation for the effects of sex composition (percent female) on earnings, with recent work testing whether the disproportionate entry of women or minorities into jobs reduces earnings or whether jobs with declining earnings disproportionately employ women or minorities (Catanzarite 2003; England, Allison, and Wu 2006). There are fewer studies that directly test how work conditions and requirements affect earnings levels or sex differences in earnings at either the worker or occupational level. Many of these studies are occupational-level analyses whose findings are questionable due to the lack of appropriate controls for worker-level determinants (e.g., human capital) that affect earnings; typically, they use aggregate measures of worker factors, an approach that suffers from a type of ecological fallacy (Krivo and Kaufman 1990). And those studies that do provide a direct test of devaluation have studied only sex differences among whites.

In this chapter, I evaluate results from two broad but direct empirical tests of devaluation processes, guided by the predictions developed in Chapter 2. I first analyze devaluation processes in terms of how employment segregation and other characteristics of positions affect the position-level *earnings* of black women, black men, white women, and white women (adjusted for group differences in human capital, family structure, geographic residence, and labor supply). An important issue is not just how these predictors affect the variation in earnings across positions but also how the magnitude of their effects differs for race-sex groups. As you will see, these analyses suggest that segregation and stereotyping do affect earnings levels. With respect to growth, skills, employment segregation, and race-gender typing (designated as core findings), the global devaluing effect of sex segregation is particularly notable, and there is primarily positive but mixed evidence for specific devaluation corresponding to the race-gender–typed measures. Results concerning desirable employment, product market structure, and links to other actors (supplementary findings) demonstrate that indicators of economic power and privilege in the product and labor markets enhance workers' earnings, especially for African Americans and women.

I then consider how these same sets of factors affect the adjusted *earnings ratios* among race-sex groups. This approach evaluates how earnings inequality varies across labor market positions as a result of devaluation and other processes.[2] For the earnings ratios, I begin with a base model (corresponding to Figure 2.4 in Chapter 2) as an initial test of my approach. This base model specifies that the effect of each predictor on earnings gaps is constant; that is, it does not depend on (vary with) the value of the other predictors. Not surprisingly, the core and supplementary findings largely echo those of the earnings-level analyses. A greater presence of a less "favored" group reduces earnings disparities among race-sex groups because it globally devalues earnings for all workers. While there is generally support for specific devaluation effects, the patterns are more complex than I had predicted. White- or male-typed skills are consistently rewarded and exacerbate earnings gaps. And some black- or female-typed skills (such as nurturance) reduce earnings disparities because they devalue earnings levels as expected. But others (e.g., clerical perception) increase earnings gaps because they reward men for female-typed skills and women are not rewarded or are even penalized. The results also highlight how economic resources and external pressures or actors work to reduce earnings disparities among groups.

I then complicate this model by considering the somewhat more speculative implications of my approach, which suggests that profitability, employment growth, and market power more broadly moderate the effects of race-gender–typed work tasks on earnings gaps. The results from this extended model reveal that only profitability systematically mutes the (de)valuing effects of race-gender typicality. In contrast, the economic resource measures diminish some (de)valuing effects but enhance others. Nevertheless, profitability, growth, and market power themselves directly reduce earnings disparities among groups in most race-gender–typed settings, especially atypical ones.

Earnings Level Results

How well do skill and growth, employment segregation and race-gender typing, desirable employment, product market structure, and links to other actors explain adjusted earnings levels for each race-sex group? The charts in Figure 5.1 summarize both the degree to which they account for earnings variations (the pie charts) and the relative importance of the five sets of predictors (the associated bar charts).[3] For each race-sex group, the model accounts for well over half of the variation in earnings levels across positions (55–64%), slightly more for women than for men. The biggest share can be attributed to the effects of employment segregation and race-gender typing, which are the primary indicators of devaluation processes. They alone account for about 30% of the total explained variation, slightly more for whites (both men and women) than for blacks. The remaining sets of factors each are roughly similar in how well they explain earnings levels (around 20% of the total explained), although desirable employment is always the next most powerful and product market structure is consistently the least powerful set.

For readers interested in the detailed numeric results, Appendix Table B5.1 presents the two-stage EGLS results for the earnings-level models.[4] The discussion here, however, is oriented around visual summaries of these findings presented in Table 5.1. Akin to the format that should be familiar from the previous chapter, Table 5.1 presents paired columns of predictions and results, which is easier to follow because the predicted direction of effect on earnings is the same for all race-sex groups. The final column summarizes the relative size of the effects across race-sex groups, with the group listed first having the largest absolute magnitude of effect and the group listed last having the smallest effect. If a race-sex group is not listed, then the predictor did not significantly affect earnings for that group. Groups joined by a pair of dashes (--) have effects that are similar in size.[5] I use initials to denote the groups: BW for black women; BM for black men; WW for white women; and WM for white men. As Table 5.1 summarizes, these predictors affect earnings in the expected way, with a few departures. Initial analyses had suggested a few more anomalies. But in the course of pondering these, I was led to the fruitful speculation that sex segregation might interact with gender-typed skill and task requirements, which led to the revised model with interactions presented here.

Core Findings

General skill and growth. General skill and growth each increase earnings levels for all groups largely as expected, and these payoffs are not the same for all groups. The positive effects of skill on earnings are greater for blacks than whites within sex and for women than men within race. In fact, and very surprisingly,

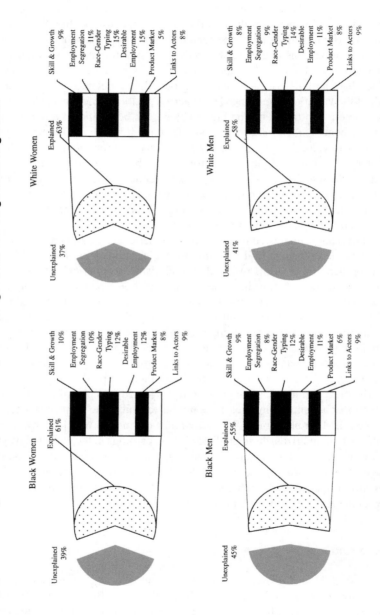

Figure 5.1 Explained Variance in Earnings Level, Two-Stage EGLS Regression

Table 5.1 Predictions and Summary of Results for Analyses of Earnings Levels with Order of Effects by Race-Sex Group

Predictors	Expected Sign	Result	Order of Effects
General skill and growth			
Skill and training	+	+	BW BM WW
Employment growth	+	+	BM--WW WM
Employment segregation			
Black men to white men	−	−	WM
White women to white men[a]	−	−	BM--WW--BW--WM
White- or male-typed work			
Status in interaction	+	∩	WM WW BM BW
Authority	+	+	WM WW--BM--BW
Math skill	+	+	WW--BW BM
Black- or female-typed work			
Physical exertion	−	−	WM--BM WW--BW
Nurturant skill	−	−	WM BW varies +to −
Physical dexterity	−	+	BM WM WW, BW varies +to −
Clerical perception	−	+	BM WM varies +to −
Routinization	−	+	BW WW
Environmental conditions	+/−	+	WW--WM--BW
Desirable employment			
Sufficient work hours	+	+	WW BW WM--BM
Unemployment rate	−	−	BW BM--WW
Self-employment rate	+	+	
Product market structure			
Market power	+	+	BW--WW--BM--WM
Profitability	+	+	BW--WW BM--WM
Economic scale	+	+	WM
Capital intensity	+	+	BM--BW--WM
Foreign involvement	+/−	+	WW--WM BW--BM
Productivity	+	−	BM--WM
Linkages to other actors			
Industry unionization	+	+	BM--BW WM--WW
Occupation unionization	+	+	BM--BW--WW--WM
Percent public sector	−	−	
Federal purchases	+/−	+	BW--WW

Notes: a. This effect of segregation is evaluated at the mean of the variables with which it interacts.

BW = black women; WW = white women; BM = black men; WM = white men

Predicted effects and findings
+Positive − Negative +/− Opposing predictions ∩ Inverted U-shaped effect

Order of effects
-- Less than 1 standard error difference in coefficients

general skill does not even have a significant effect for white men.[6] Growth similarly increases earnings more for black men than for white men, and for white women more than for white men, but fails to benefit the earnings of black women. Thus, the demand for workers indexed by growth does appear to provide some leverage for women and blacks, both in terms of gaining access to positions (as we saw in the last chapter) and in terms of equalizing earnings gaps.

Employment segregation and race-gender typing. I argued earlier that this set should exemplify the operation of both global and specific devaluation processes. Employment segregation does indeed devalue the earnings for all groups. Although the overrepresentation of blacks to whites is a significant detriment to the earnings only for white men, the overrepresentation of women to men depresses earnings for all groups.[7] Assessing the relative effects of female employment representation across groups is complicated by the fact that it interacts with several of the race-gender–typing indicators for some groups. Evaluating its effect at the mean of these interacting variables (as Table 5.1 does) initially suggests that the devaluing effects of the overrepresentation of women are fairly similar across groups. However, a slightly different story emerges by considering how this effect varies across the interacting variables. For women, the devaluation is more severe for whites than for blacks, except in positions requiring the lowest levels of dexterity and nurturant skill. While for men, the effect is more severe for blacks than for whites, except in positions requiring the lowest levels of clerical perception. Among whites, the devaluing effect of the overrepresentation of women is virtually always larger for women than for men, while the reverse is true among blacks.

Race-gender typing. The results for the race-gender–typing indicators consistently favor the prediction that white- and male-typed indicators increase earnings. Both authority and relative status in interaction raise earnings for all four race-sex groups, and math skill significantly increases earnings for all but white men. As expected, employment in such positions benefits whites more than blacks and, except for math skills, men more than women.

Turning to the results for the black- and female-typed skills, there is mixed support for the expectation that these devalue earnings. Physical exertion and nurturant skills decrease earnings as expected, and exertion does devalue earnings more for men than for women and more for whites than for blacks. Nurturant skill is consistently devaluing only for white men. For black women, nurturant skill has a less detrimental effect, devaluing earnings only at above-average levels of female overrepresentation. The consequences for men of working in female-dominated jobs requiring physical dexterity and clerical perception appear to reflect the kind of "glass elevator" process that Williams (1992) and others have argued characterize the prospects of men employed in female-typed jobs. Physical dexterity increases earnings for men but its effect on women's earnings varies with sex segregation. In positions in which men are overrepresented, dexterity has a positive effect on earnings for both black and white women, but has a devaluing effect when women are overrepresented.[8] Clerical perception also has partly unexpected effects. For black men it always enhances earnings, but for white men, it is rewarded only in jobs in which women are overrepresented; it devalues earnings for white men in jobs in which men are overrepresented.[9]

Finally, work involving poor environmental conditions is typed as black- and male-appropriate, which gives rise to opposite devaluation predictions. Except for black men, the results show that workers are compensated for poor working conditions, as has been the only consistent finding in past research supporting the compensating differentials perspective (Brown 1980). The lack of benefit for black men is consistent with a devaluation argument they are not compensated because such work is stereotypically appropriate for them.

Supplementary Findings

Desirable employment. The effects of these indicators are also relevant to my specific devaluation argument, especially in how the effects vary across race-sex groups. As predicted, a greater availability of sufficient work hours increases earnings for all groups, and such employment pays off more for women than for men. But within sex, availability of sufficient hours benefits whites more than blacks. Higher rates of unemployment lower earnings for everyone except white men. Contrary to expectations, these detrimental effects are larger for blacks than for whites and for women than for men. So there is again mixed support for the specific devaluation argument.

Product market structure. Aside from productivity, the other product-market-structure factors significantly increase earnings for at least some groups. Not surprisingly, employment in organizations with high market shares, high profitability, and a large extent of involvement in foreign markets enhances earnings for all groups. In addition, work in capital-intensive settings benefits all but white women, while work in large-scale workplaces pays off only for white men. Quite unexpected is the finding that industry-level productivity has a negative effect on earnings for men. But what is most interesting is how these central aspects of economic structure differentially reward race-sex groups, although the differences are not consistently large. Market power, profitability, and foreign involvement all appear to benefit women more than men, whereas capital intensity and economic scale pay off more for men than women. With respect to race, market power, profitability, and capital intensity increase earnings more for blacks than for whites, while foreign involvement and economic scale are more beneficial for whites than blacks. The fact that market power and profitability pay off more for blacks than whites, and for women than men, possibly reflects the overcrowding of women and blacks into the lowest-paid jobs, which depresses earnings at the bottom of the within-group pay distribution and thus increases the within-group payoff to employment in resource-rich settings. The pattern of differential returns to capital intensity parallels that of unionization (see below). This potentially represents a lesser and only more recent attention by unions to issues of sex inequality than of racial inequality (Cornfield 1991; Milkman 2007) and the historic strength of unions in the capital intensive manufacturing sector.

Linkages to other actors. As expected, unionization, either by industry or by occupation, enhances the earnings of all workers, especially for blacks and women. The pattern of effects across groups consistently shows a greater payoff for blacks than for whites and, to a lesser degree, for men than for women. Public sector employment has no effect on earnings and the extent of federal purchasing increases earnings for women but not men.

Summary and Implications for Earnings Inequality

Overall the evidence broadly supports the idea that segregation and race-gender typing differentiate the rewards attached to positions. Segregation systematically devalues the earnings paid to workers, with a higher representation of women affecting all groups to varying degrees but a higher representation of blacks depressing the earnings only of white men. This lends strong credence to the argument that segregation and crowding of women and blacks should reduce earnings inequality (increase earnings ratios relative to white men) within a position.

Beyond such global devaluation, the results provide a positive but mixed appraisal of specific devaluation (valuation) processes. Two indicators of black- or female-typed work (exertion and nurturant skills) consistently depress earnings and are more detrimental to the earnings of men than women, and of blacks than whites. This implies that such task requirements should decrease earnings inequality (increase earnings ratios). Two others have effects that vary by race-sex group and by sex segregation. Dexterity enhances earnings for men (both black and white), while for women its effect varies with the employment representation of women. In "male" jobs, women benefit from dexterity requirements, while in "female" jobs, women's earnings are devalued by dexterity requirements. Clerical perception requirements generally enhance earnings for men but are unrewarded for women. One interpretation of these effects could be that employers perceive dexterity and clerical perception as innate traits for women but as skills for men. Thus men receive a payoff to such task requirements, while women receive such payoffs only in male-dominated jobs. Contrary to the argument I developed in Chapter 2, this suggests that some female-typed skills (especially in female-dominated positions) may increase earnings inequality by sex if men's earnings are increased but women's earnings are devalued by such skills.

Also as expected, white- and male-typed skills and requirements (authority, status in interaction, math skills, and general skills) enhance earnings. While authority and status in interaction benefit men more than women and whites more than blacks, general skill has the reverse order of relative payoffs across race and sex. Applied to earnings inequality, this would suggest that general skill should decrease earning inequality (increase earnings ratios) by race and by sex but that authority and status in interaction should have the opposite effect.

While the effects of desirable employment conditions on earnings were in the expected direction, the pattern across groups was only partly consistent with expectations. Availability of sufficient hours did increase earnings more for women than men, but it was more beneficial for whites than for blacks. This implies that sufficient hours should decrease sex inequality in earnings but possibly increase racial earnings inequality. Unemployment decreased earnings more for women than for men and more for blacks than for whites, which suggests that it should increase both race and sex earnings inequality (decreasing male to female and black to white earnings ratios).

Similarly, traditional indicators of economic power and privilege in product markets had positive effects on earnings in almost every case, aside from the unexpected negative effect of productivity for men. Although the differential payoffs across race-sex groups are small, the patterns predominantly favored women over men and blacks over whites, consistent with my specific devaluation argument. With respect to earnings inequality, this would imply a narrowing of earnings inequality (higher earnings ratios) in more economically powerful work contexts.

Finally, an analogous picture emerges from the effects of unionization, especially with respect to race. Unionization increases earnings for all groups, with a clear suggestion of a greater benefit to blacks than to whites. Sex differences in payoffs to unionized work were less consistent in favoring men over women and the differences were very small. Applied to earnings inequality, the obvious implication is that unionization should decrease racial earning inequality (higher black to white earnings ratios).

Earnings Ratios: Base Model Results

The analysis of earnings ratios concentrates on the comparison of earnings gaps between white men and the other three race-sex groups, but also considers the earnings gaps between black women and black men and between black women and white women. The pie charts in Figure 5.2 show that the sets of predictors explain a small to relatively modest share of the variation in earnings gaps across positions, unlike the analyses of earnings levels just discussed or the analyses of employment segregation in the previous chapter. Their explanatory power is highest for the three contrasts to white men's earnings, especially for white women. Note that the predictors work best in explaining the sex gap in earnings among whites and are least predictive of the sex gap in earnings among blacks. Despite this, a clear pattern emerges in terms of the relative importance of the different sets of predictors shown by the bar charts in Figure 5.2. Given the results for the earnings levels, it is not surprising that employment segregation and race-gender typing are the strongest predictors of earnings gaps in each comparison. In contrast, skill and growth is always the weakest set, with the desirable employment, product market structure, and links to other actors being stronger and somewhat similar in their predictive power.

Appendix Table B5.2 presents the detailed, numeric EGLS-SUR results from the base model for the five contrasts of earnings ratios among the race-sex groups: black women to white men, black men to white men, white women to white men, black women to black men, and black women to white women.[10] The visual summary of these results is in Table 5.2 using a format that should be familiar from the last chapter. For each earnings gap (earnings ratio), the table has a pair of columns, one indicating the predicted effects for the explanatory variables and the other showing whether the empirical results in Appendix Table B5.2 support or contradict the expectation.

Core Findings

General skill and growth. Skill significantly increases earnings ratios (decreases gaps) for all but sex ratios among blacks. Thus, although the analysis of segregation in the last chapter demonstrated that higher skill levels limit access of "less-favored" groups to positions, this analysis suggests that race and sex earnings inequality is typically less among those who gain access to high skill positions. Contrary to the statistical discrimination argument, this suggests that earnings for blacks and women are not discounted more in highly skilled positions. Instead, as the earnings level analyses showed, employment in highly skilled positions provides larger payoffs for women and blacks relative to their earnings potential in the devalued, lower-skilled positions in which they are more likely to be employed. Thus, these findings run counter to both the specific devaluation argument and the statistical discrimination argument.

Employment growth has slightly inconsistent effects. It increases earnings ratios for black men relative to white men and for white women relative to white men, but decreases it for black women compared to white women. As the earnings level analysis similarly showed, employment growth is more advantageous for black men and white women than for white men, and benefits black women not at all. Indeed it is this lack of benefit that depresses the earnings ratio for black to white women. Overall, this supports the specific devaluation argument with the caveat that growth does not open a window to higher earnings for black women.

Employment segregation and race-gender typing. This set of predictors represents the primary indicators of how global and specific devaluation processes should affect earnings gaps. Net employment representation has a

Figure 5.2 Explained Variance in Earnings Ratios, SUR-EGLS Base Model

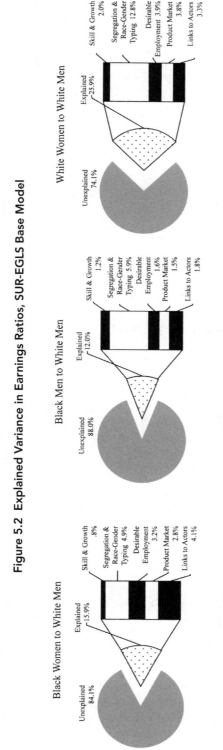

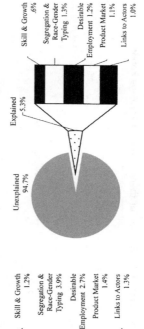

Table 5.2 Predictions and Summary of Results for the Analyses of Earnings Ratios

Predictors	Black Women: White Men		Black Men: White Men		White Women: White Men		Black Women: Black Men		Black Women: White Women	
	Predict	Result	Predict	Result	Predict	Result	Predict	Result	Predict	Result
General skill and growth										
Skill and training	+/−	**+**	+/−	**+**	+/−	**+**	+/−		+/−	**+**
Employment growth	+		+	✓	+	✓	+		+	✗
Employment segregation										
Employment segregation	+	✓	+	✗	+	✓	+		+	✓
White- or male-typed work										
Status in interaction	−	∪97%	−	∪85%	−	✓	−		−	∪96%
Authority	−	✓	−	✓	−	✗	−	✓	−	✓
Math skill	−		−	✓	−		−		−	✓
Black- or female-typed work										
Physical exertion	+	✓	+	✓	+	✓	+		+	✓
Nurturant skill	+		+		+	✓	+		+	
Physical dexterity	+		+	✗	+	✗	+	✗	+	
Clerical perception	+		+		+/0	✗	+/0		+	
Routinization	+	—	+	—	+/−		+/−		+	
Environmental conditions	+/−		+/−	✓	−	✓	+/−		+/−	
Desirable employment										
Sufficient work hours	+		+	✓	+		+		+	✗
Unemployment rate	+		+		+		+		+	✗
Self-employment rate	−	✓	−	✓	−		−	✓	−	✓

continues

Table 5.2 continued

Predictors	Black Women: White Men		Black Men: White Men		White Women: White Men		Black Women: Black Men		Black Women: White Women	
	Predict	Result	Predict	Result	Predict	Result	Predict	Result	Predict	Result
Product market structure										
Market power	+	✓	+	✓	+	✓	+	✓	+	
Profitability	+		+		+		+		+	
Economic scale										
Capital intensity										
Foreign involvement										
Productivity										
Linkages to other actors										
Industry unionization	+	✓	+	✓	+/0	✓	+/0	✓	+	
Occupation unionization	+	✓	+	✓	+/0	✓	+/0	✓	+	
Percent public sector	+	✓	+	✓	+/0	✓	+	✓	+	
Federal purchases	+/0		+/0		+/0	✓	+/0	✓	+/0	✓

Notes:
Predicted effects
+Positive −Negative +/−Opposing predictions 0 No effect Blank No prediction
Findings
✓ Predicted effect significant ✗ Opposite of prediction significant Blank No significant effect
+ Positive significant effect − Negative significant effect ∪ U-shaped effect

significant effect on earnings ratios for all but the sex gap among blacks and is positive (as expected) for three of the remaining four outcomes. The overrepresentation of the "less-favored" group increases earnings ratios (decreases gaps) for both black and white women relative to white men and for black women relative to white women. These findings accord with both the global devaluation argument and the "differential treatment breeds differential treatment" argument. At the extreme of relative representation in which a less-favored group is overrepresented, earnings are devalued for all workers, but especially for the more-favored group. At the other extreme, when the more-favored group is overrepresented, earnings discrimination against less-favored groups is more likely. Contrarily, when black men are overrepresented in a position, they earn less relative to white men in that position, but when white men are overrepresented in a position, black men earn more relative to white men. One possible explanation is that this could indicate the operation of a "glass escalator," privileging white men employed in positions with a high representation of black men.

Specific devaluation (valuation). Two sets of indicators of race and gender typing of work were expected to have opposite effects. White- or male-"appropriate" work settings were expected to decrease earnings ratios, while black- or female-"appropriate" settings were predicted to increase them. The white- or male-typed indicators are mainly significant (eleven of fifteen) and their effects are in line with the expectations, with one exception. Higher math skill requirements do decrease black-white earnings ratios (increase earnings gaps) for men and women, but they unexpectedly increase the earnings ratio for white women relative to white men. Although relative status in interaction has a U-shaped effect on all three black-white earnings ratios, this effect is nearly always negative across the range of possible scores.[11] Thus, racial earnings inequality is higher in positions requiring higher status interactions with others than in those in which workers are subordinate to others. Finally, authority has a negative effect on all five earnings ratios, indicating that race and sex earnings inequality are both higher among positions requiring the exercise of authority.

There are fewer significant effects (ten of thirty) for the indicators of black- or female-appropriate work, and they are evenly split between supporting and contradicting the predicted positive effects. The supporting effects are scattered across outcomes and predictors, except for nurturant skill. Positions requiring nurturant skill have higher earnings ratios for all three comparisons to white men's earnings because white men's earnings levels are the most devalued by nurturant skill. The significant effects of physical dexterity and clerical perception are the opposite of expectation, decreasing earnings ratios (increasing gaps), except that dexterity increases the black-to-white earnings ratio for women. Recall, however, how these predictors affected earnings levels. Dexterity decreases sex earnings ratios because it increases earnings levels for men.

For women, it increases earnings levels in male-dominated jobs while decreasing earnings in female-dominated ones. Similarly, the negative clerical-perception effects on sex earnings ratios for whites reflects the fact that clerical perception does not pay off as a skill for women but does benefit men in female-dominated jobs. These results are consistent with a specific devaluation argument in that men but not women are rewarded for some female-typed skills.

Despite a few contradictory findings, there is thus broad support for the devaluation argument that work settings that are stereotypically associated with blacks and women "equalize" earnings ratios by how they devalue earnings among race-sex groups. At a global level, a disproportionately high representation of women and blacks does reduce earnings ratios, with the puzzling exception of racial earnings gaps among men. But devaluation also operates in ways tied to the more specific content of stereotyping. Although the summary of results in Table 5.2 portrays mixed support for a devaluing effect of black- or female-typed skills and requirements, the apparently contradictory effects of dexterity and clerical perception suggest a more complicated devaluation process. These female-typed skills either are rewarded for men but not for women or increase men's earnings in all settings while benefitting women in male-dominated positions, but depressing their earnings levels in female-dominated positions. And white- or male-typed skills consistently decrease sex and race earnings ratios (increase earning gaps), in accord with a devaluation approach.

Supplementary Findings

Desirable employment. The availability of sufficient hours increases earnings ratios for both black and white women relative to white men, suggesting (as did the analysis of earnings levels) that gaining access to such work pays off more for women than for men. The same is not true for racial earnings ratios; sufficient hours has no effect on the racial gap among men and surprisingly increases the racial gap (decreases the earnings ratio) among women. The unemployment rate has a similar negative effect on racial earnings ratios among women but no effect on other earnings gaps. If black women are more likely than white women in a position to be laid off or fired, this could result in such an outcome. Self-employment has the expected negative effect on all five outcomes and is significant for all but sex gaps among whites. A greater degree of self-employment opportunity exacerbates earnings inequality among groups. Thus, not only are self-employment opportunities more accessible to more-favored groups (as we saw in the previous chapter), but less-favored groups that do gain access to positions with a high level of self-employment have lower earnings in comparison to more-favored groups. You might be wondering why gaining access to one kind of desirable employment (sufficient hours) largely reduces earnings gaps while gaining access to another (self-employment) increases earnings gaps. In making this prediction, I argued earlier that the difference lies in the fact that black and female entrepreneurs face customer discrimination and more limited access to lucrative networks and capital markets.

Product market structure. Although I expected and found that all the predictors in this set should affect earnings levels, I had specific hypotheses about earnings gaps just for market power and profitability. Only market power has any significant effect on earnings ratios, increasing the earnings ratios in every contrast, except for black women to white women, albeit the extended model in the next section finds an effect of profitability in some race-gender–typed work settings. This is consistent with the earnings level analyses that found small differentials favoring blacks and women. This could indicate a visibility process in which economic buffering provides oligopolistic firms with slack resources to overcome past discrimination or it might suggest that gaining access to such traditionally desirable employment (in terms of rewards and benefits) pays off more for blacks and women relative to their devalued earnings potential elsewhere.

Linkages to other actors. The final set of effects for linkages to other actors shows strong support for the hypotheses. Seven of the ten unionization effects are significant, all in the predicted positive direction. Except for the earnings ratio for black women to white women, each of the other earnings ratios is increased (earnings gaps decreased) by a greater degree of either occupational unionization, industrial unionization, or both. Overall, these results suggest that unionization has been instrumental in reducing many aspects of race and sex earnings inequality in the workplace.

Similarly, the two indicators of government linkages both have the expected positive effect of reducing race and sex inequality. Federal purchases has a significant effect only on the earnings ratio for white women relative to white men. But public sector employment has a positive effect on all five earnings ratios. As others have found, the public sector as an employer operates with a much more egalitarian wage system, systematically reducing sex and race earnings gaps.

Summary

Given the interconnection between race-sex group earnings levels and earnings ratios, it should be no surprise that the analyses of earnings ratios also support the argument that devaluation processes are important for understanding earnings gaps. As these two sets of analyses demonstrate, however, devaluation is not just a matter of the presence of women and blacks creating lower earnings and less between-group inequality, although such global devaluation is clearly an important component. Nor is it always a simple form of specific devaluation (valuation) in which black- or female-typed skills and conditions devalue earnings and thus minimize earning gaps or in which white- or male-typed skills and conditions are rewarded and exacerbate earnings gaps. The reality is that some specific devaluation occurs when men are rewarded for female-typed skills and women are not rewarded or are even penalized. And, in some cases, whites' (men's) earnings actually benefit less from employment in earnings-enhancing settings than do the other groups.

External pressures and linkages to other actors also contribute to understanding the pattern of earnings gaps across positions. Indeed, concentrated market power is one of the work settings in which earnings increase more for blacks and women than for white men and, consequently, in which race and sex earnings gaps decline. This is consistent with the argument that, in response to public and governmental pressure, employers used the slack resources generated by such economic buffering to overcome past inequalities, although there is no direct evidence for this interpretation. Government's role in reducing race and sex earnings inequality can also be seen in the leveling effect of the extent of federal contracting on sex earnings gaps among whites and in the lower levels of inequality within the government than in the private sector found for all five between-group contrasts. Similarly widespread are the equalizing benefits of unionization, albeit it does not reduce race earnings gaps among women.

Extending the Base Model: Moderating Factors

The base model results reaffirm the value of the race-sex queuing perspective for understanding labor market inequality, especially the importance of devaluation processes. As was true for employment segregation, the race-gender–typing indicators are the strongest predictors of both earnings levels within race-sex groups and earnings gaps among race-sex groups. The extended model considers how external pressures and resources repress or exacerbate the operation of devaluation processes. Specifically, I examine how growth, market power, and profitability moderate the effects of race-gender–typed work on earnings gaps and vice versa. My general expectation is that growth should diminish the salience of employer preferences and should increase the leverage of workers vis-à-vis employers, thereby muting the effects of race-gender–typed work. Similarly, growth's positive effect on earnings ratios should be larger in race-gender–atypical settings. Although market power and profitability should increase the salience of employer preferences, the visibility argument (supported by the previous results) suggests that this would benefit blacks and women and thus suppress devaluation effects.

I evaluated these speculations by testing for interaction effects between the set of race-gender–typing indicators and growth, market power, and profitability. These extended models keep only those interactions that were significant (for interested readers, Appendix Table B5.3 contains the detailed numeric

EGLS-SUR results for the extended model). Here I discuss Tables 5.3 and 5.4, which present visual/verbal summaries of the significant interactions from the extended models. Table 5.3 describes how the effects on earnings gaps of the race-gender–typing indicators differ across levels of growth, market power, and profitability. Table 5.4 complements this by depicting how the effects of growth, market power, and profitability vary across race-gender–typed settings. For each of the five earnings comparisons, a table entry indicates a significant interaction and describes the effect of a predictor on the relative earnings of the two groups and how it changes across levels of the moderating variable. A plus sign (+) indicates that a predictor increases the earnings of the specified race-sex group (relative to the other group in the contrast), whereas a minus sign (–) means that the predictor reduces the relative earnings of that group. A zero (0) denotes that the effect becomes zero in a moderating condition, and a U-shaped relationship is shown by (∪). When the size of a plus or minus symbol varies across the levels of the moderating variable, this indicates that the magnitude of a predictor's effect varies correspondingly.

There are two things to notice about the profitability results in contrast to the growth and market power results. The first is that profitability did not have a significant effect on any earnings ratio in the base model, unlike growth and market power, but it did have a significant effect on each of the earnings ratios in the extended, moderated-effects model. The second point is that there is much more consistency both about how profitability moderates the effects of race-gender–typing indicators and about how profitability's effects are in turn moderated by them.

Moderated Effects of Profitability and Race-Gender–Typing Indicators

How profitability conditions the effect of race-gender typing. Profitability significantly moderates the effects of status in interaction and authority in nine of ten cases, all but the negative effect of authority on the sex earnings ratio among blacks (see Table 5.3, Panel A). These indicators of white- or male-typed skills have negative effects on earnings ratios (increasing gaps) when businesses are losing money.[12] But these effects are muted or even reduced to zero when a profit is being made. Profitability also moderates the effect of environmental conditions on the sex earnings ratio among whites, changing it from a positive effect under conditions of a loss to a negative effect under conditions of a gain. Aside from this last effect, these results clearly support the idea that profitability suppresses the operation of specific devaluation processes. The inequality-producing effects for blacks (or women) of working in positions requiring white- (or male-) typed skills that are present when businesses are losing money is strongly diminished when a profit is being made.

Table 5.3 How Growth, Market Power, and Profitability Moderate the Effects of Race-Gender-Typing Indicators on Earnings Ratios

		Black Women: White Men	Black Men: White Men	White Women: White Men	Black Women: Black Men	Black Women: White Women
		R-G-T effect	R-G-T effect	R-G-T effect	R-G-T effect	R-G-T effect
Panel A: Profitability moderated by	Profit level[a]					
Status in interaction with others	Loss	∪ BW	∪ BW	∪ WW	∪ BW	∪ BW
	Gain	− BW	∪ BM	− WW	− BW	− BW
Authority	Loss	− BW	− BM	− WW		− BW
	Gain	0 BW	0 BM	0 WW		0 BW
Environmental conditions	Loss			+ WW		
	Gain			− WW		
	Growth level[a]	R-G-T effect	R-G-T effect	R-G-T effect	R-G-T effect	R-G-T effect
Panel B: Growth moderation of						
Status in interaction with others	Decline	− BW		− WW		
	Growth	+ BW		+ WW		
Authority	Decline	− BW				
	Growth	− BW				
Math skill	Decline	+ BW				− BW
	Growth	− BW				− BW
	MP level[a]	R-G-T effect	R-G-T effect	R-G-T effect	R-G-T effect	R-G-T effect
Panel C: Market power (MP) moderation of						
Authority	Low			− WW		+ BW
	High			− WW		− BW
Environmental conditions	Low		− BM			
	High		0 BM			
Physical dexterity	Low					+ BW
	High					− BW
Clerical perception	Low		− BM		+ BW	
	High		+ BW		− BM	

Notes: a. The levels of the moderating variables are defined as the mean of the moderating variable plus or minus twice its standard deviation. If the "low" value was less than the variable's minimum then the minimum was used. Similarly, if the "high" value was greater than the variable's maximum then the maximum was used.

Table 5.4 How Race-Gender–Typing Indicators Moderate the Effects of Growth, Market Power, and Profitability on Earnings Ratios

	Black Women: White Men	Black Men: White Men	White Women: White Men	Black Women: Black Men	Black Women: White Women
R-G-T level[a]	Profit effect	Profit effect	Profit effect	Profit effect	Profit effect
Panel A: Profitability moderated by					
Status in interaction with others Low	− BW	− BM	+ WW	− BW	− BW
Moderate	+ BW	+ BM	+ WW	+ BW	+ BW
High	− BW	− BM	− WW	− BW	− BW
Authority No	− BW	− BM	+ WW		− BW
Yes	+ BW	+ BM	+ WW		+ BW
Environmental conditions Poor			− WW		
Good			+ WW		
R-G-T level[a]	Growth effect	Growth effect	Growth effect	Growth effect	Growth effect
Panel B: Growth moderated by					
Status in interaction Low	+ BW		− WW		
High	+ BW		+ WW		
Authority No	+ BW				
Yes	+ BW				
Math skill Low	+ BW				+ BW
High	− BW				− BW
R-G-T level[a]	MP effect	MP effect	MP effect	MP effect	MP effect
Panel C: Market Power (MP) moderated by					
Authority No			+ WW		+ BW
Yes			+ WW		− BW
Environmental conditions Poor		− BM			
Good		+ BM			
Physical dexterity Low					+ BW
High					− BW
Clerical perception Low		− BM		+ BW	
High		+ BM		− BW	

Notes: a. For nurturant skill and authority, the levels of the moderating variables are defined as the absence (0) or presence (1) of the attribute. Otherwise, the levels of the moderating variables are defined as the mean of the moderating variable plus or minus twice its standard deviation. If the "low" value was less than the variable's minimum then the minimum was used. Similarly, if the "high" value was greater than the variable's maximum then the maximum was used. Status in interaction's moderating effect on profitability is also shown at a moderate level (its mean) to show how profitability's effect changes sign for some outcomes.

How race-gender typing conditions the effect of profitability. In tandem, the effect of profitability on earnings ratios also varies across race-gender–typed settings in a fairly, but not wholly, consistent way (Panel A of Table 5.4). In settings that are typed as "inappropriate" for the less-favored group, profitability has a positive effect on the earnings ratio, increasing the earnings of the less-favored group relative to the more-favored one. For example, in positions requiring authority, profitability increases the earnings ratio (decreases earnings gaps) for four of the five comparisons. In contrast, profitability decreases the earnings of the less-favored group relative to the more-favored one in "appropriate" settings. Similarly, in positions with poor working conditions, profitability decreases the female-male earnings ratio for whites while increasing it in positions with good working conditions. The pattern of how status in interaction with others moderates the effects of profitability is a partial exception. Its effect changes from negative in positions requiring low-status interactions to positive in those requiring moderate status relative to others.[13] But it unexpectedly changes back to negative in positions requiring the highest levels of relative status ("inappropriate" settings). With some exceptions, then, profitability reduces earnings differentials between races (sexes) in settings typed as black (female) "inappropriate," but increases earnings gaps in settings typed as "appropriate."

Moderated Effects of Growth and Race-Sex–Typing Indicators

How growth conditions the effect of race-gender typing. Panel B of Table 5.3 presents the results for the moderating effects of employment growth. Notice that growth only moderates the effects of the indicators of white- or male-typed skills, and all but one of the moderating effects is on an earnings ratio contrasting women and men. For both black and white women relative to white men, growth rather dramatically changes the effect of status in interaction on earnings ratios. In declining positions, the earnings ratios decrease (gaps increase) from low-status to moderate-status interactions, indicating that status in interaction pays off more for white men than for black or white women. But in growing positions, this effect reverses and the earnings ratios increase (disparities diminish) from low-status to moderate-status interactions.[14] This finding supports the argument that growth reduces employers' motive and ability to devalue women's earnings in gender-atypical work settings.

However, the moderating effects of growth on authority and math skill contradict this expectation. The effect of these white-male–typed skills becomes more negative (rather than less negative), such that these skills increase disparities more in growing positions compared to declining ones. Moreover, in declining positions, math skill even reverses sign and increases the earnings ratio (reduces the gap) for black women relative to white men. Following Reskin and Roos's (1990) research on women entering gender-atypical occupations, one possible explanation is that black women are more likely to gain access to race-gender–atypical positions only when these positions have become less desirable (including declining employment and earnings), which would diminish earnings inequality within such positions.

How race-gender typing conditions the effect of growth. Turning to how the effect of growth is moderated by the race-gender–typing indicators, Panel B of Table 5.4 shows that greater employment pressure usually but not always increases earnings ratios (reduces gaps) in both race-gender–typical and –atypical work settings. But only for status in interaction does growth have a greater equalizing effect in atypical than in typical settings. Surprisingly, growth has a negative effect on earnings ratios in several situations: on the sex earnings ratio for whites in positions requiring low-status interactions and on the earnings ratios for black women relative to whites (both men and women) in positions needing high math skills. Thus, there is little support for the expectation that growth should be most beneficial in atypical settings.

Moderated Effects of Market Power and Race-Gender–Typing Indicators

How market power conditions the effect of race-gender typing. The results for the moderating effects of market power in Panel C of Table 5.3 reveal an intriguing pattern. Among men, higher market power diminishes the negative effects of two race-gender–typing indicators (environmental conditions and clerical perception) on the black-white earnings ratio. But among women, higher market power heightens the negative effects of two race-gender–typing indicators (authority and dexterity) on the black-white earnings ratio. Similarly, market power moderates effects on sex earnings ratios differently for whites than for blacks. For whites, higher market power diminishes the negative effect of authority on the sex earnings ratios, while for blacks, higher market power changes the effect of clerical perception on the sex earnings ratios from positive to negative. Market power thus does not consistently mute or exacerbate specific devaluation. It reduces the devaluation created by some task requirements for men and by others for whites, while it increases some (de)valuing effects for women and others for blacks.

How race-gender typing conditions the effect of market power. Although the effect of market power on earnings ratios changes as it varies across race-gender–typed settings and across contrasts among groups, there is a clear pattern that applies to most outcomes. In settings that are "inappropriate" for a less-favored race-sex group, market power has a positive effect on earnings ratios, increasing the earnings of the less-favored group relative to the more-favored one. For example, in positions with good environmental conditions (black "inappropriate"), market power increases the black-white earnings ratio among men. But in settings which are "appropriate" for the less-favored race-sex group, market power has a negative (or less positive) effect on earnings ratios, reducing the earnings of the less-favored group relative to the more-favored one; for example, market power decreases the black-white earnings ratio among men in positions with poor environmental conditions.[15] As the previous base model results showed, market power itself broadly equalizes earnings among groups. This is still true in many race-gender–atypical settings, but it can have the opposite effect in some race-gender–typical settings.

Implications of the Extended Model Results

As in the prior chapter on employment segregation, these findings highlight the importance of external pressures and internal resources as determinants of race and sex labor market inequality. While growth does moderate the effects of all three white- or male-typed skills on earnings ratios (especially for black women relative to white men), only for status in interaction does growth mute the devaluing effects. For authority and math skills, growth magnifies the influence of specific valuation. However, employment pressures do usually increase the earnings of other race-sex groups relative to white men, although there are a few race-gender–typed settings in which the reverse occurs. Remember also from the base model results for the black-white earnings ratios for men that growth increases relative black earnings uniformly in all settings.

Slack resources, like those provided by profitability and market power, can be used either to counter or to acquiesce to internal and external pressures. Market power in particular generates visibility to both the general public and the government, which in turn can make such work settings more likely targets of external pressure. Such visibility and pressure create an incentive to use slack resources to accommodate rather than resist external pressures, although the strength of this incentive will vary with the degree of government or public pressure over time.[16] Herring's (2009) work suggests that there is also a direct profit motive as one rationale for companies to diversify their workforce. He proposes that diversity is profitable because it broadens the viewpoints used to guide business operations, resulting in higher creativity, better problem solving, and an ability to reach more diverse markets. The results from the extended model generally support the conclusion that, in recent times, slack resources have been used to reduce race and sex earnings inequality. Market power increases earnings ratios for women relative to men or for blacks to whites (among men) in gender- or race-atypical work settings, although the opposite applies to black-white earnings ratios among women. Profitability much more systematically reduces earnings gaps across a range of race- and gender-atypical work settings.

Such slack resources are not a cure-all for earnings inequality created by devaluation processes. Market power mutes the effects of some specific devaluation processes, while magnifying the effects of others. Profitability does consistently diminish the impact of devaluation processes on both race and sex earnings gaps in positions with white- or male-typed skills and requirements. This pattern is somewhat echoed in Herring's (2009) study of the value to businesses of a diverse workforce in which he finds that profitability is linked to both race diversity and sex diversity, but that market power is linked only to race diversity. It remains an open question of whether or not these effects of market power and profitability are time invariant, given how they depend in part on incentives generated by government and public pressures for more egalitarian employment processes.

What's Next?

In this chapter, I evaluated how well my race-sex queuing perspective works for understanding earnings gaps among race-sex groups. Like the analysis of employment segregation in the last chapter, findings from the base model support nearly all of the hypothesized effects, aside from a few anomalies. And the extended model illustrates the complex ways in which growth, market power, and profitability moderate the effects of race-gender typing and how their effects on earnings ratios, in turn, depend on the race-gender–typed context of work. In the next chapters I examine how broader social contexts may moderate these findings. Specifically, I consider how regional variation in social context and cultural beliefs, broadly defined, influence employment segregation and earnings gaps among race-sex groups.

Notes

1. The explanation behind this quote (as found on the Web at http://en.wikipedia .org/wiki/Wikipedia:Reference_desk_archive/Language/April_2006) is that it is a reference to the practice of cooling milk jugs by putting them in a creek. This could tempt the milkman to dilute the milk by adding water to increase profits. The proof of such fraud was a buyer finding a trout in the milk.

2. Technically, the results from the analyses of logged earnings levels and of logged earnings ratios are related but not perfectly redundant, even though the logged earnings ratio for a particular pair of race-sex groups is a linear function of the logged earnings level for each group:

$$\ln\left(\frac{E_1}{E_2}\right) = \ln\left(E_1\right) - \ln\left(E_2\right)$$

But the models for estimating the earnings levels and the earnings ratios differ in several ways that prevent the results of the earning-ratio analyses from being exact mathematical functions of the results of the earnings-level analyses. First, the analysis of earnings levels for each race-sex group includes as predictors two indicators of employment segregation (the representation of black men relative to white men and white women relative to white men), while the analysis of each earnings ratio includes only one indicator of employment segregation (the relative representation of the two groups whose earnings are compared). Second, the form of heteroskedasticity specified and corrected is different for the earnings-level analyses than for the earnings-ratio analyses. Finally, as discussed in Chapter 3, while both analyses allow for correlated errors between employment segregation and the earnings outcomes, the earnings-level analyses employ two-stage EGLS estimation techniques (a generalization of 2SLS), while the earnings-ratio analyses employ SUR-EGLS estimation techniques.

3. I noted in Chapter 4 (note 2) that there is no unique decomposition of the contributions to explained variance among the sets of predictors because a substantial portion of it is shared among the predictors in these analyses. As before, the results I present are the average of the alternative ways of attributing shared explanatory power, rescaled so they sum to the actual R^2.

4. The appendix table also provides results for the diagnostic tests for heteroskedasticity and correlated errors. The significant Lagrange multiplier (LM) statistics indicate that both error components (correlated errors within industry sectors and correlated errors within occupation segments) are different from zero and thus necessitate random effects estimation. The significant Breusch-Pagan (BP) statistics for the initial error variance indicate heteroskedasticity by group size and by sector location. The nonsignificant BP statistics for the error variance adjusted for group size suggest that this source of heteroskedasticity is properly modeled in these analyses. However, the adjusted BP statistics for segment location, while greatly reduced in size, are still significant in the analyses for all but white women. The basic findings are robust to alternative specifications of the error structure, none of which fully solves the problem.

5. If two effects differed by less than one standard error, they are considered similar in size. Note that this is a less stringent criterion than the usual test of statistical significance to help identify consistent patterns of small differences.

6. For white men, the general-skills effect becomes significant only if physical exertion and either math skill or relative status in interaction are removed from the model.

7. These analyses exclude the measure of the relative representation of black women to white men because it is so strongly associated with the other two segregation indicators (especially white women) that the regression results are unstable and imprecise if it is included. If included by itself, it has a negative effect on earnings for all groups, so I discuss the effects of employment segregation for black men as representing the effect of race segregation and the effects of segregation for white women as representing the effect of sex segregation.

8. For white women, dexterity becomes devaluing right when the balance tips from men to women. For black women, this occurs when women are about one-third more likely than men to be employed in a position.

9. Clerical perception becomes devaluing when men are about one-third more likely than women to be employed in a position.

10. These appendix tables also provide results for the diagnostic tests used to assess the problems of heteroskedasticity and correlated errors for each outcome. The significant LM statistics indicate that both error components (correlated errors within

industry sectors and correlated errors within occupation segments) are different from zero and should be specified as part of the error structure. The significant BP statistics for the initial error variance indicate heteroskedasticity by group size and by sector location. The nonsignificant BP statistics for the error variance adjusted for group size and segment location suggest that heteroskedasticity is properly modeled in three of the five analyses. For the earnings ratios for black women to white women and for black women to black men, the heteroskedasticity correction has not fully solved the problem. However, the basic findings for this outcome are robust to alternative specifications of the error structure.

11. The effect turns positive only for a small proportion of positions (3%, 15%, and 4%) with the highest levels of relative status in interaction.

12. As Panel A of Table 5.3 shows, the effect of status in interaction is U-shaped, but predominantly a negative effect when the profit level is a loss. When the profit level is a gain, this U-shaped effect flattens or becomes a smaller negative effect.

13. In the case of white women to white men, it changes from small positive to larger positive.

14. Technically, the effect of status in interaction is U-shaped in declining positions but is inverted U-shaped in growing positions. But for the vast majority of positions and for up to above-average levels of status in interaction, the effect is negative in declining positions but positive in growing ones.

15. The opposite pattern, however, characterizes the effects of market power on black-white earnings ratios among women. In this case, market power increases the black-white earnings ratio in the black-"appropriate" setting but decreases it in the black-"inappropriate" one.

16. Dobbin and Kelly (2007: 1237) argue that judicial pressure to combat sexual harassment, for example, has gradually strengthened but with mixed messages most recently, suggesting "the declining salience of judges and legislatures."

6

Regional Variation in Labor Market Inequality

The frontiers are not east or west, north or south,
but wherever a man "fronts" a fact.
—Thoreau (1985: 249)

As the last two chapters made clear, stereotyping plays a major role in understanding employment segregation and earnings gaps among race-sex groups in a variety of ways, including processes of statistical discrimination (Reskin 1993; Marini 1989; Bielby and Baron 1986), race-sex queuing (Kaufman 2002, 2001; Reskin and Roos 1990), and cultural devaluation (England et al. 1994; Steinberg 1990). Do other social contexts moderate the effects of stereotyping, and does the pattern of findings vary across contexts? In this chapter I consider how regional variation in social context and cultural beliefs, broadly defined, influence these outcomes. Researchers have used varying units to study geographic differences in labor market inequality, primarily metropolitan areas or local labor market areas (e.g., Cohen and Huffman 2003a; Huffman and Cohen 2004; McCall 2001a,b; see also the studies reviewed by Beggs and Villemez 2001), but also states (e.g., Beggs 1995) and countries (e.g., Charles and Grusky 2004). In deciding to use a comparison between the southern and the northern states, I chose to privilege detail in defining labor market positions over detail in defining geographic areas because my theoretical focus is not on regional processes and predictors per se.[1] Rather, my intent is to provide an initial demonstration of how the social context of regions may moderate the effects of stereotyping and queuing processes. As I discuss next, there are clear social and economic divides between the South and the rest of the United States, and, given the number of outcomes and predictors and the complexity of the findings, a biregional comparison makes the presentation and discussion of the results manageable.

In particular, comparing the effects of race-gender–stereotyped tasks on segregation and earnings gaps in the South versus the North should reveal the influence of regional context and address the widely articulated view that racial prejudice, sex roles, and processes of discrimination and inequality are more pronounced in the South (e.g., Firebaugh and Davis 1988; Greeley and Sheatsley 1971; Quillian 1996). As Weakliem and Biggert (1999: 874) note, "Discussions of regional differences [in political attitudes] have often focused on the contrast between the southern states and the rest of the nation, since this is the largest and historically most important division." Their analyses of a wide range of political attitudes (from sexuality and sex roles to race relations and civil liberties to government spending priorities) confirm that the South is notably more conservative across the board, even with controls for socioeconomic status, race, gender, urbanism, religion, and so on.

But other regional differences are also relevant and may manifest themselves in a comparison of effects between the South and the North. Blacks comprise a larger portion of the population and of the labor queue in the South than in the North, which should push blacks higher into the labor queue for some jobs in the South than in the North.[2] Although the South and North also differ in their industrial composition and, hence, product market structure, it is not clear if such differences in levels would necessarily translate into differences in processes and effects. Labor unions are much less prevalent in the South than the North but, conversely, blacks might be more important to unions as potential members in the South given their larger share of the labor force. If so, then unions could be more proactively egalitarian in their policies and actions in the South than in the North. Finally, the South generally faced greater pressure by civil rights organizations and by the judicial, legislative, and executive branches during the 1960s and 1970s (see the discussion in Schuman, Steeh, and Bobo 1985: 8-42), which might mute the effects of differences in the cultural context.

For simplicity, I estimate only the base models of employment segregation and earnings gaps in the South and the North to examine how the effects of the predictors vary across regions. I begin by considering North-South differences in the process of employment segregation and then discuss differences in earnings gaps. Paralleling the much more uneven regional distribution of blacks and whites than of women and men, there are greater regional differences in the processes affecting racial labor-market inequality than sex labor-market inequality. Another notable pattern are several results suggesting that there may be greater resistance to relaxing stereotyping in the South than in the North, especially in noting how the effects of skill and growth and of black- or female-typed skills and working conditions vary between the North and the South. Despite these regional differences, the results suggest that in both regions, employers rank black women at the bottom of the labor queue for the best jobs.

Employment Segregation in the North and the South

As Figure 6.1 shows, the degree to which the model as a whole can explain the various forms of employment segregation is the same for the North as for the

Figure 6.1 Explained Variance in Employment Segregation by Region, SUR-EGLS Base Model

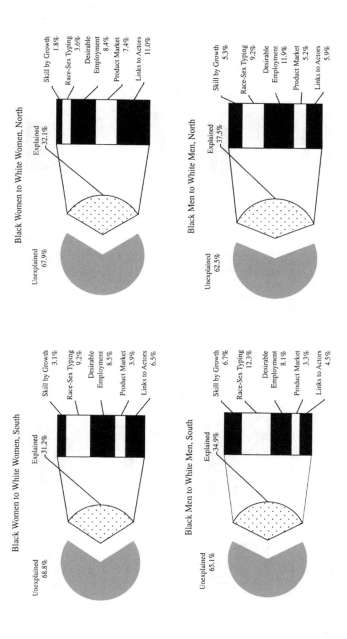

Black Women to White Women, North

Skill by Growth 1.8%
Race-Sex Typing 3.6%
Desirable Employment 8.4%
Product Market 7.4%
Links to Actors 11.0%

Explained 32.1%

Unexplained 67.9%

Black Men to White Men, North

Skill by Growth 5.3%
Race-Sex Typing 9.2%
Desirable Employment 11.9%
Product Market 5.2%
Links to Actors 5.9%

Explained 37.5%

Unexplained 62.5%

Black Women to White Women, South

Skill by Growth 3.1%
Race-Sex Typing 9.2%
Desirable Employment 8.5%
Product Market 3.9%
Links to Actors 6.5%

Explained 31.2%

Unexplained 68.8%

Black Men to White Men, South

Skill by Growth 6.7%
Race-Sex Typing 12.3%
Desirable Employment 8.1%
Product Market 3.3%
Links to Actors 4.5%

Explained 34.9%

Unexplained 65.1%

continues

Figure 6.1 continued

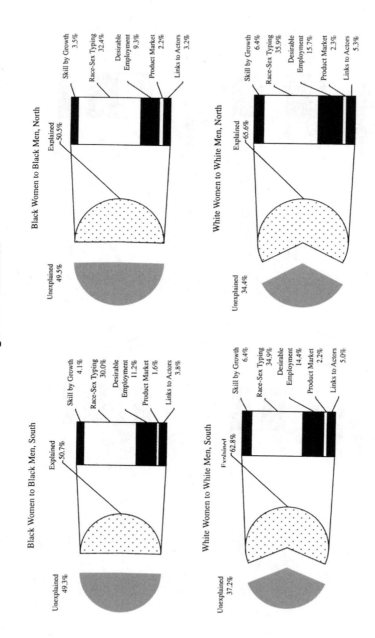

continues

141

Figure 6.1 continued

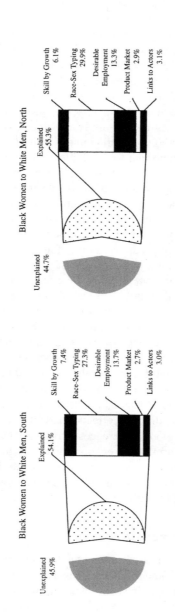

Black Women to White Men, North

Black Women to White Men, South

South. Furthermore, the pattern across types of segregation is similar to that described in Chapter 4: The base model explains about one-third of the variation across positions for race segregation within sex, but more than half of the variation for sex segregation within race and for the combined race and sex segregation contrast (black women to white men). And the pattern of relative contributions of each set of predictors is again more similar for the three sex segregation outcomes and somewhat distinct from that for race segregation within sex in both the North and the South. However, there are some regional differences in the relative contributions of the predictor sets, especially for race segregation. One difference is that the skill and growth set explains a larger relative share of southern employment segregation than of northern segregation, particularly for race segregation, and race-gender typing is a much stronger relative predictor of racial segregation in the South than in the North. In contrast, it is slightly more important for explaining variation in sex segregation in the North than in the South. Despite these differences, the race-gender–typing set and the desirable employment set are always the two most influential sets, except in predicting race segregation among women in the North. In that case, links to other actors and desirable employment are the most important, followed somewhat closely by product market structure.

These patterns of predictive power foreshadow what the analyses reveal about regional variation in the effects of predictors on segregation: There is somewhat less regional variation in the effects on sex segregation (especially among whites) and more regional variation in the effects on race segregation (especially among men). As in previous chapters, the detailed numeric results from the EGLS-SUR models are presented in appendix tables (A6.1 and A6.2), while here I orient discussion of the results around visual summaries of these findings, as presented in Table 6.1.[3] For each segregation outcome, this table presents a pair of columns, one for the North and one for the South. The table entries signify whether a predictor has a significant positive, a significant negative, or a significant U-shaped effect in each region. Shaded areas indicate when a predictor has different effects across the two regions. Given the focus of this chapter on regional differences, I forgo a detailed discussion of how predictors affect each form of segregation and emphasize differences in the effects in the predictors between the North and the South. I discuss each type of employment segregation, beginning with sex segregation within race and then turning to race segregation within sex.

Sex Segregation Among Whites

Table 6.1 shows only four differences in the determinants of the relative representation of white women to white men. The interaction between general skill and employment growth is significant only in the South. Thus growth mutes the negative effects of skill on white women's employment representation in

Table 6.1 Summary of Results for the Analyses of Employment Segregation by Region

Predictors	Black Women: White Men		Black Men: White Men		White Women: White Men		Black Women: Black Men		Black Women: White Women	
	North	South	North	South	North	South	North	South	North	South
General skill and growth										
Skill and training scale	−	−	−	−	−	−	−	−	−	−
Skill/training × growth			+	+		+				+
Employment growth rate										
Black- or female-typed work										
Physical exertion	−	−	−	+	−	−	−	−		
Nurturant skill	+	+		+		+	+	+		
Physical dexterity	+	+		−	+	+	+	+		
Clerical perception	+	+			+	+	−	+		
Environmental conditions	−	−	−	+	−	−	−	−		
Routinization	−	−			−	−			−	
White- or male-typed work										
Status in interaction	○	○	○	○	○	○	○	○	○	○
Authority	+	−			+	+	+	+	−	−
Math skill	−		−	−	−	−	−	−	−	−
Desirable employment										
Sufficient work hours	−	−	−				−			
Unemployment rate	+	+	+	+	−	−	−	−	+	+
Self-employment rate	−	−	−	−			−	−	−	−

continues

Table 6.1 continued

Predictors	Black Women: White Men		Black Men: White Men		White Women: White Men		Black Women: Black Men		Black Women: White Women	
	North	South	North	South	North	South	North	South	North	South
Product market structure										
Market power	+ +	+ +	+	+	+ +	+	+ + +	+ +	+	+
Profitability					+				+	+
Economic scale	+						+ −			
Capital intensity	−					−				+
Foreign involvement										
Productivity										
Linkages to other actors										
Industry unionization	+ +	−			−	−		−	+ + +	+ +
Occupation unionization	+ +				−	−		−	+ + +	
Percent public sector	−	−	+ −	+ −			−	−		
Federal purchases							−	−		

Notes: Shaded areas show regional differences in effects.
Table entries signify
+ Positive significant effect − Negative significant effect ∪ U shaped effect Blank No significant effect

the South but not the North. This implies that southern employers turn more readily to employing white women than do northern employers in response to a shortage of skilled white men. Both nurturant skill and capital intensity similarly have effects only in the South, hinting at a more prevalent stereotyping of such work settings as gendered work in the South than in the North.[4] Finally, profitability has a positive effect on white women's representation exclusively in the North. This implies that only in the North do employers use slack resources to respond favorably to external antidiscrimination pressures for white women, perhaps indicating a more intense preference for sex segregation among southern employers. Note that the differences in the effects of nurturant skill, capital intensity, and profitability (but not in the skill by growth interaction) are consistent with the argument that values and preferences in the South are more conducive to sex segregation.

Sex Segregation Among Blacks

For this form of employment segregation, four predictors have significant effects in the North and not the South, with three others significant only in the South (keep in mind that seven other indicators of race or gender typing have similar effects in both regions). Nurturant skill increases the representation of black women relative to black men in the South but not in the North, just as it does among whites, perhaps indicative of stronger cultural pressures on both employers and black women to conform to a "feminine" or specifically "mammy" stereotype in the South. In contrast, environmental conditions and capital intensity each has a negative effect on black women's representation only in the North. This might suggest weaker or nonexistent normative pressures against the employment of black women in hazardous conditions or in factories in the South. That is, poor environmental conditions may be considered equally acceptable for black women as for black men in the South, with the race-typing content of this working condition dominating the gender-typing one. Economic scale for the first time has a significant effect on race-sex segregation, but only in the North. This positive effect implies that the formalization and limitation of discretionary decisionmaking that accompanies large size is beneficial to the employment prospects of black women in the North. Indeed, reading across the row in Table 6.1 shows that economic scale not only has a positive effect just in the North but also solely for the representation of black women relative to the other three race-sex groups. The unemployment rate surprisingly decreases black women's representation relative to black men, but only in the North. This suggests that black women's position in the race-sex queue for positions is generally lower than that of black men in the North, but not in the South.[5] Also unexpected is that public sector employment reduces black women's representation relative to black men in the South. Since it has no effect on sex segregation among whites in either the North or the South but increases racial representation for both men and women, this implies that the public sector has operated in a more egalitarian fashion for blacks than for women, especially in the South.

Race Segregation Among Men

Table 6.1 shows considerable regional variation in the analyses of the representation of black men contrasted to white men, with seven predictors affecting only one region and only nine having significant effects in both regions. Interestingly, there is virtually no overlap between those predictors having varying effects on the employment likelihood for black men relative to white men and those having divergent effects on sex segregation. One overlap is that the interaction of general skills and employment growth is significant for black men only in the South, as it was for white women. As Figure 6.2 shows, this interaction means that growth increases the representation of black men (and white women) relative to white men in the South for jobs requiring high skills, but reduces their relative representation for jobs requiring low skills. In contrast, growth significantly raises the representation of black men in the North for all skill levels. Together these effects imply that southern employers meet increased employment demands by hiring black men and white women only if constrained by a need for skilled labor, whereas northern employers respond to employment pressures by hiring black men (but not white women) more uniformly at all skill levels. However, in both the North and the South, general skill requirements reduce black men's relative representation. Although this negative effect is diminished by employment growth only in the South, general skill has a larger negative effect in the South than in the North except at the highest growth levels. The fact that availability of sufficient work hours is only significant in the North may also reflect differences in the operation of labor queues between regions. Black men's much larger share of the labor pool in the South than the North means that they should be pushed upward in the labor queue for some of the more desirable jobs, such as those offering more hours of work.

Three of the race- or gender-typing indicators have significant effects that vary by region. In the South, greater physical exertion and more routinization increase black men's relative representation, while higher dexterity requirements reduce their representation. All of these are consistent with the argument that there is a stronger racial stereotype in the South than the North about the kinds of appropriate work situations for black men (more menial, routine, and brute force).

Finally, industry unionization has a significant negative effect on race segregation among men in the South but not the North, implying that southern unions more actively promote (or less proactively resist) racial barriers than do northern unions. Looking at the full set of union effects across outcomes in Table 6.1 strengthens this interpretation. Four of the five negative effects of industry unionization are in the South; the other negative effect is for white

Figure 6.2 Effect of Growth Rate on Employment Segregation of Black Men to White Men and of White Women to White Men, Moderated by Skill in the South

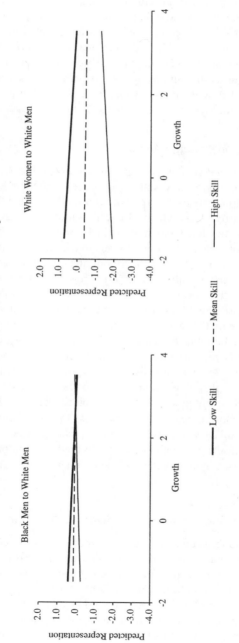

women relative to white men in the North. And for race segregation among women, industry unionization actually increases black women's representation in the North while having no effect in the South. Occupation unionization has three positive effects, all on black women's representation, only one of which is significant in the South. Thus, the regional analysis paints a very different image of how unions affect employment segregation than did the prior national analyses. It suggests that unions operate in a way that is primarily either neutral or beneficial to women and blacks in the North but predominantly detrimental to their employment representation in the South.

Race Segregation Among Women

The results for racial segregation among women (Table 6.1) show somewhat less regional variation than was the case for men, and there is little similarity in how the predictors' effects diverge between the North and the South for men. The only similarity is that physical exertion increases black women's representation relative to white women solely in the South, just as it did for black men compared to white men. This corresponds to the argument that race stereotyping is more prevalent in the South. Among the other race-gender–typing indicators, only routinization also differs across regions—it reduces black women's representation in the North but not the South. Economic scale has a positive effect just in the North on black women's representation relative to white women. Taken together with the fact that economic scale also increases their representation relative to both black men and white men, these results hint at a kind of tokenism underlying the egalitarian effects of large economic scale among northern employers. Using a visibility viewpoint, these findings suggest that large northern employers are more likely to respond to external pressures for egalitarian employment processes by hiring black women, whom they can "double count" in reporting and charting progress toward equity. Finally, as mentioned earlier, industry unionization has a positive effect on black women's representation in the North and no effect in the South, implying that northern unions operate in a more egalitarian fashion than do southern unions.

Race and Sex Segregation:
Black Women's Representation Relative to White Men

For this final, doubly contrasted form of employment segregation, five predictors have significant effects solely in the North and one is significant just in the South. Only for this outcome does authority have divergent effects between the North and the South; authority increases black women's relative employment likelihood only in the North. (Keep in mind that a similar effect, which is constant across regions, is found for the other sex-segregation outcome measures.) Economic scale also increases black women's representation relative to white men only in the North. As I argued above, this perhaps reflects not only more formalization of procedures and less discretionary decisionmaking but also a kind of strategic tokenism in the hiring process as size increases. In the North but not the South, capital intensity reduces black women's representation relative to white men just as it does relative to black men. The opposite pattern holds for white women, in which their representation compared to white men is reduced by capital intensity only in the South. Together these findings imply that factory work may be considered appropriate for black but not white women in the South, whereas there is a more uniform stereotyping of factory work as inappropriate for women in the North. The links to other actors' set of predictors evidences considerable regional variation, with three of the four effects differing. Industry unionization has a negative effect only in the South, while occupation unionization has a positive effect only in the North. As I noted earlier, this suggests a strong contrast between northern and southern unions in how they promote or hinder workplace equity. Finally, public sector employment increases black women's representation relative to white men solely in the North. Along with the effects of public sector employment on the other forms of segregation, these findings imply that the public sector has more successfully (or perhaps aggressively) striven for racial equity in their employment processes than they have for sexual equity, particularly in the South. This parallels results from DiPrete's (1989) study of the federal bureaucratic labor market in which he demonstrated greater racial then sexual equity in both initial placement but also in promotion rates.

Summary

Overall, the regional analyses indicate somewhat greater regional homogeneity in the process of sex segregation but somewhat greater regional diversity in the process of race segregation. There is considerable regional variation in the effects of the predictors on race segregation among men, especially among the indicators of race-gender typing. The same is true to a lesser degree for race segregation among women. For example, physical exertion has a negative effect on the relative representation of women to men for all three sex-segregation outcomes in both the North and the South, but it has a positive effect on the relative representation of blacks to whites (among both men and women) only in the South. This suggests stronger racial stereotyping in the South than the North.

Aside from this pattern, several other regional differences in employment segregation are especially interesting. The skill and growth effects suggest that northern employers respond to employment demand at all skill levels by opening up access to jobs for only black men; there is not a significant effect of growth on relative employment likelihoods for any other race-sex group. In contrast, southern employers respond to employment demand solely at the highest skill levels by opening up access to jobs for black men and white women, but not for black women. To me, the finding that southern employers appear to respond to employment demand only for the most skilled jobs implies a greater resistance to relaxing stereotypes in the South than the North. Similarly, nurturant skills, a key gender-typing indicator, affects sex segregation among whites and among blacks only in the South, again suggesting stronger or more prevalent normative constraints or pressures.[6]

Earnings Gaps in the North and the South

Unlike the analyses of employment segregation, the explanatory power of the base model for earnings gaps does vary across regions (see Figure 6.3). With the exception of race segregation among men, the explained variance is higher in the North than in the South, most notably for the sex gaps in earnings. Like the earlier national analyses of earnings gaps, the model's explanatory power is highest for gaps between white men and the other three race-sex groups. In addition, while the predictive power is highest for sex earnings gaps among whites (especially in the North), it is lowest for sex earnings gaps among blacks (especially in the South). The pattern of the relative importance of predictor sets (shown in the bar charts in Figure 6.3) also largely replicates the pattern from the national analyses. The employment segregation and race-gender–typing set is almost always the strongest predictor of earnings gaps, and skill/growth is almost always the weakest set, with the other sets falling between these extremes.

But there is also some regional patterning of the relative contributions of these predictor sets, most notably for racial earnings gaps. As expected, employment segregation and race-gender typing are much stronger relative predictors of racial earnings gaps in the South, and correspondingly all the other predictor sets are noticeably stronger predictors in the North. In counterpoint, even though the skill and growth set is typically the weakest, it consistently has somewhat stronger relative importance in the North than the South for predicting earnings gaps.

Regional variation in the effects of predictors on earnings gaps parallels these patterns of predictive power, with the same two sets (employment segregation/race-gender typing and skill/growth) showing the greatest regional differences. I orient discussion of these results around visual summaries of the findings presented in Table 6.2. (The detailed numeric results from the EGLS-SUR models are presented in Appendix Tables B6.3 and B6.4.)[7] For each earnings ratio, this table presents a pair of columns, one for the North and one for the South. The table entries signify whether a predictor has a significant positive, a significant negative, or a significant U-shaped effect in each region. Shaded areas indicate when a predictor has effects that differ between the regions. Given this chapter's focus on regional differences, I emphasize differences in the predictors' effects on earnings ratios between the North and the

Figure 6.3 Explained Variance in Earnings Gaps by Region, SUR-EGLS Base Model

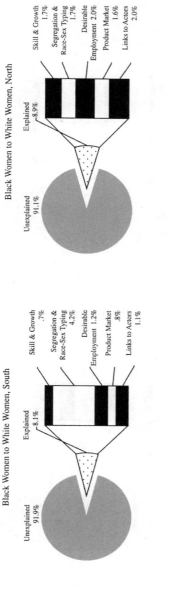

Black Women to White Women, South

Unexplained 91.9%

Explained 8.1%

Skill & Growth .7%

Segregation & Race-Sex Typing 4.2%

Desirable Employment 1.2%

Product Market .8%

Links to Actors 1.1%

Black Men to White Men, South

Unexplained 88.6%

Explained 11.4%

Skill & Growth .7%

Segregation & Race-Sex Typing 7.3%

Desirable Employment .8%

Product Market 1.2%

Links to Actors 1.4%

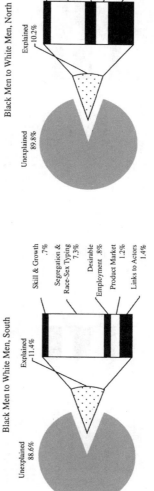

Black Women to White Women, North

Unexplained 91.1%

Explained 8.9%

Skill & Growth 1.7%

Segregation & Race-Sex Typing 1.7%

Desirable Employment 2.0%

Product Market 1.6%

Links to Actors 2.0%

Black Men to White Men, North

Unexplained 89.8%

Explained 10.2%

Skill & Growth .7%

Segregation & Race-Sex Typing 4.1%

Desirable Employment 1.2%

Product Market 1.5%

Links to Actors 2.7%

continues

Figure 6.3 continued

Black Women to Black Men, South

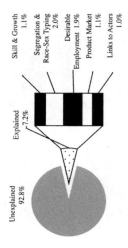

Black Women to Black Men, North

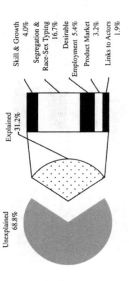

White Women to White Men, South

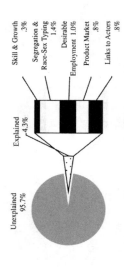

White Women to White Men, North

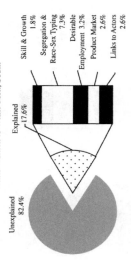

continues

Figure 6.3 continued

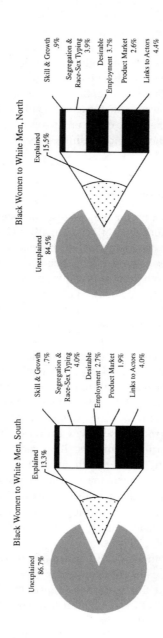

South. For consistency with the prior discussion of employment segregation among race-sex groups, I begin by discussing sex earnings gaps within race and then turn to race earnings gaps within sex.

First, however, a quick visual comparison of Table 6.2 and Table 6.1 reveals two important differences about predicting earnings gaps versus employment segregation. Given the lesser predictive power of the earnings gaps base model, it is not surprising that there are overall fewer significant effects in the earnings gap analyses and that fewer predictors consistently affect all the outcomes. Part of the inconsistency is that more of the predictors evidence higher degrees of regional variation (i.e., show regional differences for three or more of the outcome measures).

Sex Earnings Gaps Among Whites

This outcome evidences by far the greatest consistency in effects across the North and the South, with eleven effects similarly significant in both regions and only four significant in a single region. All but one of the significant predictors in the employment segregation and race-gender–typing set have consistent effects. In contrast to the other outcomes, this predictor set has greater predictive power in the North than in the South. Math skills, employment growth, and productivity all increase white women's earnings relative to white men's only in the South, while market power increases white women's relative earnings only in the North.

The regional differences in math skills and market power effects are intriguing. Contrary to how math skills consistently privilege the more-favored race-sex groups, higher math skill requirements in the South increase white women's earnings relative to white men's.[8] The market power effect is a bit more interesting. While market power consistently heightens employment access for less-favored race-sex groups (as we saw earlier in this chapter), it only selectively affects a few earnings ratios, as illustrated by how it increases white women's relative earnings in the North but not the South. This is partly in line with the social distance argument that southern employers with slack resources are more likely to express "tastes for discrimination" by maintaining social distance among race-sex groups (i.e., failing to equalize earnings gaps) rather than by creating physical distance among race-sex groups (i.e., increasing employment segregation).

Employment growth also affects queuing processes in the South and the North very differently, especially considering the earlier findings for employment segregation. In the South, growth significantly increases white women's relative earnings at all skill levels, but it increases their relative employment representation only in skilled jobs. This suggests that southern employers respond to shifts in employment demands by reducing gender pay gaps among whites at all skill levels as an incentive to avoid losing female employees to

Table 6.2 Summary of Results for the Analyses of Earnings Ratios by Region

Predictors	Black Women: White Men		Black Men: White Men		White Women: White Men		Black Women: Black Men		Black Women: White Women	
	North	South	North	South	North	South	North	South	North	South
General skill and growth										
Skill and training	+	+	+						+	+
Employment growth	+	+	+	−		+			−	+
Employment segregation										
Employment segregation	+	+	+	+	+	+			+	+
Black- or female-typed work										
Physical exertion	+		+		+ +	+ +	−	+	+	
Nurturant skill				−	+ +	+ +				
Physical dexterity	−	−	−	−	− −	− −				
Clerical perception	−	−	−	+						
Environmental conditions										
Routinization						+			+	−
White- or male-typed work										
Status in interaction	⊃	⊃	⊃	⊃	⊃	⊃				
Authority	−	−	−	−	−	−	−	−	−	−
Math skill	−	−	−	−		+			−	−
Desirable employment										
Sufficient work hours		+			+	+			+	+
Unemployment rate										−
Self-employment rate	−	−	−	−	−	−	−	−	−	−

continues

Table 6.2 continued

Predictors	Black Women: White Men North	Black Women: White Men South	Black Men: White Men North	Black Men: White Men South	White Women: White Men North	White Women: White Men South	Black Women: Black Men North	Black Women: Black Men South	Black Women: White Women North	Black Women: White Women South
Product market structure										
Market power	+			+	+					
Profitability										
Economic scale										
Capital intensity			+							
Foreign involvement										
Productivity						+				
Linkages to other actors										
Industry unionization	+		+		+	+			+	
Occupation unionization	+	+	+	+	+	+			+	+
Percent public sector							+	+		+
Federal purchases										

Notes: Shaded areas show regional differences in effects.
Table entries signify
+ Positive significant effect **—** Negative significant effect ∪ U shaped effect Blank No significant effect

better opportunities in a tighter labor market. And for jobs requiring long training times, southern employers also appear to open up access for white women
(and for black men as we saw earlier). In contrast, northern employers respond
by *increasing* the race pay gap among women, apparently as an incentive to
avoid losing white women from the (many) positions that they share with black
women (recall that there are very low levels of race employment segregation
among women).

Sex Earnings Gaps Among Blacks

Perhaps the most notable aspect of these results (as was true for the national results) is how poorly the base model predicts and explains the earnings gap between black women and black men. Only three measures have effects in both
the North and the South, and another three affect sex earnings gaps among
blacks in only one region. In the North both employment growth and physical
dexterity decrease black women's earnings relative to black men. There is a
parallel effect of employment growth on black women's earnings relative to
white women. One interpretation could be that northern employers respond to
employment growth in those jobs with many black women by creating incentives for black men and white women to stay, rather than creating incentives
for black women, who have more restricted alternative employment options. In
the South, nurturant skill increases black women's earnings relative to black
men. In contrast, nurturant skills increase earnings ratios for both black women
and white women relative to white men in both regions.

Race Earnings Gaps Among Men

This outcome shows considerable North-South differences in the base model effects. Only six predictors have similar (significant) effects in the North and the
South. Eleven more have effects that diverge in significance or sign between the
regions, with five significant only in the South and five significant only in the
North. What is most interesting and striking is that employment segregation
has opposite signed effects. This helps make sense of the national results, which
showed an unexpected negative effect of employment segregation on race earnings gaps among men but a positive effect on other earnings gaps. What we see
from the regional analyses is that the effect is positive in the North but negative
in the South. Thus, the northern effect parallels those on other earnings gaps. It
suggests that global devaluation lowers white men's earnings in "black men's
jobs" and the prospect that "differential treatment breeds differential treatment"
lowers black men's earnings in "white men's jobs," whereas in the South, the
negative effect might reflect a "glass escalator" effect. The fact that higher relative employment likelihoods for black men *decrease* their earnings relative to

white men could indicate that southern employers reward and privilege white men who are doing black men's work.

Among the set of race-gender–typing predictors, the white- or male-typed predictors all have significant and regionally invariant effects on men's race earnings gaps. But the black- or female-typed predictors have significant effects mainly in the South. Routinization increases earnings ratios (reduces gaps), indicative of devaluation, only in the South. The effects of dexterity and environmental conditions are negative only in the South, decreasing earnings ratios (increasing disparities). Although high dexterity is stereotypically associated with women's work, in the context of racial stereotypes (especially among men) low dexterity connotes black-typed work and high dexterity connotes white-typed work. Thus it affects racial earnings gaps as would a white-typed work trait by decreasing black men's earnings relative to white men's. Although poor environmental conditions are representative of black-typed work, it is the only work characteristic for which a compensating differentials hypothesis has been found to apply. A devaluation perspective would then suggest that it should benefit whites more than blacks, as it does. The fact that these are all significant only in the South bolsters the argument that racial stereotyping is more pronounced in the South than in the North.

The flip side of that argument is supported by the effects that are significant only in the North: skill, employment growth, nurturant skill, capital intensity, and industry unionization. For the most part, these effects represent processes that diminish disparities because they benefit the earnings of black men, rather than reduce gaps through devaluation processes. For example, the positive employment-growth effect suggests that northern employers respond to employment growth by using earnings as an incentive to maintain employment relationships with black men, as well as opening up access to highly skilled jobs (which the employment segregation analyses demonstrated). In contrast, faced with a tight labor market, southern employers appear to take analogous actions with respect to white women instead of black men. Similarly, industry unionization increases the relative earnings of black men in the North but not in the South. Both findings suggest less resistance to racial inclusiveness and equity in the North than in the South.

Race Earnings Gaps Among Women

Much like the results for men, there are more region-specific effects of the predictors on racial earnings gaps among women than there are uniform effects. Also similar is that most of the region-specific effects (five of seven) are for predictors representing devaluation processes: employment segregation or race- or gender-typed skills and conditions. Almost all of these devaluation predictors have effects only in the South; the sole exception is routinization's positive effect in the North. Employment segregation, authority, and math skills affect women's racial earnings gaps only in the South. The positive effect of segregation is consistent with global devaluation of black women's jobs and greater discrimination against black women in white women's jobs. In contrast, both authority and math skill (white-typed skills) diminish black women's relative earnings. These findings strengthen the implication from the analysis of racial gaps among men that stereotyping and devaluation are more pronounced in the South. While the positive industry unionization effect seen only in the North reinforces this conclusion, it is contradicted by the fact that employment growth has a negative effect solely in the North.

Race and Sex Gaps:
Black Women's Earnings Relative to White Men

The results for this double contrast of race and sex bear more similarity to those for race earnings gaps among men than they do for sex earnings gaps among either whites or blacks. Six predictors have the same signed and regionally invariant effects on both the earnings gap of black women versus white men and of black men versus white men. Of the six effects that do differ by region for black women versus white men, five also differ by region in the analyses of race earnings gaps among men (although not always in the same way). For both outcomes, dexterity has a negative effect in the South and unionization has a positive effect in the North. While employment segregation has a positive effect in the North on both earnings gaps, its effect in the South differs between the two outcomes. Both employment growth and market power have significant positive effects on both earnings gaps but in opposite regions. And, unlike the results for the race earnings gaps among men, there is no clear concentration of regional differences among sets of predictors.

Summary

Overall, these regional analyses indicate somewhat greater regional homogeneity in the processes affecting labor market inequality between women and men but somewhat greater regional diversity in the processes affecting labor market inequality between blacks and whites. In particular, there is considerable regional variation in the effects of the predictors on race employment segregation and earnings gaps among men, especially among the indicators of race-gender typing. The same is true to a lesser degree for race segregation and employment gaps among women. For example, physical exertion has a negative effect on the relative representation of women to men for all three sex-segregation outcomes in both the North and the South, but it has a positive effect on the relative representation of blacks to whites (among both men and women) only in the South, suggesting stronger racial stereotyping in the South than in the North.

Aside from this pattern, several other regional differences in employment segregation are especially interesting. The skill and growth effects suggest that northern employers respond to employment demand at all skill levels by opening up access to jobs only for black men; there is not a significant effect of growth on relative employment likelihoods for any other race-sex group. In contrast, southern employers respond to employment demand solely at the highest skill levels by opening up access to jobs for black men and white women, but not for black women. To me, the finding that southern employers appear to respond to employment demand only for the most skilled jobs implies a greater resistance to relaxing stereotypes in the South than in the North. Similarly, nurturant skill, a key gender-typing indicator, affects sex segregation among whites and among blacks only in the South, again suggesting stronger or more prevalent normative constraints or pressures.

The most interesting regional patterns in the race-sex earnings gaps are shown by the set of race- and gender-typed skills and conditions. At an abstract level, while the white- or male-typed work indicators have very consistent effects in both the North and the South, black- or female-typed work indicators reveal considerable regional variability. One interpretation could be that there is more regional uniformity in valuing white- or male-typed skills but less conformity between the North and the South in devaluing black- and female-typed skills. The results from the regional analyses of race earnings gaps, especially among men, showed this most clearly. In addition, these same analyses more broadly suggested that, in the North, race earnings gaps are affected primarily through processes that benefit the earnings levels of blacks and hence reduce earnings gaps. In contrast, in the South, race earnings gaps are affected predominantly either by processes that devalue the earnings levels of workers, thereby reducing race earnings gaps, or by those that privilege the earnings of whites, thus increasing race earnings gaps. As was the case for employment segregation, this suggests more inflexible and/or more widespread normative constraints in the South than in the North.

These results reinforce the importance of employment growth for understanding the results of queuing processes, especially in light of how employment growth affects segregation and earnings ratios for different race-sex groups. Southern employers apparently respond to excess employment demand in two ways: (1) by hiring white women and black men (but not black women) for skilled jobs; and (2) by increasing white women's and black women's earnings (but not black men's) relative to white men's at any skill level, perhaps as an incentive to avoid losing employees who might be most prone to seek better-paying jobs in a tighter labor market. In contrast, northern employers appear to respond to excess demand in three different ways: (1) by hiring black men for jobs at any skill level; (2) by increasing black men's earnings relative to *white men's;* and (3) by increasing black men's and white women's earnings relative to *black women's.* In either region, black women benefit the least from employment growth, implying that they are the group ranked the lowest in employers' race-sex queues, suggesting a double disadvantage of their race and gender statuses as a counterpart to the double privilege of white men's statuses.

Notes

1. I use "North" as a shorthand for the nonsouthern states of the United States. Although regional heterogeneity is likely within the North, I limited the comparison to South versus North for several reasons. Most important was a concern for sample sizes within labor market positions and their effects on robust estimation of segregation and earnings gaps among groups within a position. There are roughly equal numbers of blacks in the South and the North in the PUMS (Public Use Micro Samples) data, which means that region-specific estimates of the outcome measures should have similar reliabilities and robustness. Partitioning the North into additional regions would create unequal sample sizes of blacks across regions and consequently introduce regional differences into the reliability of the outcome measures.

2. For example, black women make up 19.1% of the labor force in the South but only 8.8% in the North in my 1990 PUMS sample. Similarly, black men are 13.8% of the labor force in the South but only 6.2% in the North.

3. The appendix table also reports results for the diagnostic tests for heteroskedasticity and correlated errors. The significant Lagrange multiplier (LM) statistics suggest that both error components (within industry sectors and within occupation segments) should be specified as part of the error structure. The significant Breusch-Pagan (BP) statistics for the initial error variance indicate heteroskedasticity by group size and by sector location. The BP statistics for the error variance adjusted for segment location are not significant in all the analyses. For group size, the BP statistics are not significant for eight of the ten analyses and are only marginally significant in the other two, suggesting that heteroskedasticity has been reasonably modeled in these analyses.

4. Capital intensity's effect suggests either that employers' stereotyping of factory work as a male domain is present (stronger) in the South but not in the North, or that women's aversion to factory work is more pronounced in the South than in the North.

5. According to the fundamental principles of queuing theory, queuing should operate to push the least preferred race-sex group into unemployment, more so than for other groups.

6. An alternative explanation to a broad regional effect could be that there are more traditional gender role expectations in rural areas and smaller communities, which are more prevalent in the South. However, the measurement of both employment segregation and earnings gaps do control for metropolitan versus nonmetropolitan residence (see Chapter 3 and Appendix B), which diminishes the applicability of this explanation.

7. The appendix table also reports results for the diagnostic tests for heteroskedasticity and correlated errors. The significant LM statistics suggest that both error components (within industry sectors and within occupation segments) should be specified as part of the error structure. The significant BP statistics for the initial error variance indicate heteroskedasticity by group size and sector location. The BP statistics for the error variance adjusted for segment location are not significant in all the analyses. For group size, the BP statistics are not significant for eight of the ten analyses and are only marginally significant in the other two, suggesting that heteroskedasticity has been reasonably modeled in these analyses.

8. Note that this could be a chance finding and thus should not be given too much weight. This is a standard problem of statistical inference. If the effect of math skill is in reality negative, there is a 64% probability that we would find at least one positive effect by pure random chance when making twenty independent tests (ten effects in the regional analyses of each employment segregation and earnings gaps).

7

Conclusion

Any road followed precisely to its end leads precisely nowhere.
Climb the mountain just a bit to test that it's a mountain.
From the top of the mountain, you cannot see the mountain.
—Frank Herbert (1965: 69)

I want to begin the ending of this endeavor by revisiting the two pairs of jobs discussed in the introductory chapter with the goal of better understanding the patterns of employment segregation and earnings gaps described there. I turn then to a more systematic appraisal of the contributions and implications of the integrated race-sex queuing perspective developed and empirically assessed in this book.

Recall that the jobs within each pair are similar in their general skill requirements but differ in their specific skill requirements, the types of work performed, and the social and economic contexts within which they are located. And despite the parallel overall skill levels within pairs (and adjusting for worker differences in their supply-side characteristics), the jobs differ markedly in the race-gender composition of their workers and in the earnings they receive. In the first pair, pressing machine operatives in laundries are disproportionately black women, and garbage collectors are disproportionately black men. Although pressers earn about half what garbage collectors do, white men in both jobs earn from 20% to 60% more than the other race-sex groups. In the other pair, nurses in hospitals are more likely to be white women, and pilots in air transport are more likely to be white men. There is a similar two-to-one disparity in between-job earnings, in favor of pilots. White men's earnings advantage in nursing is relatively modest (10% to 15%) but is quite substantial among pilots (30% to 200%). Keep in mind that these results rely upon statistical models that remove (control for) disparities due to variation among workers (and between race-sex groups) in their human capital, family characteristics, marital status, and geographic residence. For example, the earnings advantage of white men in these cases would average about 10% more without such controls.

163

Thus, while these supply-side factors are certainly important in explaining a share of labor market inequalities among race-sex groups, they don't help us understand the patterns just highlighted. It is also worth noting that comparing similarly gender-typed jobs (nurses to pressers and pilots to garbage collectors) shows that the jobs that are white typed earn about three times as much as those that are black typed.

If the full answer is not worker-level differences, what can explain these patterns? The findings discussed in Chapters 4 and 5 suggest that the operation of race-gender stereotyping and devaluation processes, as moderated by external pressures and internal resources, are of central importance. Consider first how these factors apply to the disproportionate representation of race-sex groups in these four jobs. Statistical discrimination and queuing would predict that the jobs in which African Americans and women are disproportionately located should be those with lower general skill and training levels, less desirable employment conditions, and task requirements stereotypically "appropriate" to their race and gender. But many of these effects could be muted by high levels of employment growth, profitability, or market power.

Why are black women employed disproportionately as pressing machine operatives in laundries? Corresponding to the queuing perspective's principles, this job has low levels of desirable employment conditions, making it a receiving position for members of race-sex groups ranked low in the labor queues for more desirable jobs. Furthermore, the low general skill but above-average physical dexterity task requirements make it stereotypically appropriate for black women, and the moderate employment decline means that a lack of such external pressure amplifies the skill effect. Black men are overrepresented among garbage collectors in sanitary services for much the same reasons. Higher-than-average unemployment makes it less desirable for race-sex groups ranked higher in labor queues. Low levels of skills and training (magnified by the declining employment growth) and routinized work make it a stereotypic fit for black workers, and a high level of physical exertion and a low level of physical dexterity make it further appropriate for black *men*.

The very different characteristics of registered nurses in hospitals and pilots in air transport can help to explain the disproportionate employment of white women as nurses and of white men as pilots. Both jobs have high general-skill requirements, which stereotypically favor the employment of whites over blacks. Because the positions have a low unemployment rate, the general race-sex ordering of the labor market queue makes these jobs receiving sites for members of more favored race-sex groups. Several of the specific skills requirements illustrate the stereotyping processes that gender these positions. In particular, the fact that nursing requires high nurturant skills and piloting requires high math skills defines the former as female appropriate and the latter as male appropriate.[1] External pressures and internal resources also play a role in producing the form of these positions' employment segregation. The stability of employment opportunities (little growth from 1980 to 1990) means that the general skills effect (favoring whites in both positions) and the math skills effect (favoring men in piloting) are not muted by external pressures to seek employees. Currently, the projected growth in demand for registered nurses in hospitals is expected to be much faster than average (Bureau of Labor Statistics 2009), which suggests that this job will become increasingly racially diverse.[2] However, the oligopolistic nature and above-average profitability of hospitals should continue to intensify the gendering effect of nurturant skills.

Turning to the ordering of earnings levels across these four positions (from pressers at the bottom to garbage collectors to nurses to pilots), two of the usual suspects, skill requirements and demand, are implicated. These jobs are similarly ordered by general skill and training levels and, with one minor switch, by employment growth, as they are by earnings. But race-sex devaluation processes are part of the story as well. In terms of global devaluation, comparisons among these jobs parallel the findings of Chapter 5 in which job-level earnings are lower for positions in which blacks or women are overrepresented. And many of the race- or gender-typed skilled contrasts among these positions are consistent with specific devaluation processes. Most notable are the positive payoffs to increasing math skills (pressers to garbage collectors to nurses to pilots) but the negative payoffs to nurturant skills (comparing nurses to pilots).

However, the theory and research you have just finished reading has more utility, I hope, than providing an explanation of the race and sex differences in employment and earnings in a few selected jobs. It is to such broader contributions that I turn next.

Implications for Theory and Research

I want to start by reiterating and then elaborating a simple but fundamental premise. Race and sex disparities in the labor market, as elsewhere in contemporary society, are structured and produced by both choice and constraint, and they reproduce, in part, preexisting inequalities that workers bring to the labor market. In this study of the patterning of these disparities across labor market positions, I extended past innovations in prior theory, research, and methodology and introduced new ones as well. I joined others in recognizing the importance of the intersection of race and sex in the creation of inequality by analyzing four race-sex groups: black women, black men, white women, and white men. Too many analyses still follow the practice of analyzing race groups (combining women and men) and sex groups (combining blacks and whites) separately.

The current literature is also characterized by a plethora of narrow models, which often fail empirically to take into account other perspectives. In Chapter 2, I developed a more comprehensive model of the employment segregation and earnings determination processes, which was tested in the empirical analyses in

Chapters 4, 5, and 6. This fuller model relied on my integration of segmented market theory and race-sex queuing theory. In this model, race and sex affect the ranking of workers in labor market queues in two distinct ways. First, as many scholars have argued, employers use "statistical discrimination" by race-sex group membership to screen out workers from many skilled positions based on real or *perceived* average intergroup differences (not individual differences) in productivity and trainability. Second, unlike past approaches, I argue that labor queues for *all* positions have distinctive orderings of race-sex groups that parallel the race- and gender-typed nature of the work performed. Consequently, all positions (not just highly skilled ones) have a race-sex–ordered labor queue that operates to allocate race-sex groups differentially into positions. Because of this segregation process, race-sex group members are located in jobs with very different job characteristics and earnings potential.

A logical and fundamental conclusion from this framework is that differentials in the allocation/queuing process should reproduce themselves as race-sex group disparities in earnings. The most obvious way in which this occurs is from structured variation in earnings corresponding to the differential job characteristics of race-sex group members, some share of which is due to their employment segregation. Much past research has also focused on what I labeled "global" devaluation processes in Chapter 2, whereby the sex or race composition of a job's incumbents devalues jobs performed primarily by women and minorities, and thus concomitantly values jobs held predominantly by white men. However, few studies have studied "specific" devaluation processes in which job skills and characteristics stereotypically labeled as female or minority produce negative or no earnings returns while those labeled as male or white are positively valued. The results presented in Chapter 5 represent the most systematic evaluation to date of both global and specific devaluation.

In methodological terms, this research provides generalizable results through its analysis of nationally representative samples of workers across the full range of labor market positions. Many prior studies have been limited by their use of case studies, geographically limited samples, or restricted sets of jobs. Equally important is that past research at the position level has typically either failed to control for worker-level factors or has committed an ecological fallacy by using aggregate controls (e.g., occupation-level mean education). I developed a superior measurement strategy (detailed in Chapter 3) to calculate position-level disparities among race-sex groups by applying a two-step, multilevel procedure to control properly for worker-level factors. I also employed a unique schema to categorize labor market segments and positions. Unlike past classifications, my definition of positions embodied the race- and sex-segregated contours of the labor market by using race- and gender-typed task requirements to define positions rather than a circular definition based upon the observed race or sex composition of positions.

Rather than attempting to summarize the multitude of findings from the sets of models presented and discussed in Chapters 4 through 6, I focus instead on the implications of those analyses. In the next section, I consider their significance for a variety of theoretical perspectives and for future research. I turn next to their import for public policy.

Employment Segregation Results

In earlier chapters, I discussed the findings from three models of employment segregation: (1) a base model that includes five sets of predictors (skill and growth, desirable employment, race-gender typing, product market structure, and linkages to other actors) and used initially to assess the utility of my integrated perspective vis-à-vis a variety of prior, more narrow perspectives; (2) an extended model, also in Chapter 4, to explore the moderating effects of external pressures and internal resources; and (3) a regional model, in Chapter 6, to consider the moderating effects of the varying social contexts between the southern and northern regions of the United States.[3]

How well do the product market structure demand-side perspectives and the skill deficits and worker preferences supply-side approaches perform as explanations of employment segregation, relative to the integrated race-sex queuing perspective? The alternative approaches are applicable in, at best, a piecemeal fashion and have only a varying degree of correspondence with the results from the base model. The *product market structure* perspectives (Becker's theory of discrimination and segmented markets theory) are pertinent to only a few predictors, and about the same number of empirical findings supported them as contradicted them. Perhaps the most central prediction of these theories, that discrimination occurs in economic arenas buffered from market forces, was the opposite of the actual effects of market power and profitability. For unionization, the findings are equivocal inasmuch as unionization reduces racial employment segregation but increases sex segregation. (In contrast, unionization uniformly reduces earnings gaps.) A *skill deficits* approach has slightly more, yet still limited, relevance to the full range of predictors, and it did largely accord with the findings for those few predictors to which it applied. However, several "female" skill indicators had effects on race segregation that could not credibly be explained by skill deficits.

The *worker preferences* interpretation applies somewhat more broadly and was also consistent with many of the empirical findings. In particular, it is a competing explanation with the race-sex queuing perspective for many of the gender-typing effects on the sex segregation outcomes. Yet almost all of these also affect race segregation, which cannot plausibly be attributed to preferences, and some have an opposite effect on the representation of black men (physical exertion and dexterity) than on the representation of women. Moreover, several effects contradict the preference approach, and it is not relevant to the explanation of some key results, such as the effects of general skill and employment growth. As I argued earlier, the plausibility of the preferences explanation relies on limited empirical evidence of actual sex differences in work values and preferences and in how these affect job choice. In fact, many scholars argue that such preferences reflect the effect of *past* market discrimination (e.g., Marini 1989; Reskin 1993). In sum, not only is the *race-sex queuing* perspective more widely applicable than the other approaches to the full set of predictors, but, aside from a few anomalies, the findings from the base model are consistent with nearly all of its expectations. In particular, the interactive effects of general skill with employment growth can be fully explained only by this approach.

The base model results also demonstrate the value of paying attention to the interplay between race and sex in the creation of employment segregation in several ways. Only one-third of the predictors affects both race and sex segregation in the same way. Another third affects both race and sex representation but with opposite-signed effects, and the remaining third affects either race or sex segregation but not both. And, despite a highly similar pattern of findings for the employment segregation of black women and of white women, each contrasted to white men, the analysis of the employment representation of black women relative to white women revealed some key differences that do not simply reflect a uniform process of racial segregation among men and women. Most importantly, unlike the case for all other race or sex comparisons, the negative effect of general skill (reducing the relative representation of black women) is not moderated and muted by employment growth nor does employment growth itself have a significant effect in opening up employment opportunities. From a queuing perspective, this implies that when employment demand lessens the salience of employers' preferences for a race-sex ordering of workers in the labor queue, it may do so more for black men and white women than it does for black women.

The results from the extended model illustrated the crucial moderating role of external pressures and internal resources on race and sex employment segregation. Employment pressures (growth) typically diminished the effects of race-gender typing on segregation, resulting in a greater representation of the race-sex group "less preferred" for the race-gender type of the position. The results also provided considerable support for the view that, in recent times, employers used slack resources to increase access to employment by blacks and women, although in a few instances market power and profitability intensified race-gender typing. The moderating role of profitability was limited to gender typing and sex segregation. But market power consistently muted the effects of race-gender–typed indicators, thereby increasing the relative representation of women to men or of blacks to whites. These findings should be a convincing demonstration of the fundamental way in which the race-sex ordering principle of a position's labor queue can be partially overridden by external pressures and internal resources.

Similarly, the regional analyses made evident how social context can moderate employment segregation processes. The results showed somewhat greater regional diversity in the process affecting the employment segregation of blacks from whites than of women from men. This was especially true for the effects of the race-gender–typing indicators on race segregation among men. In addition, the finding that southern employers appear to respond to employment demand pressures only for the most skilled jobs implies both stronger normative constraints and a greater resistance to relaxing stereotypes in the South than in the North.

Results from the Analyses of Earnings Levels and Earnings Gaps

The major focus of the earnings and earnings disparities analyses was an assessment of devaluation processes whereby work settings that are stereotypically associated with blacks and women "equalize" earnings ratios by how they devalue earnings among race-sex groups. In Chapter 2, I drew a distinction between global and specific devaluation processes. I defined "global" devaluation as a mechanism through which the presence in a position of women and minorities in large numbers leads to lower remuneration for all workers in the position and correspondingly reduces inequality within the position. In contrast, "specific" devaluation refers to processes that either devalue the rewards for skills and tasks that are stereotypically black or female "appropriate" or positively value those skills and tasks that are stereotypically white or male "appropriate." In either case, I expected the devaluing effects on earnings to be greater for whites and men, leading to the prediction that devalued skills would decrease earnings gaps but that valued skills would increase earnings gaps among race-sex groups.

To study these processes, I analyzed position-level earnings and earnings gaps and detailed the findings from three models in earlier chapters: (1) base models, in Chapter 5, analyzing both group-specific earnings levels and between-group earnings gaps with five sets of predictors (skill and growth, global and specific devaluation, desirable employment, product market structure, and linkages to other actors); (2) an extended model of earnings gaps, also in Chapter 5, to examine the moderating effects of external pressures and internal resources; and (3) a regional model of earnings gaps, in Chapter 6, to assess the moderating effects of the differing social contexts of the North and the South.

The results from the base models for earnings levels and earnings gaps provided strong evidence for the operation of devaluation processes. In global terms, the degree of employment segregation systematically reduced the earnings paid to workers. A greater concentration of women affected the earnings of all race-sex groups to slightly varying degrees but a higher representation of blacks diminished only the earnings of white men. Not surprisingly, findings from the earnings gap analyses largely parallel these effects. A disproportionately high representation of women and blacks reduced earnings ratios ("equalized" earnings), with the notable and puzzling exception of the racial earnings gaps among men.[4] Taken together, these results consistently support the argument that the segregation and crowding of women and blacks into a job narrowed earnings inequality within that job.

In addition to supporting the global devaluation expectations, the results painted a complex picture of how specific devaluation processes work, resulting in overall support for this perspective. In terms of earnings levels, two indicators of black- or female-typed work consistently depressed earnings (more so for men than women and for blacks than whites). Two others had effects that varied by race-sex group and by the degree and kind of sex segregation; men received payoffs to these two skills but women either did not or did so only if they worked in male-dominated jobs. In contrast, four white- and male-typed skills and requirements systematically enhanced earnings, although only two of them consistently worked more to the advantage of whites over blacks and of men over women. Traditional indicators of power in product and labor markets had the expected positive effects on earnings in almost every case. And the patterns of differential payoffs across race-sex groups predominantly favored women over men and blacks over whites, consistent with the specific devaluation argument. These patterns of positive versus negative payoffs to race-gender–typed work settings, as well as how the returns vary across race-sex groups, demonstrate that specific devaluation processes are certainly an important generator of average earnings differences among race-sex groups across the entire labor market.

The other side of the coin is how these processes affect earnings disparities within positions. The results from the base model similarly reveal an intricate relationship between specific devaluation indicators and earnings gaps between groups. Four of the race-gender–typing indicators have the expected devaluing (valuing) effect of decreasing (increasing) earnings gaps. But two female-typed skills increased earnings inequality, consistent with the earnings-level findings that these skills are rewarded for men but not for women or benefit women only in male-dominated positions. Given the logical and empirical connection between race-sex group earnings levels and earnings gaps, it should be no surprise that the analyses also supported the argument that devaluation processes are important for understanding earnings disparities. These findings illustrate that devaluation is not just due to a concentration of women and blacks in a position creating lower earnings and less between-group inequality, although such global devaluation is clearly important. Nor is it invariably an elementary mechanism in which black- or female-typed skills and settings devalue earnings and consequently reduce earning gaps and in which white- or male-typed skills and settings are positively valued and exacerbate earnings disparities. The reality is that specific devaluation can also occur if men are rewarded for female-typed skills whereas women are not rewarded or are even penalized. And, contrary to the devaluation perspective, in a few situations the earnings of whites (men) actually benefit less from employment in earnings-enhancing settings than do members of other race-sex groups.

The extended model results emphasize the moderating role of external pressures and internal resources and suggest another layer of complexity in the operation of devaluation processes. On the one hand, employment pressures, market power, and profitability almost uniformly minimize disparities in earnings between white men and the other race-sex groups in most (but not quite all) race-gender–typed settings. On the other hand, they are not a panacea, as revealed by how they temper the effects of race-gender–typed skills and settings on earnings gaps. Employment growth and market power mute the effects of some specific devaluation processes, while amplifying the effects of others. Profitability does consistently diminish the impact of devaluation processes on both race and sex earnings gaps in positions with white- or male-typed skills and requirements.

Taken together with the results for employment segregation, these findings seriously challenge neoclassical economic theory's contention that discrimination can only persist in those parts of the economy buffered from market forces, such as unionized labor markets and oligopolistic product markets. Unionization has mixed effects on employment segregation, but it consistently lessens earnings disparities, suggesting that nonunion settings are more prone to discrimination, especially in earnings. More importantly, market power uniformly reduces both employment segregation and earnings gaps. On the one hand, market power should increase the salience of employers' preferences for race-sex groups in the labor queue (whatever they are). But on the other hand, it provides resources that can be used to respond to external pressures from the government and citizens' groups or to changes in public opinion on racial and sexual egalitarianism. As I suggest in discussing policy implications later, this highlights the need for public policy that creates a proactive legal environment.

The social context of regions also had a moderating effect on devaluation processes. The results demonstrated a fair degree of regional homogeneity in the processes affecting earnings inequality between women and men but regional diversity in the processes generating disparities between blacks and whites. In particular, the race-gender–typing indicators exhibited considerable regional variation in how they affected racial earnings gaps, especially among men. Although the white- or male-typed work indicators had consistent effects in both the North and the South, the black- or female-typed work indicators did not. This might indicate more regional uniformity in positively valuing white- or male-typed skills but less conformity between the North and the South in devaluing black- and female-typed skills. As was the case for employment segregation, this suggests more inflexible and/or more widespread normative constraints in the South than in the North.

The North versus South analyses further highlighted the central role of employment growth in queuing processes, taking into consideration how growth affected both segregation and earnings gaps among race-sex groups. In reaction to employment pressures, southern employers appeared to adopt two strategies: (1) hiring white women and black men (but not black women) for skilled jobs;

and/or (2) increasing earnings for white women and black women (but not black men) relative to white men's at any skill level, possibly as an incentive to minimize turnover of those employees most likely to look for better-paying jobs in a tight market. In contrast, northern employers apparently used very different approaches: (1) hiring black men for jobs at any skill level; (2) increasing black men's earnings relative to *white men's;* and (3) increasing black men's and white women's earnings relative to *black women's.* Thus, in both regions, black women gained the least from employment growth. In queuing terms, this suggests that they were the group ranked at the bottom in employers' race-sex queue, suggesting a double "disadvantage" of their race and sex statuses.

Suggestions for Future Research

Perhaps the most obvious avenue for future research would be determining whether the patterns of findings summarized above have varied over time. It is an open question, for example, whether or not the effects of market power and profitability on employment segregation and earnings disparities among race-sex groups have been constant over time, given how they depend in part on incentives generated by governmental and public pressures for more egalitarian employment processes. Similarly, much of the theoretical innovation and novel findings revolve around the connections between labor market inequality and stereotypic work task requirements and work settings. The regional analyses suggested that varying social contexts and normative structures moderate these relationships. Longitudinal analyses could explore whether or not changes toward egalitarian racial and sexual beliefs and roles throughout society more broadly have had a corresponding effect in diminishing the importance of stereotyping and the devaluation of race- and gender-typed work tasks.

But the most important direction for future research would be generalizable studies documenting the existence of and beliefs about assumed differences in specific skills and working conditions among race-sex groups. I would argue that the plausibility of *each* perspective discussed here (including my own) depends on a weak empirical underpinning, with little representative evidence, concerning these issues. The skill deficits approach assumes that race-sex groups differ in specific skills; the preference approach presumes sex differences in preferences for specific skills and working conditions; and the stereotyping and queuing and devaluation approaches assume employer stereotyping of specific skills and working conditions with relatively small group differences in preferences.

A literature search yielded virtually no research on these issues using representative samples; convenience samples, typically of students, were the norm. The sole exceptions were studies on differences in math skills among groups, which show a continuing advantage for whites but a declining and now small one for men (e.g., Barres 2006; Jaynes and Williams 1989; Leahey and Guo 2001; Muller 1998), and on sex differences in preferences for part-time work, which showed higher voluntary part-time employment for women (e.g., Nardone 1995). There is scant evidence that personality, taste, or value differences among workers affect sex differences in the jobs they are given (Barry 1987; Filer 1986; Glass and Camarigg 1992; Padavic 1991). Filer (1986: 423), for example, concludes from an analysis of a single firm that

> In general, the small magnitude of the changes in the estimated coefficients [*for race and sex*] when personalities and tastes are incorporated into the analysis suggests that their importance lies primarily in providing additional information rather than in correcting the possible biases [*in how race and sex affect job choice*] discussed above.

Thus, to assess the plausibility of these explanations, we need new, generalizable data to document the presence or absence of: (1) sex differences in preferences for specific skills and working conditions; (2) disparities among race-sex groups in their possession of specific skills; (3) employer beliefs about such group differences in preferences and skills; (4) widespread employer stereotypes about the race- or gender-typed nature of specific skills and working conditions. Studying some aspects of employer beliefs and stereotypes is challenging given that social desirability effects tend to limit the expression of biases during interviews (Babbie 2008: 277). But this could be accomplished using a variant of the Implicit Association Test methodology (https://implicit .harvard.edu/implicit/).

Moreover, beyond establishing (or disputing) the existence of such preferences, beliefs, and stereotypes, we need more studies examining how organizational practices and environments enable or hinder employers and supervisors from acting on their beliefs and stereotypes. This should extend beyond the more macro moderating factors I studied (growth, market power, and profitability) to include, for example, formalization of human resources processes, staffing and recruitment methods, hiring/promoting agent discretion, regulatory/ monitoring oversight, collective bargaining provisions, grievance procedures, and criminal background screening.

New research also is needed to empirically disentangle the broadly confounded effects of preference and stereotyping on sex segregation and the more narrowly confounded effects of skill deficits and stereotyping on race segregation. Ideally, the data should be longitudinal and generalizable; cover a range of ages and racial/ethnic groups; contain detailed information on qualifications, preferences for specific skills and working conditions, and work and family histories; and have a sample size sufficient both to define and analyze detailed positions and to extend the analyses beyond black-white differences to include comparisons with and among other racial/ethnic groups. Although existing data offer some of these features, none suffices for a definitive resolution.

I also see the value of work to follow up on three intriguing findings. First, I found that there were skills (i.e., physical dexterity and clerical perception) for which men are rewarded for female-typed skills, while women are either not rewarded or are even penalized, depending on the kind of sex segregation in the position.[5] There was some indication of a glass escalator for men in female-dominated jobs and of a payoff for such skills only if they were in male-dominated jobs. In addition to trying to replicate these results with recent, broad-based data, it would be worthwhile to select for in-depth case studies (like those in Reskin and Roos 1990) a subset of jobs matched on dexterity or clerical perception but with varied gender typing to uncover the mechanisms through which this occurs. This may well require rethinking the devaluation perspective to encompass the concept that male-typed skills are universally rewarded while some female-typed skills are valued (especially for men) only in male settings.

Second, I suggested that the explanation for the effects of employment growth is that it opens up opportunities and suppresses race-gender–typing effects. I can envision several different ways of exploring this further. I would find it fascinating to select for a cohort study a variety of differing race-gender–typed jobs that have experienced recent fast growth or decline. This would document the changing race-sex composition of the jobs and determine which groups first gain (or lose) access to employment in the jobs, as well as how that priority varies with the kind of race-gender typing exhibited and by geographic locale. Another approach would be to contrast the employment segregation and earnings disparities of the same occupations in growing versus declining industries to test the expectation of persisting differentials in the face of decline but diminishing disparities when growth is high. A variant could be to study new versus established companies in the same (growing) industry, coupled with in-depth interviews with hiring agents in the companies to probe their beliefs and hiring processes.

Third, the broad-brush regional analyses in the last chapter suggested more inflexible and/or more widespread normative constraints in the South than in the North. Multilevel modeling of local labor markets would be an ideal way to study the relationship between social context and labor market inequality, perhaps combining census data on workers with measures of normative beliefs in local areas. The latter possibly could be derived from existing public opinion polls, specially commissioned brief surveys, or content analysis of local newspapers and other media.

I would also recommend an expanded use of audit studies and related methodologies, which I consider a valuable but underutilized approach. As I argued in Chapter 1, these provide perhaps the clearest and most convincing evidence of the continuing status-based differential treatment by employers of job candidates. But for this to be worthwhile, they would need to be extended along multiple dimensions, each involving unique challenges. The existing employment audit studies have been concentrated regionally in a bare handful of large metropolitan areas, making their generalizability suspect. Thus, a crucially important extension, as others have recommended (see Fix and Struyk 1993:

44), would be to conduct simultaneous audit studies across a nationally representative sample of labor market locales. Similar to Bendik's (2007) suggestions, a second pair of extensions would be particularly valuable even if restricted to a few geographic locales. One would be to assess race by sex effects and to compare these among multiple racial/ethnic groups (i.e., more than just black-white pairs or Hispanic-Anglo pairs) in the same local market. Lastly, audit studies have been limited almost exclusively to relatively low-skilled entry-level jobs identified from newspaper want ads. An obvious but difficult extension would be to incorporate a wider range of types of positions and to positions advertised and recruited through other sources. One of the challenges is the identification of a representative sample of employers (nationwide or even within a single market). However, methodologies for drawing representative samples of organizations do exist (Parcel, Kaufman, and Jolly 1991), such as that used for the National Organization Studies (Kalleberg et al. 1991; Smith, Kalleberg, and Marsden 2002). A sampling frame for larger establishments can be derived from the required filing of EEO-1 reports by establishments with one hundred or more employees as other have done (Hirsh 2009; Kalev, Dobbin, and Kelly 2006; Robinson et al. 2005).

The race-sex queuing perspective I developed and applied to employment segregation and earnings gaps should also have utility for studying other aspects of labor market inequality. Consider, for example, the long-term persistence and relative invariance over time of racial differences in unemployment, underemployment, and employment discouragement (inability ever to find a job). The unemployment rate for blacks, for example, has been virtually constant at twice the unemployment rate for whites for the last forty years (Council of Economic Advisers 1998). And since the middle 1980s, indicators of employment discouragement for young adults suggest a similar two-to-one ratio of discouragement for black males compared to white males and of at least one and a half to one (often higher) for black females compared to white females (Council of Economic Advisers 1998). According to data used in my analyses, the lion's share of employment in 1990 (nearly 75%) was in positions that were normatively typed as either "white" or "neutral" (no clear typing) according to the stereotyping characteristics discussed earlier. Thus, three-fourths of the positions had labor queues for which preferential evaluation of whites over blacks is likely to occur. Being ranked in the bottom of the labor queue can explain both why blacks are more likely than whites to be discouraged workers unable to secure job offers and why blacks are more likely than whites to become unemployed.

Finally, future research should pay continued attention to the intersection of race and sex. The results from the analyses of sex segregation among blacks closely paralleled those for sex segregation among whites, but there was much less similarity in the analyses of race segregation within the sexes. There was an analogous pattern in the earnings gaps analyses, with an even greater divergence in the process generating black-white earnings disparities within sexes than was the case for segregation. In addition, the regional analyses suggested that northern and southern employers treat race-sex groups intersectionally in response to employment growth. For example, northern employers increase black men's and white women's earnings relative to black women's, while southern employers increase white women's and black women's earnings (but not black men's) relative to white men's. These patterns, and the fact that the models are generally less predictive of racial inequality among women than of the other outcomes, indicate the need to further broaden not only possible predictors but also theory about the determinants of labor market inequality.

At the same time, I would strongly advocate moving beyond a key limitation of my work on black-white disparities to study queuing, stereotyping, and devaluation processes for Hispanics, Asians, and Native Americans. To do this properly requires rejecting pan-ethnic categorizations of Hispanic and Asian groups and recognizing that the history and treatment in the United States of Mexican Americans differs from that of Cuban Americans, of Puerto Ricans, and so on, just as it differs among Japanese Americans, Chinese Americans, Filipinos, and other Asian groups. Their inclusion would provide an opportunity to validate (or falsify) the theoretical expectations developed in Chapter 2 against a wider variety of situations. In queuing terms, I would expect such analyses to reveal a racial hierarchy with blacks at the bottom, followed by most Hispanic groups, and then most Asians, with whites occupying the most favored position (see Reskin, Hargens, and Hirsh's [2004] analyses of sixty detailed sex–race/ethnic groups).

While I would expect the same processes to be operable, some differential expectations would also be necessary. For example, the details of how jobs are "race/ethnic–typed" would vary for these groups in line with differences in how the groups are stereotyped in the United States. A devaluation perspective would suggest that some race/ethic–typed skills would be considered "natural" for groups and hence less rewarded. Along these lines, it would be interesting to determine the effects of a job's math skill requirements on the earnings of, say, Japanese Americans and Chinese Americans and its effect on the earnings gap between them and whites. Moreover, given the varying geographic concentration of racial/ethnic groups, I would anticipate considerable regional variation in the queuing and stereotyping processes. Groups more in the middle of queues for jobs in some locales may well be at the bottom of the queue for the same job in other locales due to the absence of less-favored groups, or they could be closer to the top of the queue when more-favored groups are absent. From a modeling standpoint, this suggests the need for analyses at a much more fine-grained level of geography that can incorporate the presence and size of other groups in local labor markets. Finally, the continuing immigration of and varying characteristics of migrants across racial/ethnic groups introduces additional complexity in trying to understand and predict the location of racial/ethnic groups in the labor queue. It is an intriguing question as to how the presence of immigrants affects queuing and employers' perceptions of particular groups. Do immigrants "push" nonimmigrant members of a group further up in the queue by providing a less-favored group or does an immigrant presence intensify stereotyping and statistical discrimination and drag nonimmigrants further down in the queue?

Implications for Public Policy

By highlighting the systematic, structural, and persistent nature of employment segregation and earnings disparities by race and sex, this research demonstrates the continuing need for legal remedies focused on hiring, job transfer, promotion, and wage-setting practices. Antidiscrimination statutes, while obviously important and necessary, are insufficient. As Reskin (1998: 6) summarizes in her definitive compendium of research on affirmative action, "[because] much discrimination results from employers doing business as usual, it requires employers to do more than refrain from actively discriminating—it entails proactive efforts to promote equal employment opportunities for groups traditionally subject to employment discrimination."

I have in mind the kind of process-driven rather than outcome-driven approaches distinguished by Reskin (1998). On the one hand, there are many strategies that employers can voluntarily pursue, recognizing that successful implementation requires procedural fairness and that "[b]oth the intended beneficiaries of affirmative action and workers not targeted by it stand to gain from fair personnel procedures" (p. 63). Such strategies include: (1) formalization of hiring, transfer, promotion, and wage determination processes with well-publicized internal grievance procedures to ensure fairness; (2) involved leadership providing not only public/moral commitment but also the establishment of organizational structures to set and monitor goals and achievements; and (3) the active use of sanctions and incentives to motivate change agents. Kalev, Dobbin, and Kelly's (2006) analysis of best practices demonstrates that establishing managerial responsibility for compliance heightens the effectiveness of other practices.

However, given the systemic nature of queuing and devaluation processes, reliance solely on voluntary programs by employers is insufficient. In fact, the existence of formal mechanisms in some instances may do more to provide legal cover for "business as usual" than to promote change (Hirsh 2008; Hirsh and Kornich 2008). Thus, external pressures and a proactive enforcement climate are also crucial to reduce disparities (Hirsh 2009; Hirsh and Kornich 2008; Reskin 1998). The results of my analyses indicate the roles played by external pressures and internal resources, both in directly affecting labor market inequality and in moderating the effects of other processes (especially stereotyping processes) that affect segregation and earnings disparities. Curiously, it appears that indirect pressure in a firm's legal environment (proactive enforcement) is in some ways more effective than direct pressure. Hirsh (2009) finds that discrimination charges by the Equal Employment Opportunity Commission against a particular establishment do not affect its workplace segregation whereas such charges against other establishments in an organizational field do reduce segregation in the field as a whole. Consequently, highly visible actions that signal to firms that there is a societal and legal system commitment to effective enforcement, such as the Lilly Ledbetter Fair Pay Act of 2009, should be a continuing legislative priority.[6]

These findings also have implications for the effectiveness of market-based incentives, such as increased competition or job growth, for reducing discrimination. Contrary to neoclassical economic theory (Arrow 1972, 1973; Becker 1971; Cain 1975), competition per se does *not* diminish labor market inequality in terms of either employment segregation or earnings gaps. Indeed, the opposite held true. Increasing market power was predictive of a greater relative representation of women and blacks in positions and of smaller race and sex earnings gaps within jobs. Moreover, the effects of race-gender–typed skills and requirements on employment segregation were uniformly muted in the presence of high levels of market power. For earnings gaps, market power had a less consistent effect, reducing some race-gender–typing effects but increasing others. This suggests that public policy cannot rely upon economic competition in place of regulation and monitoring to combat discrimination.

In addition to the effects of market power, several findings bolster Reskin's (1998) conclusion that favorable economic conditions foster favorable opportunities for reducing discrimination. Both employment growth and higher profitability increased the representation of women and blacks in jobs and reduced race-sex earnings disparities within positions. Although employment growth had mixed success in muting race-gender–typing effects on earnings gaps, profitability did so consistently. Moreover, both employment growth and profitability invariably dampened the effects of race-gender–typed skills and requirements on employment segregation. The bottom line is that public policies that stimulate economic growth, but not necessarily those fostering competition, are good for employers and for all workers, regardless of race or sex.

Finally, these findings could be useful to federal agencies (such as the Equal Employment Opportunity Commission and Office of Federal Contract Compliance) as well as corresponding state agencies in targeting both their enforcement efforts and policy responses (e.g., EEO training, diversity education, affirmative action, comparable worth studies, etc.). Although my broad regional analyses certainly indicate the need for closer monitoring and visible use of sanctions in the South, I would suggest that a more fine-grained analysis of geographic differences would be essential to direct enforcement resources efficiently. In addition, the results can help identify the specific types of positions (in terms of task requirements, working conditions, product market characteristics, etc.) in which segregation and earnings disparities are likely to be greatest. For example, the evidence of strong and consistent effects of global devaluation on earnings levels as well as earnings gaps suggests the need to look closely at wage setting processes in jobs with either very high or very low concentrations of women and minorities. I would also recommend a more active monitoring (and advocacy) role on the part of the EEOC or other federal entities as a means to establish an effective enforcement climate, both to discourage overt and covert discriminatory practices as well as to encourage voluntary employer efforts. In particular, the deployment of recurring, nationally representative hiring audit studies (as proposed earlier) coupled with prominent media coverage of their findings could significantly impact the enforcement climate by signaling public commitment to and concern for the reduction of labor market discrimination.

Notes

1. High clerical perception and dexterity requirements for both jobs play a less consistent role in explaining these patterns. On the one hand, they accurately predict that women should be overrepresented in nursing. But overrepresentation of men in piloting runs counter to this prediction, in large part due to the strong effect of math skills defining the position as male appropriate.

2. According to the Bureau of Labor Statistics data, demand will even be high for registered nurses outside of the hospital setting, which could magnify the growth effect as hospitals are one of the higher paying work settings for nurses.

3. As in Chapter 6, I use "northern" as a rhetorical shorthand to refer to the non-southern regions of the country that are compared to the southern region.

4. I speculated in Chapter 5 that this could indicate the operation of a "glass escalator," privileging white men employed in positions with high concentrations of black men.

5. Physical dexterity uniformly increases earnings for men. For women dexterity has a positive effect on earnings for women in positions in which men are overrepresented, but has a negative effect when women are overrepresented. Clerical perception provides no payoff for women. For black men it always enhances earnings. For white men, it is rewarded only in jobs in which women are overrepresented but devalues their earnings in jobs in which men are overrepresented.

6. This act responded to a recent Supreme Court ruling in *Ledbetter v. Goodyear Tire & Rubber Co., Inc.* (2007, No. 05-1074) that very narrowly interpreted the meaning of the 180-day limit for filing workplace discrimination claims. In the majority's opinion, the clock started from the date of the commission of the discriminatory act (e.g., the decision to set a lower salary), even when the employee did not then realize that action was discriminatory and even if the effects of that act persisted through the point at which the discrimination became apparent and a claim was filed. As the dissenting opinion noted, this "overlooks common characteristics of pay discrimination," including the lack of transparency of wage setting in most workplaces, the time needed for an employee to become aware that discrimination is taking place, and the persistent and compounding effect of disparities in base pay when increases are routinely given on a percentage basis. Such a strict construction of the meaning of the time limit effectively removed sanctions from applying to the employer for any form of employment discrimination, but especially

for pay discrimination. And it had the potential not just to fail to discourage labor market discrimination but also to provide a strong financial incentive to employers to discriminate. The Fair Pay Act amended current law to restart the 180-day limit within which to file a complaint with the issuance of each new paycheck that contains in part or in whole discriminatory pay resulting from prior actions or decisions.

Appendix A
Supplementary Details on Data and Methods

Appendix A provides additional information on the data and methods used in this study. It is not intended to be read alone, but rather should be read as a supplement offering more details and technical material. As such, it is organized with the same headings and subheadings as Chapter 3 to facilitate finding the additional details for each section.

Defining Labor Market Positions

Occupational Segments

As shown in Table 3.1 of Chapter 3, I defined forty-two occupational segments distinguished according to three criteria: classifying first by types of skill, then by level of skill, and finally by potential race and gender stereotyping. The first distinction uses four categories of the general types of skill required. Although the identification of skills for working with data, people, or things as separate dimensions of skill is fundamental to work on skill definition (Form 1987; Spenner 1990; Steinberg 1990), these dimensions empirically cluster in limited combinations. Thus I group occupations into four categories corresponding to skills for working with: (1) only things; (2) both people and things; (3) both people and data; and (4) both data and things. *Within skill types,* I classify occupations as requiring low, medium, or high levels of general skills and training. This criterion figures prominently in sociological and economic explanations of stratification and earnings (Becker 1975; Doeringer and Piore 1971; England 1992; Form 1987; Marini 1989; Spenner 1990). *Within skill types and levels,* I distinguish occupations by whether or not the work task requirements or working conditions create the potential for race typing and/or the potential for gender typing of the position. This ensures that critical boundaries for possible race and sex segregation between positions are maintained. I used the tasks and working conditions hypothesized to create race typing (Chapter 2) to define three categories of the potential for race typing: (1) black typed—if the occupation required low skill, routine work, heavy physical exertion, extreme environmental conditions, or subordinate/subservient interactions with others; (2) white typed—if the occupation required the exercise of authority, high skill, or status-superior interactions with others; (3) not clearly race typed—if it was neither black nor white typed, or if it had mixed typing. Analogously, I used the tasks and working conditions hypothesized to create gender typing to define three categories of the potential for gender typing: (1) female typed—if the occupation required physical dexterity, clerical perception, nurturant skills, or subordinate/subservient interactions with others; (2) male typed—if the occupation required the exercise of authority, heavy physical exertion, extreme environmental conditions, or mathematical skills; (3) not clearly gender typed—if it was neither female nor male typed or if it had mixed typing.

This classification system could define up to one-hundred-eight occupational segments: [four skill types] × [three skill levels] × [three race types] × [three gender types]. But not all combinations of race typing and skill level are logically possible. By definition, all low skill combinations are typed as black appropriate (removing twenty-four combinations) and all high skill positions are typed as white appropriate (removing another twenty-four combinations). Of the sixty remaining possible combinations, I actually found only the forty-two segments listed in Table 3.1. Appendix Table A.3 (located at the end of this appendix) presents the occupational segment classification for all 503 occupations as well as their 1990 Census Occupation Codes.[1]

Industrial Sectors

To define the twenty industrial sectors listed in Table 3.2, I grouped together industries that are relatively homogeneous in terms of their product type, market scope, market power, and economic scale. I first classified industries using Browning and Singelmann's (1978) definition of broad product types: (1) extractive, (2) transformative, (3) distributive services, (4) producer services, (5) social services, and (6) personal services. This schema has been widely used in labor market analyses, including those of race/ethnic and sex differences (Lyson 1991; Nelson 1994; Saenz and Vinas 1990; Tienda, Smith, and Ortiz 1987; Wynn and Mueller 1998). *Within product type,* I sorted industries into three categories according to the scope of the markets in which they operate: (1) international—if they have a substantial market presence outside of the United States; (2) domestic—if they operate only in US domestic markets without a significant presence of foreign competitors; and (3) domestic and foreign penetrated—if they operate only in US domestic markets with a significant presence of foreign competitors. *Within product type and scope,* I classified industries by the extent of their power and presence in markets. Market power consisted of two categories: oligopolistic versus competitive. Economic scale (size) also had two groupings: large scale versus small-to-medium scale.

I also distinguish a public sector, given the theoretical prediction of differences in outcomes between the private and public sectors and their varying use of profitability as a motivating goal. This approach could define up to seventy-three sectors: [six product types] × [three market scopes] × [two levels of concentration] × [two levels of size] + [one public sector].

But only twenty combinations empirically exist in my data as shown in Table 3.2. Appendix Table A.4 (found at the end of this appendix) presents the industrial sector classification for all 228 industries as well as their 1990 Census Industry Codes.[2]

Data and Methods for the Worker-Level Analyses

Measurement

As discussed in Chapter 3, I use log-linear analysis to predict the matching of workers to labor market positions and a type of regression analysis to predict workers' earnings from their position. These techniques have different requirements for how variables can be measured. Log-linear analysis is applied to a crosstabulation of a set of variables, each of which must be coded into categories. There are practical limits on the total number of cells in this crosstabulation that implicitly limits the number of categories for each variable. In contrast, regression analysis requires that the outcome be an interval measure (i.e., the measurement scale is numeric with equal intervals) but permits the use of either interval or categorical predictors. So for each interval-level predictor, I first discuss how it is measured for the regression analysis and then how it was categorized for the log-linear analyses.

Table A.1 summarizes the operationalization of the variables for each form of analysis. The labor market outcome measure for the earnings analysis is the worker's annual earnings in the preceding calendar year measured in dollars. For the employment analysis, the outcome measure is a categorical variable whose 1,917 categories indicate the labor market position in which a worker is employed. The predictors are measures of human capital, family structure, geographic residence, labor supply (only for predicting earnings), and race-sex group membership.

Human capital. There are two measures of a worker's human capital available from the census data: education and potential work experience. *Education* is the highest year of education completed. In the 1990 PUMS, this variable is coded as single-year values for those who completed nine or more years of education up to twenty years. Fewer years of education are coded into one of two

Table A.1 Measurement of Worker-Level Variables

Variable	Earnings Analysis	Employment Analysis
Labor market outcome		
Annual earnings	Dollar earnings from the labor market position in 1989	
Labor market position		1,917 categories of labor market position
Human capital		
Education	Years of education completed	1 = Less than high school
		2 = Some high school
		3 = Completed high school
		4 = Some college
		5 = Completed college or more
Potential experience	[Age] − [Education] − [6][a]	1 = 0–9 years
		2 = 10–24 years
		3 = 25–34 years
		4 = 35 or more years
Family structure		
Marital status	Dummy coded as currently married (1) versus not (0)	Same
Presence of young children	Number of own children under 6 years old living at home	1 = No children at home
		2 = 1–2 children
Presence of older children	Number of own children 6–18 years old living at home	3 = 3 or more children
Geographic residence		
Metropolitan residence	Dummy coded as metropolitan resident (1) versus not (0)	Same
State of residence	50 dummy-coded variables for state of residence plus D.C.	1 = Southern state[b]
		2 = Not a southern state
Labor supply		
Weeks worked	Number of weeks worked	Not applicable
Employment level	Usual hours worked per week	Not applicable
Race-sex group membership		
Race-sex group	1 = Black Women	Same
	2 = Black Men	
	3 = White Women	
	4 = White Men	

Notes: a. Variable value calculated as age in years minus years of education minus six.

b. The southern region consists of Alabama, Arkansas, Delaware, Florida, Georgia, Kentucky, Louisiana, Maryland, Mississippi, North Carolina, Oklahoma, South Carolina, Tennessee, Texas, Virginia, West Virginia, and the District of Columbia.

categories: one to four years or five to eight years. For those reporting five to eight years, I used published 1980 Census data on single years of education in this category to impute the 1990 category mean, separately for each race-sex group.[3] For those reporting one to four years, I assigned the category midpoint (2.5) because the published 1980 Census data did not provide detail for this category. For the log-linear analyses, education was coded into five categories representing natural breaks in the educational system: (1) less than high school, (2) some high school, (3) high school completion, (4) some college, (5) completion of college or more. The census data do not have an explicit measure of the number of years of actual work experience, so I use the common proxy of potential experience. *Potential experience* measures the maximum number of years that a worker could have worked, that is, the number of years beyond completion of education. It is defined as the worker's age minus the number of years of education he or she completed minus six (assuming that children begin education at age six). For the employment analysis, this is coded into four ranges of years as shown in Table A.1.

Family structure. I use two types of indicators of family structure: marital status and presence of children in the home. *Marital status* is a dummy indicator contrasting those who are currently married versus those who are not. *Presence of young children* is the number of own children under the age of six who live in the worker's home. *Presence of older children* is the number of own children ages six to eighteen who live in the worker's home. For the log-linear analyses, the two measures of children present in the home are collapsed into a single indicator of the number of children ages eighteen and younger present in the home—coded as none, one to two, and three or more.

Geographic residence. I use two indicators of where workers live, metropolitan residence and state of residence. *Metropolitan residence* is a dummy indicator of whether the worker lives in a standard metropolitan statistical area (SMSA) or not.[4] *State of residence* is a set of fifty dummy indicators of the state (or the District of Columbia) in which a worker resides. For the analysis of employment position this was reduced to a contrast of southern residence versus not.[5]

Labor supply. The two indicators of labor supply are used only in the regression analysis of worker's earnings and, like earnings, are measured for the preceding calendar year. *Weeks worked* is the number of weeks worked in the preceding year. *Employment level* is the number of hours per week usually worked in the preceding year, top coded at ninety-nine hours.

Race-sex group membership. I classified workers as members of the four race-sex groups (black women, black men, white women, and white men) using their self-reported race and sex. I excluded all respondents who did not identify their race as either white or black and, among whites, excluded those whose ethnic identity was Hispanic. Unlike the 2000 Census, only a single racial/ethnic identification was possible for respondents in the 1990 Census, so these exclusions are straightforward.

Predicting Employment in Labor Market Positions

I apply log-linear analysis to the eight-dimensional crosstabulation of labor market position, race-sex group membership, education, potential experience, marital status, number of children, metropolitan residence, and southern residence. The "net" effects of race-sex group membership from this multivariate analysis are thereby adjusted for (purged of) group differences in the other predictors. I then use these net effects to construct measures of employment segregation among race-sex groups. Ideally, I would run a single analysis simultaneously predicting in which of the 1,917 positions a worker is employed. But this would require analyzing a crosstabulation with 3,680,640 cells, which is beyond the program capabilities of current statistical software and would have taken an extreme amount of time even if it were not.[6] Instead, I performed a separate log-linear analysis for each labor market position: the dependent variable was a dichotomy (D_j) indicating if workers were employed in the jth labor market position or elsewhere. This entire process was repeated for the regional model used to estimate segregation in the South and the non-South.

The first log-linear model for each labor market position specified all possible four-way associations among the predictors, a two-way association between race-sex group (G) and D_j, and all possible three-way associations of D_j with the other predictors.[7] This model does not specify that race-sex group membership and human capital interact in predicting labor market position. Although employers may evaluate the credentials of race-sex groups differently in the hiring and promotion process (Bills 1988; Moss and Tilly 1996; Neckerman and Kirschenman 1991; Ridgeway 1997), this differential evaluation is part of the segregation and queuing processes that I analyze. Excluding these interactions means that the main effect of race-sex group membership on labor market position includes the effects of the differential evaluation of a group's credentials. Thus the dependent variables (defined by the odds ratio measure) vary across positions in part because of the differential evaluation of group members' credentials across positions.

In addition to this model, I also estimated a regional log-linear model specifying that the effects of race-sex group on position can be different in the South than in the non-South. That is, I added a three-way association among southern residence, race-sex group, and position.[8] It is possible to use results from these log-linear analyses to estimate how well the observed eight-dimensional table of position by race-sex group by the five predictors would be fit by these models (Kaufman 1981). The estimated likelihood ratio chi-squares comparing the observed and expected frequencies for the initial model and the regional model were not significant ($p > .50$), suggesting the models provide a good fit.

Measuring employment segregation from the worker-level results. I calculate employment segregation as *net* odds ratios using the parameters for the race-sex group by position association (GD_j) for each position (Kaufman and Schervish 1987) for five paired comparisons among race-sex groups: black women to white men, black men to white men, white women to white men, black women to black men, and black women to white women. For example, the net odds ratio for black women (BW) compared to white men (WM) in position 1888 (pressers in laundries) shown conceptually in Eq. 3.1 in Chapter 3 is calculated from the log-linear parameters as:

Eq. A.1

$$\text{Net Odds Ratio}_{BW:WM} \text{ for position } 1888 = \frac{\left(\dfrac{\tau_{IN_{1888, BW}}}{\tau_{OUT_{1888, BW}}} \right)}{\left(\dfrac{\tau_{IN_{1888, WM}}}{\tau_{OUT_{1888, WM}}} \right)} = \frac{\tau^2_{IN_{1888, BW}}}{\tau^2_{IN_{1888, WM}}}$$

where the τs are the 2-way multiplicative parameters for GD_{1888}

In the analyses in later chapters, I use the log of the odds ratio. Logging the odds ratio changes it to an additive metric and also ensures that the order of comparison (BW to WM versus WM to BW) does not affect the magnitude of the indicator. That is, odds ratios range from zero to infinity and are asymmetrically distributed around a value of 1.0. An odds ratio for BW to WM ranging from greater than 1.0 to infinity would indicate that black women have higher odds of employment in the position than white men, while an odds ratio between zero and 1.0 would indicate that black women have lower odds of employment in the position than white men. For example, an odds ratio of 2 demonstrates the same degree of difference in odds in the "positive" direction as an odds ratio of 0.5 does in the "negative" direction. In contrast, the log odds ratio ranges from minus infinity to plus infinity and is symmetrically distributed around a value of 0.0. Thus, a positive value of the logged measure would indicate a greater representation of black women than white men employed in a position, while an equally negative value would indicate an equally greater representation of white men.

I used an analogous procedure to construct the region-specific employment segregation measures using the parameters for the race-sex group by position association (GD_j), and for the South by race-sex group by position association (SGD_j) from the regional log-linear model. In this situation, I calculated two odds ratios for each pair of race-sex groups in each position, one measuring employment segregation in the South and the second employment segregation in the non-South. Using the same example as in Eq. A.1, the region-specific odds ratios for position 1888 are:

Eq. A.2   *Net Odds Ratio$_{BW:WM}$ for position 1888 in South =*

$$\frac{\left(\dfrac{\tau_{IN_{1888,\,BW}}}{\tau_{OUT_{1888,\,BW}}}\right)}{\left(\dfrac{\tau_{IN_{1888,\,WM}}}{\tau_{OUT_{1888,\,WM}}}\right)} \times \frac{\left(\dfrac{\tau_{IN_{1888,\,BW,\,South}}}{\tau_{OUT_{1888,\,BW,\,South}}}\right)}{\left(\dfrac{\tau_{IN_{1888,\,WM,\,South}}}{\tau_{OUT_{1888,\,WM,\,South}}}\right)}$$

Net Odds Ratio$_{BW:WM}$ for position 1888 in non-South =

$$\frac{\left(\dfrac{\tau_{IN_{1888,\,BW}}}{\tau_{OUT_{1888,\,BW}}}\right)}{\left(\dfrac{\tau_{IN_{1888,\,WM}}}{\tau_{OUT_{1888,\,WM}}}\right)} \times \frac{\left(\dfrac{\tau_{IN_{1888,\,BW,\,non\text{-}South}}}{\tau_{OUT_{1888,\,BW,\,non\text{-}South}}}\right)}{\left(\dfrac{\tau_{IN_{1888,\,WM,\,non\text{-}South}}}{\tau_{OUT_{1888,\,WM,\,non\text{-}South}}}\right)}$$

*where the τs are the 2-way multiplicative parameters for GD$_{1888}$
and the 3-way multiplicative parameters for SGD$_{1888}$*

Predicting Earnings from Labor Market Positions

I predicted workers' earnings from the worker-level predictors separately for each race-sex group and further specified that the returns to these predictors vary across two-digit occupational segments and across two-digit industrial sectors in an additive fashion within each group. The two-digit definition of occupational segments uses skill type and skill level to define segments, resulting in ten segments (see Table 3.1). The two-digit definition of industrial sectors uses product type and concentration to define sectors, resulting in thirteen sectors (see Table 3.2). As shown in Eq. 3.2, in Chapter 3, the regression for group g takes the form:

Eq. A.3 $Earn = \alpha + \beta_1 X + \beta_2 X * Occ + \beta_3 X * Ind +$
                         $\beta_4\, State + \beta_5\, LMP + \varepsilon$

The predictors in X (see Table A.1) include education, potential experience and its square, an education by experience interaction, marital status, presence of young children, presence of older children, metropolitan residence, weeks worked, and employment level. *Ind* includes 12 industrial sector dummy variables, *Occ* includes 9 occupational segment dummies, *State* includes 50 state-of-residence dummies, and *LMP* includes 1,916 labor-market-position dummies.

I estimated these regressions using an "unbalanced" fixed-effects model for labor market position (Greene 1997; Judge et al. 1985). This is a statistically equivalent and time efficient way to estimate the regression with 1,916 dummy variables for labor market position. Specifically, I treated labor market positions as higher-level units having a fixed effect on the individual cases (workers) nested within them. In practical terms, this is most easily and efficiently estimated by first transforming the dependent and independent variables into deviations from their means within the labor market unit. These transformed variables then are used to perform a regression to estimate β_1, β_2, β_3, and β_4. The estimated values of β_5 for the effects of labor market positions can then be calculated using the estimates of β_1, β_2, β_3, and β_4 and the labor market position means of the variables (see Greene 1997: 617):

Eq. A.4
$$\beta_{5,\,LMP} = E\bar{a}rn_{LMP} - \left[\beta_1 \bar{X}_{LMP} + \beta_2 \bar{X}_{LMP} * Occ_{LMP} + \beta_3 \bar{X}_{LMP} * Ind_{LMP} + \beta_4 St\bar{a}te_{LMP} \right.$$

Occ_{LMP} and Ind_{LMP} are specified to indicate in which occupational segment and industrial sector a labor market position is classified. Note that this method constrains α in Eq. A.3 to zero because it estimates an effect for every category of labor market position instead of using one as a reference category. An analogous fixed-effects model was used for the regional earnings determination analyses.

Measuring adjusted earnings gaps. To calculate the adjusted earnings gap between black men (BM) and white men (WM) in position 318, as described conceptually in Eq. 3.3 of Chapter 3, I calculated the ratio of predicted BM earnings to predicted WM earnings using the estimated coefficients for each group from Eq. A.3 and A.4 along with the total sample means of the predictors in X ($\bar{X}_T$) and of the state dummies ($St\bar{a}te_T$):

Eq. A.5
$$Earnings\ Gap_{BM:WM}\ for\ position\ 318 = \frac{E\hat{a}rn_{BM}\ for\ position\ 318}{E\hat{a}rn_{WM}\ for\ position\ 318}$$

$$where\ E\hat{a}rn_{BM}\ for\ position\ 318 = \left[\beta_{1,\,BM} + \beta_{2,\,BM,\,318} + \beta_{3,\,BM,\,318} \right] \bar{X}_T + \beta_{4,\,BM}\,St\bar{a}te_T + \beta_{5,\,BM,\,318}$$

$$E\hat{a}rn_{WM}\ for\ position\ 318 = \left[\beta_{1,\,WM} + \beta_{2,\,WM,\,318} + \beta_{3,\,WM,\,318} \right] \bar{X}_T + \beta_{4,\,WM}\,St\bar{a}te_T + \beta_{5,\,WM,\,318}$$

$\beta_{2,BM,318}$ are the coefficients for black men for the interaction between X and Occ corresponding to the occupational segment for position 318.
$\beta_{3,BM,318}$ are the coefficients for black men for the interaction between X and Ind corresponding to the industrial sector for position 318.

$\beta_{2,WM,318}$ are the coefficients for white men for the interaction between X
   and *Occ* corresponding to the occupational segment for position 318.
$\beta_{3,WM,318}$ are the coefficients for white men for the interaction between X
   and *Ind* corresponding to the industrial sector for position 318.
$\beta_{5,BM,318}$ and $\beta_{5,WM,318}$ are the fixed-effects on earnings for black men and
   for white men for position 318.

Supplementary analyses also use the levels of predicted race-sex group specific
earnings (such as those calculated in Eq. A.5) as the outcome.

Data and Methods for the Position-Level Analyses

Data Sources and Sample Selection

I used a variety of sources for the industrial- and occupational-level variables.
The major sources were the *1987 Enterprise Statistics* (US Bureau of the Census 1989b), *Statistics of Income: Corporation Income Tax Returns for 1989–
1991* (US Department of the Treasury 1994, 1995, 1996), *U.S. Industrial Outlook* (US Department of Commerce 1990), and the England and Kilbourne
(1988) compilation of the *Dictionary of Occupational Titles* (4th edition). The
industry-level data that I compiled and use for this analysis are publically available on the Web through the Inter-University Consortium for Political and Social Research (ICPSR).[9] The sample size of 1,917 excludes forty-nine positions
for which there were too few workers from any of the race-sex groups to obtain
stable estimates of the labor market position's outcome measures of employment segregation and earnings gaps. Specifically, I excluded positions if there
were fewer than five workers from any of the race-sex groups.

Measurement

Table 3.5 in Chapter 3 presented summary information on the measurement of
the position-level variables, including the data source(s) used for each. In each
section below, I discuss additional details about measurement for each cluster
of variables.

General skills and training. I initially constructed separate scales of general
skills required and of the training time required to obtain skills, which I then av-
eraged together to avoid severe collinearity problems.

Skill complexity. This combines *Dictionary of Occupational Titles (DOT)* indicators of the extent of complexity in three skill areas (people, data, and things)
with the extent of general educational skills required for job performance.

Training time. Training time uses the *DOT* indicator of the months required to learn the skills in preparation for the specific job.

Growth and employment type rates. This cluster consists of employment growth and indicators of three different aspects of the availability of desirable jobs: those offering sufficient levels of employment, those providing small chances for job insecurity, and those offering the opportunity to be your own boss.

Employment growth. I measure growth as the increase (decrease) from 1980 to 1990 using the ratio of the number of workers employed in a position in 1990 to the number of workers in 1980 in the PUMS data. I adjusted the 1990 counts downward by a factor of <5/6> because I used a 6% sample for 1990 and a 5% sample for 1980. I log the ratio to specify that growth and decline represent equivalent metric changes and to reduce skewness.

Sufficient work. I define sufficient hours as the opportunity to work more than thirty hours per week. I measure this by the percent of the labor force in a position who work more than thirty hours per week.

Unemployment rate. The extent of unemployment is a common measure of job insecurity. I calculate it as the percent of the labor force in a position who are unemployed.

Self-employment. Self-employment, measured as the percent of the labor force in a position who are self-employed, is the obvious indicator of the opportunity to work independently.

Race- and gender-typed work tasks. As discussed in Chapter 2, race-typed tasks and conditions correspond to jobs requiring heavy physical labor, poor working conditions, menial or subservient tasks, status-superior interactions, skill, and authority. Gender-typed tasks and conditions include all of these (except skill) as well as physical dexterity, clerical perception, nurturant skills, and mathematical skills.

Physical exertion. For this variable, I combined a *DOT* indicator of the presence of four types of physical demands of work (climbing or balancing; stooping, kneeling, crouching or crawling; reaching, handling, fingering or feeling; seeing) with a *DOT* indicator of the degree of strength required (ranging from sedentary to very heavy).

Environmental conditions. To measure poor working conditions, I use a *DOT* indicator of the presence of six environmental situations that make demands on a worker's physical capacities (extreme cold; extreme heat; wet or humid conditions; excessive noise or vibrations; hazardous conditions; fumes, gases, dust, or poor ventilation).

Routinization. One meaning of menial work is the performance of routine and repetitive tasks. This scale includes *DOT* indicators of repetitive or short-cycle job tasks, the variety of job duties (reverse-coded), and a required worker preference for routine work tasks.

Status in interaction. This refers to the types of interaction with others in the workplace (either coworkers or clients) required by the occupation, ranging from subordinate to superordinate. It is measured by a reverse-coding of the *DOT* indicator of complexity in dealing with people, for which a value of zero now represents taking instructions or helping and a value of eight now represents mentoring.

Authority. The exercise of authority over others is a second way in which work can require status-superior interactions. I use England et al.'s (1994) measure of whether or not an occupation requires the exercise of supervisory responsibility, which they coded from the 1980 Census Occupational Titles.

Physical dexterity. To measure overall dexterity requirements, I combined *DOT* indicators of the degree of three kinds of dexterity required by a job: finger dexterity, manual dexterity, and motor coordination. Each item was reverse-coded from the original indicator; high values now represent high dexterity (top 10% of the population) and low values are low dexterity (bottom 10%).

Clerical aptitude. For this variable I use the *DOT* indicator of the degree of clerical perception (aptitude) required to perform or learn job tasks. I reversed the coding so that higher values represent higher required aptitudes.

Nurturant work. The idea of nurturant skill as a female-typed skill is central in the literature on sex segregation and comparable worth. I use England et al.'s (1994) measure, a dummy indicator of whether nurturing is a major task requirement for an occupation.

Math skills. To measure a job's requirement for math skills, I use the *DOT* indicator of the degree of numerical aptitude required to perform or learn job tasks. Again, this was reverse-coded such that high values correspond to high aptitudes.

Product market structure. This cluster consists of measures of the power, economic scale, and character of the production process of industries as well as their involvement in economic globalization.

Market power. This indicator is the average of the concentration of sales in the eight largest selling firms in an industry and the concentration of employment in the eight largest employing firms in an industry. The sales concentration ratio measures the proportion of total sales in an industry for which the eight largest selling firms account. Employment concentration is defined analogously.

Profitability. I measure the extent of profits by the average of two indicators of profitability, each a three-year average to reduce the influence of short-term fluctuations. I use net income relative to assets and net income relative to business receipts to measure profitability.

Economic scale. I originally constructed separate measures of the physical size of industries and the financial size of industries. I made them into a single measure because their separate use created collinearity problems and because preliminary analyses suggested that each affects the outcomes similarly. *Physical size* combines mean employment size of firms with several indicators of the percent of large employers in an industry. *Financial size* includes per firm averages of sales, assets, net income, and value added in an industry.

Capital intensity. This item reflects the use of capital relative to labor in the production process and is measured by mean total assets per employee and mean depreciable assets per employee.

Foreign involvement. This refers to the involvement of US firms in markets outside of the United States. It combines indicators of foreign dividends earned per company, foreign tax credits per company, and the value of exports per company.

Foreign penetration. This item complements the foreign involvement measure by indexing the presence of non-US companies in the US domestic market in 1990. The scale consists of three data-based indicators and one content-coded indicator of the presence of foreign competition in an industry's US domestic markets. The quantitative indicators are the average value of imports per firm in an industry, the value of imports as a share of an industry's total commodity output, and an industry's share of imports from *all* industries. The fourth indicator was content coded from the *U.S. Industrial Outlook* using a seven-point scale of the penetration of foreign competitors into an industry.[10] Note that the foreign penetration scale was used in the definition of industrial sectors but not as a predictor.

Productivity. Productivity is the extent to which the work performed in an industry increases the economic worth of the output beyond the worth of the inputs. The scale combines the average value added per employee with the value added as a percentage of total output.

Linkages to other actors. This final set of indicators captures the potential influence on labor market processes of actors other than private employers or the workers, namely unions and government. The government can be a labor market actor as an employer or as a regulator of other employers.

Industry unionization and occupation unionization. I measure the presence of unions separately for industries and for occupations. I use the proportion of an industry's labor force who are union members and the proportion of an occupation's labor force who are union members, constructed by Reynolds (1997) from *Current Population Survey* (CPS) data from 1985 to 1989 (US Bureau of the Census 1985, 1986, 1987, 1988, 1989a). He utilized Kokkelenberg and Sockell's (1985) measurement procedures but updated them using CPS data for more recent years.

Public sector. Workers employed in the public sector include more than just those who work in public sector industries. I define public sector workers as those who either work in one of the public sector industries (see Table A.4) or report their class of worker in the PUMS as employed for federal, state, or local government. I measure this by the percent of the labor force in a position employed in the public sector.

Federal purchases. Federal purchases is a measure of the extent of linkages between an industry and the federal government, which could subject the hiring, promotion, and remuneration processes in an industry to scrutiny by the Office of Federal Contract Compliance. The scale combines the value of federal purchases per company in the industry with federal purchases as a percent of industry output.

Estimation Issues

There are five statistical issues that have the potential to affect the analyses of employment segregation and earnings gaps: (1) missing data, (2) collinearity among the predictors, (3) heteroskedasticity of the errors across positions, (4) correlated errors between pairs of positions in the same analysis, and (5) errors for the same position being correlated between the analyses for employment segregation and earnings gaps.

In discussing these issues, I use the same concrete example as in Chapter 3 (Eq. 3.4) of a typical model that contrasts white women (WW) to white men (WM) in terms of employment segregation (*ES*) and earnings gaps (*EG*) as well as the group-specific predicted earnings for white women and white men (*Eârn*):

Eq. A.6a $$ES_i^{WW:WM} = \beta_1{}' \underline{X}_{1,i} + \varepsilon_{1,i}$$

Eq. A.6b $$EG_i^{WW:WM} = \gamma_2\, ES_i^{WW:WM} + \beta_2{}' \underline{X}_{2,i} + \varepsilon_{2,i}$$

Eq. A.6c $$Eârn_i^{WW} = \gamma_3\, ES_i^{WW:WM} + \delta_3\, ES_i^{BM:WM} + \beta_3{}'\, \underline{X}_{3,i} + \varepsilon_{3,i}$$

Eq. A.6d $$Eârn_i^{WM} = \gamma_4\, ES_i^{WW:WM} + \delta_4\, ES_i^{BM:WM} + \beta_4{}'\, \underline{X}_{4,i} + \varepsilon_{4,i}$$

Missing data. Corresponding to Cohen and Cohen's (1983: 284–289) procedure, I first used mean substitution to estimate values for cases that had missing information for a predictor. In the analyses, I then controlled for possible biases due to this mean substitution by including as predictors (in X_1 or X_2) dummy variables indexing for each predictor whether or not a case had been mean substituted. I do not report the results for these missing data presence indicators in the result tables; they are not substantively interesting, and this helps simplify already large tables. But one, or usually more, of these correction factors have significant effects in each model, indicating that the correction is needed.

Collinearity. I used Belsley, Kuh, and Welsch's (1980) diagnostic measures, condition indices and coefficient variance decomposition proportions, to determine possible collinearity concerns.[11] I resolved the two substantial collinearity problems found by combining general skills and training time into a single scale and by combining physical size and financial size into a single scale. While there are occasionally several other high condition indices (greater than 30) in the analyses, the variance decomposition proportions indicate that this collinearity did not degrade the estimation of the coefficients, so these collinearities are not consequential.[12]

Heteroskedasticity, correlated errors within an equation, and EGLS estimation. To apply ordinary least squares (OLS) regression to any of the models in Eq. A.6, I would have to assume that the error variance for, say $\varepsilon_{1,i}$, is $Var(\underline{\varepsilon}_1) = \sigma_1^2 I$. That is, I would have to assume that the $\varepsilon_{1,i}$ are homoskedastic (have equal variance across positions) and have zero autocorrelation (are not correlated between pairs of positions). Suppose instead that $Var(\underline{\varepsilon}_{1,i}) = \sigma_1^2 \Omega$, specifying either heteroskedasticity or autocorrelation or both. The consequence of this violation of the assumptions is that the OLS estimator remains unbiased but is inefficient (Greene 1997: 498). However, the coefficient standard errors and significance tests that are *actually* reported by any statistical software using OLS in this situation are biased (Greene 1997: 498–499). The reason for this seeming contradiction is that statistical software always uses the formula $Var(\underline{\beta}_1) = \sigma_1^2 (X_1'X_1)^{-1}$ which is only valid if $Var(\underline{\varepsilon}_1) = \sigma_1^2 I$. If $Var(\underline{\varepsilon}_1) = \sigma_1^2 \Omega$, then the formula which should be used (assuming you can separately calculate an estimate of Ω) is: $Var(\underline{\beta}_1) = \sigma_1^2 [(X_1'X_1)^{-1} (X_1'\Omega X_1) (X_1'X_1)^{-1}]$.

For the regression models in Eq. A.6a–d, the disturbances are virtually certain to be heteroskedastic because the dependent variable is calculated from aggregate parameters and is based on varying numbers of workers in the position (Hanushek and Jackson 1977: 143). In addition, I consider the possibility that there is heteroskedasticity across industrial sectors and occupational segments. I use a Breusch-Pagan (BP) statistic to test for the initial presence of each of these forms of heteroskedasticity and then to test for the effectiveness of my subsequent correction for heteroskedasticity (Greene 1997: 552–554).

It also is quite plausible that positions located in the same industrial sector or the same occupational segment would have correlated errors. That is, positions in the same industrial sector (occupational segment) are likely to be subject to a similar set of unmeasured, idiosyncratic processes that affect employment and wage setting. I use a Lagrange multiplier (LM) statistic to test for the existence of such correlated errors (Greene 1997: 629).

In all of the analyses reported earlier, the diagnostic tests indicate that there is in fact both heteroskedasticity and autocorrelation. Thus, if I were to apply OLS estimation, the results for these models from standard OLS software would report biased estimates of the standard errors of the coefficients and hence biased significance tests. There are two possible solutions: (1) calculate the OLS standard errors correctly, which would result in an inefficient estimator; (2) use estimated generalized least squares (EGLS), which would provide unbiased and efficient estimates. I use EGLS because it is both a more efficient estimator and, in practical terms, is as easy if not easier to do than to calculate the OLS standard errors correctly. Specifically I estimate a two-component "unbalanced" random-effects model in LIMDEP (Greene 1998) with a heteroskedastic error variance. The random-effects model specifies that positions in the same industry sector j have correlated errors and those in the same occupation segment k have correlated errors.[13] For the analyses of employment segregation and earnings gaps (Eq. A.6a and A.6b), I further specified the error variance for the comparison of white women to white men in position i in industry sector j and occupation segment k as heteroskedastic by group (σ^2_{WW}, σ^2_{WM}), group size ($N_{WW,i}$, $N_{WM,i}$), industry sector (σ^2_j), and occupation segment (σ^2_k):

Eq. A.7
$$\sigma^2_{ijk} = \left(\frac{\sigma^2_{WW}}{N_{WW,i}} + \frac{\sigma^2_{WM}}{N_{WM,i}} \right) \times \sigma^2_j \times \sigma^2_k$$

For the analyses of group-specific earnings levels (Eq. A.6c and A.6d), I specified the error variance for white women (and analogously for white men) in position i in industry sector j and occupation segment k as heteroskedastic by group (σ^2_{WW}), group size ($N_{WW,i}$), industry sector (σ^2_j), and occupation segment (σ^2_k):

Eq. A.8
$$\sigma^2_{ijk} = \left(\frac{\sigma^2_{WW}}{N_{WW,i}} \right) \times \sigma^2_j \times \sigma^2_k$$

Correlated errors between equations. Three of the four models in Eq. A.6a–d include other endogenous variables (employment segregation between the groups) as predictors. This creates the potential for the error term for employment segregation ($\varepsilon_{1,i}$) to be correlated with the errors for the outcomes of which employment segregation is a predictor ($\varepsilon_{2,i}$, $\varepsilon_{3,i}$, and $\varepsilon_{4,i}$). If so, then equation-by-equation OLS (or EGLS) estimates of the earnings gap or earnings level models are biased and inconsistent (Greene 1997: 710). For some of the analyses, this issue is in-consequential because the magnitude of the correlations of errors between equations is small enough to ignore. As a diagnostic, I calculate four sets of estimates of the magnitude of this correlation for each analysis: (1) the correlation between the errors from the reduced form models (i.e., excluding employment segregation from the prediction of earnings gaps); (2) the correlation between the errors from the structural models estimated using no correction for between-equation correlated errors; (3) the smallest value consistent with the reduced form estimates; and (4) the largest value consistent with the reduced form estimates.

For example, the variance and covariance of the errors for the reduced form equations corresponding to the structural equations shown in Eq. A.6a and A.6b place theoretical limits on the possible values for γ (the effect of employment segregation) and for ρ (the correlation between $\varepsilon_{1,i}$ and $\varepsilon_{2,i}$). Using consistent estimates of the reduced form error variances and covariance, I can calculate empirical limits on the possible values for ρ.

To develop this, it is easiest if I first rewrite Equations A.6a and A.6b as a structural system in matrix notation:

Eq. A.9
$$Y\Gamma + XB = E$$
$$\text{where } Y = \begin{bmatrix} ES^{WW:WM} & EG^{WW:WM} \end{bmatrix}, \Gamma = \begin{bmatrix} 1 & -\gamma_2 \\ 0 & 1 \end{bmatrix}, X = \begin{bmatrix} X_1 & X_2 \end{bmatrix},$$
$$B = \begin{bmatrix} -\beta_1 & 0 \\ 0 & -\beta_2 \end{bmatrix}, \text{ and } E = \begin{bmatrix} \varepsilon_1 & \varepsilon_2 \end{bmatrix}$$

The corresponding reduced form equations for this system are:

Eq. A.10
$$Y = -XB\Gamma^{-1} + E\Gamma^{-1}$$

The variance-covariance matrix for the structural errors (E) is:

Eq. A.11
$$\Sigma_S = \begin{bmatrix} \sigma_1^2 & \rho\sigma_1\sigma_2 \\ \rho\sigma_1\sigma_2 & \sigma_2^2 \end{bmatrix}$$

and the variance-covariance matrix for the corresponding reduced form errors ($E\Gamma^{-1}$) is:

Eq. A.12

$$\Sigma_R = \begin{bmatrix} \sigma_{1,R}^2 & \rho_R \, \sigma_{1,R} \, \sigma_{2,R} \\ \rho_R \, \sigma_{1,R} \, \sigma_{2,R} & \sigma_{2,R}^2 \end{bmatrix}$$

Next write Σ_R as a function of Γ and Σ_S (Greene 1997: 722):

Eq. A.13

$$\Sigma_R = (\Gamma^{-1})' \Sigma_S \Gamma^{-1} =$$

$$\begin{bmatrix} \sigma_1^2 & \rho \, \sigma_1 \, \sigma_2 + \gamma_2 \, \sigma_2^2 \\ \rho \, \sigma_1 \, \sigma_2 + \gamma_2 \, \sigma_2^2 & \sigma_2^2 + 2\gamma_2 \rho \, \sigma_1 \, \sigma_2 + \gamma_2^2 \sigma_1^2 \end{bmatrix}$$

Eq. A.13 thus describes the equivalencies between the four unknown structural parameters (one in Γ and three in Σ_S) and the three estimable parameters in Σ_R.

By choosing a range of hypothetical values for γ_2, I can use the three equivalencies in Eq. A.13 to derive the range of possible values for the three unknown parameters in Σ_S corresponding to the range of values for γ_2. I used Maple 6.01 to solve the three equations that are nonlinear in the unknown parameters. I estimated values for Σ_R from OLS residuals from the reduced form models in Eq. A.10 for each of the five comparisons of groups; this yields consistent estimates of Σ_R (Greene 1997: 721). I limited possible solutions from Maple to those that produced: (1) real-number values as opposed to complex-number values; (2) positive values for σ_1 and σ_2; and (3) values in the range [–1.0, 1.0] for ρ. I specified the range of hypothetical values for γ as [–1, 1]. This range is reasonable both because the earnings gap and the employment segregation measures are logged ratios with similar ranges of values and because I find possible values for ρ, σ_1, and σ_2 corresponding only to a much narrower range of values for γ [–0.25, 0.25]. Values of γ outside this range always produced impossible values (as defined above) for ρ or σ_2.

For each of the four estimated values of the error correlation, I calculate whether it significantly differs from zero using Fisher's z test (Knoke, Bohrnstedt, and Mee 2002: 190). For example, Table A.2 presents these diagnostics for the base analyses of earnings gaps. For three of the five analyses, it is reasonable to assume that the errors between equations are uncorrelated. But for the analyses of black men compared to white men and of black women compared to black men, the correlations are too large to ignore.

The classic solution to this problem is to employ some variation of an instrumental variables or two-stage least squares (2SLS) approach (Greene 1997: 710–711). This requires that there are one or more instruments available in the analysis; that is, predictors in X_1 that are not also in X_2. The estimation of Eq. A.6b, then, could use the predicted values of $ES_i^{WW:WM}$ in place of its observed values to get consistent estimates, but this solution is only as good as the set of instruments used to predict $ES_i^{WW:WM}$. Although I do have some possible instrumental variables in all of the models (the interaction between skill and growth in this instance), they are somewhat weak instruments in terms of the absolute size of their effects on employment segregation. I experimented with using

Table A.2 Estimates of Between-Equation Error Correlations for Base Models of Employment Segregation and Earnings Gaps

| | Range Consistent with Reduced Form Data | | Actual Correlation from | |
| | Smallest Absolute | Largest Absolute | Structural Reduced Form | No correction |
Analysis for	Correlation p	Correlation p	Correlation p	Correlation p
Black women to white men	0.003	0.041	0.015	−0.022
Black men to white men	0.163 *	0.537 *	0.165 *	0.041
White women to white men	−0.030	−0.056 *	−0.034	−0.033
Black women to black men	−0.082 *	−0.176 *	−0.085 *	−0.015
Black women to white women	0.026	−0.041	−0.005	0.006

$*p < 0.05$, two-tailed

this approach but there was extremely high collinearity between the predicted employment segregation measure and the other predictors, which degraded many of the coefficient estimates.[14]

Instead, I take advantage of the fact that this is a triangular system of equations; that is, I specify that employment segregation affects earnings gaps but do not specify a reciprocal effect of earnings gaps on employment segregation. For triangular systems, a seemingly unrelated regressions (SUR) model gives consistent estimates under two conditions (Greene 1997: 737):

1. The SUR model is estimated iteratively until the estimates converge, first using estimates of the variances and covariance of $\varepsilon_{1,i}$ and $\varepsilon_{1,i}$ to estimate the SUR coefficients and then using the SUR coefficients to re-estimate Σ (the variances and covariances of the errors).
2. It is crucial to begin the iterative process with a consistent estimate of Σ. This can be calculated from the residuals from OLS estimation of Eq. A.6a and 2SLS estimation of Eq. A.6b (Lahiri and Schmidt 1978: 1219).[15] Thus, for the analyses presented earlier, I use the SUR model to estimate results when the diagnostics suggest that the errors for employment segregation and earnings gaps are correlated.

A similar problem arises in the estimation of the models for group-specific earnings levels (Eq. A.6c and A.6d). Unlike the earnings gap analyses in which a single other endogenous variable corresponding to employment segregation for that pair of groups is included, each earnings level analysis always includes

Table A.3 1990 Census Occupations and Segment Codes

Occupation Title	Census Code	Segment Code[a]	Census Recode
Executive, administrative, and managerial			
Legislators	3	4213	
Chief executives and general administrators, public administration	4	4232	
Administrators and officials, public administration	5	4232	
Administrators, protective services	6	4222	
Financial managers	7	4332	
Personnel and labor relations managers	8	4332	
Purchasing managers	9	4232	
Managers, marketing, advertising, and public relations	13	4332	
Administrators, education, and related fields	14	4332	
Managers, medicine, and health	15	4332	
Managers, food serving, and lodging establishments	17	4232	19
Managers, properties, and real estate	18	4232	16
Postmasters and mail superintendents	16	4222	17
Funeral directors	19	4232	18
Managers, service organizations, n.e.c.	21	4232	19
Managers and administrators, n.e.c.	22	4232	19
Management related occupations			
Accountants and auditors	23	5332	
Underwriters	24	4233	
Other financial officers	25	4332	
Management analysts	26	5332	
Personnel, training, and labor relations specialists	27	4312	
Purchasing agents and buyers, farm products	28	4213	
Buyers, wholesale and retail trade exc. farm products	29	4233	
Purchasing agents and buyers, n.e.c.	33	4213	
Business and promotion agents	34	4312	
Construction inspectors	35	5233	5233
Inspectors and compliance officers, exc. construction	36	5233	
Management related occupations, n.e.c.	37	4213	4213
Engineers, architects, and surveyors			
Architects	43	4332	
Aerospace engineers	44	5332	
Metallurgical and materials engineers	45	5332	
Mining engineers	46	5333	
Petroleum engineers	47	5332	
Chemical engineers	48	5332	
Nuclear engineers	49	5332	
Civil engineers	53	5332	
Agricultural engineers	54	5332	
Electrical and electronic engineers	55	5332	
Industrial engineers	56	5332	
Mechanical engineers	57	5332	
Marine and naval architects engineers	58	5332	
Engineers, n.e.c.	59	5332	
Surveyors and mapping scientists	63	5223	
Mathematical and computer scientists			
Computer systems analysts and scientists	64	5332	
Operations and systems researchers and analysts	65	4233	
Actuaries	66	5332	
Statisticians	67	5332	
Mathematical scientists, n.e.c.	68	5332	
Natural scientists			
Physicists and astronomers	69	5332	
Chemists, exc. biochemists	73	5332	
Atmospheric and space scientists	74	5233	
Geologists and geodesists	75	5333	
Physical scientists, n.e.c.	76	5332	
Agricultural and food scientists	77	5332	

continues

Table A.3 continued

Occupation Title	Census Code	Segment Code[a]	Census Recode
Biological and life scientists	78	5332	
Forestry and conservation scientists	79	4213	
Medical scientists	83	5332	
Health diagnosing occupations			
Physicians	84	4332	
Dentists	85	4332	
Veterinarians	86	4332	
Optometrists	87	4332	
Podiatrists	88	4312	
Health diagnosing practitioners, n.e.c.	89	4312	
Health assessment and treating occupations			
Registered nurses	95	4213	
Pharmacists	96	6233	
Dieticians	97	4312	
Respiratory therapists	98	4312	
Occupational therapists	99	4312	
Physical therapists	103	4312	
Speech therapists	104	4312	
Therapists, n.e.c.	105	4312	
Physicians' assistants	106	4213	
Teachers, postsecondary			
Earth, environmental and marine science teachers	113	4332	
Biological science teachers	114	4332	
Chemistry teachers	115	4332	
Physics teachers	116	4332	
Natural science teachers, n.e.c.	117	4332	
Psychology teachers	118	4332	
Economics teachers	119	4332	
History teachers	123	4332	
Political science teachers	124	4332	
Sociology teachers	125	4332	
Social science teachers, n.e.c.	126	4332	
Engineering teachers	127	4332	
Mathematical science teachers	128	4332	
Computer science teachers	129	4332	
Medical science teachers	133	4332	
Health specialties teachers	134	4332	
Business, commerce, and marketing teachers	135	4332	
Agriculture and forestry teachers	136	4332	
Art, drama, and music teachers	137	4332	
Physical education teachers	138	4312	
Education teachers	139	4332	
English teachers	143	4332	
Foreign language teachers	144	4332	
Law teachers	145	4332	
Social work teachers	146	4332	
Theology teachers	147	4332	
Trade and industrial teachers	148	4332	
Home economics teachers	149	4332	
Teachers, postsecondary, n.e.c.	153	4332	
Postsecondary teachers, subject not specified	154	4332	
Teachers, except postsecondary			
Teachers, prekindergarten and kindergarten	155	4213	
Teachers, elementary school	156	4312	
Teachers, secondary school	157	4312	
Teachers, special education	158	4312	
Teachers, n.e.c.	159	4312	
Counselors, educational and vocational	163	4312	
Librarians, archivists, and curators			
Librarians	164	4213	
Archivists and curators	165	4213	
Social scientists and urban planners			
Economists	166	4332	
Psychologists	167	4332	
Sociologists	168	4332	

continues

Table A.3 continued

Occupation Title	Census Code	Segment Code[a]	Census Recode
Social scientists, n.e.c.	169	4312	
Urban planners	173	4332	
Social, recreation, and religious workers			
Social workers	174	4312	
Recreation workers	175	4312	
Clergy	176	4312	
Religious workers, n.e.c.	177	4312	
Lawyers and judges			
Lawyers	178	4332	
Judges	179	4332	
Writers, artists, entertainers, and athletes			
Authors	183	4312	
Technical writers	184	4312	
Designers	185	5213	
Musicians and composers	186	5312	
Actors and directors	187	4213	
Painters, sculptors, craft-artists, and artist printmakers	188	5312	
Photographers	189	4233	
Dancers	193	4323	
Artists, performers and related workers, n.e.c.	194	4312	
Editors and reporters	195	4312	
Public relations specialists	197	4312	
Announcers	198	4213	
Athletes	199	4333	
Health technologists and technicians			
Clinical lab technologists and technicians	203	5233	
Dental hygienists	204	4233	
Health record technologists and technicians	205	4213	
Radiologic technicians	206	4233	
Licensed practical nurses	207	4213	
Health technologists and technicians, n.e.c.	208	5233	

Occupation Title	Census Code	Segment Code[a]	Census Recode
Engineering and related technologists and technicians			
Electrical and electronic technicians	213	5213	
Industrial engineering technicians	214	5233	
Mechanical engineering technicians	215	5233	
Engineering technicians, n.e.c.	216	5233	
Drafting occupations	217	5233	
Surveying and mapping technicians	218	5223	
Science technicians			
Biological technicians	223	5233	
Chemical technicians	224	5233	
Science technicians, n.e.c.	225	5233	
Technicians, except health, engineering, and science			
Airplane pilots and navigators	226	5233	
Air traffic controllers	227	4332	
Broadcast equipment operators	228	6233	
Computer programers	229	5332	
Tool programmers, numerical control	233	5332	
Legal assistants	234	4233	
Technicians, n.e.c.	235	5233	
Sales occupations			
Supervisors and proprietors, sales occupations	243	4232	
Sales representatives, finance and business services			
Insurance sales occupations	253	4233	
Real estate sales occupations	254	4213	
Securities and financial services sales occupations	255	4332	
Advertising and related sales occupations	256	4213	
Sales occupations, other business services	257	4233	

continues

Table A.3 continued

Occupation Title	Census Code	Segment Code[a]	Census Recode
Sales representatives, commodities			
except retail			
Sales engineers	258	4332	
Sales representatives, mining, manufacturing, and wholesale	259	4233	
Sales workers, retail and personal services			
Sales workers, motor vehicles, and boats	263	4213	
Sales workers, apparel	264	4213	
Sales workers, shoes	265	4213	
Sales workers, furniture, and home furnishings	266	4213	
Sales workers, radio, TV, hi-fi, and appliances	267	4213	
Sales workers, hardware, and building supplies	268	4213	
Sales workers, parts	269	4213	
Sales workers, other commodities	274	4213	
Sales counter clerks	275	4213	
Cashiers	276	6213	
Street and door-to-door sales workers	277	4233	
News vendors	278	6233	
Sales related occupations			
Demonstrators, promoters, and model sales	283	4233	
Auctioneers	284	4213	
Sales support occupations, n.e.c.	285	4233	
Supervisors, administrative support occupations			
Supervisors, general office	303	4232	
Supervisors, computer equipment operators	304	5232	
Supervisors, financial records processing	305	5232	
Chief communications operators	306	6222	
Supervisors, distribution, scheduling, and adjusting clerks	307	6222	
Computer equipment operators			
Computer operators	308	5213	
Peripheral equipment operators	309	5213	
Secretaries, stenographers, and typists			
Secretaries	313	4213	
Stenographers	314	5213	
Typists	315	6213	
Information clerks			
Interviewers	316	4233	
Hotel clerks	317	4213	
Transportation ticket and reservation agents	318	4213	
Receptionists	319	4213	
Information clerks, n.e.c.	323	6213	
Records processing occupations, except financial			
Classified ad clerks	325	4233	
Correspondence clerks	326	4233	
Order clerks	327	4233	
Personnel clerks, exc. payroll and timekeeper	328	5213	
Library clerks	329	4233	
File clerks	335	5213	
Records clerks	336	5233	
Financial records processing occupations			
Bookkeepers, accounting, and auditing clerks	337	5233	
Payroll and timekeeping clerks	338	5213	
Billing clerks	339	5213	
Cost and rate clerks	343	5233	
Billing, posting, and calculating machine operators	344	5211	
Duplicating, mail and other office machine operators			
Duplicating machine operators	345	3131	
Mail preparing and paper handling machine operators	346	5131	
Office machine operators, n.e.c.	347	5131	
Communication equipment operators			
Telephone operators	348	6233	
Communication equipment operators, telegraphers, n.e.c.	353	6213	

continues

Table A.3 continued

Occupation Title	Census Code	Segment Code[a]	Census Recode	Occupation Title	Census Code	Segment Code[a]	Census Recode
Mail and message distributing occupations				*Private households service occupations*			
Postal clerks, exc. mail carriers	354	4213		Launderers and ironers	403	3131	
Mail carriers, postal service	355	5233		Cooks, private household	404	5233	
Mail clerks, exc. postal service	356	5131		Housekeepers and butlers	405	5233	
Messengers	357	6131		Child care workers, private household	406	4113	
Material recording, scheduling, and distributing clerks, n.e.c.				Private household cleaners, and servants	407	5133	
Dispatchers	359	4233		*Protective service occupations*			
Production coordinators	363	6233		Supervisors, firefighting, and fire prevention occupations	413	5222	
Traffic, shipping, and receiving clerks	364	5233		Supervisors, police, and detectives	414	4222	
Stock and inventory clerks	365	5233		Supervisors, guards	415	4222	
Meter readers	366	3233		*Firefighting and fire prevention occupations*			
Weighers, measurers, checkers, and samplers	368	5133		Fire inspection and fire prevention occupations	416	5221	
Expediters	373	6233		Firefighting occupations	417	5221	
Material recording, scheduling, and distribution clerks, n.e.c.	374	4233		*Police and detectives*			
Adjusters and investigators				Police and detectives, public service	418	4233	
Insurance adjusters, examiners, and investigators	375	4213		Sheriffs, bailiffs, and other law enforcement officers	423	4233	
Investigators and adjusters, exc. insurance	376	4233		Correctional institution officers	424	4131	
Eligibility clerks, social welfare	377	4312		*Guards*			
Bill and account collectors	378	4233		Crossing guards	425	4133	
Miscellaneous administrative support				Guards and police, exc. public service	426	4131	
General office clerks	379	4233		Protective service occupations, n.e.c.	427	4233	
Bank tellers	383	6233		*Food preparation and service occupations*			
Proofreaders	384	5213		Supervisors, food preparation, and service occupations	433	5222	
Data-entry keyers	385	5213		Bartenders	434	6213	
Statistical clerks	386	5213		Waiters and waitresses	435	4113	
Teachers' aides	387	4213		Cooks	436	5233	
Administrative support occupations, n.e.c.	389	6233		Food counter, fountain, and related occupations	438	4131	

continues

Table A.3 continued

Occupation Title	Census Code	Segment Code[a]	Census Recode
Kitchen workers, food preparation	439	3131	
Waiters'/waitresses' assistants	443	6131	
Misc. food preparation occupations	444	3131	
Health service occupations			
Dental assistants	445	6213	
Health aides, exc. nursing	446	4213	
Nursing aides, orderlies, and attendants	447	6223	
Cleaning and building service occupations, except household			
Supervisors, cleaning, and building service workers	448	5222	
Maids and housemen	449	3121	
Janitors and cleaners	453	3121	
Elevator operators	454	6111	
Pest control occupations	455	6233	
Personal service occupations			
Supervisors, personal service occupations	456	4222	
Barbers	457	6213	
Hairdressers and cosmetologists	458	6213	
Attendants, amusement and recreation facilities	459	6213	463
Guides	461	6213	464
Ushers	462	6213	465
Public transportation attendants	463	6113	466
Baggage porters and bellhops	464	6111	467
Welfare service aides	465	4231	468
Family childcare providers	466	4113	468
Early childhood teacher's assistants	467	4213	
Child care workers, n.e.c.	468	4113	
Personal service occupations, n.e.c.	469	4213	
Farm operators and managers			
Farmers, exc. horticultural	473	5221	
Horticultural specialty farmers	474	5221	
Managers, farms, exc. horticultural	475	6222	
Managers, horticultural specialty farms	476	4222	
Farm occupations, except managerial			
Supervisors, farm workers	477	5222	
Farm workers	479	3121	478
Marine life cultivation workers	483	3121	479
Nursery workers	484	3121	
Related agricultural occupations			
Supervisors, related agricultural occupations	485	5222	
Groundskeepers and gardeners, exc. farm	486	3121	
Animal caretakers, exc. farm	487	3133	
Graders and sorters, agricultural products	488	3121	
Inspectors, agricultural products	489	5233	
Forestry and logging occupations			
Supervisors, forestry, and logging workers	494	5222	
Forestry workers, exc. logging	495	5233	
Timber cutting and logging occupations	496	3121	
Fishing, hunters, and trappers			
Captains and other officers, fishing vessels	497	6222	
Fishers	498	3121	
Hunters and trappers	499	3121	
Mechanics and repairers			
Vehicle and mobile equipment mechanics and repairers			
Supervisors, mechanics, and repairers	503	6222	
Automobile mechanics, exc. apprentices	505	5221	
Automobile mechanic apprentices	506	5221	
Bus, truck, and stationary engine mechanics	507	5221	
Aircraft engine mechanics	508	5221	
Small engine repairers	509	5223	
Automobile body and related repairers	514	5221	
Aircraft mechanics, ex. engine	515	5221	
Heavy equipment mechanics	516	5221	

continues

Table A.3 continued

Occupation Title	Census Code	Segment Code[a]	Census Recode	Occupation Title	Census Code	Segment Code[a]	Census Recode
Farm equipment mechanics	517	5221		*Construction trades, except supervisors*			
Industrial machinery repairers	518	5221		Brickmasons and stonemasons, exc. apprentices	563	5221	
Machinery maintenance occupations	519	3121		Brickmason and stonemason apprentices	564	5221	
Electrical and electronic equipment repairers				Tile setters, hard, and soft	565	5221	
Electronic repairers, communications, and industrial equipment	523	5233		Carpet installers	566	5221	
Data processing equipment repairers	525	5233		Carpenters, exc. apprentices	567	5221	
Household appliance and power tool repairers	526	5223		Carpenter apprentices	569	5221	
Telephone installers and repairers	529	5223		Drywall installers	573	3221	
Misc. electrical and electronic equipment repairers	533	5223		Electricians, exc. apprentices	575	5223	
Heating, air conditioning, and refrigeration mechanics	534	5221		Electrician apprentices	576	5223	
Miscellaneous mechanics and repairers				Electrical power installers and repairers	577	5223	
Camera, watch, and musical instrument repairers	535	5213		Painters, construction and maintenance	579	5221	
Locksmiths and safe repairers	536	5221		Paperhangers	583	5221	
Office machine repairers	538	5233		Plasterers	584	5221	
Mechanical controls and valve repairers	539	5223		Plumbers, pipefitters, and steamfitters, exc. apprentices	585	5221	
Elevator installers and repairers, n.e.c.	543	5221		Plumber, pipefitter, and steamfitter apprentices	587	5221	
Millwrights	544	5221		Concrete and terrazzo finishers	588	5221	
Specified mechanics and repairers, n.e.c.	547	5221		Glaziers	589	5221	
Not specified mechanics and repairers	549	5221		Insulation workers	593	3221	
Construction trades				Paving, surfacing, and tamping equipment operators	594	3221	
Supervisors, brickmasons, stonemasons, and tile setters	553	5222		Roofers	595	5221	
Supervisors, carpenters and related workers	554	5222		Sheetmetal duct installers	596	5221	
Supervisors, electricians, and power transmission installers	555	5222		Structural metal workers	597	5221	
Supervisors, painters, paperhangers, and plasterers	556	5222		Drillers, earth	598	3221	
Supervisors, plumbers, pipefitters, and steamfitters	557	5222		Construction trades, n.e.c.	599	3121	
Supervisors, construction, n.e.c.	558	6222		*Extractive occupations*			
				Supervisors, extractive occupations	613	6233	
				Drillers, oil well	614	3121	
				Explosives workers	615	5221	
				Mining machine operators	616	3121	
				Mining occupations, n.e.c.	617	3121	

continues

Table A.3 continued

Occupation Title	Census Code	Segment Code[a]	Census Recode
Precision production occupations			
Supervisors, production occupations	628	3121	633
Tool and die makers, exc. apprentices	634	5213	
Tool and die maker apprentices	635	5213	
Precision assemblers, metal	636	3131	
Machinists, exc. apprentices	637	5231	
Machinist apprentices	639	5221	
Boilermakers	643	5221	
Precision grinders, fitters, and tool sharpeners	644	3131	
Patternmakers and model makers, metal	645	5233	
Lay-out workers	646	5221	
Precious stones and metals workers (jewelers)	647	5233	
Engravers, metal	649	5233	
Sheet metal workers, exc. apprentices	653	5221	
Sheet metal worker apprentices	654	5221	
Misc. precision metal workers	655	5213	
Precision woodworking occupations			
Patternmakers and model makers, wood	656	5233	
Cabinet makers and bench carpenters	657	5233	
Furniture and wood finishers	658	5221	
Misc. precision woodworkers	659	5221	
Precision textile, apparel, and furnishings machine workers			
Dressmakers	666	5233	
Tailors	667	5233	
Upholsterers	668	3221	
Shoe repairers	669	5233	
Misc. precision apparel and fabric workers	674	6233	
Precision workers, assorted materials			
Hand molders and shapers, exc. jewelers	675	5233	
Patternmakers, lay-out workers, and cutters	676	5233	
Optical goods workers	677	5233	
Dental lab and medical appliance technicians	678	5313	
Bookbinders	679	5233	
Electrical and electronic equipment assemblers	683	3131	
Misc. precision workers, n.e.c.	684	5233	
Precision food production occupations			
Butchers and meat cutters	686	3231	
Bakers	687	5233	
Food batchmakers	688	5233	
Precision inspectors, testers, and related workers			
Inspectors, testers, and graders	689	5233	
Adjusters and calibrators	693	3131	
Plant and system operators			
Water and sewage treatment plant operators	694	5221	
Power plant operators	695	5233	
Stationary engineers	696	5221	
Misc. plant and system operators	699	3233	
Metalworking and plastic working machine operators			
Lathe and turning machine set-up operators	703	5233	
Lathe and turning machine operators	704	3131	
Milling and planing machine operators	705	3131	
Punching and stamping press machine operators	706	5121	
Rolling machine operators	707	3131	
Drilling and boring machine operators	708	3131	
Grinding, abrading, buffing, and polishing machine operators	709	3131	
Forging machine operators	713	5233	
Numerical control machine operators	714	3131	
Misc. metal, plastic, stone, and glass working machine operators	715	5233	
Fabricating machine operators, n.e.c.	717	3131	
Metal and plastic processing machine operators			
Molding and casting machine operators	719	5233	
Metal plating machine operators	723	5233	

continues

Table A.3 continued

Occupation Title	Census Code	Segment Code[a]	Census Recode
Heat treating equipment operators	724	3231	
Misc. metal and plastic processing machine operators	725	5233	
Woodworking machine operators			
Wood lathe, routing, and planing machine operators	726	3131	
Sawing machine operators	727	3131	
Shaping and joining machine operators	728	3233	
Nailing and tacking machine operators	729	3131	
Misc. woodworking machine operators	733	3233	
Printing machine operators			
Printing press operators	734	5233	
Photoengravers and lithographers	735	5233	
Typesetters and compositors	736	5233	
Misc. printing machine operators	737	5233	
Textile, apparel, and furnishings machine operators			
Winding and twisting machine operators	738	3131	
Knitting, looping, taping, and weaving machine operators	739	3131	
Textile cutting machine operators	743	3131	
Textile sewing machine operators	744	3131	
Shoe machine operators	745	3131	
Pressing machine operators	747	3131	
Laundering and dry cleaning machine operators	748	3131	
Misc. textile machine operators	749	3131	
Machine operators, assorted materials			
Cementing and gluing machine operators	753	5233	
Packaging and filling machine operators	754	3131	
Extruding and forming machine operators	755	5233	
Mixing and blending machine operators	756	3131	
Separating, filtering, and clarifying machine operators	757	5233	

Occupation Title	Census Code	Segment Code[a]	Census Recode
Compressing and compacting machine operators	758	3233	
Painting and paint spray machine operators	759	3221	
Roasting and baking machine operators	763	5233	
Washing, cleaning, and pickling machine operators	764	3233	
Folding machine operators	765	5233	
Furnace, kiln, and oven operators, exc. food	766	3121	
Crushing and grinding machine operators	768	3233	
Slicing and cutting machine operators	769	3131	
Motion picture projectionists	773	5233	
Photographic process machine operators	774	5233	
Miscellaneous and not specified machine operators			
Misc. and not specified machine operators	777	5233	
Machine operators, not specified	779	5233	
Fabricators, assemblers, and hand working occupations			
Welders and cutters	783	5221	
Solderers and blazers	784	3131	
Assemblers	785	3131	
Hand cutting and trimming occupations	786	3131	
Hand molding, casting, and forming occupations	787	5233	
Hand painting, coating, and decorating occupations	789	5221	
Hand engraving and printing occupations	793	5233	
Misc. hand working occupations	795	5233	
Production inspectors, testers, samplers, and weighers			
Production inspectors, checkers, and examiners	796	5133	
Production testers	797	5131	
Production samplers and weighers	798	3121	
Graders and sorters, exc. agricultural	799	3131	
Motor vehicle operators			
Supervisors, motor vehicle operators	803	6222	
Truck drivers, heavy	804	6233	

continues

Table A.3 continued

Occupation Title	Census Code	Segment Code[a]	Census Recode	Occupation Title	Census Code	Segment Code[a]	Census Recode
Truck drivers, light	805	6233		Industrial truck and tractor equipment operators	856	3131	
Driver-sales workers	806	6233		Misc. material moving equipment operators	859	3131	
Bus drivers	808	6233		*Handlers, equipment cleaners, helpers, and laborers*			
Taxicab drivers and chauffeurs	809	6113		Supervisors, handlers, equipment cleaners, and laborers, n.e.c.	864	5223	863
Parking lot attendants	813	6111		Helpers, mechanics, and repairers	865	3121	864
Motor transportation occupations, n.e.c.	814	3121		*Helpers, construction and extractive occupations*			
Rail transportation occupations				Helpers, construction trades	866	5221	865
Railroad conductors and yardmasters	823	4233		Helpers, surveyor	867	3121	866
Locomotive operating occupations	824	5233		Helpers, extractive occupations	868	3121	867
Railroad brake, signal, and switch operators	825	3223		Construction laborers	869	3121	
Rail vehicle operators, n.e.c.	826	3133		Production helpers	874	5233	873
Water transportation occupations				*Freight, stock, and material handlers*			
Ship captains and mates, exc. fishing boats	828	6222		Garbage collectors	875	3121	
Sailors and deckhands	829	3121		Stevedores	876	3121	
Marine engineers	833	5221		Stock handlers and baggers	877	3131	
Bridge, lock, and lighthouse tenders	834	6133		Machine feeders and offbearers	878	3131	
Material moving equipment operators				Freight, stock, and material handlers, n.e.c.	883	3121	
Supervisors, material moving equipment operators	843	6222		Garage and service station related occupations	885	6233	
Operating engineers	844	3221		Vehicle washers and equipment cleaners	887	3131	
Longshore equipment operators	845	3121		Hand packers and packagers	888	3131	
Hoist and winch operators	848	3131		Laborers, exc. construction	889	3131	
Crane and tower operators	849	3131					
Excavating and loading machine operators	853	3221					
Grader, dozer, and scraper operators	855	3221					

Note: a. Each digit of the segment code represents one of the four criteria used to define occupational segments. The first digit is Skill Type: (3) Things; (4) Data and People; (5) Data and Things; (6) People and Things. The second digit is Skill Level: (1) Low; (2) Medium; (3) High. The third digit is Potential Gender-Type: (1) Female; (2) Male; (3) Not Clearly Gender-typed. The final digit is Potential Race-Type: (1) Black; (2) White; (3) Not Clearly Race-typed.

Table A.4 1990 Census Industry Codes and Segment Classification

Industry Title	Census Code	Sector Code[a]	Census Recode	Industry Title	Census Code	Sector Code[a]	Census Recode
Agriculture, forestry, and fisheries				*Apparel and other finished textile products manufacturing*			
Agricultural production, crops	10	1222		Apparel and accessories, exc. knit	151	2322	
Agricultural production, livestock	11	1222		Misc. fabricated textile products	152	2322	
Veterinary services	12	1222	20	*Paper and allied products manufacturing*			
Agricultural services, exc. horticultural	30	1222	20	Pulp, paper, and paperboard mills	160	2311	
Landscape and horticultural services	20	1222	21	Misc. paper and pulp products	161	2219	
Forestry	31	1222	30	Paperboard containers and boxes	162	2219	
Fishing, hunting, and trapping	32	1222	31	*Printing, publishing, and allied industries manufacturing*			
Mining				Newspaper publishing and printing	171	2219	
Metal mining	40	1212		Printing, publishing, and allied industries, exc. newspapers	172	2219	
Coal mining	41	1212		*Chemicals and allied products manufacturing*			
Oil and gas extraction	42	1112		Plastics, synthetics, and resins	180	2111	
Nonmetallic mining and quarrying, exc. fuel	50	1212		Drugs	181	2111	
Construction				Soaps and cosmetics	182	2111	
Construction	60	2322		Paints, varnishes, and related products	190	2112	
Food and kindred products manufacturing				Agricultural chemicals	191	2112	
Meat products	100	2219		Industrial and misc. chemicals	192	2111	
Dairy products	101	2219		*Rubber and miscellaneous plastics products manufacturing*			
Canned, frozen, preserved fruits and vegetables	102	2311		Tires and inner tubes	210	2311	
Grain mill products	110	2111		Other rubber products and plastics footwear and belting	211	2311	
Bakery products	111	2219		Misc. plastics products	212	2222	
Sugar and confectionery products	112	2111		*Leather and leather products manufacturing*			
Beverage industries	120	2311		Leather tanning and finishing	220	2322	
Misc. food preparations and kindred products	121	2112		Footwear, exc. rubber and plastic	221	2322	
Not specified food industries	122	2222		Leather products, exc. footwear	222	2322	
Tobacco manufactures	130	2111		*Lumber and wood products manufacturing, except furniture*			
Textile mill products manufacturing				Logging	230	2222	
Knitting mills	132	2219		Sawmills, planing mills, and millwork	231	2322	
Dyeing and finishing textiles, exc. work and knit goods	140	2311					
Carpets and rugs	141	2222					
Yarn, thread, and fabric mills	142	2311					
Misc. textile mill products	150	2322					

continues

Table A.4 continued

Industry Title	Census Code	Sector Code[a]	Census Recode
Wood buildings and mobile homes	232	2222	
Misc. wood products	241	2322	
Furniture and fixtures	242	2322	
Stone, clay, glass, and concrete products manufacturing			
Glass and glass products	250	2311	
Cement, concrete, gypsum, and plaster products	251	2322	
Structural clay products	252	2112	
Pottery and related products	256	2112	
Misc. nonmetallic mineral and stone	262	2322	
Metal industries manufacturing			
Blast furnaces, steelworks, rolling, and finishing mills	270	2311	
Iron and steel foundries	271	2219	
Primary aluminum industries	272	2311	
Other primary metal industries	280	2311	
Cutlery, handtools, and general hardware	281	2112	
Fabricated structural metal products	282	2222	
Screw machine products	290	2112	
Metal forgings and stampings	291	2219	
Ordnance	292	2219	
Misc. fabricated metal products	300	2322	
Not specified metal industries	301	2222	
Machinery manufacturing, except electrical			
Engines and turbines	310	2111	
Farm machinery and equipment	311	2112	
Construction and material handling machines	312	2111	
Metal working machinery	320	2112	
Office and accounting machines	321	2111	
Computer and related equipment	322	2111	
Machinery, exc. electrical, n.e.c.	331	2112	
Not specified machinery	332	2112	
Electrical machinery, equipment, and supplies manufacturing			
Household appliances	340	2111	
Radio, TV, and communication equipment	341	2111	
Electrical machinery, equipment, and supplies, n.e.c.	342	2111	
Not specified electrical machinery, equipment, and supplies			
Transportation equipment manufacturing			
Motor vehicles and motor vehicle equipment	351	2111	
Aircraft and parts	352	2111	
Ship, boat building, and repairing	360	2219	
Railroad locomotives and equipment	361	2311	
Guided missiles, space vehicles, and parts	362	2111	
Cycles and misc. transportation equipment	370	2311	
Professional, photographic equipment and watches manufacturing			
Scientific and controlling instruments	371	2111	
Medical, dental and optical instruments and supplies	372	2111	
Photographic equipment and supplies	380	2111	
Watches, clocks, and clockwork operated devices	381	2111	
Not specified professional equipment	382	None	
Toys, amusement, and sporting goods	390	2322	
Misc. manufacturing industries	391	2322	
Not specified manufacturing industries	392	None	
Transportation			
Railroads	400	3211	
Bus service and urban transit	401	3212	
Taxicab service	402	3212	
Trucking service	410	3222	
Warehousing and storage	411	3212	

continues

Table A.4 continued

Industry Title	Census Code	Sector Code[a]	Census Recode
US Postal Service	412	3211	
Water transportation	420	3112	
Air transportation	421	3112	
Pipelines, exc. natural gas	422	3211	
Services incidental to transportation	432	3222	
Communications			
Radio and television broadcasting	440	4212	
Telephone communications	441	4212	
Telegraph and misc. communication services	442	4212	
Utilities and sanitary services			
Electric light and power	450	2219	460
Gas and steam supply systems	451	2219	461
Electric and gas and other combinations	452	2219	462
Water supply and irrigation	470	2219	
Sanitary services	471	2219	
Not specified utilities	472	2222	
Wholesale trade (durable goods)			
Motor vehicles and equipment	500	3222	
Furniture and home furnishings	501	3222	
Lumber and construction materials	502	3222	
Professional and commercial equipment and supplies	510	3222	
Metals and minerals, exc. petroleum	511	3222	
Electrical goods	512	3222	
Hardware, plumbing, and heating supplies	521	3222	
Not specified electrical and hardware	522	None	
Machinery, equipment, and supplies	530	3222	
Scrap and waste materials	531	3212	
Misc. wholesale, durable goods	532	3212	
Wholesale trade (nondurable goods)			
Paper and paper products	540	3222	
Drugs, chemicals, and allied products	541	3212	
Apparel, fabrics, and notions	542	3222	
Groceries and related products	550	3222	
Farm products—raw materials	551	3222	
Petroleum products	552	3112	
Alcoholic beverages	560	3222	
Farm supplies	561	3212	
Misc. wholesale, nondurable goods	562	3212	
Not specified wholesale trade	571	3222	
Retail trade			
Lumber and building material retailing	580	3222	
Hardware stores	581	3222	
Retail nurseries and garden stores	582	3222	
Mobile home dealers	590	3222	
Department stores	591	3211	
Variety stores	592	3211	
Misc. general merchandise stores	600	3211	
Grocery stores	601	3211	
Dairy products stores	602	3222	
Retail bakeries	610	3222	
Food stores, n.e.c.	611	3222	
Motor vehicle dealers	612	3222	
Auto and home supply stores	620	3222	
Gasoline service stations	621	3222	
Misc. vehicle dealers	622	3222	
Apparel and accessory stores, exc. shoe	623	3212	630
Shoe stores	630	3222	631
Furniture and home furnishings stores	631	3222	632
Household appliance stores	632	3222	640
Radio, TV, and computer stores	633	3222	640
Music stores	640	3222	
Eating and drinking places	641	3222	
Drug stores	642	3212	

continues

Table A.4 continued

Industry Title	Census Code	Sector Code[a]	Census Recode
Liquor stores	650	3222	
Sporting goods, bicycles, and hobby stores	651	3222	
Book and stationery stores	652	3222	
Jewelry stores	660	3222	
Gift, novelty, and souvenir shops	661	3222	682
Sewing, needlework, and piece goods stores	662	3222	661
Mail order houses	663	3222	662
Vending machine operators	670	3222	
Direct selling establishments	671	3222	
Fuel dealers	672	3222	
Retail florists	681	3222	
Misc. retail stores	682	3222	
Not specified retail trade	691	3222	
Finance, insurance, and real estate			
Banking	700	4222	
Savings institutions, including credit unions	701	4222	
Credit agencies, n.e.c.	702	4222	
Security, commodity brokerage, and investment companies	710	4222	
Insurance	711	4222	
Real estate, including real estate–insurance offices	712	4222	
Business and repair services			
Advertising	721	4222	
Services to dwellings and other buildings	722	4212	
Commercial research, development, and testing labs	730	5212	891
Personnel supply services	731	4222	
Business management and consulting services	892	4212	732
Computer and data processing services	732	4222	740
Detective and protective services	740	4222	741
Business services, n.e.c.	741	4222	742

Industry Title	Census Code	Sector Code[a]	Census Recode
Automotive rental and leasing, w/o driver	742	4212	750
Automotive parking and carwashes	750	4212	
Automotive repair and related services	751	6222	
Electrical repair shops	752	6222	
Misc. repair services	760	6222	
Personal services			
Private households	761	6222	
Hotels and motels	762	6222	
Lodging places, exc. hotels and motels	770	6222	
Laundry, cleaning, and garment services	771	6222	
Beauty shops	772	6222	
Barber shops	780	6222	
Funeral service and crematories	781	6212	
Shoe repair shops	782	6212	
Dressmaking shops	790	6222	
Misc. personal services	791	6212	
Entertainment and recreation services			
Theaters and motion pictures	800	6212	
Video tape rental	801	4222	742
Bowling centers	802	6222	801
Misc. entertainment and recreation services	810	6222	802
Professional and related services			
Offices and clinics of physicians	812	5222	
Offices and clinics of dentists	820	5222	
Offices and clinics of chiropractors	821	5222	
Offices and clinics of optometrists	822	5222	
Offices and clinics of health practitioners, n.e.c.	830	5222	
Hospitals	831	5212	
Nursing and personal care facilities	832	5212	
Health services, n.e.c.	840	5222	
Legal services	841	5222	
Elementary and secondary schools	842	5222	

continues

Table A.4 continued

Industry Title	Census Code	Sector Code[a]	Census Recode	Industry Title	Census Code	Sector Code[a]	Census Recode
Colleges and universities	850	5222		Accounting, auditing, and bookkeeping services	890	5212	
Vocational schools	851	5222		Research, development, and testing services	891	5212	
Libraries	852	5222		Misc. professional and related services	893	5222	892
Educational services, n.e.c.	860	5222		*Public administration*			
Job training and vocational rehabilitation services	861	5212		Executive and legislative offices	900	5999	
Child day care services	862	5212		General government, n.e.c.	901	5999	
Family child care homes	863	6222	770	Justice, public order, and safety	910	5999	
Residential care facilities, without nursing	870	5212		Public finance, taxation, and monetary policy	921	5999	
Social services, n.e.c.	871	5212		Administration of human resources programs	922	5999	
Museums, art galleries, and zoos	872	5212	881	Administration of environmental quality and housing programs	930	5999	
Labor unions	873	5222		Administration of economic programs	931	5999	
Religious organizations	880	5222		National security and international affairs	932	5999	
Membership organizations	881	5212					
Engineering, architectural, and surveying services	882	5222					

Note: a. Each digit of the sector code represents one of the four criteria used to define industrial sectors. The first digit is Product Type: (1) Extractive; (2) Transformative; (3) Distributive Services; (4) Producer Services; (5) Social Services; (6) Personal Services. The second digit is Market Scope: (1) International; (2) Domestic; (3) Domestic with Foreign Penetration; (9) Not applicable (government). The third digit is Concentration: (1) Oligopoly; (2) Competitive; (9) Not applicable (government). The final digit is Economic Scale: (1) Large; (2) Small to Medium; (9) Mixed or Not applicable (government).

the same two other endogenous variables, the employment segregation of white women from white men and of black men from white men (see the discussion in Chapter 5 for the rationale for this model specification). Because the collinearity diagnostics did not suggest the same problems with using instrumental variables, and in order to provide consistency across the four earnings level analyses, I used a 2SLS estimation approach to estimate the group-specific earnings level models.

Notes

1. I used a minor revision of the 1990 Census occupation codes to maintain comparability with the 1980 Census occupation codes in order to facilitate the measurement of employment growth from 1980 to 1990. The revisions are presented in the last column of Table A.3.

2. The industry coding I used is a slight modification of the 1990 Census industry codes, which preserves comparability with the 1980 Census industry codes for valid measurement of employment growth. The modifications are shown in the last column of Table A.4.

3. The category means are 7.28 for white females, 7.23 for white males, 6.85 for black females, and 6.76 for black males. I calculated these from data in Table 262 from the *1980 Census of Population, Vol. 1, Characteristics of the Population, Chapter D, Part 1, Section A* (US Bureau of the Census 1983).

4. There was a minor variation on this coding for the cases from the 1990 1% PUMS, which identifies residence for cases using public use metropolitan areas (PUMAs) rather than SMSAs. Some of these cases are classified as residing in a mixed metropolitan-nonmetropolitan area. For these cases, I used the geographic equivalency data (US Census Bureau 1994c) to calculate the proportion of all residents in the PUMA in a metropolitan area. I assigned this imputed mean to the mixed cases for the regression analysis and used the imputed modal category to define metropolitan residence for the log-linear analyses.

5. Although a more detailed measurement of geographic residence is possible (i.e., identifying state of residence as is done in the earnings analysis), this had to be balanced against the level of detail used to define labor market positions to ensure that the crosstabulation of position by residence (and by the other predictors) was not too sparse. Priority was given to detail in the definition of positions rather than detail in geography.

6. The approach I used required over thirty-nine days of continuous processing to estimate the set of initial models for 1990 and slightly more time for the regional models.

7. In Goodman's notation, the model is:

$$(EPMC) (EPMR) (EPMS) (EPMG) (EPCR) (EPCS) (EPCG) (EPRS) (EPRG) (EPSG)$$
$$(EMCR) (EMCS) (EMCG) (EMRS) (EMRG) (EMSG) (ECRS) (ECRG) (ECSG) (ERSG)$$
$$(PMCR) (PMCS) (PMCG) (PMRS) (PMRG) (PMSG) (PCRS) (PCRG) (PCSG) (PRSG)$$
$$(MCRS) (MCRG) (MCSG) (MRSG) (CRSG) (EPDj) (EMDj) (ECDj) (ERDj) (ESDj)$$
$$(PMDj) (PCDj) (PRDj) (PSDj) (MCDj) (MRDj) (MSDj) (CRDj) (CSDj) (RSDj) (GDj)$$

where E is education, P is potential experience, M is marital status, C is children present, R is metropolitan residence, S is southern residence, and G is race-sex group.

8. The model is the same as that specified in note 7 above, except that the last term, GD_j, is replaced by SGD_j.

9. The ICPSR Web address is http://www.icpsr.umich.edu/. The data are archived as Study Number 1225, *1980 and 1990 Industrial Structure Measures*. Users of these data should acknowledge my research support from the National Science Foundation (Grant Number SBR-9422800) and the role of ICPSR as distributor of the data.

10. Two coders independently read the reports on each industry's market and activities, written by economic experts in the industry, and assigned values on foreign penetration from zero (no penetration) to six (substantial presence of foreign competition). Intercoder reliability was extremely high (a correlation of 0.92) with relatively few differences between coders of more than one category (9.5%).

11. To the best of my knowledge, these diagnostics have not been developed for EGLS models, so I evaluated them using an OLS regression model equivalent to each EGLS model I estimated. Because the OLS regression models are unbiased but inefficient in this situation, this provides a reasonable guesstimate of collinearity problems for the corresponding EGLS models.

12. In all of the analyses, there is also a near dependency involving some of the dummy variables for the presence of missing data, but these are inconsequential for the coefficients of interest.

13. As detailed earlier, a labor market position can sometimes span more than one of the twenty industry segments or the forty-two occupational segments. However, each labor market position lies entirely within a more aggregated definition of thirteen industry sectors (collapsing across the market scope criterion) and ten occupational segments (collapsing across the race- and gender-typed criteria). Labor market positions within the same aggregated sector or segment were specified as having correlated errors and a common error variance.

14. For example, for the base analysis of black men to white men, the squared multiple correlation of predicted employment segregation with the other predictors (excluding the instrument) is greater than 0.98, indicating that the instrumental variable provides extremely little additional variation.

15. The collinearity problem with the 2SLS estimation noted earlier affects the stability and precision of the individual coefficients, but it does not affect the precision of the predicted value of y nor the estimation of the residuals (Allsion 1999: 142–145).

Appendix B
Numeric Results Tables

The Appendix provides the tables of detailed numeric results for the analyses reported in Chapters 4, 5 and 6.

Table B4.1 SUR-EGLS Regressions of Employment Segregation[a] on Skills, Growth and Employment Rates, Race and Gender Typing, Product Market Structure, and Linkages to Other Actors[b]

Predictors	Black Women: White Men		Black Men: White Men		White Women: White Men		Black Women: Black Men		Black Women: White Women	
	b	Beta	b	Beta	b	Beta	b	Beta	b	Beta
General skills and growth										
Skills and training	-.7072** (.1068)	-.43	-.1206** (.0455)	-.17	-.6207** (.0903)	-.41	-.4941** (.0901)	-.36	-.1201** (.0498)	-.17
Skills and training × growth	.0875* (.0459)	.03	.0434* (.0193)	.03	.0806* (.0369)	.02	.0479 (.0399)	.02	-.0208 (.0227)	-.01
Growth rate	-.0402 (.0499)	-.01	.0163 (.0218)	.01	-.0258 (.0431)	-.01	-.0431 (.0431)	-.02	-.0172 (.0238)	-.01
Race- and gender-typing										
Environmental conditions	-.1869** (.0668)	-.07	-.1210† (.0269)	-.10	-.1715** (.0571)	-.06	-.0804 (.0592)	-.03	-.0329 (.0330)	-.03
Physical exertion	-1.1483** (.0711)	-.59	.0564* (.0294)	.07	-1.1510** (.0608)	-.63	-1.1740** (.0610)	-.72	.0498 (.0336)	.06
Routinization	-.3440† (.0669)	-.18	.1032** (.0283)	.13	-.2873++ (.0569)	-.16	-.4117++ (.0571)	-.26	-.0584 (.0317)	-.05
Status in interactions	-.4580++ (.0880)	-.37	-.1172++ (.0366)	-.22	-.4737++ (.0751)	-.41	-.3506++ (.0766)	-.34	-.0081 (.0430)	-.01
Squared status in interactions	.0763** (.0115)	.34	.0345** (.0050)	.35	.0643** (.0098)	.30	.0408** (.0098)	.21	.0136** (.0056)	.14
Authority	.1639 (.0887)	.03	-.0484 (.0399)	-.02	.2010† (.0760)	.04	.1631† (.0752)	.04	.0060 (.0414)	.00
No authority, part-time	-.1269 (.1054)	-.03	-.0561 (.0471)	-.03	-.1604 (.0913)	-.04	-.0943 (.0900)	-.03	.0308 (.0489)	.02
Physical dexterity	.1996** (.0420)	.08	-.0762++ (.0182)	-.08	.1985** (.0354)	.09	.2662* (.0357)	.14	-.0179 (.0200)	-.02
Nurturant skill	.2107* (.1187)	.03	.0623 (.0557)	.02	.1853* (.1022)	.03	.1634* (.0969)	.03	-.0293 (.0523)	-.01
Clerical perception	.6004** (.0811)	.23	.0683 (.0358)	.06	.6656** (.0703)	.28	.5261** (.0700)	.25	-.0230 (.0389)	-.02

continues

Table B4.1 continued

Predictors	Black Women: White Men b	Beta	Black Men: White Men b	Beta	White Women: White Men b	Beta	Black Women: Black Men b	Beta	Black Women: White Women b	Beta
Math skills	-.9863** (.1048)	-.36	-.3388++ (.0455)	-.29	-.6380** (.0890)	-.25	-.6985** (.0908)	-.30	-.3284** (.0507)	-.27
Desirable employment										
Percent sufficient work	-.0357** (.0038)	-.30	-.0064** (.0017)	-.13	-.0466** (.0032)	-.42	-.0297** (.0032)	-.30	.0079† (.0018)	.15
Percent unemployed	.0300** (.0089)	.07	.0358** (.0038)	.19	.0010 (.0077)	.00	-.0080 (.0078)	-.02	.0298** (.0042)	.16
Percent self-employed	-.0321** (.0029)	-.20	-.0115** (.0011)	-.17	-.0174** (.0024)	-.12	-.0209** (.0025)	-.15	-.0147** (.0014)	-.21
Product market structure										
Market power	.2359++ (.0434)	.12	.1293++ (.0190)	.15	.1294++ (.0375)	.07	.0955++ (.0372)	.06	.0773++ (.0208)	.09
Profitability	.1082+ (.0487)	.03	-.0317 (.0220)	-.02	.1174++ (.0423)	.04	.1169++ (.0411)	.04	-.0213 (.0236)	-.02
Economic scale	.0396 (.0252)	.02	.0101 (.0124)	.01	.0165 (.0223)	.01	.0328 (.0215)	.02	.0252 (.0136)	.03
Capital intensity	-.1192++ (.0420)	-.05	.0010 (.0185)	.00	-.1045++ (.0358)	-.05	-.1140++ (.0367)	-.05	-.0066 (.0227)	-.01
Foreign involvement	.0473 (.0455)	.02	.0306 (.0215)	.03	.0091 (.0394)	.00	.0162 (.0371)	.01	.0499+ (.0232)	.05
Productivity	.0178 (.0445)	.01	.0131 (.0197)	.01	.0090 (.0381)	.00	-.0145 (.0386)	-.01	-.0054 (.0220)	-.01
Linkages to other actors										
Industry unionization	-.5432† (.2055)	-.05	-.0665 (.0862)	-.02	-.6693++ (.1769)	-.07	-.4554+ (.1812)	-.05	.2864** (.0997)	.06
Occupation unionization	.0862 (.2693)	.01	-.0635 (.1133)	-.01	-.5206+ (.2335)	-.04	-.1458 (.2317)	-.01	.5489** (.1304)	.10

continues

Table B4.1 continued

Predictors	Black Women: White Men		Black Men: White Men		White Women: White Men		Black Women: Black Men		Black Women: White Women	
	b	Beta	b	Beta	b	Beta	b	Beta	b	Beta
Percent public sector	.0049* (.0022)	.09	.0096** (.0009)	.42	-.0025 (.0019)	-.05	-.0048† (.0019)	-.11	.0076** (.0011)	.32
Federal purchases	-.0134++ (.0029)	-.06	-.0061++ (.0012)	-.07	-.0104++ (.0024)	-.05	-.0083++ (.0026)	-.05	-.0019 (.0015)	-.02
Constant	4.2474		1.2418		4.4785		3.2849		-.1292	
Between-equation correlation	-.061		.283		-.276		-.081		-.062	
Lagrange multiplier test	442.475‡		583.880‡		66.781‡		177.453‡		621.019‡	
Breusch-Pagan tests for	Initial	Adjusted	Initial	Adjusted	Initial	Adjusted	Initial	Adjusted	Initial	Adjusted
Group size	34.518‡	1.269	61.816‡	1.166	21.621‡	.808	42.666‡	.888	69.611‡	1.960
Sectors	130.933‡	8.762	109.483‡	13.876	122.046‡	10.205	136.947‡	15.790	142.738‡	9.521
$R^2 y,\hat{y}$	.555		.521		.629		.541		.459	
N	1916		1916		1916		1916		1916	

Notes: a. Employment segregation controls for worker differences in human capital, family structure, and geographic residence.
b. Dummy indicators for missing value substitutions are not reported.

*p < .05, one-tailed + p < .05, two-tailed †p < .05, two-tailed, where effects were opposite of predictions
**p < .01, one-tailed ++p < .01, two-tailed ‡p < .05 for the LM and Breusch-Pagan tests

Table B4.2 SUR-EGLS Regressions of Employment Segregation[a] on Skills, Growth and Employment Rates, Race and Gender Typing, Product Market Structure, and Linkages to Other Actors with Significant Interactions[b]

Predictors	Black Women: White Men		Black Men: White Men		White Women: White Men		Black Women: Black Men		Black Women: White Women	
	b	Beta	b	Beta	b	Beta	b	Beta	b	Beta
General skills and training										
Skills and training	-.6928** (.1039)	-.42	-.1202** (.0452)	-.17	-.5643** (.0883)	-.37	-.4597** (.0874)	-.34	-.1222** (.0482)	-.17
Skills and training × growth	-.1255 (.0893)	-.04	.0490* (.0198)	.03	.1086 (.0995)	.03	-.1082 (.0754)	-.04	-.0287 (.0225)	-.02
Growth rate	-.1102 (.0740)	-.03	.0200 (.0217)	.01	.9943+ (.4042)	.33	-.1915++ (.0707)	-.07	-.0126 (.0236)	-.01
Race- and gender-typing										
Environmental conditions	-.0985 (.0681)	-.03	-.1280† (.0268)	-.10	-.0944* (.0574)	-.04	-.0025 (.0597)	.00	-.0331 (.0327)	-.03
Physical exertion	-1.1188** (.0698)	-.57	.0545* (.0292)	.07	-1.1373** (.0596)	-.63	-1.1599** (.0595)	-.71	.0574* (.0328)	.07
Routinization	-.4026† (.0680)	-.21	.1010** (.0281)	.12	-.3230++ (.0564)	-.18	-.4431++ (.0563)	-.28	-.0327 (.0309)	-.04
Status in interactions	-.4179++ (.0861)	-.34	-.1088++ (.0364)	-.21	-.4848++ (.0731)	-.42	-.3444++ (.0753)	-.33	-.0060 (.0420)	-.01
Squared status in interactions	.0647** (.0114)	.28	.0328** (.0049)	.34	.0628** (.0097)	.30	.0309** (.0098)	.16	.0155** (.0054)	.16
Authority	-.2953** (.1155)	-.06	-.0450 (.0511)	-.02	-.3583** (.1001)	-.08	-.2923** (.0961)	-.07	.0324 (.0481)	.01
No authority, part-time	.0855 (.0886)	.02	-.0464 (.0396)	-.03	.1174 (.0755)	.03	.1332 (.0756)	.04	.0053 (.0406)	.00
Physical dexterity	.2007** (.0409)	.09	-.0735** (.0181)	-.07	.1780** (.0346)	.08	.2618** (.0347)	.13	-.0064 (.0197)	-.01
Nurturant skill	.2652* (.1262)	.04	.0674 (.0557)	.03	.2332* (.1012)	.04	.2469** (.1008)	.05	-.0449 (.0510)	-.02
Clerical perception	.5527** (.0798)	.22	.0683 (.0356)	.06	.6560** (.0685)	.28	.5082** (.0688)	.24	-.0270 (.0382)	-.02

continues

Table B4.2 continued

Predictors	Black Women: White Men b	Beta	Black Men: White Men b	Beta	White Women: White Men b	Beta	Black Women: Black Men b	Beta	Black Women: White Women b	Beta
Math skills	-.9544** (.1022)	-.35	-.3549** (.0454)	-.30	-.6832** (.0878)	-.27	-.6887** (.0890)	-.30	-.3325** (.0497)	-.28
Desirable employment										
Percent sufficient work	-.0374** (.0037)	-.31	-.0061** (.0017)	-.12	-.0473** (.0032)	-.43	-.0323** (.0032)	-.32	.0080† (.0018)	.15
Percent unemployed	.0314** (.0087)	.07	.0380** (.0038)	.20	.0020 (.0076)	.00	-.0130 (.0078)	-.04	.0296** (.0042)	.15
Percent self-employed	-.0347** (.0028)	-.21	-.0115** (.0012)	-.17	-.0183** (.0023)	-.12	-.0245** (.0026)	-.18	-.0161** (.0014)	-.23
Product market structure										
Market power	.2751++ (.0429)	.14	-.0071 (.0344)	-.01	.1525++ (.0370)	.08	.1406++ (.0371)	.09	.0991++ (.0304)	.12
Profitability	1.2962++ (.2171)	.42	-.0333 (.0222)	-.03	1.0811++ (.1509)	.37	.8892++ (.1586)	.34	-.0241 (.0234)	-.02
Economic scale	.0445 (.0259)	.03	.0083 (.0126)	.01	.0204 (.0219)	.01	.0386 (.0217)	.03	.0274+ (.0136)	.04
Capital intensity	-.1087++ (.0416)	-.04	.0002 (.0185)	.00	-.0959++ (.0345)	-.04	-.0944++ (.0364)	-.05	-.0055 (.0227)	-.01
Foreign involvement	.0069 (.0449)	.00	.0302 (.0215)	.03	-.0300 (.0385)	-.01	-.0304 (.0369)	-.01	.0421 (.0231)	.04
Productivity	-.0034 (.0436)	.00	.0143 (.0196)	.01	-.0013 (.0367)	.00	-.0296 (.0377)	-.01	.0009 (.0217)	.00
Linkages to other actors										
Industry unionization	-.5145† (.2060)	-.05	-.0719 (.0870)	-.02	-.7207++ (.1739)	-.08	-.4339+ (.1803)	-.05	.2730** (.0993)	.06
Occupation unionization	.0646 (.2652)	.01	-.0525 (.1128)	-.01	-.4769+ (.2284)	-.04	-.2161 (.2261)	-.02	.4966** (.1287)	.09
Percent public sector	.0032 (.0022)	.06	.0099** (.0009)	.43	-.0045† (.0018)	-.09	-.0060† (.0019)	-.13	.0079** (.0011)	.33

continues

Table B4.2 continued

Predictors	Black Women: White Men b	Beta	Black Men: White Men b	Beta	White Women: White Men b	Beta	Black Women: Black Men b	Beta	Black Women: White Women b	Beta
Federal purchases	-.0131++ (.0028)	-.06	-.0062++ (.0012)	-.07	-.0092++ (.0023)	-.05	-.0075++ (.0025)	-.04	-.0021 (.0015)	-.02
Moderating interactions										
Growth										
Routinization	-.3319++ (.0952)	-.10			-.2764++ (.0782)	-.09	-.2632+ (.0835)	-.09		
Environmental conditions	.3620++ (.0915)	.09			.3018++ (.0867)	.08	.3371++ (.0811)	.10		
Authority							.1008 (.1170)	.01		
No authority, part-time							.3077++ (.1097)	.05		
Nurturant skill					.3558++ (.1314)	.04				
Math skills					.4179++ (.1424)	-.37				
Profit										
Routinization	-.1525+ (.0624)	-.04								
Status in interactions							-.1636++ (.0835)	-.14		
Squared status in interactions							.0289+ (.0119)	.11		
Authority	-.2586 (.1549)	-.02			-.2026 (.1290)	-.02	-.1197 (.1356)	-.01		
No authority, part-time	-.3833++ (.1411)	-.05			.4101++ (.1167)	-.06	-.4394++ (.1156)	-.07		
Nurturant skill	.4242+ (.2152)	.03					.4241+ (.1810)	.04		
Clerical perception	-.3941++ (.0719)	-.36			.3165++ (.0503)	-.31	-.1994++ (.0646)	-.22		

continues

Table B4.2 continued

Predictors	Black Women: White Men		Black Men: White Men		White Women: White Men		Black Women: Black Men		Black Women: White Women	
	b	Beta	b	Beta	b	Beta	b	Beta	b	Beta
Market power										
Environmental conditions			.0851++ (.0219)	.08						
Physical exertion	.1259++ (.0351)	.05			.1140++ (.0289)	.05	.0863++ (.0303)	.04		
Status in interactions			.1102++ (.0256)	.25					.0251 (.0235)	.06
Squared status in interactions			-.0162++ (.0043)	-.16					-.0132++ (.0039)	-.13
Authority	-.3102++ (.0978)	-.04	-.1038+ (.0468)	-.03	-.2148+ (.0848)	-.03	-.2557++ (.0801)	-.04		
No authority, part-time	-.3273+ (.1284)	-.05	.0321 (.0583)	.01	-.4488++ (.1118)	-.07	-.2718++ (.1062)	-.05		
Nurturant skill					.2875++ (.1045)	.04				
Constant	4.419		1.245		4.698		3.591		-.101	
Between-equation correlation	-.095		.242		-.239		-.096		-.173	
Lagrange multiplier test	531.138‡		534.911‡		116.270‡		221.901‡		628.428‡	
Breusch-Pagan tests for	Initial	Adjusted	Initial	Adjusted	Initial	Adjusted	Initial	Adjusted	Initial	Adjusted
Group size	42.491‡	1.684	60.885‡	1.583	25.590‡	.954	53.073‡	.820	73.319‡	2.090
Sectors	134.868‡	10.149	110.989‡	13.896	144.005‡	13.544	143.459‡	19.674	151.134‡	11.224
R^2 $y, \hat{y}$	.569		.524		.649		.563		.464	
N	1916		1916		1916		1916		1916	

Notes: a. Employment segregation controls for worker differences in human capital, family structure, and geographic residence.

b. Dummy indicators for missing value substitutions are not reported.

* $p < .05$, one-tailed $^{+}p < .05$, two-tailed $^{†}p < .05$, two-tailed, where effects were opposite of predictions

** $p < .01$, one-tailed $^{++}p < .01$, two-tailed

‡ $p < .05$ for the LM and Breusch-Pagan tests

Table B5.1 Two-Stage EGLS Regressions of Earnings Levels[a] on Skills and Growth, Race and Gender Typing, Desirable Employment, Product Market Structure, and Linkages to Other Actors[b]

Predictors	Black Women		Black Men		White Women		Black Women	
	b	Beta	b	Beta	b	Beta	b	Beta
General skills and growth								
Skills and training	.0968** (.0168)	.36	.0412** (.0161)	.17	.0299* (.0148)	.11	.0112 (.0175)	.04
Employment growth	.0082 (.0077)	.02	.0263** (.0063)	.05	.0243** (.0063)	.05	.0114* (.0062)	.02
Employment segregation								
Black men to white men	-.0019 (.0368)	.00	-.0446 (.0330)	-.13	-.0346 (.0324)	-.09	-.1436** (.0345)	-.39
White women to white men	-.0196* (.0115)	-.11	-.0307** (.0100)	-.19	-.0229** (.0095)	-.13	-.0781** (.0159)	-.46
White- or male-typed work								
Status in interactions	.0242 (.0153)	.12	.0398** (.0133)	.22	.0544** (.0130)	.27	.0679** (.0140)	.35
Squared status in interactions	-.0051** (.0021)	-.14	-.0038 (.0025)	-.11	-.0073** (.0020)	-.20	-.0068** (.0027)	-.19
Authority	.0443** (.0139)	.05	.0575** (.0141)	.08	.0617** (.0121)	.07	.1167** (.0152)	.15
No authority, part-time	.0325* (.0152)	.05	.0185 (.0140)	.03	.0228* (.0128)	.03	.0250* (.0147)	.04
Math skills	.0879** (.0212)	.19	.0340* (.0196)	.08	.1042** (.0181)	.23	.0297 (.0208)	.07
Black- or female-typed work								
Physical exertion	-.0289* (.0158)	-.09	-.0499** (.0135)	-.17	-.0337** (.0131)	-.11	-.0586** (.0145)	-.19
Nurturant skill	-.0006 (.0169)	.00	-.0244 (.0184)	-.03	-.0189 (.0149)	-.02	-.0498** (.0210)	-.05
Physical dexterity	.0181** (.0076)	.05	.0323** (.0070)	.09	.0006 (.0065)	.00	.0210** (.0074)	.06
Clerical perception	.0032 (.0143)	.01	.0283* (.0130)	.07	.0140 (.0120)	.03	.0336* (.0147)	.08

continues

Table B5.1 continued

Predictors	Black Women		Black Men		White Women		Black Women	
	b	Beta	b	Beta	b	Beta	b	Beta
Routinization	.0434** (.0103)	.14	.0127 (.0092)	.05	.0196** (.0090)	.06	.0068 (.0097)	.02
Environmental conditions	.0225* (.0113)	.05	.0126 (.0083)	.03	.0303** (.0092)	.07	.0299** (.0083)	.07
Desirable employment								
Percent sufficient work	.0047** (.0008)	.24	.0034** (.0007)	.19	.0062** (.0006)	.32	.0035** (.0007)	.19
Percent unemployed	-.0063** (.0019)	-.09	-.0033* (.0015)	-.05	-.0028* (.0016)	-.04	.0017 (.0016)	.02
Percent self-employed	-.0003 (.0006)	-.01	.0002 (.0006)	.01	.0005 (.0005)	.02	.0005 (.0006)	.02
Product market structure								
Market power	.0247** (.0083)	.08	.0170** (.0069)	.06	.0186** (.0070)	.06	.0170** (.0068)	.06
Profitability	.0336** (.0079)	.07	.0217** (.0073)	.05	.0320** (.0066)	.06	.0165* (.0073)	.03
Economic scale	-.0057 (.0049)	-.02	.0034 (.0038)	.01	.0000 (.0037)	.00	.0069* (.0037)	.03
Capital intensity	.0142* (.0083)	.03	.0143** (.0053)	.04	.0053 (.0061)	.01	.0122** (.0049)	.03
Foreign involvement	.0180** (.0075)	.04	.0171** (.0051)	.05	.0240** (.0064)	.06	.0232** (.0047)	.06
Productivity	.0000 (.0072)	.00	-.0116* (.0058)	-.03	-.0080 (.0059)	-.02	-.0100* (.0057)	-.03
Linkages to other actors								
Industry unionization	.3445** (.0343)	.20	.3499** (.0273)	.23	.3141** (.0274)	.19	.3146** (.0266)	.19

continues

Table B5.1 continued

Predictors	Black Women b	Black Women Beta	Black Men b	Black Men Beta	White Women b	White Women Beta	Black Women b	Black Women Beta
Occupation unionization	.1425** (.0414)	.07	.1500** (.0340)	.08	.1344** (.0350)	.06	.1269** (.0355)	.06
Percent public sector	-.0004 (.0005)	-.04	-.0005 (.0004)	-.07	-.0006 (.0004)	-.07	-.0003 (.0004)	-.03
Federal purchases	.0015** (.0005)	.04	.0006 (.0004)	.02	.0012** (.0004)	.04	-.0006 (.0004)	-.02
Interactions with sex segregation								
Dexterity by WFWM	-.0137** (.0046)	-.05			-.0190** (.0038)	-.06		
Clerical perception by WFWM							.0256** (.0055)	.03
Nurturant skill by WFWM	-.0359** (.0136)	-.04						
Constant	8.982		9.397		8.736		9.467	
Lagrange multiplier test	23.687‡		283.913‡		369.313‡		233.749‡	
Breusch-Pagan tests for	Initial	Adjusted	Initial	Adjusted	Initial	Adjusted	Initial	Adjusted
Group size	416.69‡	1.30	95.50‡	.01	53.46‡	.05	8.77‡	.01
Sectors	117.79‡	70.14‡	458.83‡	33.92‡	101.48‡	30.35	640.76‡	37.99‡
Buse's R²	.621		.552		.636		.581	
N	1916		1916		1916		1916	

Notes: a. Earnings levels controls for worker differences in human capital, family structure, geographic residence, and labor supply.
b. Dummy indicators for missing value substitution are not reported.
+p < .05, two-tailed ++ p < .01, two-tailed
‡p < .05 for the LM and Breusch-Pagan tests

Table B5.2 SUR-EGLS Regressions of Earnings Gaps[a] on Skills, Growth and Employment Rates, Race and Gender Typing, Product Market Structure, and Linkages to Other Actors[b]

Predictors	Black Women: White Men		Black Men: White Men		White Women: White Men		Black Women: Black Men		Black Women: White Women	
	b	Beta	b	Beta	b	Beta	b	Beta	b	Beta
General skills and training										
Skills and training	.0768† (.0197)	.38	.0299† (.0131)	.23	.0252 (.0146)	.17	.0164 (.0165)	.09	.0570† (.0110)	.38
Growth and employment rates										
Growth rate	-.0062 (.0087)	-.02	.0122+ (.0057)	.05	.0116 (.0064)	.04	-.0144 (.0080)	-.04	-.0140+ (.0062)	-.05
Percent sufficient work	.0017† (.0007)	.11	-.0005 (.0005)	-.05	.0046† (.0005)	.42	.0009 (.0006)	.07	-.0017** (.0004)	-.15
Percent unemployed	-.0015 (.0014)	-.03	-.0005 (.0009)	-.02	.0011 (.0011)	.03	-.0002 (.0014)	.00	-.0028† (.0012)	-.07
Percent self-employed	-.0024** (.0005)	-.12	-.0023** (.0003)	-.18	-.0005 (.0003)	-.03	-.0013** (.0005)	-.07	-.0014** (.0003)	-.09
Race- and gender-typing										
Routinization	.0187 (.0119)	.08	.0106 (.0078)	.07	-.0026 (.0090)	-.02	.0045 (.0104)	.02	.0139* (.0073)	.08
Environmental conditions	-.0204* (.0114)	-.06	-.0278† (.0065)	-.12	-.0056 (.0082)	-.02	.0033 (.0109)	.01	-.0116 (.0088)	-.04
Physical exertion	.0211 (.0129)	.09	.0029 (.0078)	.02	.0586† (.0098)	.33	-.0040 (.0118)	-.02	-.0090 (.0081)	-.05
Status in interactions	-.0467++ (.0161)	-.30	-.0438++ (.0099)	-.44	-.0040 (.0114)	-.04	-.0183 (.0142)	-.14	-.0318++ (.0104)	-.28
Squared status in interactions	.0052** (.0022)	.19	.0076** (.0017)	.42	.0005 (.0017)	.03	.0004 (.0018)	.02	.0038** (.0012)	.18
Authority	-.0959** (.0168)	-.18	-.0631** (.0122)	-.18	-.0810** (.0126)	-.20	-.0388** (.0140)	-.08	-.0239** (.0101)	-.06
No authority, part-time	.0094 (.0180)	.01	-.0040 (.0127)	-.01	.0077 (.0138)	.02	.0116 (.0162)	.02	.0073 (.0117)	.02

continues

Table B5.2 continued

Predictors	Black Women: White Men b	Beta	Black Men: White Men b	Beta	White Women: White Men b	Beta	Black Women: Black Men b	Beta	Black Women: White Women b	Beta
Physical dexterity	-.0139 (.0076)	-.05	-.0040 (.0053)	-.02	-.0332† (.0055)	-.15	-.0141† (.0066)	-.06	.0104+ (.0046)	.05
Nurturant skill	.0556** (.0208)	.07	.0302 (.0167)	.06	.0453** (.0170)	.08	.0270 (.0175)	.04	.0074 (.0118)	.01
Clerical perception	-.0198 (.0144)	-.06	-.0210+ (.0099)	-.10	-.0427† (.0106)	-.18	-.0062 (.0128)	-.02	.0078 (.0093)	.03
Math skills	-.0265 (.0198)	-.08	-.0435** (.0131)	-.20	.0312† (.0142)	.12	.0053 (.0171)	.02	-.0512** (.0124)	-.20
Product market structure										
Market power	.0232++ (.0074)	.10	.0196++ (.0046)	.13	.0097 (.0051)	.05	.0133+ (.0066)	.06	.0025 (.0053)	.01
Profitability	-.0030 (.0087)	-.01	-.0012 (.0057)	.00	-.0009 (.0062)	.00	-.0041 (.0079)	-.01	-.0087 (.0062)	-.03
Economic scale	-.0071 (.0055)	-.03	-.0017 (.0029)	-.01	.0000 (.0038)	.00	-.0062 (.0052)	-.03	-.0066 (.0046)	-.04
Capital intensity	-.0004 (.0080)	.00	.0047 (.0042)	.02	-.0058 (.0055)	-.03	-.0111 (.0080)	-.04	.0012 (.0073)	.01
Foreign involvement	-.0086 (.0060)	-.03	-.0024 (.0045)	-.01	-.0001 (.0054)	.00	.0042 (.0072)	.02	-.0022 (.0065)	-.01
Productivity	.0109 (.0082)	.04	.0086 (.0051)	.05	.0068 (.0058)	.03	.0133 (.0076)	.05	.0084 (.0061)	.04
Linkages to other actors										
Industry unionization	.1069** (.0367)	.08	.0412 (.0226)	.05	.0643+ (.0263)	.07	.0136 (.0345)	.01	.0213 (.0282)	.02
Occupation unionization	.1683** (.0480)	.10	.0602* (.0300)	.06	.1455* (.0355)	.12	.0767 (.0434)	.06	.0500 (.0327)	.04
Percent public sector	.0017** (.0004)	.25	.0012** (.0002)	.27	.0013** (.0003)	.26	.0011** (.0004)	.20	.0006* (.0003)	.12

continues

Table B5.2 continued

Predictors	Black Women: White Men b	Black Women: White Men Beta	Black Men: White Men b	Black Men: White Men Beta	White Women: White Men b	White Women: White Men Beta	Black Women: Black Men b	Black Women: Black Men Beta	Black Women: White Women b	Black Women: White Women Beta
Federal purchases	.0006	.02	.0001	.01	.0010++	.05	-.0003	-.01	-.0003	-.02
	(.0005)		(.0003)		(.0003)		(.0005)		(.0004)	
Employment segregation	.0159++	.13	-.0378++	-.20	.0371++	.38	.0003	.00	.0125+	.06
	(.0038)		(.0057)		(.0031)		(.0041)		(.0060)	
Constant	-.3893		.1222		-.7850		-.3276		.2995	
Between-equation correlation	-.061		.283		-.276		-.081		-.062	
Lagrange multiplier test	5.946		49.782‡		46.003‡		5.162		6.516‡	
Breusch-Pagan tests for	Initial	Adjusted	Initial	Adjusted	Initial	Adjusted	Initial	Adjusted	Initial	Adjusted
Group size	233.244‡	1.811	33.586‡	2.805	12.336‡	2.752	381.612‡	6.425‡	650.850‡	9.464‡
Sectors	105.615‡	32.523	310.588‡	24.479	284.154‡	21.060	140.808‡	42.361‡	201.993‡	103.620‡
R^2 $y, \hat{y}$	.183		.134		.193		.052		.054	
N	1916		1916		1916		1916		1916	

Notes: a. The earnings gap controls for worker differences in human capital, family structure, geographic residence, and labor supply.
b. Dummy indicators for missing value substitutions are not reported.
*p < .05, one-tailed +p < .05, two-tailed †p < .05, two-tailed, where effects were opposite of predictions
**p < .01, one-tailed ++p < .01, two-tailed ‡p < .05 for the LM and Breusch-Pagan tests

Table B5.3 SUR-EGLS Regressions of Earnings Gaps[a] on Skills and Growth, Desirable Employment Rates, Race and Gender Typing, Product Market Structure, Linkages to Other Actors, and Significant Interactions[b]

Predictors	Black Women: White Men		Black Men: White Men		White Women: White Men		Black Women: Black Men		Black Women: White Women	
	b	Beta	b	Beta	b	Beta	b	Beta	b	Beta
General skills and growth										
Skills and training	.0765†	.38	.0266†	.20	.0162	.11	.0113	.06	.0530†	.35
	(.0195)		(.0130)		(.0144)		(.0164)		(.0109)	
Growth rate	.0763	.19	.0116+	.05	-.0116	-.04	-.0143	-.04	.0397	.13
	(.0436)		(.0056)		(.0115)		(.0080)		(.0270)	
Employment segregation										
Employment segregation	.0220++	.18	-.0263++	-.14	.0323++	.33	.0027	.02	.0416++	.20
	(.0038)		(.0057)		(.0031)		(.0041)		(.0059)	
White- or male-typed work										
Status in interactions	-.0330+	-.21	-.0430++	-.44	-.0021	-.02	-.0156	-.12	-.0304++	-.27
	(.0164)		(.0099)		(.0116)		(.0142)		(.0101)	
Squared status in interactions	.0054**	.19	.0082**	.45	.0014	.07	.0013	.05	.0044**	.21
	(.0023)		(.0017)		(.0018)		(.0018)		(.0012)	
Authority	-.0946**	-.15	-.0549**	-.14	-.0732**	-.16	-.0408**	-.07	-.0182*	-.04
	(.0174)		(.0124)		(.0127)		(.0139)		(.0101)	
No authority, part-time	.0231	.04	-.0066	-.02	.0214	.05	.0147	.03	.0109	.03
	(.0183)		(.0131)		(.0153)		(.0161)		(.0120)	
Math skills	-.0249	-.07	-.0395**	-.18	.0289†	.11	.0143	.05	-.0329**	-.13
	(.0200)		(.0129)		(.0139)		(.0172)		(.0126)	
Black- or female-typed work										
Physical exertion	.0313†	.13	.0013	.01	.0547†	.31	.0037	.02	-.0076	-.04
	(.0128)		(.0077)		(.0097)		(.0118)		(.0080)	
Nurturant skill	.0449*	.06	.0287	.06	.0422**	.08	.0180	.03	.0070	.01
	(.0208)		(.0164)		(.0168)		(.0175)		(.0115)	
Physical dexterity	-.0119	-.04	-.0006	.00	-.0304†	-.14	-.0129	-.05	.0165++	.08
	(.0075)		(.0052)		(.0055)		(.0066)		(.0047)	
Clerical perception	-.0208	-.07	-.0210+	-.10	-.0400†	-.17	-.0037	-.01	.0077	.03
	(.0143)		(.0098)		(.0104)		(.0128)		(.0091)	
Environmental conditions	-.0230*	-.06	-.0279†	-.12	-.0136	-.05	.0020	.01	-.0115	-.04
	(.0114)		(.0065)		(.0085)		(.0109)		(.0088)	

continues

Table B5.3 continued

Predictors	Black Women: White Men b	Beta	Black Men: White Men b	Beta	White Women: White Men b	Beta	Black Women: Black Men b	Beta	Black Women: White Women b	Beta
Routinization	.0246* (.0118)	.10	.0092 (.0077)	.06	-.0043 (.0088)	-.02	.0057 (.0103)	.03	.0152* (.0072)	.09
Desirable employment										
Percent sufficient work	.0023† (.0007)	.15	-.0003 (.0004)	-.03	.0045† (.0005)	.41	.0010 (.0006)	.08	-.0017** (.0004)	-.16
Percent unemployed	-.0004 (.0015)	-.01	-.0006 (.0009)	-.02	.0012 (.0011)	.03	-.0003 (.0014)	-.01	-.0036† (.0012)	-.09
Percent self-employed	-.0017** (.0005)	-.08	-.0019** (.0003)	-.15	-.0004 (.0003)	-.02	-.0010* (.0005)	-.06	-.0007* (.0004)	-.05
Product market structure										
Market power	.0201++ (.0073)	.08	-.0414+ (.0166)	-.27	.0064 (.0052)	.04	.0695++ (.0181)	.33	.0033 (.0053)	.02
Profitability	-.0304 (.0161)	-.08	-.0094 (.0098)	-.04	.0071 (.0153)	.02	-.0244 (.0149)	-.07	-.0251 (.0131)	-.09
Economic scale	-.0058 (.0055)	-.03	-.0019 (.0029)	-.01	-.0005 (.0038)	.00	-.0049 (.0052)	-.03	-.0060 (.0047)	-.04
Capital intensity	-.0009 (.0080)	.00	.0042 (.0041)	.02	-.0075 (.0055)	-.03	-.0112 (.0080)	-.04	.0014 (.0074)	.01
Foreign involvement	-.0085 (.0062)	-.03	-.0023 (.0044)	-.01	.0021 (.0054)	.01	.0022 (.0072)	.01	-.0047 (.0066)	-.02
Productivity	.0127 (.0082)	.04	.0093 (.0051)	.05	.0066 (.0058)	.03	.0134 (.0075)	.05	.0083 (.0062)	.04
Linkages to other actors										
Industry unionization	.1090** (.0366)	.09	.0436* (.0225)	.05	.0653+ (.0263)	.07	.0026 (.0346)	.00	.0097 (.0283)	.01
Occupation unionization	.1822** (.0478)	.11	.0683* (.0296)	.07	.1450++ (.0350)	.12	.0774 (.0431)	.06	.0446 (.0321)	.04
Percent public sector	.0016** (.0004)	.23	.0011** (.0002)	.25	.0014** (.0003)	.28	.0011** (.0004)	.19	.0003 (.0003)	.06

continues

Table B5.3 continued

Predictors	Black Women: White Men b	Beta	Black Men: White Men b	Beta	White Women: White Men b	Beta	Black Women: Black Men b	Beta	Black Women: White Women b	Beta
Federal purchases	.0006 (.0005)	.02	.0001 (.0003)	.01	.0009++ (.0003)	.04	-.0003 (.0005)	-.01	-.0003 (.0004)	-.02
Moderating interactions										
Growth										
Status in interactions	.0675++ (.0220)	.32			.0309+ (.0131)	.20				
Squared status in interactions	-.0108++ (.0039)	-.19			-.0064+ (.0030)	-.15				
Authority	-.0533 (.0290)	-.05								
No authority, part-time	-.0521+ (.0218)	-.05								
Math skills	-.0497+ (.0202)	-.33							-.0200+ (.0098)	-.18
Profit										
Environmental conditions					-.0273+ (.0129)	-.06				
Status in interactions	.0370++ (.0142)	.21	.0132 (.0098)	.12	.0124 (.0114)	.10	.0303+ (.0121)	.20	.0193+ (.0096)	.15
Squared status in interactions	-.0093++ (.0023)	-.25	-.0036+ (.0018)	-.15	-.0048++ (.0019)	-.17	-.0064++ (.0019)	-.20	-.0042++ (.0013)	-.15
Authority	.1024++ (.0318)	.08	.0502+ (.0240)	.06	.0728++ (.0252)	.07			.0356 (.0187)	.04
No authority, part-time	.0234 (.0223)	.02	-.0123 (.0167)	-.02	-.0161 (.0182)	-.02			.0354++ (.0132)	.05
Market power										
Environmental conditions			.0157++ (.0057)	.08						
Authority					.0022 (.0136)	.00			-.0384++ (.0099)	-.06

continues

Table B5.3 continued

Predictors	Black Women: White Men b	Beta	Black Men: White Men b	Beta	White Women: White Men b	Beta	Black Women: Black Men b	Beta	Black Women: White Women b	Beta
No authority, part-time					.0423+ (.0167)	.07			.0093 (.0132)	.01
Physical dexterity									-.0146++ (.0037)	-.05
Clerical perception			.0207++ (.0058)	.33			-.0221++ (.0065)	-.27		
Constant	-.4696		.0893		-.7844		-.3713		.2621	
Between-equation correlation	-.095		.242		-.239		-.096		-.173	
Lagrange multiplier test	7.775‡		49.427‡		48.718‡		6.491‡		6.149‡	
Breusch-Pagan tests for	Initial	Adjusted	Initial	Adjusted	Initial	Adjusted	Initial	Adjusted	Initial	Adjusted
Group size	238.784‡	1.742	33.965‡	2.681	15.138‡	1.969	387.188‡	6.504‡	656.150‡	8.497‡
Sectors	98.967‡	33.970‡	300.800‡	23.296	272.254‡	18.521	144.496‡	41.559‡	211.998‡	106.448‡
R^2 y,ŷ	.197		.162		.219		.056		.046	
N	1916		1916		1916		1916		1916	

Notes: a. The earnings gap controls for worker differences in human capital, family structure, geographic residence, and labor supply.
b. Dummy indicators for missing value substitutions are not reported.
*p < .05, one-tailed +p < .05, two-tailed †p < .05, two-tailed, where effects were opposite of predictions
**p < .01, one-tailed ++ p < .01, two-tailed ‡p < .05 for the LM and Breusch-Pagan tests

Table B6.1 SUR-EGLS Regressions of Employment Segregation[a] on Skills and Growth, Race and Gender Typing, Desirable Employment, Product Market Structure, and Linkages to Other Actors[b]—Northern States

Predictors	Black Women: White Men b	Beta	Black Men: White Men b	Beta	White Women: White Men b	Beta	Black Women: Black Men b	Beta	Black Women: White Women b	Beta
General skill and growth										
Skill and training scale	-.7095** (.1080)	-.42	-.1224** (.0522)	-.16	-.6117** (.0898)	-.41	-.4977** (.0890)	-.36	-.1602** (.0543)	-.20
Skills and training × growth	.0668 (.0477)	.02	.0159 (.0237)	.01	.0514 (.0374)	.02	.0484 (.0410)	.02	-.0345 (.0262)	-.02
Growth rate	.0061 (.0520)	.00	.0583+ (.0256)	.04	-.0052 (.0434)	.00	-.0219 (.0454)	-.01	.0063 (.0279)	.00
Black- or female-typed work										
Physical exertion	-1.1506** (.0747)	-.57	-.0525 (.0369)	-.06	-1.1175** (.0609)	-.62	-1.0784** (.0628)	-.65	-.0463 (.0398)	-.05
Nurturant skill	.2236* (.1172)	.04	.0431 (.0582)	.02	.1520 (.1012)	.03	.1267 (.0950)	.02	.0057 (.0550)	.00
Physical dexterity	.2226** (.0430)	.09	.0030 (.0210)	.00	.2009** (.0354)	.09	.2364** (.0366)	.12	-.0037 (.0225)	.00
Clerical perception	.6688** (.0839)	.25	.0677 (.0416)	.06	.6538** (.0702)	.28	.5907** (.0718)	.27	.0187 (.0451)	.01
Environmental conditions	-.2261** (.0731)	-.08	-.1060† (.0352)	-.08	-.2065** (.0583)	-.08	-.1598** (.0635)	-.06	.0116 (.0423)	.01
Routinization	-.3825† (.0693)	-.19	.0182 (.0338)	.02	-.2686++ (.0574)	-.15	-.3978++ (.0580)	-.25	-.0849† (.0360)	-.09
White- or male-typed work										
Status in interactions	-.4260++ (.0920)	-.33	-.1092+ (.0437)	-.19	-.4600++ (.0753)	-.40	-.3633++ (.0788)	-.35	-.0584 (.0501)	-.10
Squared status in interactions	.0667** (.0115)	.28	.0286++ (.0057)	.27	.0636** (.0097)	.30	.0395** (.0095)	.21	.0171** (.0061)	.15

continues

Table B6.1 continued

Predictors	Black Women: White Men b	Beta	Black Men: White Men b	Beta	White Women: White Men b	Beta	Black Women: Black Men b	Beta	Black Women: White Women b	Beta
Authority	.2071† (.0891)	.04	.0332 (.0430)	.01	.2160† (.0753)	.05	.1714† (.0758)	.04	.0801 (.0455)	.03
No authority, part-time	−.1248 (.1085)	−.03	−.0896 (.0537)	−.05	−.1830+ (.0911)	−.05	−.0731 (.0925)	−.02	.0304 (.0548)	.01
Math skills	−.7865** (.1076)	−.28	−.2854** (.0513)	−.23	−.6065** (.0881)	−.24	−.5328** (.0921)	−.23	−.1467** (.0574)	−.11
Desirable employment										
Sufficient work hours	−.0361** (.0039)	−.29	−.0122** (.0019)	−.22	−.0478** (.0032)	−.44	−.0258** (.0033)	−.26	.0074† (.0020)	.13
Unemployment rate	.0254** (.0094)	.06	.0379** (.0048)	.19	−.0015 (.0079)	.00	−.0169† (.0083)	−.05	.0315** (.0051)	.15
Self-employment rate	−.0300** (.0029)	−.18	−.0122** (.0013)	−.16	−.0181** (.0023)	−.12	−.0187** (.0026)	−.14	−.0125** (.0016)	−.16
Product market structure										
Market power	.2141++ (.0461)	.10	.1371++ (.0236)	.15	.1128++ (.0375)	.06	.0830+ (.0405)	.05	.0588+ (.0249)	.06
Profitability	.1087+ (.0502)	.03	−.0435 (.0256)	−.03	.1301++ (.0420)	.05	.1220++ (.0437)	.05	−.0246 (.0272)	−.02
Economic scale	.0739++ (.0275)	.04	.0204 (.0151)	.03	.0245 (.0220)	.02	.0599+ (.0237)	.04	.0445+ (.0175)	.05
Capital intensity	−.1060+ (.0488)	−.04	.0296 (.0253)	.02	−.0637 (.0372)	−.03	−.1350++ (.0439)	−.06	−.0364 (.0319)	−.03
Foreign involvement	.0542 (.0694)	.01	.0634 (.0357)	.04	−.0463 (.0552)	−.01	.0012 (.0651)	.00	.1231++ (.0450)	.07
Productivity	.0833 (.0469)	.03	.0565+ (.0228)	.05	.0109 (.0388)	.00	.0136 (.0409)	.01	.0386 (.0252)	.03

continues

Table B6.1 continued

Predictors	Black Women: White Men b	Beta	Black Men: White Men b	Beta	White Women: White Men b	Beta	Black Women: Black Men b	Beta	Black Women: White Women b	Beta
Linkages to other actors										
Industry unionization	-.1866	-.02	.0829	.02	-.5863++	-.06	-.1713	-.02	.3488**	.07
	(.2168)		(.1046)		(.1772)		(.1950)		(.1204)	
Occupation unionization	.5844*	.04	.1882	.03	-.4096	-.03	.1581	.01	.7583**	.12
	(.2800)		(.1358)		(.2342)		(.2367)		(.1523)	
Percent public sector	.0075**	.14	.0114**	.46	-.0033	-.07	-.0034	-.07	.0112**	.42
	(.0024)		(.0011)		(.0019)		(.0020)		(.0013)	
Federal purchases	-.0138++	-.06	-.0064++	-.06	-.0095++	-.05	-.0092++	-.05	-.0018	-.02
	(.0032)		(.0016)		(.0025)		(.0030)		(.0019)	
Constant	3.2856		1.4752		4.5066		2.2383		-.8766	
Between-equation correlation	-.061		.029		-.176		-.096		-.022	
Lagrange multiplier test	438.241‡		597.077‡		59.219‡		95.244‡		594.130‡	
Breusch-Pagan tests for	Initial	Adjusted	Initial	Adjusted	Initial	Adjusted	Initial	Adjusted	Initial	Adjusted
Group size	48.791‡	2.473	109.583‡	.105	26.202‡	.787	85.821‡	3.238	173.831‡	6.122‡
Sectors	123.918‡	10.804	81.058‡	11.047	125.044‡	10.003	119.026‡	21.617	158.663‡	16.954
Buse's R^2	.553		.375		.656		.505		.321	
N	1869		1869		1869		1869		1869	

Notes: a. Employment segregation controls for worker differences in human capital, family structure, and geographic residence.
b. Dummy indicators for missing value substitutions are not reported.

*p < .05, one-tailed +p < .05, two-tailed †p < .05, two-tailed, where effects were opposite of predictions
**p < .01, one-tailed ++p < .01, two-tailed ‡p < .05 for the LM and Breusch-Pagan tests

Table B6.2 SUR-EGLS Regressions of Employment Segregation[a] on Skills and Growth, Race and Gender Typing, Desirable Employment, Product Market Structure, and Linkages to Other Actors[b]—Southern States

Predictors	Black Women: White Men		Black Men: White Men		White Women: White Men		Black Women: Black Men		Black Women: White Women	
	b	Beta	b	Beta	b	Beta	b	Beta	b	Beta
General skill and growth										
Skills and training scale	-.7495**	-.44	-.1275**	-.17	-.6655**	-.43	-.5191**	-.36	-.1342**	-.16
	(.1169)		(.0520)		(.0960)		(.1025)		(.0578)	
Skills and training × growth	.0644	.02	.0469*	.03	.0743*	.02	.0142	.00	-.0337	-.02
	(.0501)		(.0223)		(.0403)		(.0446)		(.0269)	
Growth rate	-.0394	-.01	-.0199	-.01	-.0203	-.01	-.0066	.00	-.0179	-.01
	(.0547)		(.0258)		(.0457)		(.0486)		(.0279)	
Black- or female-typed work										
Physical exertion	-1.1110**	-.55	.1178**	.13	-1.1029**	-.65	-1.2267**	-.70	.1434**	.14
	(.0788)		(.0346)		(.0651)		(.0693)		(.0407)	
Nurturant skill	.2634*	.04	.0104	.00	.2505**	.04	.2624**	.05	-.0747	-.02
	(.1282)		(.0615)		(.1067)		(.1090)		(.0577)	
Physical dexterity	.1854**	.08	-.1262++	-.11	.2084**	.09	.2906**	.14	-.0441	-.04
	(.0460)		(.0211)		(.0378)		(.0403)		(.0236)	
Clerical perception	.5651**	.21	.0597	.05	.6771**	.28	.4771**	.21	-.0620	-.05
	(.0890)		(.0417)		(.0746)		(.0795)		(.0464)	
Environmental conditions	-.1901**	-.06	-.1787†	-.13	-.1479**	-.05	-.0303	-.01	-.0493	-.03
	(.0747)		(.0322)		(.0617)		(.0678)		(.0411)	
Routinization	-.3848†	-.19	.0934**	.10	-.3503++	-.19	-.4467++	-.26	.0009	.00
	(.0740)		(.0330)		(.0611)		(.0655)		(.0372)	
White- or male-typed work										
Status in interactions	-.5269++	-.41	-.1982++	-.34	-.5395++	-.46	-.3388++	-.31	.0150	.02
	(.0970)		(.0426)		(.0798)		(.0873)		(.0514)	
Squared status in interactions	.0838**	.36	.0437**	.41	.0704**	.33	.0351**	.17	.0129*	.11
	(.0128)		(.0056)		(.0104)		(.0113)		(.0067)	

continues

Table B6.2 continued

Predictors	Black Women: White Men b	Beta	Black Men: White Men b	Beta	White Women: White Men b	Beta	Black Women: Black Men b	Beta	Black Women: White Women b	Beta
Authority	.1709 (.0961)	.03	-.0676 (.0461)	-.03	.2155† (.0798)	.04	.1708† (.0846)	.04	-.0053 (.0469)	.00
No authority, part-time	-.1135 (.1147)	-.03	-.0440 (.0543)	-.02	-.1737 (.0964)	-.04	-.0898 (.1011)	-.02	.0126 (.0560)	.01
Math skills	-1.0932** (.1140)	-.39	-.4067** (.0520)	-.31	-.6730** (.0941)	-.26	-.7782** (.1029)	-.32	-.3755** (.0588)	-.27
Desirable employment										
Sufficient work hours	-.0371** (.0041)	-.30	-.0023 (.0019)	-.04	-.0464** (.0019)	-.41	-.0347** (.0041)	-.33	.0056† (.0031)	.09
Unemployment rate	.0280** (.0097)	.06	.0359** (.0046)	.17	.0020 (.0083)	.00	-.0074 (.0087)	-.02	.0303** (.0052)	.14
Self-employment rate	-.0328** (.0031)	-.20	-.0109** (.0013)	-.14	-.0157** (.0025)	-.10	-.0213** (.0029)	-.15	-.0154** (.0016)	-.19
Product market structure										
Market power	.2367++ (.0479)	.12	.0939++ (.0229)	.10	.1568++ (.0404)	.08	.1208++ (.0416)	.07	.0587+ (.0250)	.06
Profitability	.1226+ (.0533)	.04	.0037 (.0259)	.00	.0822 (.0453)	.03	.1150+ (.0459)	.04	.0264 (.0278)	.02
Economic scale	.0336 (.0278)	.02	.0141 (.0138)	.02	.0116 (.0248)	.01	.0200 (.0242)	.01	.0244 (.0153)	.03
Capital intensity	-.0651 (.0482)	-.02	.0094 (.0225)	.01	-.1174++ (.0414)	-.05	-.0545 (.0425)	-.02	.0381 (.0289)	.03
Foreign involvement	-.0925 (.0708)	-.02	-.0372 (.0336)	-.02	-.0870 (.0596)	-.02	-.0663 (.0638)	-.02	.0244 (.0438)	.01
Productivity	-.0112 (.0490)	.00	.0029 (.0236)	.00	-.0054 (.0408)	.00	-.0106 (.0440)	.00	-.0098 (.0261)	-.01

continues

Table B6.2 continued

Predictors	Black Women: White Men b	Black Women: White Men Beta	Black Men: White Men b	Black Men: White Men Beta	White Women: White Men b	White Women: White Men Beta	Black Women: Black Men b	Black Women: Black Men Beta	Black Women: White Women b	Black Women: White Women Beta
Linkages to other actors										
Industry unionization	-.7564† (.2267)	-.07	-.2122† (.1019)	-.04	-.7119++ (.1902)	-.07	-.5054+ (.2031)	-.05	.1504 (.1199)	.03
Occupation unionization	-.0657 (.2975)	.00	-.1667 (.1310)	-.03	-.4446 (.2487)	-.04	-.2253 (.2640)	-.02	.3773** (.1542)	.06
Percent public sector	.0026 (.0025)	.05	.0087** (.0011)	.34	-.0026 (.0020)	-.05	-.0066† (.0022)	-.14	.0054** (.0013)	.20
Federal purchases	-.0150++ (.0033)	-.07	-.0079++ (.0015)	-.08	-.0110++ (.0027)	-.05	-.0074+ (.0030)	-.04	-.0024 (.0019)	-.02
Constant	4.9774		1.2738		4.5852		4.1248		.3789	
Between-equation correlation	.011		.301		-.187		-.027		-.078	
Lagrange multiplier test	254.486‡		235.096‡		53.430‡		154.713‡		176.886‡	
Breusch-Pagan tests for	Initial	Adjusted	Initial	Adjusted	Initial	Adjusted	Initial	Adjusted	Initial	Adjusted
Group size	50.062‡	1.044	70.109‡	.840	21.799‡	.301	51.144‡	11.291‡	216.695‡	2.238
Sectors	128.327‡	8.487	80.805‡	17.064	116.746‡	8.709	130.373‡	17.403	106.748‡	27.034
Buse's R^2	.541		.349		.628		.507		.312	
N	1869		1869		1869		1869		1869	

Notes: a. Employment segregation controls for worker differences in human capital, family structure, and geographic residence.

b. Dummy indicators for missing value substitutions are not reported.

*p < .05, one-tailed +p < .05, two-tailed †p < .05, two-tailed, where effects were opposite of predictions

**p < .01, one-tailed ++p < .01, two-tailed ‡p < .05 for the LM and Breusch-Pagan tests

Table B6.3 SUR-EGLS Regressions of Earnings Gaps[a] on Skills, Growth and Employment Rates, Race and Gender Typing, Product Market Structure, and Linkages to Other Actors[b]—Northern States

Predictors	Black Women: White Men		Black Men: White Men		White Women: White Men		Black Women: Black Men		Black Women: White Women	
	b	Beta	b	Beta	b	Beta	b	Beta	b	Beta
General skill and growth										
Skills and training	.0690† (.0240)	.25	.0386† (.0180)	.21	.0215 (.0146)	.14	.0038 (.0227)	.01	.0593† (.0151)	.25
Employment growth	-.0123 (.0117)	-.02	.0195+ (.0084)	.05	.0094 (.0062)	.03	-.0266+ (.0116)	-.05	-.0170+ (.0084)	-.04
Employment segregation										
Employment segregation	.0153++ (.0052)	.10	.0276++ (.0073)	.11	.0366++ (.0030)	.35	.0104 (.0062)	.05	.0002 (.0076)	.00
Black- or female-typed work										
Physical exertion	.0200 (.0178)	.06	.0217* (.0118)	.10	.0672† (.0093)	.36	.0067 (.0175)	.02	-.0105 (.0120)	-.04
Nurturant skill	.0486* (.0251)	.05	.0367 (.0198)	.05	.0471** (.0178)	.08	-.0099 (.0231)	-.01	.0021 (.0158)	.00
Physical dexterity	-.0118 (.0098)	-.03	.0112 (.0073)	.04	-.0410† (.0055)	-.18	-.0192† (.0096)	-.05	.0179++ (.0066)	.05
Clerical perception	-.0260 (.0193)	-.06	-.0161 (.0140)	-.06	-.0458† (.0105)	-.19	-.0122 (.0191)	-.03	-.0080 (.0134)	-.02
Environmental conditions	-.0422** (.0170)	-.09	-.0244† (.0104)	-.07	-.0285** (.0077)	-.10	-.0196 (.0173)	-.04	.0038 (.0136)	.01
Routinization	.0042 (.0156)	.01	.0041 (.0112)	.02	-.0073 (.0088)	-.04	.0053 (.0153)	.02	.0194* (.0105)	.07
White- or male-typed work										
Status in interactions	-.0522+ (.0215)	-.25	-.0229 (.0144)	-.17	-.0397++ (.0111)	-.34	-.0133 (.0212)	-.06	.0054 (.0149)	.03
Squared status in interactions	.0066** (.0027)	.18	.0048* (.0022)	.19	.0061** (.0019)	.28	.0009 (.0025)	.02	-.0017 (.0017)	-.05

continues

Table B6.3 continued

Predictors	Black Women: White Men b	Beta	Black Men: White Men b	Beta	White Women: White Men b	Beta	Black Women: Black Men b	Beta	Black Women: White Women b	Beta
Authority	-.0636** (.0200)	-.08	-.0414** (.0151)	-.07	-.0953** (.0127)	-.20	-.0383* (.0193)	-.04	.0070 (.0133)	.01
No authority, part-time	-.0019 (.0234)	.00	-.0118 (.0178)	-.02	.0042 (.0137)	.01	.0308 (.0231)	.04	-.0003 (.0163)	-.00
Math skills	-.0581** (.0248)	-.13	-.0321* (.0176)	-.10	-.0098 (.0140)	-.04	-.0185 (.0244)	-.04	-.0205 (.0172)	-.05
Desirable employment										
Percent sufficient work	.0006 (.0009)	.03	-.0003 (.0006)	-.02	.0018† (.0005)	.16	.0014 (.0009)	.07	.0006 (.0006)	.03
Percent unemployed	.0007 (.0022)	.01	-.0016 (.0015)	-.03	.0007 (.0010)	.02	.0007 (.0021)	.01	-.0023 (.0017)	-.04
Percent self-employed	-.0036** (.0007)	-.13	-.0014** (.0005)	-.08	-.0015** (.0003)	-.09	-.0023** (.0007)	-.08	-.0014** (.0005)	-.06
Product market structure										
Market power	.0267+ (.0107)	.08	.0089 (.0074)	.04	.0110+ (.0049)	.06	.0135 (.0104)	.04	.0066 (.0076)	.02
Profitability	-.0156 (.0118)	-.03	-.0077 (.0086)	-.02	-.0040 (.0060)	-.01	-.0064 (.0117)	-.01	-.0017 (.0086)	-.00
Economic scale	-.0053 (.0070)	-.02	.0007 (.0041)	.00	.0026 (.0036)	.02	-.0049 (.0072)	-.02	-.0058 (.0061)	-.02
Capital intensity	.0088 (.0128)	.02	.0167+ (.0072)	.06	-.0088 (.0053)	-.04	-.0115 (.0135)	-.03	.0130 (.0114)	.03
Foreign involvement	-.0075 (.0184)	-.01	-.0087 (.0105)	-.02	-.0067 (.0072)	-.02	.0011 (.0194)	.00	-.0005 (.0169)	-.00
Productivity	.0087 (.0112)	.02	.0137 (.0075)	.05	.0052 (.0056)	.02	.0030 (.0109)	.01	.0108 (.0083)	.03

continues

Table B6.3 continued

Predictors	Black Women: White Men b	Beta	Black Men: White Men b	Beta	White Women: White Men b	Beta	Black Women: Black Men b	Beta	Black Women: White Women b	Beta
Linkages to other actors										
Industry unionization	.1543** (.0485)	.09	.0909** (.0346)	.08	-.0346 (.0253)	-.04	-.0171 (.0512)	-.01	.1206** (.0380)	.08
Occupation unionization	.1857** (.0634)	.09	.0814* (.0438)	.06	.0827+ (.0338)	.07	.0462 (.0634)	.02	.0841* (.0450)	.05
Percent public sector	.0021** (.0005)	.23	.0011** (.0004)	.19	.0011** (.0003)	.21	.0015** (.0005)	.17	.0003 (.0004)	.04
Federal purchases	.0009 (.0008)	.02	.0007 (.0005)	.03	.0007+ (.0003)	.03	-.0001 (.0008)	.00	.0007 (.0007)	.02
Constant	-.1451		.0047		.0196		-.2032		-.3064	
Between-equation correlation	-.061		.029		-.176		-.096		-.022	
Lagrange multiplier test	.4968		56.5104‡		55.4735‡		2.2224		1.0195	
Breusch-Pagan tests for	Initial	Adjusted	Initial	Adjusted	Initial	Adjusted	Initial	Adjusted	Initial	Adjusted
Group size	455.1741‡	4.8121	649.2318‡	3.5554	13.9062‡	1.6628	865.1004‡	6.6473‡	717.6004‡	13.6124‡
Sectors	245.1104‡	65.1160‡	1657.9979‡	32.5609	386.4649‡	13.0618	1042.3811‡	80.8727‡	410.7548‡	135.2870‡
Buse's R²	.155		.102		.312		.072		.089	
N	1869		1869		1869		1869		1869	

Notes: a. The earnings gap controls for worker differences in human capital, family structure, geographic residence, and labor supply.

b. Dummy indicators for missing value substitutions are not reported.

*p < .05, one-tailed +p < .05, two-tailed †p < .05, two-tailed, where effects were opposite of predictions

**p < .01, one-tailed ++p < .01, two-tailed ‡p < .05 for the LM and Breusch-Pagan tests

Table B6.4 SUR-EGLS Regressions of Earnings Gaps[a] on Skills, Growth and Employment Rates, Race and Gender Typing, Product Market Structure, and Linkages to Other Actors[b]—Southern States

Predictors	Black Women: White Men b	Beta	Black Men: White Men b	Beta	White Women: White Men b	Beta	Black Women: Black Men b	Beta	Black Women: White Women b	Beta
General skill and growth										
Skill and training	.0667† (.0240)	.27	.0341 (.0175)	.20	.0216 (.0179)	.12	.0259 (.0203)	.12	.0517† (.0144)	.27
Employment growth	-.0037 (.0115)	-.01	.0031 (.0083)	.01	-.0007 (.0080)	-.00	-.0007 (.0105)	-.00	.0010 (.0080)	.00
Employment segregation										
Employment segregation	-.0004 (.0045)	-.00	-.0640++ (.0067)	-.29	.0276++ (.0037)	.25	-.0055 (.0046)	-.04	.0179++ (.0064)	.08
Black- or female-typed work										
Physical exertion	-.0051 (.0162)	-.02	-.0007 (.0109)	.00	.0579† (.0123)	.28	-.0050 (.0144)	-.02	-.0203 (.0107)	-.09
Nurturant skill	.1006** (.0261)	.11	.0072 (.0214)	.01	.0328* (.0196)	.05	.0729** (.0215)	.09	.0255 (.0151)	.04
Physical dexterity	-.0222† (.0093)	-.06	-.0182† (.0072)	-.07	-.0349† (.0069)	-.14	-.0145 (.0082)	-.05	.0181++ (.0060)	.07
Clerical perception	-.0027 (.0180)	-.01	-.0109 (.0138)	-.04	-.0471† (.0134)	-.17	-.0001 (.0159)	.00	.0195 (.0119)	.07
Environmental conditions	-.0229 (.0149)	-.05	-.0337† (.0094)	-.11	-.0047 (.0105)	-.02	.0013 (.0137)	.00	-.0138 (.0117)	-.04
Routinization	.0087 (.0149)	.03	.0177* (.0107)	.09	.0100 (.0112)	.05	-.0014 (.0128)	-.01	.0142 (.0094)	.06
White- or male-typed work										
Status in interactions	-.0657++ (.0198)	-.35	-.0690++ (.0137)	-.53	-.0165 (.0143)	-.13	-.0288 (.0174)	-.17	-.0134 (.0133)	-.09
Squared status in interactions	.0073** (.0027)	.22	.0105** (.0023)	.44	.0039* (.0022)	.16	.0009 (.0022)	.03	.0001 (.0016)	.00

continues

Table B6.4 continued

Predictors	Black Women: White Men b	Beta	Black Men: White Men b	Beta	White Women: White Men b	Beta	Black Women: Black Men b	Beta	Black Women: White Women b	Beta
Authority	-.1213** (.0203)	-.16	-.0883** (.0162)	-.16	-.0766** (.0149)	-.14	-.0398* (.0176)	-.06	-.0561** (.0128)	-.10
No authority, part-time	.0244 (.0234)	.04	.0059 (.0179)	.01	.0401+ (.0169)	.09	-.0038 (.0202)	-.01	-.0059 (.0148)	-.01
Math skills	-.0720** (.0243)	-.18	-.0689** (.0176)	-.24	.0344† (.0173)	.12	-.0161 (.0212)	-.04	-.0572** (.0158)	-.18
Desirable employment										
Percent sufficient work	.0021† (.0009)	.12	-.0005 (.0006)	-.04	.0027† (.0006)	.22	.0012 (.0008)	.07	.0003 (.0006)	.03
Percent unemployed	-.0010 (.0020)	-.02	.0010 (.0014)	.02	.0019 (.0014)	.04	-.0010 (.0018)	-.02	-.0032† (.0015)	-.06
Percent self-employed	-.0034** (.0006)	-.14	-.0021** (.0004)	-.12	-.0012** (.0004)	-.07	-.0016** (.0005)	-.07	-.0011** (.0004)	-.06
Product market structure										
Market power	.0175 (.0094)	.06	.0144+ (.0068)	.07	.0047 (.0067)	.02	.0125 (.0085)	.05	.0058 (.0071)	.03
Profitability	-.0009 (.0110)	.00	.0070 (.0083)	.02	-.0093 (.0080)	-.03	.0008 (.0103)	.00	.0094 (.0078)	.03
Economic scale	-.0096 (.0069)	-.04	-.0007 (.0041)	.00	-.0054 (.0048)	-.03	-.0088 (.0068)	-.04	-.0020 (.0059)	-.01
Capital intensity	-.0100 (.0110)	-.03	-.0022 (.0063)	-.01	-.0101 (.0076)	-.04	-.0066 (.0111)	-.02	.0043 (.0101)	.01
Foreign involvement	-.0035 (.0148)	-.01	-.0027 (.0093)	-.01	.0049 (.0103)	.01	-.0044 (.0148)	-.01	-.0101 (.0135)	-.02
Productivity	.0200 (.0110)	.06	.0102 (.0076)	.04	.0167+ (.0075)	.07	.0170 (.0101)	.05	.0014 (.0078)	.01

continues

Table B6.4 continued

Predictors	Black Women: White Men		Black Men: White Men		White Women: White Men		Black Women: Black Men		Black Women: White Women	
	b	Beta	b	Beta	b	Beta	b	Beta	b	Beta
Linkages to other actors										
Industry unionization	.0409	.03	−.0251	−.02	−.0029	.00	.0183	.01	.0518	.04
	(.0474)		(.0331)		(.0336)		(.0455)		(.0365)	
Occupation unionization	.1936**	.10	.0725*	.05	.1208++	.09	.0577	.03	.0710*	.05
	(.0610)		(.0418)		(.0442)		(.0545)		(.0419)	
Percent public sector	.0025**	.31	.0016**	.28	.0019**	.33	.0010*	.14	.0002	.03
	(.0005)		(.0003)		(.0004)		(.0005)		(.0003)	
Federal purchases	.0004	.01	.0001	.00	.0005	.02	.0001	.00	.0006	.03
	(.0007)		(.0005)		(.0005)		(.0006)		(.0005)	
Constant	−.3294		.2563		−.4491		−.3455		−.0691	
Between-equation correlation	.011		.301		−.187		−.027		−.078	
Lagrange multiplier test	25.855‡		21.277‡		37.074‡		7.296‡		2.005	
Breusch-Pagan tests for	Initial	Adjusted	Initial	Adjusted	Initial	Adjusted	Initial	Adjusted	Initial	Adjusted
Group size	123.447‡	4.079	23.719‡	4.185	30.217‡	.312	230.729‡	5.840	492.775‡	16.008‡
Sectors	120.321‡	16.389	261.644‡	17.105	185.724‡	13.777	182.759‡	28.135	272.270‡	55.769‡
Buse's R^2	.133		.114		.176		.043		.081	
N	1869		1869		1869		1869		1869	

Notes: a. The earnings gap controls for worker differences in human capital, family structure, geographic residence, and labor supply.
b. Dummy indicators for missing value substitutions are not reported.

*p < .05, one-tailed +p < .05, two-tailed †p < .05, two-tailed, where effects were opposite of predictions
**p < .01, one-tailed ++p < .01, two-tailed ‡p < .05 for the LM and Breusch-Pagan tests

References

Ainsworth-Darnell, James W., and Douglas B. Downey. 1998. "Assessing the Opposi-
tional Culture Explanation for Racial-Ethnic Differences in School Performance."
American Sociological Review 63: 536–553.

Allison, Paul D. 1999. *Multiple Regression: A Primer.* Thousand Oaks, CA: Pine Forge
Press.

Althauser, Robert P., and Michael Wigler. 1972. "Standardization and Component Analysis." *Sociological Methods and Research* 1: 97–135.

Arrow, Kenneth J. 1972. "Models of Job Discrimination." Pp. 83–102 in *Racial Discrimination in Economic Life,* edited by Anthony H. Pascal. Lexington, MA: D. C.
Heath.

———. 1973. "The Theory of Discrimination." Pp. 3–33 in *Discrimination in Labor
Markets,* edited by Orley Ashenfelter and Albert Rees. Princeton, NJ: Princeton
University Press.

Ashenfelter, Orley. 1972. "Racial Discrimination and Trade Unionists." *Journal of Political Economy* 80: 435–463.

Asher, Martin, and Joel Popkin. 1984. "The Effect of Gender and Race Differentials on
Public-Private Wage Comparisons: A Study of Postal Workers." *Industrial & Labor
Relations Review* 38: 16–25.

Babbie, Earl. 2008. *The Basics of Social Research,* 4th ed. Belmont, CA: Thomson.

Baron, James N., and William T. Bielby. 1980. "Bringing the Firms Back In: Stratification, Segmentation, and the Organization of Work." *American Sociological Review*
45: 737–765.

———. 1986. "The Proliferation of Job Titles in Organizations." *Administrative Science Quarterly* 31: 561–586.

Baron, James N., Brian S. Mittman, and Andrew E. Newman. 1991. "Targets of Opportunity: Organizational and Environmental Determinants of Gender Integration
Within the California Civil Service, 1979–1985." *American Journal of Sociology*
96: 1362–1401.

Baron, James N., and Andrew E. Newman. 1990. "For What It's Worth: Organizations,
Occupations, and the Value of Work Done by Women and Nonwhites." *American
Sociological Review* 55: 155–175.

Barres, Ben A. 2006. "Does Gender Matter?" *Nature* 442: 133–136.

Barry, Janis. 1987. "Compensatory Wages for Women Production Workers at Risk." Pp.
69–91 in *Women and Work: An Annual Review,* vol. 2, edited by Laurie Larwood,
Ann Stromberg, and Barbara Gutek. Beverly Hills, CA: Sage.

Beck, E. M. 1980. "Labor Unions and Racial Income Inequality: A Time Series Analysis of the Post World War II Period." *American Journal of Sociology* 85: 791–814.

Beck, E. M., P. M. Horan, and C. M. Tolbert II. 1978. "Stratification in Dual Economy: A Sectoral Model of Earnings Differentiation." *American Sociological Review* 43: 704–720.

———. 1980. "Industrial Segmentation and Labor Market Discrimination." *Social Problems* 2: 113–130.

Becker, Gary S. 1971. *The Economics of Discrimination,* 2nd ed. Chicago: University of Chicago Press.

———. 1975. *Human Capital: A Theoretical and Empirical Analysis, with Special Reference to Education.* New York: National Bureau of Economic Research, distributed by Columbia University Press.

———. 1991. *A Treatise on the Family.* Cambridge: Harvard University Press.

Beggs, John J. 1995. "The Institutional Environment: Implications for Race and Gender Inequality in the U.S. Labor Market." *American Sociological Review* 60: 612–633.

Beggs, John J., and Wayne J. Villemez. 2001. "Regional Labor Markets." Pp. 503–530 in *Sourcebook of Labor Markets: Evolving Structures and Processes,* edited by Ivar Berg and Arne Kalleberg. New York: Plenum Press.

Belsley, David, Edwin Kuh, and Roy Welsch. 1980. *Regression Diagnostics: Identifying Influential Data and Sources of Collinearity.* New York: John Wiley and Sons.

Bendick, Marc Jr. 2007. "Situation Testing for Employment Discrimination in the United States of America." *Horizons Strategiques* 5 (July): 17–39.

Bergmann, Barbara R. 1974. "Occupational Segregation, Wages, and Profits When Employers Discriminate by Race or Sex." *Eastern Economic Journal* 1: 103–110.

———. 1986. *The Economic Emergence of Women.* Cambridge, MA: Basic Books, Harper Collins.

Berk, S. F. 1985. *The Gender Factory: The Apportionment of Work in American Households.* New York: Plenum.

Bertrand, Marianne, and Sendhir Mullainathan. 2004. "Are Emily and Greg More Employable than Lakisha and Jamal? A Field Experiment on Labor Market Discrimination." *American Economic Review* 94: 991–1013.

Betz, Nancy E., Lenore W. Harmon, and Fred W. Borgen. 1996. "The Relationships of Self-Efficacy for the Holland Themes to Gender, Occupational Group Membership, and Vocational Interests." *Journal of Counseling Psychology* 43: 90–98.

Bianchi, Suzanne M., M. A. Milkie, Liana C. Sayer, and J. P. Robinson. 2000. "Is Anyone Doing the Housework? Trends in the Gender Division of Household Labor." *Social Forces* 79: 191–228.

Bibb, Robert, and William H. Form. 1977. "The Effects of Industrial, Occupational, and Sex Stratification on Wages in Blue-Collar Markets." *Social Forces* 55: 974–996.

Bielby, William T., and James N. Baron. 1986. "Men and Women at Work: Sex Segregation and Statistical Discrimination." *American Journal of Sociology* 91: 759–799.

Bielby, Denise D., and William T. Bielby. 1988. "She Works Hard for the Money: Household Responsibilities and the Allocation of Work Effort." *American Journal of Sociology* 93: 1031–1059.

Bills, David B. 1988. "Educational Credentials and Hiring Decisions: What Employers Look for in New Employees." *Research in Social Stratification and Mobility* 7: 71–97.

Blank, Rebecca M. 1985. "An Analysis of Workers' Choice Between Employment in the Public and Private Sectors." *Industrial & Labor Relations Review* 38: 211–224.

Blau, Peter M., and Otis Dudley Duncan. 1967. *The American Occupational Structure.* New York: Wiley.

Bluestone, Barry. 1970. "The Tripartite Economy: Labor Markets and the Working Poor." *Poverty and Human Resources* 5: 15–35.

Bobo, Lawrence, James Johnson, Melvin Oliver, Reynolds Farley, Barry Bluestone, Irene Browne, Sheldon Danziger, Gary Green, Harry Holzer, Maria Krysan, Michael Massagli, Camille Zubrinsky Charles, Joleen Kirschenman, Philip Moss, and Chris Tilly. 2000. *Multi-City Study of Urban Inequality, 1992–1994.* [Atlanta, Boston, Detroit, and Los Angeles] [Computer file]. ICPSR02535-v.3. Ann Arbor, MI: Inter-University Consortium for Political and Social Research [distributor]. doi: 10.3886/ICPSR02535.

Bonacich, Edna. 1975. "Abolition, the Extension of Slavery, and the Position of Free Blacks: A Study of Split Labor Market in the United States, 1830–1863." *American Journal of Sociology* 81: 601–628.

———. 1976. "Advanced Capitalism and Black-White Relations in the United States." *American Sociological Review* 47: 34–51.

Bound, John, and Richard B. Freeman. 1989. "Black Economic Progress: Erosion of the Post-1965 Gains in the 1980s?" Pp. 32–49 in *The Question of Discrimination: Racial Inequality in the U.S. Labor Market,* edited by Steven Shulman and William Darity Jr. Middletown, CT: Wesleyan University Press.

Braddock, Jomillis Henry II, and James M. McPartland. 1987. "How Minorities Continue to Be Excluded from Equal Employment Opportunities: Research on Labor Market and Institutional Barriers." *Journal of Social Issues* 43: 5–39.

Bridges, Judith S. 1989. "Sex Differences in Occupational Values." *Sex Roles* 20: 205–211.

Bridges, William P. 1982. "The Sexual Segregation of Occupations: Theories of Labor Stratification in Industry." *American Journal of Sociology* 88: 270–295.

Bridges, William P., and Robert L. Nelson. 1989. "Markets in Hierarchies: Organizational and Market Influences on Gender Inequality in a State Pay System." *American Journal of Sociology* 95: 616–658.

Brines, Julie. 1993. "The Exchange Value of Housework." *Rationality and Society* 5: 302–340.

———. 1994. "Economic Dependency, Gender, and the Division of Labor at Home." *American Journal of Sociology* 100: 652–688.

Brown, Charles C. 1980. "Equalizing Differences in the Labor Market." *Quarterly Journal of Economics* 64: 113–134.

Brown, Charles C., James Hamilton, and James L. Medoff. 1990. *Employers Large and Small.* Cambridge, MA: Harvard University Press.

Browne, Irene. 1997. "Explaining the Black-White Gap in Labor Force Participation Among Women Heading Households." *American Sociological Review* 62: 236–252.

Browning, Harley, and Joachim Singelmann. 1978. "The Emergence of a Service Society: The Significance of the Sectoral Transformation of the U.S. Labor Force." *Politics and Society* 8: 481–509.

Buchmann, Claudia. 2006. "Status Attainment." In *The Blackwell Encyclopedia of Sociology,* edited by George Ritzer. Williston, VT: Blackwell Publishing.

Budig, Michelle. 2002. "Male Advantage and the Gender Composition of Jobs: Who Rides the Glass Escalator?" *Social Problems* 49: 258–277.

Bureau of Labor Statistics. 2009. US Department of Labor, Occupational Outlook Handbook, 2008–2009 ed., Registered Nurses, on the Internet at http://www.bls.gov/oco/ocos083.htm (accessed December 3, 2009).

Burman, George R. 1973. "The Economics of Discrimination: The Impact of Public Policy." Ph.D. diss., University of Chicago, Graduate School of Business.

Cain, G. G. 1975. "The Challenge of Dual and Radical Theories of the Labor Market to Orthodox Theory." *American Economic Review* 65: 16–22.

Carlson, Susan M. 1992. "Trends in Race/Sex Occupational Inequality: Conceptual and Measurement Issues." *Social Problems* 39: 268–290.

Cassirer, Naomi, and Barbara F. Reskin. 2000. "High Hopes: Organizational Position, Employment Experiences, and Women's and Men's Promotion Aspirations." *Work and Occupations* 27: 438–463.

Catanzarite, Lisa. 2003. "Race-Gender Composition and Occupational Pay Degradation." *Social Problems* 50: 14–37.

Charles, Maria. 2005. "National Skill Regimes, Postindustrialism, and Sex Segregation." *Social Politics* 12: 289–316.

Charles, Maria, and David B. Grusky. 2004. *Occupational Ghettos: The Worldwide Segregation of Women and Men.* Stanford: Stanford University Press.

Cohen, Jacob, and Patricia Cohen. 1983. *Applied Multiple Regression/Correlation Analysis for the Behavioral Sciences.* Hillsdale, NJ: Erlbaum.

Cohen, Philip N., and Matt L. Huffman. 2003a. "Occupational Segregation and the Devaluation of Women's Work Across U.S. Labor Markets." *Social Forces* 81: 881–908.

———. 2003b. "Individuals, Jobs, and Labor Markets: The Devaluation of Women's Work." *American Sociological Review* 68: 443–463.

Coleman, Major G. 2004. "Racial Discrimination in the Workplace: Does Market Structure Make a Difference?" *Industrial Relations* 43: 660–689.

Comanor, William S. 1973. "Racial Discrimination in American Industry." *Economica* 40: 363–378.

Cornfield, Daniel B. 1991. "The US Labor Movement: Its Development and Impact on Social Inequality and Politics." *Annual Review of Sociology* 17: 27–49.

Cotter, David A., JoAnn DeFiore, Joan M. Hermsen, Brenda M. Kowalewski, and Reeve Vanneman. 1997. "All Women Benefit: The Macro-Level Effect of Occupational Integration on Gender Earnings Inequality." *American Sociological Review* 62: 714–734.

Council of Economic Advisers. 1998. *Changing America: Indicators of Social and Economic Well-Being by Race and Hispanic Origin.* Washington, DC: The Council of Economic Advisers.

Darity, William A. Jr., and Samuel L. Myers Jr. 1998. *Persistent Disparity: Race and Economic Inequality in the United States Since 1945.* Northampton, MA: Edward Elgar.

Day, Susan X., and James Rounds. 1998. "Universality of Vocational Interest Structure Among Racial and Ethnic Minorities." *American Psychologist* 53: 728–736.

Daymont, Thomas N., and Robert L. Kaufman. 1979. "Measuring Industrial Variation in Racial Discrimination Using Log-Linear Models." *Social Science Research* 8: 41–62.

DiPrete, Thomas A. 1989. *The Bureaucratic Labor Market.* New York: Plenum Press.

DiPrete, Thomas A., and Claudia Buchmann. 2006. "The Growing Female Advantage in College Completion: The Role of Family Background and Academic Achievement." *American Sociological Review* 71: 515–541.

DiPrete, Thomas A., and David B. Grusky. 1990. "Structure and Trend in the Process of Stratification for American Men and Women." *American Journal of Sociology* 96: 107–143.

Dobbin, Frank, and Erin L. Kelly. 2007. "How to Stop Harassment: Professional Construction of Legal Compliance in Organizations." *American Journal of Sociology* 112: 1203–1243.

Doeringer, Peter B., and Michael J. Piore. 1971. *Internal Labor Markets and Manpower Analysis.* Lexington, MA: D. C. Heath.

Domanski, Henryk. 1990. "Dynamics of Labor Market Segmentation in Poland, 1982–1987." *Social Forces* 69: 423–438.

Doyle, Arthur Conan, Sir. 1960. "The Sign of Four." In *The Complete Sherlock Holmes*. New York: Doubleday. (Orig. pub. 1895.)

Duncan, Otis Dudley, and Beverly Duncan. 1955. "A Methodological Analysis of Segregation Indexes." *American Sociological Review* 20: 210–217.

Edelman, Lauren B. 2004. "Rivers of Law and Contested Terrain: A Law and Society Approach to Economic Rationality." *Law & Society Review* 38: 181–198.

England, Paula. 1992. *Comparable Worth: Theories and Evidence*. New York: Aldine de Gruyter.

England, Paula, Paul Allison, and Yuxiao Wu. 2006. "Does Bad Pay Cause Occupations to Feminize, Does Feminization Reduce Pay, and How Can We Tell with Longitudinal Data?" *Social Science Research* 36: 1237–1256.

England, Paula, Melissa S. Herbert, Barbara Stanek Kilbourne, Lori Reid, and Lori Mc-Creary Megdal. 1994. "The Gendered Valuation of Occupations and Skills: Earning in 1980 Census Occupations." *Social Forces* 73: 65–100.

England, Paula, and Barbara Stanek Kilbourne. 1988. "Occupational Measures from the Dictionary of Occupational Titles for 1980 Census Detailed Occupations." Ann Arbor, MI: Inter-University Consortium for Political and Social Research Machine Readable Data Set.

England, Paula, Lori L. Reid, and Barbara Stanek Kilbourne. 1996. "The Effect of the Sex Composition of Jobs on Starting Wages in an Organization: Findings from the NLSY." *Demography* 33: 511–521.

Farkas, George, Paula England, Keven Vicknair, and Barbara Kilbourne. 1997. "Cognitive Skill, Skill Demands of Jobs, and Earnings Among Young European-American, African-American, and Mexican-American Workers." *Social Forces* 75: 913–940.

Featherman, David L., and Robert M. Hauser. 1976. "Changes in the Socioeconomic Stratification of the Races 1962–1973." *American Journal of Sociology* 82: 621–651.

Fernandez , Roberto M., and Isabel Fernandez-Mateo. 2006. "Networks, Race, and Hiring." *American Sociological Review* 71: 42–71.

Fernandez, Roberto M., and Marie Louise Mors. 2008. "Competing for Jobs: Labor Queues and Gender Sorting in the Hiring Process." *Social Science Research* 37: 1061–1080.

Fernandez , Roberto M., and M. Lourdes Sosa. 2005. "Gendering the Job: Networks and Recruitment at a Call Center." *American Journal of Sociology* 111: 859–904.

Ferree, Myra Marx. 1991. "The Gender Division of Labor in Two-Earner Marriages: Dimensions of Variability and Change." *Journal of Family Issues* 12: 158–180.

Fields, Judith, and Edward N. Wolff. 1991. "The Decline of Sex Segregation and the Wage Gap, 1970–80." *Journal of Human Resources* 26: 608–622.

Filer, Randall K. 1986. "The Role of Personality and Taste in Determining Occupational Structure." *Industrial and Labor Relations Review* 39: 412–424.

Firebaugh, Glenn, and Kenneth E. Davis. 1988. "Trends in Anti-Black Prejudice, 1972–1984: Region and Cohort Effects." *American Journal of Sociology* 94: 251–272.

Fix, Michael, and Raymond J. Struyk, eds. 1993. *Clear and Convincing Evidence: Measurement of Discrimination in America*. Washington, DC: Urban Institute.

Form, William. 1987. "On the Degradation of Skills." *Annual Review of Sociology* 13: 29–47.

Gabin, Nancy F. 1985. "Women and the United Auto Workers' Union in the 1950s." Pp. 259–279 in *Women, Work, and Protest: A Century of U.S. Women's Labor History*, edited by Ruth Milkman. Boston: Routledge and Kegan Paul.

———. 1990. *Feminism in the Labor Movement: Women and the United Auto Workers, 1935–1975.* Ithaca, NY: Cornell University Press.

Gabriel, Stuart, and Stuart Rosenthal. 1996. "Commutes, Neighborhood Effects, and Earnings: An Analysis of Racial Discrimination and Compensating Differentials." *Journal of Urban Economics* 40: 61–83.

Galle, O. R., C. H. Wiswell, and J. A. Burr. 1985. "Racial Mix and Industrial Productivity." *American Sociological Review* 50: 20–33.

Ganzeboom, Harry B. G., Donald J. Treiman, and Wout C. Ultee. 1991. "Comparative Intergenerational Stratification Research: Three Generations and Beyond." *Annual Review of Sociology* 17: 277–302.

Gati, Itamar, Samuel H. Osipow, and Michal Givon. 1995. "Gender Differences in Career Decision Making: The Content and Structure of Preferences." *Journal of Counseling Psychology* 42: 204–216.

Glass, Jennifer. 1990. "The Impact of Occupational Segregation on Working Conditions." *Social Forces* 68: 779–796.

Glass, Jennifer, and Valerie Camarigg. 1992. "Gender, Parenthood, and Job-Family Compatibility." *American Journal of Sociology* 98: 131–151.

Glass, Jennifer, Marta Tienda, and Shelley A. Smith. 1988. "The Impact of Changing Employment Opportunity on Gender and Ethnic Earnings Inequality." *Social Science Research* 17: 252–276.

Goldscheider, Frances K., and Linda J. Waite. 1991. *New Families, No Families? The Transformation of the American Home.* Berkeley: University of California Press.

Goldstein, H. 1995. *Multilevel Statistical Models,* 2nd ed. New York: Halsted Press.

Gordon, David M. 1972. *Theories of Poverty and Underemployment.* Lexington, MA: Heath.

Greeley, Andrew M., and Paul B. Sheatsley. 1971. "Attitudes Toward Racial Integration." *Scientific American* 225: 13–19.

Greene, William H. 1997. *Econometric Analysis,* 3rd ed. Upper Saddle River, NJ: Prentice Hall.

———. 1998. *LIMDEP Version 7.0.* Plainview, NY: Econometric Software.

Greenstein, Theodore N. 1996. "Gender Ideology and Perceptions of the Fairness of the Division of Household Labor: Effects on Marital Quality." *Social Forces* 74: 1029–1042.

Grodsky, Eric, and Devah Pager. 2001. "The Structure of Disadvantage: Individual and Occupational Determinants of the Black-White Wage Gap." *American Sociological Review* 66: 542–567.

Groshen, Erica L. 1991. "The Structure of the Female/Male Wage Differential: Is It Who You Are, What You Do, or Where You Work?" *Journal of Human Resources* 26: 457–472.

Gunderson, Morley. 1989. "Male-Female Wage Differentials and Policy Responses." *Journal of Economic Literature* 27: 46–72.

Gupta, Saurabh, Terence J. G. Tracey, and Paul A. Gore Jr. 2008. "Structural Examination of RIASEC Scales in High School Students: Variation Across Ethnicity and Method." *Journal of Vocational Behavior* 72: 1–13.

Hachen, D. S. 1992. "Industrial Characteristics and Job Mobility Rates." *American Sociological Review* 57: 39–55.

Hanushek, Eric A., and John E. Jackson. 1977. *Statistical Methods for Social Scientists.* New York: Academic Press.

Hartmann, Heidi I. 1976. "Capitalism, Patriarchy, and Job Segregation by Sex." *Signs* 1: 137–169.

Haveman, Robert H., Andrew Bershadker, and Jonathan A. Schwabish. 2003. *Human*

Capital in the United States from 1975 to 2000: Patterns of Growth and Utilization. Kalamazoo, MI: Upjohn Institute for Employment Research.

Hedges, Larry V., and Amy Nowell. 1998. "Black-White Test Score Convergence Since 1965." Pp. 149–181 in *The Black-White Test Score Gap,* edited by Christopher Jencks and Meredith Phillips. Washington, DC: Brookings.

Herbert, Frank. 1965. *Dune.* New York: Chilton.

Herring, Cedric. 2009. "Does Diversity Pay?: Race, Gender, and the Business Case for Diversity." *American Sociological Review* 74: 208–224.

Herzog, A. Regula. 1982. "High School Seniors' Plans and Values: Trends in Sex Differences 1976 Through 1980." *Sociology of Education* 55: 1–13.

Hill, Richard C. 1974. "Unionization and Racial Income Inequality in the Metropolis." *American Sociological Review* 39: 507–522.

Hirsh, C. Elizabeth. 2008. "Settling for Less? Organizational Determinants of Discrimination-Charge Outcomes." *Law & Society Review* 42: 239–274.

———. 2009. "The Strength of Weak Enforcement: The Impact of Discrimination Charges, Legal Environments, and Organizational Conditions on Workplace Segregation." *American Sociological Review* 74: 245–271.

Hirsh, C. Elizabeth, and Sabino Kornrich. 2008. "The Context of Discrimination: Workplace Conditions, Institutional Environments, and Sex and Race Discrimination Charges." *American Journal of Sociology* 113: 1394–1432.

Hodson, Randy D. 1983. *Workers' Earnings and Corporate Economic Structure.* New York: Academic Press.

Hodson, Randy D., and Robert Kaufman. 1982. "Economic Dualism: A Critical Review." *American Sociological Review* 47: 727–739.

Holzer, Harry J. 1998. "Employer Hiring Decisions and Antidiscrimination Policy." Pp. 223–257 in *Generating Jobs: How to Increase Demand for Less-Skilled Workers,* edited by R. Freean and Paul Gottschalk. New York: Russell Sage.

Holzer, H. J., Keith Ihlanfeldt, and David Sjoquist. 1994. "Work, Search, and Travel Among White and Black Youth." *Journal of Urban Economics* 35: 320–345.

Holzer, Harry J., Stephen Raphael, and Michael A. Stoll. 2004. "Will Employers Hire Former Offenders? Employer Preferences, Background Checks, and Their Determinants." Pp. 205–246 in *Imprisoning America: The Social Effects of Mass Incarceration,* edited by Mary Patillo, David Weiman, and Bruce Wester. New York: Russell Sage.

Huffman, M. L., and P. N. Cohen. 2004. "Racial Wage Inequality: Job Composition Effects Across U.S. Labor Markets." *American Journal of Sociology* 109: 902–936.

Huffman, Matt L., and Steven C. Velasco. 1997. "When More Is Less: Sex Composition, Organizations, and Earnings in U.S. Firms." *Work and Occupations* 24: 214–244.

Hundley, Greg. 2000. "Male/Female Earnings Differences in Self-Employment: The Effects of Marriage, Children, and the Household Division of Labor." *Industrial and Labor Relations Review* 54: 95–114.

Husserl, Edmund. 1931. *Ideas: General Introduction to Pure Phenomenology,* translated by W. R. Boyce Gibson. New York: Macmillan.

Ihlanfeldt, Keith, and David Sjoquist. 1998. "The Spatial Mismatch Hypothesis: A Review of Recent Studies and Their Implications for Welfare Reform." *Housing Policy Debate* 9: 849–892.

Jacobs, Jerry A. 1989. "Long-Term Trends in Occupational Segregation by Sex." *American Journal of Sociology* 95: 160–173.

———. 2001. "Evolving Patterns of Sex Segregation." Pp. 535–550 in *Sourcebook on Labor Markets: Evolving Structures and Processes,* edited by Ivar Berg and Arne L. Kalleberg. New York: Kluwer Academic/Plenum.

Jacobs, Jerry A., and Ronnie J. Steinberg. 1990. "Compensating Differentials and the Male-Female Wage Gap." *Social Forces* 69: 439–468.

Jacobs, Lawrence R., and Theda Skocpol, eds. 2005. *Inequality and American Democracy: What We Know and What We Need to Learn.* New York: Russell Sage.

Jaynes, Gerald David, and Robin M. Williams Jr., eds. 1989. *A Common Destiny: Blacks and American Society.* Washington, DC: National Academy Press.

Jencks, Christopher, Lauri Perman, and Lee Rainwater. 1988. "What Is a Good Job? A New Measure of Labor Market Success." *American Journal of Sociology* 93: 1322–1357.

Jencks, Christopher, and Meredith Phillips, eds. 1998. *The Black-White Test Score Gap.* Washington, DC: Brookings.

Johnson, George, and Gary Solon. 1986. "Estimates of the Direct Effects of Comparable Worth Policy." *American Economic Review* 76: 1117–1125.

Johnson, Monica Kirkpatrick. 2002. "Social Origins, Adolescent Experiences, and Work Value Trajectories During the Transition to Adulthood." *Social Forces* 80: 1307–1340.

Judd, Patricia C., and Patricia A. Oswald. 1997. "Employment Desirability: The Interactive Effects of Gender-Type Profile, Stimulus Sex, and Gender-Typed Occupation." *Sex Roles* 37: 467–476.

Judge, George G., W. E. Griffiths, R. Carter Hill, Helmut Lütkepohl, and Tsoung-Chao Lee. 1985. *The Theory and Practice of Econometrics,* 2nd ed. New York: Wiley.

Kain, John F. 1968. "Housing, Segregation, Negro Employment and Metropolitan Decentralization." *The Quarterly Journal of Economics* 82: 175–197.

———. 1992. "The Spatial Mismatch Hypothesis: Three Decades Later." *Housing Policy Debate* 3: 371–460.

Kalev, Alexandra, Frank Dobbin, and Erin Kelly. 2006. "Best Practices or Best Guesses? Diversity Management and the Remediation of Inequality." *American Sociological Review* 71: 589–917.

Kalleberg, Arne L., and Ivar Berg. 1987. *Work and Industry: Structures, Markets, and Processes.* New York: Plenum Press.

———. 1994. "Work Structures and Markets: An Analytic Framework." Pp. 3–17 in *Industries, Firms, and Jobs: Sociological and Economic Approaches,* expanded ed., edited by George Farkas and Paula England. Hawthorne, NY: Aldine de Gruyter.

Kalleberg, Arne L., David Knoke, Peter V. Marsden, and Joe L. Spaeth. 1991. *National Organizations Survey, 1991* [Computer file]. Champaign, IL: University of Illinois, Survey Research Laboratory [producer], 1993. Ann Arbor, MI: Inter-University Consortium for Political and Social Research [distributor], 1994.

Kalleberg, Arne L., Michael Wallace, and Robert P. Althauser. 1981. "Economic Segmentation, Worker Power, and Income Inequality." *American Journal of Sociology* 87: 651–683.

Kaufman, Robert L. 1981. "Racial Discrimination and Labor Market Segmentation." Ph.D. diss., University of Wisconsin, Madison.

———. 1983. "A Structural Decomposition of Black-White Earnings Differentials." *American Journal of Sociology* 89: 585–611.

———. 1986. "The Impact of Industrial and Occupational Structure on Black-White Employment Allocation." *American Sociological Review* 51: 310–323.

———. 1993. "Decomposing Longitudinal from Cross-Unit Effects in Panel and Pooled Cross-sectional Designs." *Sociological Methods and Research* 21: 482–504.

———. 2001. "Race and Labor Market Segmentation." Pp. 645–668 in *Sourcebook on Labor Markets: Evolving Structures and Processes,* edited by Ivar Berg and Arne L. Kalleberg. New York: Kluwar Academic/Plenum.

————. 2002. "Assessing Alternative Perspectives on Race and Sex Employment Segregation." *American Sociological Review* 67: 547–572.

Kaufman, Robert L., and Thomas N. Daymont. 1981. "Racial Discrimination and the Social Organization of Industries." *Social Science Research* 10: 225–255.

Kaufman, Robert L., and Randy Hodson, and Neil D. Fligstein. 1981. "Defrocking Dualism: A New Approach to Defining Industrial Sectors." *Social Science Research* 10: 1–31.

Kaufman, Robert L., and Paul G. Schervish. 1986. "Using Adjusted Crosstabulations to Interpret Log-Linear Relationships." *American Sociological Review* 51: 717–733.

————. 1987. "Variations on a Theme: More Uses of Odds Ratios to Interpret Log-Linear Parameters." *Sociological Methods and Research* 16: 218–255.

Kessler-Harris, Alice. 1985. "Problems of Coalition-Building: Women and Trade Unions in the 1920s." Pp. 110–138 in *Women, Work, and Protest: A Century of U.S. Women's Labor History,* edited by Ruth Milkman. Boston: Routledge and Kegan Paul.

Kilbourne, Barbara S., George Farkas, Kurt Beron, Dorothea Weir, and Paula England. 1994a. "Returns to Skill, Compensating Differentials, and Gender Bias: Effects of Occupational Characteristics on the Wages of White Women and Men." *American Journal of Sociology* 100: 689–719.

Kilbourne, Barbara S., Paula England, and Kurt Beron. 1994b. "Effects of Individual, Occupational, and Industrial Characteristics on Earnings: Intersections of Race and Gender." *Social Forces* 72: 1149–1176.

King, Mary C. 1992. "Occupational Segregation by Race and Gender, 1940–1988." *Monthly Labor Review* 115: 30–37.

Kmec, Julie A. 2005. "Setting Occupational Sex Segregation in Motion: Demand-Side Explanations of Sex Traditional Employment." *Work and Occupations* 32: 322–354.

Kmec, Julie A., and Lindsey B. Trimble. 2009. "Does It Pay to Have a Network Contact? Social Network Ties, Workplace Racial Context, and Pay Outcomes." *Social Science Research* 38: 266–278.

Knoke, David, George W. Bohrnstedt, and Alisa Potter Mee. 2002. *Statistics for Social Data Analysis,* 4th ed. Itasca, IL: F. E. Peacock.

Kokkelenberg, Edward C., and Donna R. Sockell. 1985. "Union Membership in the United States, 1973–1981." *Industrial and Labor Relations Review* 38: 497–543.

Krivo, Lauren J., and Robert L. Kaufman. 1990. "Estimating Macro Relationships Using Micro Data." *Sociological Research and Methods* 19: 196–224.

Lahiri, Kajal, and Peter Schmidt. 1978. "On the Estimation of Triangular Structural Systems." *Econometrica* 46: 1217–1221.

Lang, Kevin, and William T. Dickens. 1994. "Neoclassical and Sociological Perspectives on Segmented Labor Markets." Pp. 65–88 in *Industries, Firms, and Jobs,* edited by George Farkas and Paula England. New York: Aldine de Gruyter.

Leahey, Erin, and Guang Guo. 2001. "Gender Differences in Mathematical Trajectories." *Social Forces* 80: 713–732.

Leonard, Jonathan S. 1984. "Employment and Occupational Advance Under Affirmative Action." *Review of Economics and Statistics* 66: 377–385.

————. 1985. "The Effects of Unions on the Employment of Blacks, Hispanics, and Women." *Industrial and Labor Relations Review* 39: 115–132.

————. 1994. "Use of Enforcement Techniques in Eliminating Glass Ceiling Barriers." Report to the Glass Ceiling Commission, US Department of Labor.

Levine, Jeffrey, Edward G. Carmines, and Paul M. Sniderman. 1999. "The Empirical Dimensionality of Racial Stereotypes." *Public Opinion Quarterly* 63: 371–384.

Libeau, Vera A. 1977. "Minority and Female Membership in Referral Unions." Research

Report No. 55, Equal Employment Opportunity Commission. Washington, DC: US Government Printing Office.

Lippa, R. 1998. "Gender-Related Individual Differences and the Structure of Vocational Interests: The Importance of the People-Things Dimension." *Journal of Personality and Social Psychology* 74: 996–1009.

Loscocco, Karyn A. 1990. "Reactions to Blue-Collar Work: A Comparison of Women and Men." *Work and Occupations* 17: 152–177.

Lueptow, L. B. 1980. "Social Structure, Social Change, and Parental Influence in Adolescent Sex-Role Socialization: 1964–1975." *Journal of Marriage and the Family* 42: 93–103.

Lyson, Thomas A. 1985. "Race and Sex Segregation in the Occupational Structures of Southern Employers." *Social Science Quarterly* 66: 281–295.

———. 1991. "Shifts, Occupational Recomposition, and the Changing Sexual Division of Labor in the Five Largest U.S. Cities, 1910–1930." *Sociological Forum* 6: 157–177.

Macpherson, David A., and Barry T. Hirsch. 1995. "Wages and Gender Composition: Why Do Women's Jobs Pay Less?" *Journal of Labor Economics* 13: 426–471.

Marini, Margaret M. 1989. "Sex Differences in Earnings in the United States." *Annual Review of Sociology* 15: 343–380.

Marini, Margaret M., and Pi-Lang Fan. 1997. "The Gender Gap in Earnings at Career Entry." *American Sociological Review* 62: 588–604.

Marshall, Ray. 1965. *The Negro and Organized Labor.* New York: Wiley.

———. 1974. "The Economics of Racial Discrimination: A Survey." *Journal of Economic Literature* 12: 849–871.

Martin, Jack K., and Steven A. Tuch. 1993. "Black-White Differences in the Value of Job Rewards Revisited." *Social Science Quarterly* 74: 884–901.

May, Martha. 1985. "Bread Before Roses: American Workingmen, Labor Unions, and Family Wage." Pp. 1–21 in *Women, Work, and Protest: A Century of U.S. Women's Labor History,* edited by Ruth Milkman. Boston: Routledge and Kegan Paul.

McBrier, Debra B. 2003. "Gender and Career Dynamics Within a Segmented Professional Labor Market: The Case of Academia." *Social Forces* 81: 1201–1266.

McCall, Leslie. 2000a. "Gender and the New Inequality: Explaining the College/Noncollege Wage Gap." *American Sociological Review* 65: 234–255.

———. 2000b. "Explaining Levels of Within-Group Wage Inequality in U.S Labor Markets." *Demography* 37: 415–430.

———. 2001a. *Complex Inequality: Gender, Class, and Race in the New Economy.* New York: Routledge.

———. 2001b. "Sources of Racial Wage Inequality in Metropolitan Labor Markets: Racial, Ethnic, and Gender Differences." *American Sociological Review* 66: 520–541.

McCrary, Michael. 1998. "'Same Song, Different Verse': Processes of Race-Sex Stratification and Self-Employment Success." *Research in Social Stratification and Mobility* 16: 319–350.

Merton, Robert K. 1949. *Social Theory and Social Structure.* New York: Free Press.

Milkman, Ruth. 1985. "Women Workers, Feminism, and the Labor Movement Since the 1960s." Pp. 300–322 in *Women, Work, and Protest: A Century of U.S. Women's Labor History,* edited by Ruth Milkman. Boston: Routledge and Kegan Paul.

———. 1987. *Gender at Work: The Dynamics of Job Segregation by Sex During World War II.* Chicago: University of Illinois.

———. 2007. "Two Worlds of Unionism: Women and the New Labor Movement." Pp. 63–80 in *The Sex of Class: Women Transforming American Labor,* edited by Dorothy Sue Cobble. Ithaca: Cornell University Press.

Mincer, Jacob, and Solomon W. Polachek. 1974. "Family Investment in Human Capital: Earnings of Women." *Journal of Political Economy* 82: 76–108.

Moss, Philip, and Chris Tilly. 1996. "Soft Skills and Race: An Investigation of Black Men's Employment Problems." *Work and Occupations* 23: 252–276.

———. 2001. *Stories Employers Tell: Race, Skill, and Hiring in America.* New York: Russell Sage.

Muller, Chandra. 1998. "Gender Differences in Parental Involvement and Adolescents' Mathematics Achievement." *Sociology of Education* 71: 336–356.

Mullis, R. L., Ann K. Mullis, and D. Gerwels. 1998. "Stability of Vocational Interests Among Adolescents and Young Adults." *Adolescence* 33: 699–707.

Nardone, Thomas. 1995. "Part-Time Employment: Reasons, Demographics, and Trends." *Journal of Labor Research* 16: 275–292.

Neckerman, Kathryn M., and Joleen Kirschenman. 1991. "Hiring Strategies, Racial Bias, and Inner-City Workers." *Social Problems* 38: 801–815.

Nelson, Joel I. 1994. "Work and Benefits: The Multiple Problems of Service Sector Employment." *Social Problems* 41: 240–256.

Neumark, David. 1999. "Labor Market Information and Wage Differentials by Race and Sex." *Industrial Relations* 38: 414–445.

O'Neill, June. 2003. "The Gender Gap in Wages, Circa 2000." *American Economic Review* 93: 309–315.

Padavic, Irene. 1991. "Attraction of Male Blue-Collar Jobs for Black and White Women: Economic Need, Exposure, and Attitudes." *Social Science Quarterly* 72: 33–49.

Padavic, Irene, and Barbara Reskin. 2002. *Women and Men at Work,* 2nd ed. Thousand Oaks, CA: Pine Forge.

Pager, Devah. 2003. "The Mark of a Criminal Record." *American Journal of Sociology* 108: 937–975.

———. 2007. "The Use of Field Experiments for Studies of Employment Discrimination: Contributions, Critiques, and Directions for the Future." *Annals of the American Academy of Political and Social Science* 609: 104–133.

Pager, Devah, and Lincoln Quillian. 2005. "Walking the Talk? What Employers Say Versus What They Do." *American Sociological Review* 70: 355–380.

Pager, Devah, Bruce Western, and Bart Bonikowski. 2009. "Discrimination in a Low-Wage Labor Market: A Field Experiment." *American Sociological Review* 74: 800–820.

Parcel, Toby L. 1979. "Race, Regional Labor Markets, and Earnings." *American Sociological Review* 44: 262–279.

———. 1989. "Comparable Worth, Occupational Labor Markets, and Occupational Earnings: Results from the 1980 Census." Pp. 134–152 in *Pay Equity: Empirical Inquiries,* edited by Robert T. Michael, Heidi Hartmann, and Brigid O'Farrell. Washington, DC: National Academy Press.

Parcel, Toby L., Robert L. Kaufman, and Leeann Jolly. 1991. "Going Up the Ladder: Multiplicity Sampling to Create Linked Macro-Micro Organizational Samples." Pp. 43–79 in *Sociological Methodology,* vol. 21, edited by Peter V. Marsden.

Parcel, Toby L., and Charles W. Mueller. 1989. "Temporal Change in Occupational Earnings Attainment, 1970–1980." *American Sociological Review* 54: 622–634.

Petersen, Trond, and Laurie A. Morgan. 1995. "Separate and Unequal: Occupation Establishment Sex Segregation and the Gender Wage Gap." *American Journal of Sociology* 101: 329–365.

Petersen, Trond, and Ishak Saporta. 2004. "The Opportunity Structure for Discrimination." *American Journal of Sociology* 109: 852–901.

Petersen, Trond, Ishak Saporta, and Marc-David L. Seidel. 2000. "Offering a Job: Meritocracy and Social Networks." *American Journal of Sociology* 106: 763–816.

Phillips, S. D., and A. R Imhoff. 1997. "Women and Career Development: A Decade of Research." *Annual Review of Psychology* 45: 31–59.

Quillian, Lincoln. 1996. "Group Threat and Regional Change in Attitudes Toward African-Americans." *American Journal of Sociology* 102: 816–860.

Raphael, Steven. 1998. "The Spatial Mismatch Hypothesis of Black Youth Joblessness: Evidence from the San Francisco Bay Area." *Journal of Urban Economics* 43: 79–111.

Raphael, Steven, and Michael A. Stoll. 2006. "Modest Progress: The Narrowing Spatial Mismatch Between Blacks and Jobs in the 1990s." In *Redefining Urban and Suburban America: Evidence from Census 2000,* edited by Bruce Katz, Alan Berube, and Robert Lang. Washington, DC: Brookings Institution.

Raudenbush, Stephen W., and Anthony S. Bryk. 2002. *Hierarchical Linear Models: Applications and Data Analysis Methods,* 2nd ed. Thousand Oaks, CA: Sage.

Raudenbush, Stephen W., Anthony S. Bryk, Yuk Fai Cheong, and Richard Congdon. 2001. *HLM 5: Hierarchical Linear and Nonlinear Modeling,* 2nd ed. Lincolnwood, IL: Scientific Software International.

Raudenbush, Stephen W., and R. Kasim. 1998. "Cognitive Skill and Economic Inequality: Findings from the National Adult Literacy Survey." *Harvard Educational Review* 68: 33–79.

Reid, Lori L. 1998. "Devaluing Women and Minorities: The Effects of Race/Ethnic and Sex Composition of Occupations on Wage Levels." *Work and Occupations* 25: 511–536.

Reskin, Barbara F. 1988. "Bringing the Men Back In: Sex Differentiation and the Devaluation of Women's Work." *Gender and Society* 2: 58–81.

———. 1993. "Sex Segregation in the Workplace." *Annual Review of Sociology* 19: 241–270.

———. 1998. *The Realities of Affirmative Action in Employment.* Washington, DC: American Sociological Association.

———. 2003. "Including Mechanisms in Our Models of Ascriptive Inequality: 2002 Presidential Address." *American Sociological Review* 68: 1–21.

Reskin, Barbara F., Lowell Hargens, and Elizabeth Hirsh. 2004. "Picturing Segregation: The Structure of Occupational Segregation by Sex, Race, Ethnicity, and Hispanicity." Paper presented at the 2004 Annual Meetings of the American Sociological Association, San Francisco. http://www.allacademic.com/meta/p110079_index.html.

Reskin, Barbara, Debra B. McBrier, and Julie A. Kmec. 1999. "The Determinants and Consequences of Workplace Sex and Race Composition." *Annual Review of Sociology* 25: 235–261.

Reskin, Barbara F., and Irene Padavic. 1999. "Sex, Race, and Ethnic Inequality in United States Workplaces." Pp. 343–374 in *Handbook of the Sociology of Gender,* edited by Janet Saltzman Chafetz. New York: Plenum.

Reskin, Barbara F., and Patricia A. Roos. 1987. "Sex Segregation and Status Hierarchies." Pp. 1–21 in *Ingredients for Women's Employment Policy*, edited by Christine Bose and Glenna Spitze. Albany: SUNY University Press.

———. 1990. *Job Queues, Gender Queues: Explaining Women's Inroads into Male Occupations.* Philadelphia: Temple University Press.

———. 1993. "1970–1990 Trends in Occupational Sex and Race Composition." Funded grant proposal, National Science Foundation.

Reskin, Barbara F., and Catherine E. Ross. 1992. "Jobs, Authority, and Earnings Among Managers: The Continuing Significance of Sex." *Work and Occupations* 19: 342–365.

Reynolds, John R. 1997. "Job Stress and Industrial Conditions in the 1980s: Direct, Indirect, and Conditional Effects of Macroeconomic Structure on Workers' Psychological Well-Being." Ph.D. diss., Ohio State University, Department of Sociology.

Ridgeway, Cecilia L. 1997. "Interaction and the Conservation of Gender Inequality: Considering Employment." *American Sociological Review* 62: 218–235.

Rindfuss, Ronald R., C. Gray Swicegood, and Rachel A. Rosenfeld. 1987. "Disorder in the Life Course: How Much and Does It Matter?" *American Sociological Review* 52: 785–801.

Robinson, Corre L., Tiffany Taylor, Donald Tomaskovic-Devey, Catherine Zimmer, and Matthew W. Irvin Jr. 2005. "Studying Race or Ethnic and Sex Segregation at the Establishment Level: Methodological Issues: Substantive Opportunities Using EEO-1 Reports." *Work and Occupations* 32: 5–38.

Roos, Patricia A., and Joan E. Manley. 1996. "Staffing Personnel: Feminization and Change in Human Resource Management." *Sociological Focus* 29: 245–261.

Rosenfeld, Rachel A. 1983. "Sex Segregation and Sectors: An Analysis of Gender Differences in Returns from Employer Changes." *American Sociological Review* 48: 637–655.

Rosenfeld, Rachel A., and Kenneth I. Spenner. 1992. "Occupational Sex Segregation and Women's Early Career Job Shifts." *Work and Occupations* 19: 424–449.

Rowe, R., and W. E. Snizek. 1995. "Gender Differences in Work Values: Perpetuating the Myth." *Work and Occupations* 22: 215–229.

Saenz, Rogelio, and Jamie Vinas. 1990. "Chicano Geographic Segregation: A Human Ecological Approach." *Sociological Perspectives* 33: 465–481.

Sakamoto, Arthur, and Meichu D. Chen. 1991. "Inequality and Attainment in a Dual Labor Market." *American Sociological Review* 56: 295–308.

Sayer, Liana C. 2005. "Gender, Time, and Inequality: Trends in Women's and Men's Paid Work, Unpaid Work, and Free Time." *Social Forces* 84: 285–303.

Schuman, Howard, Charlotte Steeh, and Lawrence Bobo. 1985. *Racial Attitudes in America: Trends and Interpretations.* Cambridge, MA: Harvard University Press.

Schutt, Randall K. 1987. "Craft Unions and Minorities: Determinants of Change in Admission Practices." *Social Problems* 34: 388–402.

Sewell, William H., Archibald O. Haller, and Alejandro Portes. 1969. "The Educational and Early Occupational Attainment Process." *American Sociological Review* 34: 82–92.

Shelton, Beth Anne. 1992. *Women, Men, and Time: Gender Differences in Paid Work, Housework, and Leisure.* New York: Greenwood Press.

Shelton, Beth Anne, and Daphne John. 1996. "The Division of Household Labor." *Annual Review of Sociology* 22: 299–322.

Shepherd, William G. 1970. *Market Power and Economic Welfare.* New York: Random House.

Smith, James D., and Finis R. Welch. 1977. "Black-White Male Wage Ratios: 1960–1970." *American Economic Review* 67: 323–338.

Smith, Tom W., Arne L. Kalleberg, and Peter V. Marsden. 2002. *National Organizations Survey, 2002* [Computer file]. ICPSR04074-v1. Chicago, IL: National Opinion Research Center (NORC) [producer], 2003. Ann Arbor, MI: Inter-University Consortium for Political and Social Research [distributor], 2004.

Sorensen, Aage B., and Arne L. Kalleberg. 1981. "An Outline of a Theory of Matching Persons to Jobs." Pp. 39–74 in *Sociological Perspectives on Labor Markets,* edited by Ivar Berg. New York: Academic Press.

Sorensen, Elaine. 1990. "The Crowding Hypothesis and Comparable Worth Issue: A Survey and New Results." *Journal of Human Resources* 25: 55–89.

Spenner, Kenneth I. 1990. "Skill: Meanings, Methods, and Measures." *Work and Occupations* 17: 399–421.

Stainback, Kevin. 2008. "Social Contacts and Race/Ethnic Job Matching." *Social Forces* 87: 857–886.

Steinberg, Ronnie J. 1990. "Social Construction of Skill: Gender, Power, and Comparable Worth." *Work and Occupations* 17: 449–482.

Stockard, Jean. 1999. "Gender Socialization." Pp. 215–227 in *Handbook of the Sociology of Gender,* edited by Janet Saltzman Chafetz. New York: Kluwar Academic/Plenum.

Strom, Sharon Hartman. 1985. "'We're No Kitty Foyles': Organizing Office Workers for the Congress of Industrial Organizations, 1937–1950." Pp. 206–234 in *Women, Work, and Protest: A Century of U.S. Women's Labor History,* edited by Ruth Milkman. Boston: Routledge and Kegan Paul.

Sullivan, Teresa A., and Stephen D. McCracken. 1988. "Black Entrepreneurs: Patterns and Rates of Return to Self-Employment." *National Journal of Sociology* 2: 167–185.

Szafran, R. F. 1982. "What Kinds of Firms Hire and Promote Women and Blacks? A Review of the Literature." *Sociological Quarterly* 23: 171–190.

Taeuber, Alma F., Karl E. Taeuber, and Glen G. Cain. 1966. "Occupational Assimilation and the Competitive Process: A Reanalysis." *American Journal of Sociology* 72: 273–285.

Taylor, Patricia A., Patricia A. Gwartney-Gibbs, and Reynolds Farley. 1986. "Changes in the Structure of Earnings Inequality by Race, Sex, and Industrial Sector, 1960–1980." *Research in Social Stratification and Mobility* 5: 105–138.

Thoreau, Henry David. 1927. *The Heart of Thoreau's Journals,* edited by Odell Shepard. Boston: Houghton Mifflin. (Citation to p. 246 from the journal entry c. November 11–14, 1850.)

———. 1985. *A Week on the Concord and Merrimack Rivers; Walden, or, Life in the Woods; The Maine Woods; Cape Cod.* New York: Library of America. (Citation to p. 249 from the chapter on Thursday.)

Thurow, Lester C. 1975. *Generating Inequality.* New York: Basic Books.

Tienda, Marta, Shelley A. Smith, and Vilma Ortiz. 1987. "Industrial Restructuring, Gender Segregation, and Sex Differences in Earnings." *American Sociological Review* 52: 195–210.

Tigges, Leann M. 1987. *Changing Fortunes: Industrial Sectors and Workers' Earnings.* New York: Praeger.

Tolbert, Charles M., Patrick M. Horan, and E. M. Beck. 1980. "The Structure of Economic Segmentation: A Dual Economy Approach." *American Journal of Sociology* 85: 1095–1116.

Tolbert, Pamela S., and Phyllis Moen. 1998. "Men's and Women's Definitions of 'Good' Jobs." *Work and Occupations* 25: 168–194.

Tomaskovic-Devey, Donald. 1993. *Gender and Racial Inequality at Work: The Sources and Consequences of Job Segregation.* Ithaca, NY: ILR Press.

Tomaskovic-Devey, Donald, and Sheryl Skaggs. 1999. "An Establishment-Level Test of the Statistical Discrimination Hypothesis." *Work and Occupations* 26: 422–445.

Tracey, T. J. G. 1997. "RANDALL: A Microsoft FORTRAN Program for a Randomization Test of Hypothesized Order Relations." *Educational and Psychological Measurement* 57: 164–168.

Turner, Margery, Michael Fix, and Raymond Struyk. 1991. *Opportunities Denied, Opportunities Diminished: Discrimination in Hiring.* Washington, DC: Urban Institute.

US Bureau of the Census. 1983. *1980 Census of Population and Housing Public Use Microdata Sample A (PUMS A).* Machine Readable Data File. Washington, DC: US Bureau of the Census.

———. 1985. *Current Population Survey, May 1985.* Machine Readable Data File. Washington, DC: US Bureau of the Census.

————. 1986. *Current Population Survey, May 1986*. Machine Readable Data File. Washington, DC: US Bureau of the Census.

————. 1987. *Current Population Survey, May 1987*. Machine Readable Data File. Washington, DC: US Bureau of the Census.

————. 1988. *Current Population Survey, May 1988*. Machine Readable Data File. Washington, DC: US Bureau of the Census.

————. 1989a. *Current Population Survey, May 1989*. Machine Readable Data File. Washington, DC: US Bureau of the Census.

————. 1989b. *1987 Enterprise Statistics*. Washington, DC: US Government Printing Office.

————. 1994a. *1990 Census of Population and Housing 1% Public Use Microdata Sample (PUMS)*. Machine Readable Data File. Washington, DC: US Bureau of the Census.

————. 1994b. *1990 Census of Population and Housing 5% Public Use Microdata Sample (PUMS)*. Machine Readable Data File. Washington, DC: US Bureau of the Census.

————. 1994c. *1990 Public Use Microdata Sample (PUMS) 1% and 5%—United States Geographic Equivalency Files*. Machine Readable Data File. Washington, DC: US Bureau of the Census..

————. 2009. *Educational Attainment in the United States: 2007, Current Population Report P20-560*. Washington, DC: US Bureau of the Census.

US Commission on Civil Rights. 1982. "Nonreferral Unions and Equal Employment Opportunity." Washington, DC: US Government Printing Office.

US Department of Commerce. 1990. *US Industrial Outlook for 1990*. Washington, DC: US Government Printing Office.

————. 1994. *Input-Output Accounts of the US Economy, 1987 Benchmark*. Machine Readable Data File. Washington, DC: US Government Printing Office.

US Department of the Treasury. 1994, 1995, 1996. *Statistics of Income: Corporation Income Tax Returns for 1989–1991*. Washington, DC: US Government Printing Office.

Villemez, Wayne J., and William P. Bridges. 1988. "When Bigger Is Better: Differences in the Individual-Level Effect of Firm and Establishment Size." *American Sociological Review* 53: 237–255.

Wagner, Eric F. 1982. "Personality Differences as Measured by the Hand Test Among Holland Types for Females." *Perceptual and Motor Skills* 55: 710.

Wallace, M., and C. F. Chang. 1990. "Barriers to Women's Employment: Economic Segmentation in American Manufacturing." *Research in Social Stratification and Mobility* 9: 337–361.

Weakliem, David L., and Robert Biggert. 1999. "Regional and Political Opinion in the Contemporary United States." *Social Forces* 77: 863–886.

West, Candace, and Don Zimmerman. 1987. "Doing Gender." *Gender and Society* 1: 125–151.

Wharton, Amy S. 1986. "Industry Structure and Gender Segregation in Blue Collar Occupations." *Social Forces* 64: 1025–1031.

————. 1989. "Gender Segregation in Private-Sector, Public-Sector, and Self-Employed Occupations, 1950–1981." *Social Science Quarterly* 70: 923–940.

Williams, Christine L. 1992. "The Glass Escalator: Hidden Advantages for Men in the 'Female' Professions." *Social Problems* 39: 253–267.

Wilson, William Julius. 1996. *When Work Disappears: The World of the New Urban Poor*. New York: Knopf.

Wright, Rosemary, and Jerry A. Jacobs. 1994. "Male Flight from Computer Work: A

New Look at Occupational Resegregation and Ghettoization." *American Sociological Review* 59: 511–536.

Wynn, Tor, and Charles W. Mueller. 1998. "Product Characteristics, Human Capital, and Labor Market Segments: Services and the Distribution of Rewards in Labor Market Transactions." *Sociological Quarterly* 39: 597–622.

Yinger, John. 1995. *Closed Doors, Opportunities Lost: The Continuing Costs of Housing Discrimination*. New York: Russell Sage.

Zucker, Lynne G., and Carolyn Rosenstein. 1981. "Taxonomies on Institutional Structure: Dual Economy Reconsidered." *American Sociological Review* 46: 869–884.

Index

advertising methods, 31
affirmative action, 54, 92, 177
African Americans: blacks as larger
percentage of workforce in the South,
138, 161(n2); black-typed employment,
3, 40–41, 43, 48–50, 87, 164; constraint
theory about black job seekers, 48–49;
and distinction between craft-type and
industrial-type unions, 53; educational
and academic aspirations, 56(n10); and
government employment, 53–54; high
value of job security, 109(n15); labor
force participation and commitment
of black women compared to white
women, 90; mathematics skills and
skills deficit approach, 109(n14); and
mismatch between geographic location
of jobs and workers, 20; new
opportunities in war conditions, 51;
stereotypes about black employees,
108(n10); unemployment, underemployment, and employment
discouragement, 175. *See also*
discrimination; race- and gender-typed
employment; race-sex queuing theory;
race-typed employment; regional
variation in labor market inequality;
statistical discrimination; *headings
beginning with* earnings disparities *or*
employment segregation
airline pilots and navigators, 2–3, 58, 61,
163–165
Asians, 75(n5), 176
audit studies on race and preferential
evaluations, 1–2, 19, 174–175

authority: measurement of, 70, 72, 192;
predictions about, 44–45, 49; and
employment segregation and earnings
gap. *See also* race- and gender-typed
employment

Baron, James N., 16(n13), 24
Becker, Gary S., 26–27, 94; theory of
discrimination, 13, 92, 167
Belsley, David, 195
Bendick, Marc, Jr., 1, 175
Berg, Ivar, 17
Beron, Kurt, 46
Bianchi, Suzanne M., 21
Bielby, William T., 16(n13), 24
Biggert, Robert, 138
Braddock, Jomillis Henry, II, 30
Browning, Harley, 60
Bush, George H. W., 92

capital intensity, 52; and factory work,
161(n4); measurement of, 71–72, 193;
and worker preferences, 93, 161(n4)
Census of Population Public Use
Microdata Samples (PUMS; 1990),
57, 62–63, 161(nn 1,2), 200–214,
215(nn 1–4)
clerical perception: and devaluation of
labor, 135(n9); differing rewards for
men and women, 112, 173–174,
179(n5); as "female"-typed skill, 24,
49; measurement of, 70, 72; not
recognized/valued as a skill, 111;
predictions about, 44–45, 49; and
employment segregation and earnings

263

gap. *See also* race- and gender-typed employment

COEA. *See* Council of Economic Advisors

cognitive schemas, and worker preferences, 23–24

Cohen, Jacob, 195

Cohen, Patricia, 195

collinearity, 74, 195

comparable worth concept, 13

compensating differentials approach (trade-off between wages and job amenities), 22–24, 33–34, 158

competitive markets. *See* market power

competitive theory of discrimination, 26–27

Council of Economic Advisors (COEA), 8

criminal records, 2, 108(n11)

Day, Susan X., 25

demand-side perspectives on employment segregation and earnings gap, 25–34, 92, 94. *See also* devaluation of labor; product market structure; race-sex queuing theory; statistical discrimination

desirable employment. *See* employment conditions

devaluation of labor, 33–34, 44–46, 55(n7); "compensable differences" vs. "gendered devaluation of work," 33–34, 158; devaluation of labor in positions with concentrated less-favored employees, 39–40, 50, 112, 116, 117; differential treatment leading to differential treatment, 39, 157; and earnings gap, 111, 124–127, 135(nn 8,9), 157–158, 160; and environmental conditions of employment, 117; "global" vs. "specific" devaluation, 166, 169–172; and labor market position characteristics, 43, 48; mechanisms of, 49–50; men but not women rewarded for female-typed skills, 112, 116, 118, 127, 170, 173–174, 179(n5); predictions about, 45–46, 48–50; and race- and gender-typed jobs, 33–34, 40–41, 49–50, 111, 124–127, 135(nn 8,9); and regional variation in earnings gap, 157–158,

160; social construction of skill and skill-earnings relationship, 34, 50; summary and implications, 164–166, 169–171. *See also* earnings disparities, analysis of results

DiPrete, Thomas A., 149

discrimination, 13, 50–51, 167; advantages for nondiscriminating firms, 26, 107; antidiscrimination pressure, and regional variation in employment segregation, 138; antidiscrimination pressure from government and citizens' groups, 31, 51, 54, 73, 90–91, 171; "competition reduces discrimination" argument, 26–27; "competition reduces discrimination" argument, refuted, 92, 167, 171, 178; customers' tastes for, 26–27, 32, 38, 48; differential treatment leading to differential treatment, 39, 157; employers' tastes for, 26, 154; legacy of discrimination, 56(n11); policy implications, 177–179; and product market structure, 26–27, 50–51, 92, 167, 171; race-sex queuing and earnings gap, 39–40; and regional variation in earnings gap, 154; social distance in the workplace rather than segregation between workplaces, 27, 31, 39, 51, 106, 154; statistical discrimination, 27–29; and stereotypes about black employees, 108(n10); tokenism, 148–149; and unionization, 27, 91–92, 167; workers' tastes for, 26–27, 32, 38, 48. *See also* gender-typed employment; race- and gender-typed employment; race-sex queuing theory; race-typed employment

Dobbin, Frank, 136(n16), 177

earnings disparities, analysis of results, 165, 166; atypical occupations, 132, 133; base model results for earnings ratios, 112, 119–127, 136(n15); earnings level results, 113–119; employment conditions, 112, 117, 119, 120–122, 125–126; employment segregation and race-gender typing, 112, 114–122, 124–125, 166; extended model results, 127–134, 171; federal contracts/purchases, 114–115, 118,

126; general skill and growth, 113–115, 120–122; interaction of growth and race-gender typing, 129–133; interaction of market power and race-gender typing, 126, 129, 132–134; interaction of profitability and race-gender typing, 112, 126, 128–131, 133–134; product market structure, 112, 114–115, 117–121, 123, 126; public sector employment, 114–115, 118, 126; specific devaluation of labor, 111, 124–127, 132, 135(nn 8,9); strongest and weakest predictors, 150; summary and implications, 118–119, 126–127, 163–167, 169–172; unionization, 114–115, 118–119, 126

earnings disparities, connections to employment segregation. *See* employment segregation, and earnings gap

earnings disparities, explanations for, 3; composition component of earnings gap (between-group differences in factors that affect earnings), 9–10, 13; decomposition of earnings gaps among race-sex groups, 9–10; devaluation of labor in positions with concentrated less-favored employees, 39–40, 112, 116–117, 165; earnings gap across labor market positions, 39–41; impact of sex differences in initial placement on earnings gap, 30; overview of demand-side perspectives, 17, 25–34; overview of integrated perspective, 38–41; overview of supply-side perspectives, 17–25; reasons for decrease in wages for "female"-typed jobs, 12–13; returns component of earnings gap (between-group differences in payoffs to factors affecting earnings), 9–11; segregation component of earnings gap (impact of differential distribution of groups across labor divisions), 9–11. *See also* devaluation of labor; race- and gender-typed employment

earnings disparities, policy recommendations, 177–179, 179(n6)

earnings disparities, predictions about: employers' linkages to other actors, 42, 45; employment growth, 42, 45, 47, 127; estimation issues and error

sources, 73–75; family structure, 10, 42, 45; general skill and training requirements, 42–46; geographic residence, 10, 42; growth and employment conditions, 45; human capital, 10, 42; and labor market position characteristics, 48; labor supply, 10, 42; overview of predictors, 10; predictions about connection to employment segregation, 45–46; predictions of two-level model, 43–55; product market structure, 42, 45, 51; public sector employment, 54; race- and gender-typed tasks, 42, 45; race-sex groups, 42

earnings disparities, research methodology and data analysis, 57–75, 181–199. *See also* research methodology and data analysis

earnings disparities, statistics on, 7–9, 11–12, 16(nn 10,11,12), 67–69

ecological fallacy, 111

economic buffering. *See* market power

economic prosperity. *See* employment growth; profitability

economic scale, 52; and definition of labor market positions, 60–61; measurement of, 71, 73, 193

education. *See* human capital/status attainment; skill level of jobs; training and skill development

EEOC. *See* Equal Employment Opportunity Commission

employers: advertising methods, 31; employee referrals, 31, 90; job applicants' use of social networks, 31, 90; staffing and recruitment practices, 31–32; suggestions for further research, 173. *See also* intensity of employer preferences; job applicants; race-sex queuing theory; salience of employer preferences; statistical discrimination

employers' linkages to other actors: base model results for employment segregation across labor market positions, 79–80, 82, 91–92; and description of two-level model, 42–43; earnings gap and race- and gender-typed employment, 112, 114–115, 118–119, 126; and earnings gap by region, 151–153, 156, 158–159; measurement of, 71, 73, 194; predictions about, 44–45, 52–54; and regional variation in employment segregation, 139–141, 144–146, 148–149. *See also* federal contracts/purchases; government; public sector employment; unionization

employment conditions (sufficient work hours, unemployment rate, self-employment rate): base model results for employment segregation across labor market positions, 79–80, 82, 88, 90, 94, 95; differing value of job security, 109(n15); and earnings gap in race-sex-typed employment, 112, 117, 119, 120–122, 125–126; measurement of, 70, 72, 191; and nurses and airline pilots, 164; predictions about, 44–48; and regional variation in earnings gap, 151–153, 155, 158; and regional variation in employment segregation, 139–141, 143, 145–146

employment discouragement, 175

employment growth, 176; and atypical occupations, 132; and description of two-level model, 42–43; and earnings gap, 120–122, 129–133; and employment segregation, 79, 81, 83–87, 95–96, 108(nn 6,7); interaction with race-gender typing, 98, 100, 102–103, 109(n18), 129–133, 168, 176; measurement of, 70, 72, 108(n5), 191; predictions about, 44–48, 83; and regional variation in earnings gap, 150–155, 157–161; and regional variation in employment segregation, 171–172; and routinized skills, 109(n18); and salience and intensity of employer preferences, 36, 46–47, 83–84, 96, 168; suggestions for further research, 174. *See also* labor supply

employment segregation, analysis of results, 33, 77–109, 168–169; base model results, 78–96; desirable employment, 79–80, 82, 88, 90; extended model results, 96–107, 168–169; general skills by growth and segregation across labor market positions, 79, 81, 83–87, 95–96,

108(nn 6,7); implications for other explanations, 92–95; implications of extended model results, 106–107; interaction of employment growth and race-gender typing, 98, 100, 102–103; interaction of market power and race-gender typing, 99, 101, 104–106; interaction of profitability and race-gender typing, 98, 100, 103–104; intersection of race and gender, 95–96; linkages to other actors, 79–80, 82, 91–92; product market structure, 79, 82, 90–91; race-gender typing, 79–83, 87–89, 96; regional variations, 138–150, 168–169; summary and implications, 163–169

employment segregation, and earnings gap, 7–12; conclusions about, 169–172; earnings gap and race-gender typing, 112, 114–122, 124–125, 166; predictions, 45–46; regional variations, 150–155, 157–160

employment segregation, explanations for, 3, 166–167; "competition reduces discrimination" argument, 26–27, 92, 167, 171, 178; constraint explanation, 48–49; interplay of race and gender, 168; moderation by societal contexts, especially regional differences between North and South, 15, 137–138, 171–172; overview of demand-side perspectives, 17, 25–34; overview of integrated perspective, 34–55; overview of supply-side perspectives, 17–25; social distance in the workplace rather than segregation between workplaces, 27, 31, 39, 51, 106, 154

employment segregation, policy recommendations, 177–179

employment segregation, predictions about, 43–55; estimation issues and error sources, 73–75; general skill and training requirements, 43–46; growth and employment conditions, 44, 46–48; linkages to other actors, 52–54; product market structure, 44, 50–52; race- and gender-typed tasks, 44, 48–50

employment segregation, statistics on: and index of dissimilarity, 4, 5; measuring employment segregation from worker-level results, 64–66;

observed vs. net segregation, 5–6; overview of evidence, 4–7

England, Paula, 46

environmental conditions of employment. *See* working environment

Equal Employment Opportunity Commission (EEOC), 54, 178

factory work, 93, 145, 149, 161(n4)

Fair Pay Act of 2009, 178, 180(n6)

family structure: and assumptions about women's preferences, 6, 21–23, 36–37; and description of two-level model, 42; earnings gap and consequences for household division of labor, 22; lack of evidence for compatibility of actual employment and family responsibilities, 23, 37; measurement from PUMS data, 64, 184–185; and observed earnings vs. adjusted earnings, 68; and prediction of earnings, 10, 66; reasons for division of labor, 21–22

Fan, Pi-Lang, 30

federal contracts/purchases: base model results for employment segregation across labor market positions, 82, 92; earnings gap in race- and gender-typed settings, 114–115, 118, 126; measurement of, 71, 73, 194; predictions about, 44, 53–54. *See also* employers' linkages to other actors

female-typed employment: base model results for employment segregation across labor market positions, 87, 93; and debate over women's preferences for vs. restrictions to female-typed jobs, 23–24; and devaluation of labor, 34, 40–41; examples of "female"-typed skills and conditions, 24, 109(n18); and general skill and training requirements, 43; and lack of evidence for compatibility of actual employment and family responsibilities, 23, 37; men but not women rewarded for female-typed skills, 112, 116, 118, 127, 170, 173–174, 179(n5); predictions about, 44–45, 49–50

Fernandez, Roberto M., 90

Filer, Randall K., 25, 173

foreign involvement, foreign penetration, 52; measurement of, 71, 73, 193

garbage collectors, 2–3, 57, 61, 68, 163–165

gender: and family responsibilities, 21–22; gender role socialization, 23–24; gender schemas, 23–24; and household division of labor, 22; household power dynamics, 22; impact of sex differences in initial placement on earnings gap, 30; intersection with race in base model results for employment segregation across labor market positions, 104–106; and McCall's approach to local economies, 20; and worker preferences, 21–26, 93–94. *See also* female-typed employment; male-typed employment; men; race-sex queuing theory; women

gender-atypical occupations, 132, 133

gender-typed employment, 14; base model results for employment segregation across labor market positions, 81, 87–88; and definition of occupational segments, 58–60; and devaluation of labor, 33–34, 40–41; interaction of growth, profitability, and market power and gender typing, 96–107; and "mammy" stereotype, 145; men but not women rewarded for female-typed skills, 112, 116, 118, 127, 170, 173–174, 179(n5); and ordering principle of labor queues, 32, 33, 35–36, 38; predictions about, 44–45, 47–50; reasons for decrease in wages for "female"-typed jobs, 12–13; and routinized skills, 109(n18); and salience and intensity of employer preferences, 47; social construction of skill and skill-earnings relationship, 111; and worker preferences, 21–26, 93–94

general skills. *See* skill level of jobs

geographic residence, 14; and analysis of evidence for employment segregation, 4; and intensity of employer preferences, 34; measurement from PUMS data, 64, 185, 215(n5); mismatch between geographic location of jobs and workers, 20; and observed earnings vs. adjusted earnings, 68; and prediction of earnings, 10, 66; regional differences in racial prejudice, 15; and two-level model (worker level, labor market position level), 42. *See also* regional variation in labor market inequality

glass escalator/elevator effect, 116, 174, 179(n4)

government, 14; antidiscrimination pressure on companies, 31, 51–52, 54, 73, 90–91, 138, 171; policy implications, 177–179; predictions about, 44–45, 53–54. *See also* employers' linkages to other actors; federal contracts/purchases; public sector employment

Herring, Cedric, 107, 133–134
heteroskedasticity, 74, 108(n4), 109(n17), 135(n2), 136(n10), 161(nn 3, 7), 195–196
Hirsh, C. Elizabeth, 54, 178
Hispanics, 75(n5), 176
Holzer, Harry J., 108(n11)
housework, 21–22
human capital/status attainment, 18–19; and audit studies on race and preferential evaluations, 19; and description of two-level model, 42; human capital thesis of compensating differentials (trade-off between wages and job amenities), 22–24, 33–34, 55(n2); lower earnings for "female"-type work not explained by human capital deficiencies, 13; measurement from PUMS data, 64, 183–184; and observed earnings vs. adjusted earnings, 68; and prediction of earnings, 10, 66; and race-sex queuing, 37–39; and race-sex stereotyping, 18, 19; skills deficit approach, 92–93, 109(n14), 167, 172–173; and statistical discrimination, 27–28. *See also* skill level of jobs

ICPSR. *See* Inter-University Consortium for Political and Social Research
Ihlanfeldt, Keith, 20
immigrants, 176–177
index of dissimilarity, 4, 5, 15(n5), 64–65

industrial configuration of job market, 20
industry: and definition of labor market positions, 60–61, 182–183. *See also* employers; product market structure
integrated perspective on employment segregation and earnings gap, 34–55; description of two-level model, 41–43; dilemmas of multilevel data structure, 41; fundamental principles, 35–41; predictions of two-level model, 43–55; research methodology and data analysis, 57–75, 181–215; summary and implications, 163–179. *See also* earnings disparities, analysis of results; employment segregation, analysis of results; labor market position level model; race-sex queuing theory; worker-level model
intensity of employer preferences, 34, 38–39; defined, 33; and employment growth, 46–47, 83–84; and labor market position characteristics, 43; predictions about, 46; and skill level of jobs, 43, 46, 84; and wartime conditions, 51
intersection of race and gender, 12, 95–96, 148–149, 159, 161, 165, 175–176
Inter-University Consortium for Political and Social Research (ICPSR), 69, 76(n10)

Jacob, Jerry A., 33
job applicants: audit studies on race and preferential evaluations, 1–2, 19, 174–175; criminal records, 2, 108(n11); employee referrals, 31, 90; likelihood of accepting a job offer, 37; queuing mechanisms in hiring, 29–30; social network contacts, 31, 90; and staffing and recruitment practices, 31–32. *See also* human capital/status attainment; skill level of jobs; statistical discrimination; supply-side perspectives on employment segregation and earnings gap; worker preferences
job security/insecurity. *See* employment conditions
jobs. *See* employment conditions; employment growth; labor market positions; skill level of jobs; task

requirements of occupations; working environment
John, Daphne, 21
Johnson, Lyndon B., 54
Johnson, Monica Kirkpatrick, 24

Kalev, Alexandra, 177
Kallenberg, Arne L., 17
Kasim, R., 19
Kelly, Erin L., 136(n16), 177
Kilbourne, Barbara S., 46
King, Mary C., 4
Kmec, Julie A., 31
Kornrich, Sobino, 54
Kuh, Edwin, 195

labor market position level model:
base model results for earnings ratios, 119–127; base model results for employment segregation, 78–96; data and methods for, 69–75; estimation issues and error sources, 73–75, 194–199; extended model results for earnings ratios, 124–127; extended model results for employment segregation, 96–107; measurement of components, 69–73, 190–194
labor market positions, 13, 58; defined, 43, 57–62, 181–183, 200–214; and description of two-level model, 41–43; influence of position characteristics on earnings gaps, 43; issues with job-level studies, 16(n14); measuring employment from worker-level results, 64–66, 187–188; overly broad or circularly defined labor market segments, 13; predicting earnings from labor market positions, 66–69, 188–189; predicting employment in labor market positions, 64–66, 186–187. *See also* skill level of jobs; task requirements of occupations
labor supply: and description of two-level model, 42; measurement from PUMS data, 64, 184–185; and observed earnings vs. adjusted earnings, 68; and prediction of earnings, 10, 66
labor unions. *See* unionization
Ledbetter v. Goodyear Tire & Rubber Co., Inc., 179(n6)

Lilly Ledbetter Fair Pay Act of 2009, 178, 180(n6)
Lippa, R., 25

male-typed employment: base model results for employment segregation across labor market positions, 87; examples of "male"-typed skills and conditions, 24, 109(n18); and general skill and training requirements, 43; higher value of labor, 34, 41; predictions about, 44–45, 49–50. *See also* authority; earnings disparities, analysis of results; mathematical skills; physical labor; status in interaction; working environment
"mammy" stereotype, 145
Manley, Joan E., 33
manual dexterity. *See* physical dexterity
Marini, Margaret M., 30
market power (oligopolistic vs. competitive), 14, 27, 29–31; and competitive theory of discrimination, 26–27; conclusions about, 167–168, 171; and definition of labor market positions, 60–61; and earnings gap, 112, 126, 127, 129, 132–134, 136(n15); and employment segregation, 90–91, 92, 95, 104–107; and hospitals, 165; inconsistencies among studies, 55(n6); measurement of, 71–72, 193; mixed findings on race and sex segregation, 30–31; predictions about, 50–52; and race-gender typing, 99, 101, 104–106, 112, 126, 127, 129, 132–134; refutation of "competition reduces discrimination" argument, 92, 167, 171, 178; and regional variation in earnings gap, 154; and salience of employer preferences, 34; and visibility of successful companies, 51, 106
market structures and forces. *See* product market structure
mathematical skills: as "male"-typed skill, 24, 49, 164; measurement of, 70, 72, 192; and ordering principle of labor queues, 35; payoffs of, 165; predictions about, 44–45, 49; and skills deficit approach, 109(n14);

studies on, 172. *See also* gender-typed employment
McCall, Leslie, 20
McPartland, James M., 30
men: glass escalator/elevator effect, 116, 174, 179(n4); men but not women rewarded for female-typed skills, 112, 116, 118, 127, 170, 173–174, 179(n5). *See also* family structure; gender-typed employment; male-typed employment; race- and gender-typed employment
Merton, Robert K., 34
missing data, 74, 195
MLwiN program, 56(n9)
Mors, Marie Louise, 90
Moss, Philip, 18, 47

Native Americans, 176
neoclassical economic theory, 171, 178
Nixon, Richard M., 92
nurses, 2–3, 57, 61, 163–165, 179(n2)
nurturant skills: and devaluation of labor, 34, 50; as "female"-typed skill, 24, 49, 164; measurement of, 70, 72, 192; negative payoffs of, 111, 165; and ordering principle of labor queues, 35; predictions about, 44–45, 49. *See also* gender-typed employment

occupations. *See* employment conditions; employment growth; labor market positions; skill level of jobs; task requirements of occupations; working environment
odds ratios, observed vs. net, 65–66, 187–188
Office of Federal Contract Compliance (OFCC), 54
O'Neill, June, 55(n1)

Padavic, Irene, 92
Pager, Devah, 2
part-time employment, and worker preferences, 36–37, 172–173
physical dexterity: as black/female-typed skill, 24, 49, 164; and devaluation of labor, 135(n8); measurement of, 70, 72, 192; men but not women rewarded for, 173–174, 179(n5); not recognized as valued skill, 111; and ordering

principle of labor queues, 35, 164; predictions about, 44–45, 49. *See also* gender-typed employment
physical labor: as black/male-typed skill, 24, 164; measurement of, 70, 72, 191; and ordering principle of labor queues, 36; predictions about, 44–45, 48–49. *See also* gender-typed employment
policy implications, 177–179
postindustrial local economies, 20
pressing machine operatives, 2–3, 57, 59, 61, 65, 75(n8), 163–165
product market structure (market power, profitability, economic scale, capital intensity, foreign involvement/penetration, productivity), 92, 103–104, 107, 156; and antidiscrimination pressure, 90–91; and base model results on employment segregation across labor market positions, 79, 82, 90–92, 94–95; conclusions about, 167–168, 170–171, 178; and definition of labor market positions, 60–61; and description of two-level model, 42–43; and discrimination, 50–51, 92, 167; earnings gap and interaction of market power and race-gender typing, 129, 132–134; earnings gap and interaction of profitability and race-gender typing, 128–131, 133–134; earnings gap and race- and gender-typed employment, 112, 114–115, 117–120, 121, 123, 126; earnings gap by region, 151–154, 156, 158–159; and hospitals, 165; inconsistencies among employment segregation studies, 55(n6); interaction with race-gender typing, 96–107; measurement of, 71–73, 192–193; predictions about, 44–45, 50–52; and race-sex queuing, 29–30, 34, 36; and refutation of "competition reduces discrimination" argument, 92, 167, 171, 178; and regional variation in employment segregation, 139–141, 144–145, 148–149; segmented market perspectives, 29–31; and statistical discrimination, 28; and visibility of successful companies, 51, 106. *See also* market power; profitability
productivity, 52; measurement of, 71, 73, 193. *See also* product market structure

profitability (slack resources), 30–31, 168; advantages of workforce diversity, 107, 133–134; and base model results on employment segregation across labor market positions, 90–91, 104, 107; conclusions about, 167–168; earnings gap and interaction with race-gender typing, 112, 126, 128–131, 133–134; employment segregation and interaction with race-gender typing, 98, 100, 103–104; mixed findings on race and sex segregation, 30–31; predictions about, 50–52; and race-sex queuing, 36; and regional variation in earnings gap, 154; and visibility of successful companies, 51, 106. *See also* product market structure

public policy, 177–179

public sector employment: and base model results on employment segregation, 82, 91–92, 95; earnings gap and race- and gender-typed employment, 114–115, 118, 126; measurement of public sector labor force, 71, 73, 194; and regional variation in employment segregation, 145–146, 149

PUMS. *See* Census of Population Public Use Microdata Samples

queuing mechanisms in hiring. *See* race-sex queuing theory

race: audit studies on race and preferential evaluations, 1–2, 19, 174–175; intersection with gender in base model results for employment segregation across labor market positions, 95–96; and mismatch between geographic location of jobs and workers, 20; racial differences in geographic location, 4; racial differences in labor market inputs, 4. *See also* African Americans; discrimination

race- and gender-typed employment, 43, 112, 166, 168–169; base model results for employment segregation, 79–83, 87–89, 96; earnings gap and atypical occupations, 132, 133; earnings gap and interaction with employment growth, 129–133; earnings gap and interaction with profitability, 112, 126, 128–131, 133–134; employment segregation and earnings gap, 112, 114–122, 124–125; employment segregation and interaction with growth, profitability, and market power, 97–107, 168–169; measurement of, 70, 72, 191–192; men but not women rewarded for female-typed skills, 112, 116, 118, 127, 170, 173–174, 179(n5); predictions about, 44, 48–50; and regional variation in employment segregation, 139–141, 143, 145–150, 168–169; and skill level of jobs, 83; stereotypes about black employees, 108(n10); suggestions for further research, 172–177; summary and implications, 163–172. *See also* gender-typed employment; race-sex queuing theory

race-sex queuing theory, 3, 13, 32–55, 82, 161(n5); and antidiscrimination legislation, 54; compared to other explanations, 94–95; and context-specific discrimination, 38; defined/described, 32; and earnings gap, 38–39, 166; and employment growth, 33, 38–39, 46, 72, 83, 160–161; factors considered in ranking, 32; fundamental principles in integrated perspective, 35–41; and gender- or race-"appropriate" jobs, 36, 38, 49, 83, 166; and general skill and training requirements, 43–44; and human capital (worker qualifications), 37–39; intensity of employer preferences, 33, 34, 38–39, 43, 46–47, 84; and labor market structure, 36; labor queue, 38–39; moderating effects of external pressure, 106; ordering principles, described, 33–39; predictions, 43–55; and product market structure, 51; and public sector employment, 91; and regional variation in effects of employment growth, 154; and regional variation in job queue, 138, 172; shape of job queue, 33, 38–39; structural properties of labor queues, 32–33; suggestions for further research, 175; summary and implications, 164–172; variation in labor queues across product and labor markets, 36; variation of job queues across potential workers, 36–37. *See also* employment segregation, analysis of results; statistical discrimination

race-sex stereotyping: audit studies on race and preferential evaluations, 1–2, 19, 174–175; and definition of occupational segments, 58–60; "mammy" stereotype, 145; and "soft" skills, 18; suggestions for further research, 173–174. *See also* race- and gender-typed employment

race-typed employment, 14; and definition of occupational segments, 58–60; and description of two-level model, 42–43; and devaluation of labor, 33–34, 40–41; and general skill and training requirements, 43; and ordering principle of labor queues, 33, 35–36, 38; predictions about, 47–50; and salience and intensity of employer preferences, 47

Raphael, Stephen, 108(n11)

Raudenbush, Stephen W., 19

Reagan, Ronald, 92

regional variation in labor market inequality, 137–162, 171–172, 175; and antidiscrimination pressure on companies, 138; blacks as larger percentage of workforce in the South, 138, 161(n2); conclusions about, 149–150, 168–169, 171–172, 176; definition of regions, 161(n1); earnings gap, 150–160; employment segregation and, 138–150; and policy recommendations, 178–179; race earnings gaps among men, 157–158; race earnings gaps among women, 158–159; race segregation among men, 146–148; race segregation among women, 148; representation of black women relative to white men, 148–149; sex earnings gaps among blacks, 157; sex earnings gaps among whites, 154–157; sex segregation among blacks, 145–146; sex segregation among whites, 142–145; social contexts, 15, 137–138, 171–172; suggestions for further research, 174, 176; and tokenism, 148–149; and

traditional gender role expectations, 161(n6); and unionization, 138, 146, 148–149; variation in job queue, 138. *See also* geographic residence

research methodology and data analysis, 13–14, 57–75, 76(n10), 136(n10), 166, 181–216; Census of Population Public Use Microdata Samples (PUMS; 1990), 58, 62–63; data and methods for position-level analyses, 69–75, 190–215; data and methods for worker-level analysis, 57, 62–69, 183–190; definition of labor market positions, 57–62, 181–183; earnings ratios, 134(n2); estimation issues and error sources, 73–75, 108(n4), 109(n17), 134–135(n2), 136(n10), 161(nn 3, 7), 194–199; measurement of position-level components, 69–73, 76(n11); measuring adjusted earnings gap, 67–69, 189–190; measuring employment segregation from worker-level results, 64–67, 187–188; observed earnings vs. adjusted earnings, 68–69, 189–190; observed vs. net odds ratios, 65–66, 187–188; predicting earnings from labor market positions, 66–69, 188–189; regional model, 67; "unbalanced" fixed-effects model, 67. *See also* earnings disparities, analysis of results

Reskin, Barbara F., 32–34, 91, 131, 177

RIASEC typology, 25

Ridgeway, Cecilia L., 23

Roos, Patricia A., 32–34, 132

Rounds, James, 25

routinized tasks: as black-typed skill, 164; and employment growth, 109(n18); measurement of, 70, 72, 192; predictions about, 44–45

Rowe, R., 24

salience of employer preferences, 33; and antidiscrimination legislation, 54; defined, 34; and employment growth, 36, 83–84, 96, 102; and labor market position characteristics, 43; predictions about, 46, 51; and product market structure, 36, 51, 171; and skill level of jobs, 84; and wartime conditions, 51

segmented market theory, 13, 29–31; and

base model results on employment segregation across labor market positions, 92, 94; defined/described, 29; and queuing model, 29–30, 34. *See also* product market structure

segregation. *See headings beginning with* employment segregation

self-employment rate. *See* employment conditions

self-selection into jobs. *See* worker preferences

Shelton, Beth Anne, 21

SIC. *See* Standard Industrial Classification (SIC) codes

Singelmann, Joachim, 60

Sjoquist, David, 20

skill level of jobs: definition of high skill level, 108(n8); and definition of occupational segments, 58–60; and devaluation of labor in skilled positions, 41; higher payoff of skills for less-favored sex-race groups, 46; measurement of, 70, 72, 190–191; and ordering principle of labor queues, 35; predictions about, 46; and race- and gender-typed jobs, 43; and salience and intensity of employer preferences, 43, 46, 84; skills deficit approach, 92–93, 109(n14), 167, 172–173; and statistical discrimination, 27–28, 38, 83; suggestions for further research, 173–174; and two-level model for employment segregation and earnings gap, 43–46, 79, 81, 83–87, 92–93. *See also* human capital/status attainment; task requirements of occupations; training and skill development

skill levels and employment growth: discrimination reduced in highly skilled jobs under employment growth conditions, 83, 92, 106; and earnings gap, 113–115, 120–122; and employment segregation, 79, 81, 83–87, 92–93, 95–96, 108(nn 6,7); and pressing machine operators and garbage collectors, 164; and regional variation in earnings gap, 149–155, 157–161, 169; and regional variation in segregation, 139–143, 146–147, 149–150, 171–172, 176; suggestions for further research, 173–174; as

weakest predictor of earnings gap, 150

Snizek, W. E., 24

social distance in the workplace rather than segregation between workplaces, 27, 31, 39, 51, 106, 154

social network contacts of job applicants, 31, 90

spacial mismatch. *See* geographic residence

staffing and recruitment practices, 26, 31–32, 90, 173

Standard Industrial Classification (SIC) codes, 72

statistical discrimination, 27–29, 33; and devaluation of labor in skilled positions, 41; employers' beliefs about potential productivity of workers, 27–28, 32, 38, 44; and labor market position characteristics, 43; and market structures and forces, 28; and ordering principle of labor queues, 32, 36, 38, 44, 166; predictions about, 46, 164; and skill level of jobs, 27–28, 38, 46, 83; and wage setting, 46

status in interaction: base model results for employment segregation across labor market positions, 88–89, 109(n16); and gender-typed employment, 24; measurement of, 70, 72, 192; predictions about, 44–45, 48–49; and profitability, 136(nn 12,13)

stereotyping. *See* gender-typed employment; race- and gender-typed employment; race-sex stereotyping; race-typed employment

Stoll, Michael A., 108(n11)

supply-side perspectives on employment segregation and earnings gap, 17–25, 24; and crowding, 24; human capital thesis of compensating differentials (trade-off between wages and job amenities), 22–24, 33–34, 55(n2); and human capital/status attainment, 18–19; mechanisms for turning sex-segregated job choices into sex-linked wage differences, 24; and spacial mismatch between geographic location of jobs and workers, 20; skills deficit approach, 92–93, 109(n14), 167, 172–173; small sex- or race-linked differences in work values, 24; small sex-linked differences in vocational interests, 25; suggestions for further research, 172–174; work experience, 18–19; worker preferences, 21–25, 93–94, 172–173. *See also* family structure; human capital/status attainment; job applicants; labor supply; skill level of jobs

task requirements of occupations, 14; and definition of occupational segments, 58–60; and description of two-level model, 42–46; measurement of, 70, 72, 190–192; and ordering principle of labor queues, 35–36. *See also* authority; clerical perception; mathematical skills; nurturant skills; physical dexterity; physical labor; routinized tasks; skill level of jobs; status in interaction; working environment
Tilly, Chris, 18, 47
tokenism, 148–149
Tomaskovic-Devey, Donald, 16(n13), 16(n15), 49
training and skill development: and employers' beliefs about potential worker productivity, 30; and employment growth, 79, 81, 83–87; measurement of, 70, 72, 190; predictions about, 46–47; and salience and intensity of employer preferences, 46. *See also* human capital/status attainment; skill level of jobs; statistical discrimination
transportation infrastructure, 20
Turner, Margery, 1, 19, 46–47

unemployment, underemployment, and employment discouragement, 175
unionization, 14; conclusions about, 167; and discrimination, 27, 91–92, 167; distinction between craft-type and industrial-type unions, 53, 146, 148; earnings gap and race- and gender-typed employment, 114–115, 118–119, 126; and employment segregation, 82, 91–92, 94–95; measurement of, 71, 73, 194; predictions about, 44–45, 53–

54; and profiles of example race-gender-typed jobs, 2–3; and regional variation in earnings gap, 156, 158–159; and regional variation in race segregation, 138, 146, 148–149. *See also* employers' linkages to other actors

veterans, 54

War on Poverty, 54
Weakliem, David L., 138
Welsch, Roy, 195
whites. *See* glass escalator/elevator effect; race; race- and gender-typed employment; race-sex queuing theory; regional variation in labor market inequality; statistical discrimination; *headings beginning with* earnings disparities *or* employment segregation
white-typed employment: and general skill and training requirements, 43, 84; higher value of labor, 41; predictions about, 48–50; and profiles of example race-gender-typed jobs, 3
Williams, Christine L., 116
women: and assumptions about women's preferences, 21–23, 36–37; and distinction between craft-type and industrial-type unions, 53; and government employment, 53–54; lack of evidence for compatibility of actual employment and family responsibilities, 23, 37; new opportunities in war conditions, 51; and part-time employment, 36–37. *See also* family structure; female-typed employment; gender-typed employment; race- and gender-typed employment
work experience, 18–19, 37. *See also* human capital/status attainment
work hours, sufficient. *See* employment conditions
worker preferences, 21–25; conclusions about, 167–168; effect mitigated by constraints imposed by employers, 6, 49; family responsibilities, 21–23; gendered preferences for certain skills and working conditions, 23–26; human capital thesis of compensating

differentials (trade-off between wages and job amenities), 22–23, 33–34, 55(n2); implications of base model results on employment segregation across labor market positions, 93–94; and part-time employment, 36–37, 172–173; small or no sex- or race-linked differences in overall structure of preferences, 25, 37; suggestions for further research, 172–173; variation of job queues across potential workers, 36–37; weak association with job choices, 16(n9)

worker productivity: and queuing for jobs where productivity is uncertain/difficult to measure, 32, 38. *See also* statistical discrimination

worker qualifications. *See* human capital/ tatus attainment; skill level of jobs

worker-level factors. *See* family structure; geographic residence; human capital/ status attainment; labor supply

worker-level model, 41–43; measuring employment segregation from worker-level results, 64–66, 187–188; predicting employment in labor market positions, 64–66, 186–187; research methodology and data analysis, 57–69, 183–190

working environment, 14; compensating differentials for hazardous jobs, 55(n2); and definition of occupational segments, 58–60; and gender-typed employment, 24; measurement of, 70, 72, 191–192; predictions about, 44–45, 48, 50; and profiles of example race-gender-typed jobs, 2–3; and unemployment rate, 48

World War II, 51

Wright, Rosemary, 33

About the Book

Women and minorities have entered higher-paying occupations, but their overall earnings still lag behind those of white men. Why? Looking nationwide at workers across all employment levels and occupations, Robert Kaufman examines the unexpected ways that prejudice and workplace discrimination continue to plague the labor market.

Kaufman probes the mechanisms by which race and sex groups are sorted into "appropriate" jobs, showing how the resulting segregation undercuts earnings. He also uses an innovative integration of race-sex queuing and segmented-market theories to show how economic and social contexts shape these processes. His authoritative analysis reveals how race, sex, stereotyping, and devaluation interact to create earnings disparities, shedding new light on a vicious cycle that continues to leave women and minorities behind.

Robert L. Kaufman is professor of sociology at Temple University.